The Ghosts of Virginia

Volume V

by L. B. Taylor, Jr.

Photographs by the Author
Illustrations by
Brenda Goens

Copyright © 2000 by L. B. Taylor, Jr.
Printed in the U.S.A. by Progress Printing Co., Inc.

ISBN 1-928966-01-2

Contents

THE SHENANDOAH VALLEY — AND WEST

CENTRAL VIRGINIA

Author's Note

The odyssey continues!

No sooner had I completed the manuscript for "The Ghosts of Virginia, Volume IV" (1998), when the calls and letters began coming in. "Have you heard about the ghost at . . . .? Did you know about the haunted house located in . . . .? After many of the talks I gave throughout the commonwealth, people would come up and relate true supernatural encounters they had experienced. The file began to grow. And what amazed me, and still does to this day, is the variety of manifestations and historic anecdotes that surfaced. The material was fresh and absorbing. Even after writing close to a million words about ghosts in Virginia, I found still more of the unusual and fascinating.

I decided to write a volume V in the series!

I took some trips to gather data first-hand. I had a wonderful venture down through the southwest section of Virginia — to Wytheville, Abingdon, Bristol, Big Stone Gap and Wise County, across to Pounding Mill (find that on the map!), and Marion. I interviewed dozens of people. I pored through the files of such folklore archivists as Raymond Burgin and others. I visited the home of legendary Old Dominion writer and novelist, John Fox, Jr., and saw the outdoor drama based on his book, "The Trail of the Lonesome Pine." There appears to be a spirit in the Fox house in Big Stone Gap. I collected a legend at the Natural Tunnel.

On another trek, I headed north. I crossed the Potomac and interviewed historians at Point Lookout State Park in southeast Maryland. I wrote a couple of chapters on this area, which may well be among the most haunted sections in the United States.

I traveled off interstate 95 to such historic homes as The Oatlands and Morven Park, near Leesburg. Each has a haunting tale to tell.

I did book signings at: the Pungo Strawberry Festival in Virginia Beach; the Heart of the Lake Festival in Clarksville; the Tomato Festival in Hanover; the Newport News Fall Festival; and at other events. I was rewarded with still more "inexplicable incidents."

As with the previous books, volume V includes accounts of some famous Virginians and others: Thomas Jefferson at Poplar Forest; General George Pickett at Hollywood Cemetery in

Richmond; John Singleton Mosby in northern Virginia; the "real" John Henry; 17th century colonial governor William Berkeley and his nemesis, Nathanial Bacon; and writer Ellen Glasgow of Richmond; among others. And I included the "non-ghost" of Meriwether Lewis.

And there are a number of historic houses involved: the afore-mentioned Poplar Forest, Oatlands, and Morven Park; the house where Stonewall Jackson died; the Cole-Digges House and the Cornwallis Cave in Yorktown; Federal Hill in Fredericksburg; plus the Cold Harbor battlefield near Richmond; and on and on.

I did further research in Colonial Williamsburg and came up with a new script for the popular nightly ghost tour there. I revisit-ed the archives of state libraries, and spent endless hours in used bookshops, searching through the out-of-print volumes on Virginiana. And I was rewarded. In an old autobiography of Virginia writer Marion Harland, I found a riveting true account of a lost spirit in her childhood home; in a 100-year-old diary of a Civil War veteran, I discovered a chilling recollection of a ghost at a man-sion in Chantilly. It was spell binding. On the back shelves of the main library in Roanoke I found a copy of a privately published book on the houses of Madison County. It had several cryptic refer-ences to residing spirits there.

And so, volume V began to take form.

I shouldn't be at this point, but I still am continually amazed at the tremendously growing popularity of ghostly tales in the com-monwealth. When I began my venture into tracking the haunting legends of Virginia in 1983, it was a much different scene. Many people who had experienced various forms of psychic phenomena were very reluctant to talk about them. Hotel, motel, restaurant and bed and breakfast owners absolutely denied any existence of spirits in their establishments.

Today, after the publication of my series of books and other authors' accounts, ghosts have become an "in" subject. During Halloween week in 1998, for example, there were ghost tours held in Richmond, Norfolk, Portsmouth, Petersburg, Springfield, Lexington, Salem, Madison and even in tiny Big Stone Gap. There were probably others which I didn't hear about. In the vicinity of Williamsburg alone, spooky events were held at the historic planta-tions of Sherwood Forest, Berkeley, Shirley, Edgewood, North Bend, and Piney Grove, and at the York River State Park. There now are two, and sometimes three or more, nightly ghost tours, year-round, in Williamsburg, and even Colonial Williamsburg got into the act by holding a session of haunting tales at Carter's Grove.

That same week in October 1998, the number one title on the Washington Post list of best sellers was "The Vampire Armand," by Anne Rice — "A character who returns to tell his haunted tale." Number two on the list was "Bag of Bones" by Stephen King — "A Love Story Filled with Ghosts." Danielle Steel also had a smash hit called "The Ghost," in which a man moves into an old house and falls in love with the apparition of a woman who died more than 200 years ago! And best selling author R. L. Stine, father of the "Goosebumps" series of thrillers, has set literary records with his dozens of books for young people.

Today, many of the people who scoffed at the supernatural years ago, now seek recognition for their otherworld entities. The hotel, motel, restaurant, and bed and breakfast owners now even advertise that guests may encounter a ghost or two during their stay. The people at Berkeley Plantation in Charles City County once told me they had no ghosts. Some years later, after my books were published, the late Malcolm Jamieson, then owner of Berkeley, called and scolded me for not including their spirits. Seems they had some after all! The owners of the Bedrock Inn, in Pounding Mill, Virginia, north of Abingdon, called and invited me down to investigate their ghost (included in this book).

Why such interest?

I believe there is a fascination with the unexplained. There is an unabated curiosity with the unknown. That helps explain the enduring popularity of such lasting television programs as "Unsolved Mysteries," and "Sightings," and the continuing proliferation of horror movies involving ghosts. People like to be scared! Plus, there is a deep abiding interest in preserving the lore and legend of Virginia. Some of these heirloom traditions have been told and retold by families for 300 years and longer. Our forefathers who came from England, Scotland, Ireland, and other lands brought some of these accounts with them. They are part of our heritage.

Author C. J. S. Thompson, who wrote "The Mystery of Lore and Apparitions" in 1930, said ghost stories have been told for thousands of years because, "they have always responded to some innate longing in human nature to pierce the veil which hides the future after death. Stories of apparitions and ghosts have thus appealed to mankind at all times and in all countries, and will doubtless continue to do so until man's craving to know something of the unseen world is satisfied."

Thompson adds that the "multitude" of people have a love of the marvelous and supernatural, a curiosity with regard to future events, and a strong propensity to extend their hopes and fears beyond the limits of this world - that is irresistible.

The renowned parapsychologist, Dr. Hans Holzer, who has written scores of books on ghostly encounters, says, "I welcome this resurgence of curiosity in worlds beyond the physical . . ." He adds: "Ever since the dawn of humankind, people have believed in ghosts. The fear of the unknown, the certainty that there was something somewhere out there, bigger than life, beyond its pale, and more powerful than anything walking on earth, has persisted through the ages . . ."

As I have said repeatedly through this series of volumes, I do not make the case for or against ghosts. Some believe in them, some don't, and most of us, I am sure, are uncertain. Dunninger, a magician who appeared on television 30 or so years ago, had a favorite expression about spirits: "To those who believe, no explanation is necessary. To those who don't believe, no explanation is possible."

But whether or not one believes, it is an indisputable fact that the interest in ghosts has greatly increased in recent years. Perhaps it will lead to more openness among those who have actual experiences, and, eventually we will learn more about the true nature of something we have long wondered about.

As with all the other books in this series, the research and writing of V was a labor of love. I enjoyed every minute of it.

Let me extend my deep appreciation to all the Virginians and others who made this book possible by sharing their ghostly encounters with me.

Introduction

The Reverend Dr. W. A. R. Goodwin is the man most responsible for the modern restoration of Colonial Williamsburg. In the late 1920s he convinced philanthropist John D. Rockefeller, Jr., to spend millions of dollars to preserve a most important segment of American history — to rebuild and restore the town that served as the Colonial capital of Virginia from 1699 to 1780. It was a massive undertaking, but today, each year, more than a million tourists come to Colonial Williamsburg to see what life was like here in the 18th century.

Dr. Goodwin once wrote Rockefeller a letter. In it, he said: "In Williamsburg we always have the ghosts which abide, even when the distinguished men of the present come, stay for a day, and depart. I have always felt sorry for the people who live in Williamsburg who are incapable of holding companionship with the ghosts."

Of course, Dr. Goodwin's comment is open to wide interpretation. Many, however, believe he was speaking more than just figuratively.

Ghosts do seem to abound, not just in the colonial area of Williamsburg, but throughout the Old Dominion. One has only to skim through the 11 books in this series on hauntings in Virginia. Herein alone are approximately 1,000 separate encounters with spirits of one form or another, ranging from the last decade of the 20th century all the way back to the early settlers in the commonwealth.

Why? There may be a number of reasons. First, the pioneering immigrants here brought over tales of the supernatural, the origins of which date back for hundreds of years. Such stories, or personal experiences, have been handed down in families through the generations. They are still told in the mountains and foothills, the valleys and hollows all across the state.

Virginia has probably experienced more tragedy and trauma than any other state in the nation. Indian wars raged for nearly 200 years, from the early 1600s through the late 18th century. There was the Revolutionary War. And then the American Civil War, where thousands of young men died well before their time on commonwealth soil. Ghosts are often associated with untimely deaths.

And there are the houses, the wonderful houses. Hundreds of

them 100, 200 and 300 years old and more, still exist. Hauntings seem to occur more often in ancient homes. Experts on psychic phenomena say if ghosts exist, one reason is they are still tied to a family homesite. As one paranormal specialist put it, "Unwilling to depart with the physical world, such human personalities continue to stay in the very spot where their tragedy or their emotional attachment had existed prior to physical death."

Do ghosts exist?

No one can answer that question with any certainty. Thousands of Virginians have said they have had real, and sometimes frightening, ghostly encounters. But how do you prove it? The question has been argued for 5,000 years or longer, and remains unresolved.

"Where are the dead?" asks Lord Halifax in his book on ghosts, published in 1944. "Are they still amongst us, possessed of that undefined, mysterious existence which the ancient world attributed to the ghosts of the departed? . . . Between this world and that which escapes our senses? We can neither explain the connecting link, nor admit an impassable barrier."

To this, parapsychologist Hans Holzer, who has written nearly 100 books on the subject, adds: "Ghosts cannot be explained away, nor will they disappear. They continue to appear frequently all over the world . . . For ghosts are indeed nothing more or nothing less than a human being trapped by special circumstances in this world while already being of the next. Or, to put it another way, a human being whose spirit is unable to leave the earthly surroundings because of unfinished business or emotional entanglements."

Author Thompson writes: "Belief in apparitions is nearly as old as the world itself, or at least can be traced as far back as the earliest period of which we have record.

Apparitions or the appearance of spirits of the dead to the living, have been credited in all ages and by almost every people, while even among the barbarous tribes, the belief in a communication between man and the departed exists.

Holzer, and others knowledgeable on the subject, believe, "in years to come, we will deal with apparitions as 'ordinary events,' part and parcel of the human experience. . . If you are one of the many who enter a haunted house and have a genuine experience in it, be assured that you are a perfectly normal human being." Holzer says nothing is more democratic than such an experience — because it happens "all the time to just about every conceivable type of person."

If ghosts exist, what is a ghost? Past volumes in this series have offered dozens of possible definitions. The most common remains thus: a ghost appears to be a surviving emotional memory of someone who has died, most likely traumatically and or tragically, but is unaware of his or her death.

But no one — no one! — knows for sure.

What cannot be denied, however, even by the staunchest skeptic, is the fascination which the subject of ghosts commands. There is an enthralling lure of mystery, romance, adventure, and otherworldliness. What happens when we die? Do some of us linger on, in between? What could be more compelling, more alluring than the answers to such ageless questions. Perhaps someday we will find out.

Until then, enjoy the following chapters as "historic entertainment."

A word about the organization of this book: Geographically, we start in northern Virginia, cross over the Potomac River briefly to include chapters of heavily haunted sites in southern Maryland, then come back to head toward the Shenandoah Valley, southward, and westward over the West Virginia line. Next comes central Virginia, then down into the southwestern section of the commonwealth. From here we go east across the southern area, north through Tidewater, and finally, west again to the greater Richmond area.

Interspersed between these regions are summary chapters on: Spectral Vignettes; Letters from the Author's Mailbag; Indian Legends and Lore; Civil War ghosts; and a "catchall" section labeled Miscellaneous.

It is time for the journey to begin.

Enjoy!

The Lonely Grave in the Sunken Garden

(Northern Virginia)

(Author's note: Ordinarily, when I write about a ghost I like to know a little about the circumstances. Like, if the haunting is in a house, where is that house located? What is its history? Who might the spirit be? Things like that.

But when I came across a spectral account of an unusual nature which occurred more than 120 years ago, although the details of the site were missing, the recording of the event itself was so rapturously compelling, I had to include it.

It all started while I was browsing through a half-century old issue of Tyler's Quarterly Historical and Genealogical Magazine at the Rockefeller Library at Colonial Williamsburg one winter afternoon. I came across an item that caught my eye. A gentleman named Joseph Bristow went one summer day to an auction of the contents of a "Victorian mansion," presumably either in Washington or northern Virginia — the date and site were not mentioned.

Bristow bought an antique trunk. He said he didn't know why he bought it — "just one of those things we do sometimes without any apparent reason." He described the trunk as being from the 1870s period ("one of those oval top affairs with painted galvanized tin sides and mysterious interiors lined with decorated paper.")

e took it home and that evening broke the lock. There was no key. Inside, he found: an

old hoopskirt with real whalebone stays; a crystal pendant; a set of dueling pistols in a leather case; "and in one corner underneath all this impediment, a fragment of a diary and a bundle of old letters. "Old letters and a fragment of a diary!" he said. "This was the piece de excellence."

From the letters, this much is known:

The haunting experience occurred to a young lady, whose name he could not ascertain, during the summer of 1878. She apparently lived in a house in Washington, D. C. at the time, and occasionally crossed the Potomac River to visit her friend, named Geraldine, somewhere in northern Virginia at a house she called "The Hall." There is a reference in a letter written by Geraldine, of an "old mansion on the seven-terraced hill of Bull Run," which, if this was "The Hall," would put it in the vicinity of Manassas.

The following is excerpted from a letter the nameless young lady wrote in September 1878, to another friend. It was in the packet Bristow found in the old trunk.

"Have just returned to the city (D.C.) from a long visit with Geraldine at The Hall. Had a fine time but the old house was so spooky! Even the orchard had a grave by the sundial near the sunken garden. The white stone over it, resting on four brick pillars was unmarked — no name, no date.

"Geraldine said that there was a mystery connected with the grave about which she knew little, for her people would not talk about it. It seems, however, that one of Geraldine's ancestors had been guilty of some kind of a sin and had been buried in that lonely place away from the others — people can be so silly! There is more false pride among Virginians than anyone else on earth!

" . . . One night while we were both asleep I was awakened at about midnight; someone was playing on a stringed instrument of some kind. It sounded away off; at first I thought I was dreaming — but no, it was not a dream.

"Down through the well of the old circular stairway the notes came twinkling through the darkness — notes that sounded like the feet of mice running across stiff glazed paper. Someone was singing — a voice unsubstantial and barely audible, such as one occasionally hears at twilight when the world is quiet and hushed, when you know all the time that there is no voice there at all — nothing but old memories coming down the years.

"Down through the well of the stairway these old memories came; I turned over and tried to go back to sleep — but couldn't. I woke Geraldine and asked her to listen but she appeared irritated and only told me to go back to sleep.

"I lay awake for a long time listening to the faint sounds. Outside the moon was caught in the branches of an old oak and was struggling to free itself. Finally I could stand it no longer and slowly got out of bed so as not to wake Geraldine, and went out into the hall.

"Around about me was the smell of ancient woodwork, slanting gray shadows, and the white glimmer of painted doors, doors that had waited for over 200 years for the coming of this very moment — all was quiet, except for the twinkling notes coming down the well of the circular stairway. I could make them out — now. Someone was singing:

"'Oft in the stilly night, ere slumber's chain has bound me,
Fond memory brings the light of other days around me.
When I remember all the friends so link't to-get-her
I've seen around me fall, like leaves in wintry winter
I feel like one who treads alone some banquet hall . .'

"Slowly I began to climb the stairs up toward the room from whence came the notes of the stringed instrument and the unsubstantial voice of a dream. A bat was flying through the halls bumping itself against the walls. I reached the topmost floor. The alcove window at the head of the stairs was crisscrossed by cobwebs slanting across the face of the moon. Through the dusty panes far down in the hollow below I could see the burial ground of the slaves with its white wooden headboards. A mist was rising from the bottom-land, taking on strange forms as it ascended through the starlight.

"There was a shower of minor notes from the strings of an old instrument. I turned — before me was the closed door of a room extending back under the eaves. Someone was singing:

"'The light of other days is faded and all their glories past.
For grief with heavy wing hath shaded the hopes too bright to last.
The world which morning's mantle clouded, shines forth with purer rays,
But the heart ne'er feels, in sorrow shrouded, the light of other days.'

"Slowly, I opened the door.

"The moonlight coming in through a dormer window was shining on an old dust-covered harpsichord. The keys were moving!

" . . . a shadowy figure of a young woman was standing at the keyboard, a young woman with a mass of wonderful hair arranged in a high Marie Antoinette headdress — but through her billowy white Rose Bertin gown I could see the cracks in the ancient plaster of the opposite wall!

"The music ceased; she turned and looked at me for a moment and then held out a white hand in an imploring sort of way. From her sleeve, a lace handkerchief fell to the floor and lay a spot of white on the wide dusty planking. I stooped to pick it up but there was nothing there but a white moonbeam eluding my fingers, playing over the flooring as the breeze outside moved the branches of the old oak.

"I looked up — the lady was gone.

"There may not have been a figure there at all — I was not quite sure. It may, after all, have been nothing but pure hallucination engendered by the time, the hour, and the place. Slanting gray shadows and the white glimmer of old painted woodwork slowly resumed their wonted sway over hall and stair. I returned to bed. I had not been afraid at any time for the figure, if there were a figure, was a friendly one. Uncle Frank always said I had more nerve than any girl he ever knew — that I should have been a boy.

"I said nothing about my adventure. The family did not appear interested and always changed the conversation when the unusual aspects of the mansion were mentioned — this, apparently, was a forbidden subject. But I couldn't help but feel sorry for the girl out in that lonely grave by the sunken garden, away off from the other dead people, for I felt that she was connected in some manner with the mystery. . . "

(Exactly one year, to the day, September 20, 1879, the young lady wrote another letter to her friend.)

"We drove out to The Hall today.

"The Rhus was blooming on the fences and the trumpet-vines displaying their scarlet blossoms at the intersections — as they did last year when I was with Geraldine. But this fall she was away at school so we did not go up to the mansion but had Henry stop the carriage at the sunken garden.

"The honeysuckle had been allowed to invade the depression covering walls and stone-seats and ancient sundial. Geraldine was away or this would never have happened. The white unmarked stone over the lonely grave was littered with nibbled nut-shells left by squirrels. . . The girl sleeping below in her lonely crypt was not alone as long as these noisy little friends were running nervously overhead — but in winter when they were not there and instead there is snow and ice and the cold winds are whistling through the bare trees, it must be Hell down below. Or did she know or care — I wonder?

"When we die, do we become one with the wind and the cold and the ice? The old Norse believed in Gods who came down from the frozen North and I have heard our ministers tell wonderful tales about other hereafters — I don't believe any of them know.

"But I do know that there is a girl sleeping below this stone and that she will never come back unless I can bring her back in my thoughts . . .

"Last year when I was here sleeping in Geraldine's room and heard someone playing on an old harpsichord in the room under the eaves — no one but I heard; no one but I saw the unknown with her high Marie Antoinette headdress and Rose Bertin gown through which appeared the cracks in the plaster of the opposite wall. No one but I saw her drop her handkerchief to the dusty planking where it lay a white woven thing of Irish point-lace with the letter 'M' embroidered with light blue thread in one corner or that when I stooped to pick it up there was nothing there at all but a moonbeam playing over the flooring as the wind outside moved the tree branches.

"Irish point-lace can be soiled by dust but moonbeams cannot — the dust of ages on that floor could not soil my lady's handkerchief <u>that night!</u> Then, standing here this afternoon by that lonely grave, I realized for the first time that I had received a message from the girl below:

"'Do not look for me in things mundane for I belong to the moonlight which cannot be soiled and where words hurt not, neither is there heat or cold nor sound or wind but only quiet and life unending.'

"And I knew also that the poet Henry King had seen her or he could never have written those lines:

"'Marry my body to that dust
It so much loves, and fills the room
My heart keeps empty in thy tomb . . .
Each minute is a short degree . . .
Through which to Thee I swiftly glide,
And slow howe'er my marches be,
I shall at last sit down by Thee.'"

The Phantom Footsteps of Morven Park

(Leesburg)

(Author's note: I don't often write about footsteps anymore. Let me explain. Footsteps are by far the most common manifestation in the realm of psychic phenomena. There are literally hundreds, perhaps more, instances of mysterious footsteps heard in houses all across the commonwealth — from Alexandria to Big Stone Gap. Writing about them, from a journalistic standpoint, would get boringly repetitious pretty fast. So what I have done is to try to seek out the unusual ghostly encounters, the bizarre, the odd, the strange. My second goal has been to tie such lore in with historical backgrounds of famous persons, houses and sites where possible.

But when I heard about the footsteps at Morven Park, a mansion located a mile outside of Leesburg in northern Virginia, I decided to include them in this book — for two reasons. First, Morven Park itself is a Virginia historic landmark with its own fascinating background, although it is not as well known to the general public as are other houses of lesser stature. And second, these particular footsteps were so distinct and so compelling, it was hard to ignore them.)

The home is majestic. Beyond lodge gates and nearly a mile of tree-lined drive, the large, two-story house extends to an unusual length and is ornamented by a Doric portico. Says the Virginia

Landmarks Register: "The sprawling mansion, dramatically set against the Catoctin mountain range, has had a complicated architectural history. Buried within the existing fabric is a 1780s farmhouse. Judge Thomas Swann enlarged the house after he bought it in 1808. Thomas Swann, Jr., later governor of Maryland, remodeled the house into a grandiose combination of the Greek Revival and Italianate styles, converting it into a romantic revival villa of almost English scale.

Robert Lancaster, in his book, "Historic Virginia Homes and Churches," describes Morven Park as "one of the finest estates in all Virginia." It covers 1,200 acres.

The present meticulously restored interior is centered by a Renaissance great hall, Jacobean dining room, and a French drawing room. The furnishings are of varied styles and times, including 16th century Flemish tapestries, Renaissance pieces, silver and glass, fine paintings and porcelain figurines. Upstairs there are bedrooms, an office, and a massive ballroom.

There is also a museum — devoted to that grand old Virginia tradition, fox hunting. The north wing contains a collection of paintings, bronzes and photographs, plus artifacts and literature — all portraying famous hounds, huntsmen and hunts in North America and England. The oldest treasure here is a gracefully curved 1731 hunting horn carried by colonial governor Samuel Ogle of Maryland.

There is more. One of the largest personal collections of horse-drawn vehicles, the Winmill collection, has been on display at Morven Park since 1970. It contains coaches, breaks, phaetons, surreys, carts and sleighs, as well as a funeral hearse and a charcoal burning fire engine.

And then there are the gardens. They alone are worth a visit. They were the pride and joy of Marguerite Davis, wife of Westmoreland Davis, who bought the house in 1903. The garden contains what is said to be the largest living stand of boxwoods in the United States.

The Davises began collecting boxwoods in the 1930s. Once, while traveling by train, Mr. Davis spotted a strip of land along the track that had a long row of boxwood plants growing on it. He bought the land and had all the plants removed and shipped to Morven Park. It took two railroad cars.

The gardens also contain a wide variety of magnolias, hollies and flowering trees. A reflecting pool leads to the final resting places of the Davises — a brick mausoleum covered with ivy and

Morven Park

surrounded by seasonal flowers.

Westmoreland Davis himself was a fascinating character. He was 44 when he bought Morven Park in 1903. He had been a highly successful lawyer in New York and had amassed a fortune. In Virginia he became involved in politics, and although he was virtually unknown to old line politicians, he was elected governor in 1918. He served one term, but it was noteworthy for the widely praised fiscal management system he installed. He also reformed the commonwealth's archaic prison system, improved schools, upgraded farms by encouraging use of the latest scientific methods, and enforced prohibition. But Davis was an independent, and not a member of the existing party machines. In 1922 he lost in a race for the U.S. Senate because he dared to buck the Floyd-Byrd leaders. He became embittered and was a harsh critic of later governors and their administrations.

Although he was frequently curt and caustic, Davis and his wife nevertheless hosted numerous lavish parties for the high society of Virginia. Hence Morven Park gained, in the first third of the 20th century, a reputation as having "a nice tradition of gracious hospitality."

In the early 1990s, Bill Myzk became the first curator of

Morven Park. He was no stranger to psychic phenomena. A few years earlier, for example, in 1988, while living in Orange County, he came face to face with the apparition of "half a woman!" His wife saw the vision, too, and it frightened her, but for some reason it didn't scare Bill.

Other things happened. His son had a horse clock. Something kept knocking the clock over on its side. Bill asked his son if he was doing it. He wasn't. Even after Bill moved to an apartment, he kept finding the clock on its side. He never found an explanation for it.

"I used to hear a telephone ringing in the apartment," Bill remembers. "I thought that strange — because I didn't have a phone at the time. I mentioned it to my landlord, and he got a ladder and we went up to the attic and he showed me an old crank-type telephone that had been there for years. It wasn't connected. We had some valuable porcelain. One night I heard this loud crashing sound. It was like some of the porcelain and the horse clock were being smashed to pieces. It also sounded like books were falling out of the bookcase. I went into the room where all this noise occurred, and there was absolutely nothing out of place."

This happened twice. On the second occasion Bill had been dusting books and they were stacked high on a table. He left the room and heard what sounded like a table collapsing and books being flung all over. He ran back in and again found everything exactly as he had left it, not a single book on the floor. The only time he got frightened was when he saw eerie light "slats" emanating from his son's closet. There was no light in the closet. "I thought someone had broken into the house, but when I looked inside there was no one there," he said.

After Bill Myzk took the job at Morven Park he became wrapped up in the work. "No one had ever taken a real inventory of the place before," he says. "I would go around in the house by myself late and night or very early in the morning. There was no one else around at the time. I found things there that no one knew about. One time I found some original drapery in the back of a closet."

One Saturday in February 1995, Bill was in the house taking notations on a clipboard at about 6 a.m. He thought he was alone. "I was upstairs when I heard the distinct sound of a man's footsteps coming from Mrs. Davis' bedroom. I was a couple of rooms over from there. My first reaction was irritation. We had a groundskeeper who sometimes came in early, and I thought it was him. I was a little irritated because I like to work early in the solitude, and this man liked to talk a lot and I wasn't particularly in the mood for that.

"The footsteps moved from that bedroom, across the open wooden floor, heading towards Governor Davis' bedroom. Then I heard the steps moving across the ballroom, toward me. About halfway across that room, the steps stopped, and I thought maybe the groundskeeper had stopped to look out the window. A few seconds went by, and I finally said 'hello.' There was no answer. So I went across the ballroom, heading toward the bedroom. From there I could see across most of the back of the upper floors. There was no one there. I ran back through the bedrooms, the ballroom and the governor's office. Nothing. I went downstairs, but I didn't see anyone. We were closed to the public, so there shouldn't have been anyone else in the house."

Bill continues: "I went back upstairs to Mrs. Davis' bedroom. I remember there was a spectacular view. There were about 50 glass prisms in the room and the sun shining through gave off a very colorful view. Then I heard the footsteps again, moving across the ballroom. There are no rugs or carpets in there, so there was a definite resounding echo. They were moving toward the governor's bedroom. I raced in there, but the room was empty. I could only smile to myself. The steps were as clear as a bell. I wasn't imagining them. It was someone walking up there from room to room at a normal pace. And it definitely was a man's footsteps. I could hear them from a distance and then they kept getting closer. The sounds got louder. But each time I looked, I saw nothing. Later I asked the handyman if he had been in the house that morning. He said he hadn't. I never could explain it."

A year later there was a recurrence. Bill: "It was a Monday in the fall. The house was closed on Mondays. I was standing at the head of the back stairway, leaning on the railing, taking notes on my clipboard. Suddenly, I heard footsteps. They were coming from the entrance way down the stairs. They originated at the back door, and it sounded like someone in a hurry. They went past the kitchen and then into the formal dining room and faded away. Then I realized no one had opened the back door. I would have heard that. I thought it might be my secretary, Sally, so I went downstairs and looked through all the rooms. There was no one there. I called Sally and asked her if she had been in the house. She said no."

Bill adds that once he was in the ballroom late at night during a thunderstorm. Thunder was crackling. "It was pretty dark, the mansion is not well lit at night. It can be a dreary place, especially during a storm. I don't know what it was, but I got a real uneasy feeling. It was like there was a presence about. But I never saw anything. I have heard stories from others about sightings of the governor in the mansion. I don't know. I do know that the footsteps I heard were very real."

Bill says that although the governor and Mrs. Davis often entertained, that he was not an outgoing person. He was private, withdrawn, and even suspicious, once hiring his own security guard who lived in the house. "It is an interesting place," Bill notes, "and sometimes at night it can have a spooky atmosphere all its own. It's a beautiful house, but there's nothing happy about it. The Davises had no children, and this is a big house that needed children."

Does Bill think it might have been the governor who came back to walk through the mansion to see if everything was being kept up. "Could be," he says. "All I know is that on those two occasions someone or something was there. I thought I was alone each time, but I know I wasn't."

Is Historic Oatlands Haunted?

(Loudoun County, near Leesburg)

hen Robert "King" Carter, arguably the great-est land baron in the history of Virginia, died in 1732 (the same year George Washington was born) his will covered 65 printed pages. He left an estate of 330,000 acres of "choice land;" 100 horses, 2,000 cattle and pigs; 1,000 slaves; 10,000 pounds of ster-ling; and a great quantity of silver pieces. He was buried near Irvington, in the cemetery at Christ Church, which had originally been built by his father and he had rebuilt.

Carter descendants continued the legacy, and today there are at least three "Carter houses" still flourishing and open to the public. They include Carter Hall in Clarke County, Carter's Grove near Williamsburg, and Shirley Plantation in Charles City County between Williamsburg and Richmond.

Another fabulous mansion, long in the King Carter family, and now a "museum property" of the National Trust for Historic Preservation, is Oatlands, located on highway 15 about six miles south of Leesburg. It is open to the public daily from late March through December.

Oatlands was built early in the 19th century by George Carter, the great grandson of King Carter. George was born in 1777, the 15th of 17 children (13 girls and four boys). According to the Virginia Landmarks Register, house construction was begun in 1804. It took more than 20 years to complete it. The complex of manor home, out-buildings and formal gardens forms, "one of the nation's most elaborate Federal estates. . . the house has a lightness and elegance matched by few other dwellings of the period."

It took two decades to finish the work because George Carter spared no expense, and apparently didn't care how much time was involved. As one example of such extravagance, for the portico, Carter sent to New York to master carver Henry Farnum for the fashioning of the Corinthian capitals from chestnut wood. They were brought down on flatboats, overland in oxcarts, and put in place five years after being ordered.

Carter added a gristmill, a miller's residence, a brick manufactory, blacksmith shop, store, school and church. Oatlands became a 3,000-acre working plantation, a veritable village in itself. But the good times lasted only a relatively few years. Although the mansion was spared from burning by Union troops during the Civil War, it caused financial chaos for the Carters. After the war Oatlands became a refuge for relatives, friends and emancipated slaves left homeless. Beset by mounting debt, George Carter II opened his home as a summer boarding house — a country resort for affluent Washingtonians. Loudoun County became a vacation retreat for people living in cities to the east. There were horse races in Leesburg and a renowned spa in nearby Snickersville (now Bluemont). Among the regular guests was Phoebe Hearst, the mother of William Randolph Hearst, the newspaper tycoon.

Oatlands

Even this, however, was not enough to keep up with the massive expenses required to operate the mansion, and the Carter family was forced to sell. In 1903, William Corcoran Eustis and his wife, Edith, bought the property. He was a descendent of the philanthropic Corcoran Gallery family. It was said that Edith took one look at the gardens and recommended buying the plantation without looking inside the house. She later wrote: "The garden was falling into ruins; bricks were crumbling, weeds crowding the flowers, and yet the very moss-grown paths seemed to say 'We are still what we were'." She completely restored the four-acre walled garden.

Under the Eustises, Oatlands regained its former grandeur, and in the 1920s and 30s became a "focal point for prominent Washingtonians." There were lavish country weekends, garden parties, and periodical visits from such prominent leaders as Franklin Roosevelt and General George Marshall.

Mr. Eustis died in 1921, and Mrs. Eustis lived at Oatlands until her death in 1964. Their daughters presented the house and land to the National Trust for Historic Preservation a year later, and it was designated a national historic landmark in 1972.

Is Oatlands haunted? Some employees there today say no. A cashier in the gift shop, who has worked at the site for 31 years, says she has heard nothing of a supernatural nature. A supervisor, the wife of Frank Raflo, who wrote a book on the ghosts of Loudoun County, says likewise.

Yet there seems justifiable grounds for the presence of a spirit or spirits considering the history of the house. Among possible candidates: George Carter, who built Oatlands, and then was beset by overwhelming financial difficulties; any number of refugees crowded together in the dark days at the end of the Civil War; or perhaps a distraught tenant during the boarding house days.

And then there was Charles Minnegerode of Richmond, who married a Carter daughter, Virginia. They had 11 children. Charles was wounded during the war, and afterwards became a failure in business ventures. He shot himself at Oatlands, and when the Episcopal Church refused to bury him, his daughter, Marietta Minnegerode Andrews wrote, "Where else to apply (but to) Aunt Kate and Uncle George who put him down in the Carter tomb with the rest of the family."

Historical interpreters, when pressed on the subject, admit that they have sometimes "felt a presence" in the back bedroom upstairs, although they don't know who or what it may be. And then there is the portrait of William Eustis' father, which hangs prominently in the

A Psychic Circle? Jean Jackson of Columbus, Ohio, says her husband took this photo a few years ago on the grounds at Oatlands. She adds that her son is a professional photographer, and when he saw the picture he asked to see the negative, believing there would be a circular spot on it, explaining the phenomena. There was no spot on the negative. "He was bewildered," she says.

large room just inside the front door. The man's eyes seem to follow onlookers as they cross the floor. And, as the interpreters will point out, his left shoe appears to turn toward a person no matter where one stands in the room, left of the portrait, center, or right of it. Curious.

One who believes spirits may linger at Oatlands is Jean Jackson of Columbus, Ohio. She visited the mansion in July 1997, and later wrote the author, saying, "I have had many psychic experiences in Virginia. I studied two years with the English psychic Kat Frain, then seven years with Grace Reeves. If there is a ghost around, I always know it."

She enclosed the above photograph.

There reportedly are ghosts at Carter Hall, Carter's Grove, and Shirley Plantation.

Is Oatlands haunted? Judge for yourself!

CHAPTER 4

Devil Joel and the Ghost Slave

(Loudoun County)

uring the first half of the 19th century the meanest man in Loudoun County, perhaps in all of northern Virginia, was an individual named Joel Osborne. Actually, he was known as Devil Joel Osborne because there apparently was a custom in those days in this region at least that anyone who habitually used profane language was commonly given the sobriquet "Devil" in front of their name, and Joel, more than anyone around, surely earned that distinction.

He was a hard, embittered and cruel man. For obvious reasons, he never married and lived alone on a farm near the little village of Woodrow. Devil Joel's only companion was an old slave named Ben who lived a dreadful life. He was continually mistreated by his sinister master.

It has been documented in the "Bulletin of the Historical Society of Loudoun County," and in the 1958 book, "Tales of Old Virginia," by Joseph V. Nichols, just how harsh things were at the Osborne farm. There was no rest for Ben. He plowed, weeded, cultivated, and cleared the ground during the week, and on Sundays and at times when the land was too wet to work, Devil Joe made Ben dig out rocks from the stony soil and stack them up in piles that were six feet high and eight feet in diameter. It was said there were at one time at least a dozen of these piles surrounding the farmhouse.

Whenever Devil Joel had been drinking, which was often, or when he thought Ben wasn't piling rocks fast enough, he had a nasty habit of banging Ben over the head with a club. This usually knocked the slave to the ground and sometimes rendered him unconscious. Slowly, Ben would recover, stagger to his feet and continue his arduous task. Ben's friends and even some of Devil Joel's relatives urged the poor slave to escape, but he never managed to summon enough courage to do so.

As the years went by, and Devil Joel's drinking became heavier, the beatings increased. Finally, one particularly rainy day, as the two sat in a wagon husk waiting for the storm to let up, Devil Joel became enraged for no apparent reason and struck Ben a heavy blow with a hoe handle, again knocking him senseless. But this time Ben didn't get up. He was dead.

Curiously, Devil Joel was brought before the county justices and no charges were filed. It was determined, according to the law at the time, that if a slave owner accidently wounded or killed one of his slaves   if there had been no intent to kill — there was no crime. Devil Joel was free.

At least he was free according to commonwealth law. But perhaps there is a higher authority sitting in judgment. For after that brutal act, Devil Joel became a haunted man. He could not sleep at night. He had, he said, terrifying nightmares. He seemed to be withering away. His relatives became so worried about his condition that a cousin, Joseph Osborne, temporarily moved in with Devil Joel to see if he could determine what was happening to him.

The two men slept in the same room with both doors bolted shut. One night Joseph was awakened at midnight. He looked up and heard Devil Joel cursing Ben. Joseph lit a candle and saw his disturbed cousin thrashing about at nothing that could be seen. Devil Joel then backed away, fell onto his bed, and begged the apparitional Ben to leave him alone. Joseph shook him, but he was shaking violently and perspiration was running down his face.

These ghostly visitations at night went on for several months, causing the frightened Devil Joel to drink more and more, and one night in a delirium, at age 55, he died.

There is a post-script to this affair. In the days following the Civil War, several ex-slaves in the area swore that on certain bright Sunday evenings, as they passed by the Osborne farm, they could see the visions of Devil Joel, sitting on a stump with a big club in his hands, and Ben, nearby, stacking rocks in a neat pile.

Phantasmal Entities in Prince William

(Prince William County)

(Author's note: As I said so many times, I love delving into old Virginia history books. I was therefore excited to find a volume I hadn't seen before at the Big Flea Market at the Capitol Expo Center in Chantilly, Virginia, in August 1998. The book was "Prince William — The Story of Its Places and Its People." It was originally compiled by members of the Writers' Program of the Work Progress Administration in 1941. It was full of historical vignettes and anecdotes . . . just the kind of fascinating minutia that absorbs me. Here are some excerpts. Prince William County, by the way, is located south of Fairfax County and north of Stafford County, and includes Dale City, Manassas, and Quantico.)

ome of the more interesting accounts involved tombstones. The oldest tombstone in the county belongs to a woman named Rose Peters. Her inscription reads as follows:

"In memory of Rose Peters who departed this life the
    10th of September 1690
She is gone, o she is gone to everlasting rest, to
    Christ our Blessed Savior who loves sinners best"

There is this footnote: "Nothing, however, is definitely known of Rose Peters except that she was a sinner. The records show that a woman by the name of Rose Peters was escorted out of

Middlesex in 1685 because of conduct offensive to her neighbors. Whether or not poor Rose continued her sinful career in Prince William before going to 'everlasting rest' must remain a matter of conjecture."

Northeast of Bel Aire, an historic old home, is the site of Smithfield. Here, a man named Peter Trone and his wife are buried in a small graveyard. His tombstone reads:
"Sacred to the memory of Peter Trone who departed this life
  March 23rd 1832, in the 63rd year of his age.

> Hark from the tomb a doleful sound
> mine ears attend a cry,
> Ye living men come view the ground
> where you must shortly lie"

Next to this is his wife's stone:
"Sacred to the memory of Sarah Ann Trone, relict of Peter Trone,
  who departed this life May 16th, 1857, in the 89th year of her age.

> Princess, this clay must be your bed
> in spite of all your towers,
> the tall, the wise, the reverend head
> must lie as low as ours"

There are a couple of colorful tombstones off state road 234 at a site once known as the old Tansill Place.

"In Memory of Jesse Evans, who died 11th of June 1814, aged 56 yrs, 9 mo, 27 days.

Pale Death he gave the Fatal blow
The stroke was certain
The effect sure
Fearing pain death kept me opprest,
— mercy kindly gave me rest."

The second one:

"In memory of James G. Evans.

He was born Dec. 6th, 1785 and departed this life Oct 2d, 1816 in the 31st year of his age.

Stoop down my thoughts that used to rise,
Converse a while with death
Think how a gasping mortal lyes
And pants away his breath,
His quivering lip hangs feebly down
His pulse is faint and few,
Then speechless, with a doleful groan,
He bids the world adieu."

And then there is this warning on the tombstone of a woman named Patsy Groves, who died at age 26, in 1815:

"my friends, I bid you all adieu
the debt i owe is now come due.
in peace i lived, in peace i died.
i hope my aviou has not been denied.
farewell, friends, for i am gone,
amend your lives and follow on"

And in a family burial plot of the descendants of Jesse Ewell, near Haymarket, is this cryptic and poignant legend on the tomb of a one-year-old child named Alberta Ewell, who died in 1853:

"Like early dew, she sparkled, and was exhaled."

There are a few old houses, or ruins of houses, where, if there are no ghosts, there probably should be. Near the community of Groveton, for instance, are the remains of a house once known as "Folly Castle." It was so named by a man who "disapproved the goings-on of the young folk gathering here for frolics. It was not until 1899, however, that a fire put an end to Folly Castle and frivolity. Now a few flowers that bloom with perennial insistence where there was once a lovely garden, a pear tree believed to have been brought from England . . . the old foundations and chimney, and a burying ground — without a stone to tell its story — are reminders of Folly Castle's long ago."

Somewhere off county road 608 is a place known 60 years ago as Fairview, and once owned by an apparent tyrant named Jerry Herndon. Here is what the WPA writers said about it: "Stories lingering about Fairview have to do with the mistreatment by Herndon of his six sons and his few slaves. It seems that his sons were never allowed to know their own ages and were kept illiterate so that Herndon might obtain several years of additional labor after maturity had been reached. Jeremiah Herndon quickly converted his profits into gold and hid them securely until 1872, when an ex-slave, who had little love for the family, discovered the hiding place, killed Herndon and his wife, and made away with the cherished possessions of this Midas of Prince William.

"When the Negro spent some of the gold, however, he was caught, and was tried and hung at Brentsville. Various excavations still discernible in the basement of the house are explained by the accepted belief that Herndon had hidden more gold than was discovered by his murderer. No one, it seems, found a single sparkling coin."

Now for the ghosts. In the vicinity of Haymarket stands an old house called "Snow Hill." Above the cellar are 12 rooms, with finely executed woodwork. "Of interest also are the poplar paneling, the winding stairway, the unusual mantel, crucifix doors, and heavy brass locks." It dates to the second half of the 18th century, and, apparently, was built on the site of an ancient Indian burial ground.

"The ghost of an Indian chief still haunts the cellar of Snow Hill — forgetful never, it seems, that a white man committed the sacrilege of building upon a spot held sacred by the Indians. A huge poplar tree, which furnished wood enough for the beautiful paneling, once stood here; its roots, the old folks say, used to be visible in the cellar. The stalwart chief, so the story goes, was killed beneath this tree while protesting the white man's desecration and was buried under a mound that is still clearly outlined. Indian relics are found roundabout, and many a person will testify that the ghost of the chief is far from appeased."

Nearby is another house known simply as "The Shelter," also believed to be more than 200 years old. The WPA writers: "Here is another of the many Prince William houses that cherish their ghosts. A butler, long dead, is known upon occasion to open a heavy door that leads into the dining room. Another spectral visitor is accompanied by strange noises and moving lights. This is the ghost of a very old woman, a member of a disagreeable family whom the neighbors called the "Rattlesnake Grahams." Her body was borne to the burying ground by relatives because neither horses nor oxen would perform the service. Her unhappy spirit for many years dwelt in a large tree, upon which even tenacious ivy would not cling."

At a crossroads called Catharpin stands "Oakwood," a house that was originally built about 1830. "This was the home of a much beloved woman known throughout Prince William as Miss Sally Ball. Apparently she took as her model the 'virtuous' woman described in the last chapter of Proverbs, who was proficient in many vocations but particularly stretched out her hand to the poor and needy. There are those who still remember 'Miss Sally.' One old gentleman of Prince William recalls that when he was a small boy a false prophet predicted the end of the world. Immediately the lad fled to 'Miss Sally,' believing that with her he would be safe.

"In the old burying ground to the east of the house is the grave of a young man, William Bronaught, who was accidentally shot on a hunting trip while visiting Oakwood. Of course, he comes back now and then — as many a neighbor will attest. For some reason the ghost chooses to ride in a cart and to mingle his groans with the howling of a hunting dog."

Off county road 626 once stood a large brick house called "Berea." Here lived Sophia Carter (1778-1832), the daughter of Robert "King" Carter's grandson, Councillor Robert Carter. "Persistent stories in Prince William attest that this Sophia was a woman worth remembering. A strong will she had and sagacity, it seems, and also many petty vanities and idiosyncrasies. In great state she would make yearly visits to her Carter relatives at Pittsylvania and Sudley.

"Hours on end — so it is said — she would primp before her mirror, never appearing in public unless she was the pink of fashion. In her later years she would sit in the great hall, calling for maids to bring her fresh kerchiefs and a variety of lace caps. When she died, it was found that she had left money for the support of a 'female' charity school for destitute orphans.

"South of the site of the house Sophia Carter sleeps in the burying ground, her grave marked by a single tombstone. It is not strange that the ghost of so strong-minded a woman should linger about the place. For years after her death those who slept in her bedroom would find that during the night sheets and blankets were stolen from above them; and a woman with a lighted candle used to walk to the storeroom each night to be certain that the door was locked."

And, finally, there is the site of Sudley Mill. It, too, is, or was, haunted. Here's what the WPA writers found: "After mid-eighteenth century and all through the nineteenth, farmers from far and wide brought their corn to be ground. In ante-bellum days, ox carts, great Conestoga wagons with their six-horse teams, and men on horseback with sacks of grain swinging behind them, would be lined along the road awaiting their turn. Mills in those days were gossipy centers. Here news was dispensed to be grape-vined throughout the surrounding community.

"It is safe to say that there was a tavern close by, for men who wandered from home after days in the field were always athirst for the sort of refreshments mine host could serve. The Sudley Mill continued to operate through the first decade of the twentieth century.

"It stood idle for 30 years. Then its owner, an elderly lady who had an unreasonable objection to the ghost that frequented the spot, had it torn down. Whether or not the spirits departed is still a matter of local conjecture.

"Yet it is thought that Sam still comes back now and then to be quite certain that all his gold was discovered by the person for whom it was intended. Sam, it seems, was a slave of Landon Carter of Woodlawn, once owner of the mill. Because he was too old to work at strenuous labor, Mr. Carter put him in charge of the store near the mill and allowed him to keep the profits for himself. Having no need for money, Sam converted greenbacks to gold and was saving enough to purchase his and his wife's freedom when death put an end to his ambition.

"On the third morning after Sam's funeral one Mr. Fortune, then the miller, came upon the old Negro standing before him and insisting that $500 worth of gold would be found in a tar bucket on the third story of the mill. Mr. Fortune relayed the story to Mr. Carter. An investigation followed, and sure enough there was the gold exactly where Sam had said it would be. Upon the head of poor Mr. Fortune, however, fell condemnation of the pious members of the Sudley Methodist Church, who had him brought to trial in the presence of a gaping crowd of his neighbors.

"It was the minister who put an end to the matter by declaring that, although the story was most fantastic, Mr. Fortune undoubtedly believed it to be true and should not be convicted as a liar.

"There are people in Prince William who still think that the elderly lady showed the better part of valor when she caused the large stone structure to be razed."

The Happy Host of Federal Hill

(Fredericksburg)

I f there is a ghost at Federal Hill in Fredericksburg — the house owner, Mrs. Bess Lanier, doesn't happen to believe in such things, although she readily admits many others have claimed to have seen apparitions there — then it may well be the jolliest specter in all of Virginia. He allegedly is none other than Alexander Spotswood, former governor of the colony, explorer, military expert, aristocrat and bon vivant. He is said to appear, to those who have seen him, standing by the dining room sideboard, smiling, and mixing his favorite liquid concoctions. On occasion, he has even lifted a glass in a toast — either to startled onlookers, or to his own portrait which hangs on a nearby wall. No one is really quite sure. In fact, people at the Fredericksburg Visitor Center have called Spotswood a "ghostly spirit full of spirits."

This colorful Scotsman, who was born in 1676, is said by some biographers and historians to have administered one of the most notable terms in the entire colonial era when he was Virginia's chief executive from 1710 to 1722. He pursued a more enlightened and humane policy toward the Indians. He had a low tolerance for outlaws, and is the man responsible for the death of the notorious pirate Edward Teach, better known as Blackbeard. Williamsburg flourished under his ruling guidance. One colonial scholar summed up Spotswood's career by writing: "The 12 years of his governorship were full of energy, and much was done for the bet-

Federal Hill

terment of the colony."

He also was noted as being somewhat of an adventurer, and he never turned down an invitation to a good party. It was Alexander Spotswood, who, in 1716, gathered up a group of "convivial gentlemen" and set out to explore the Blue Ridge Mountains. The expedition — the first such attempted by Englishmen — included 63 men, 74 horses, an assortment of dogs and a "vast quantity of alcoholic beverages." They fought off hornets and rattlesnakes, shot bear and deer for their suppers, and generally had a grand old time.

After reaching what they perceived to be the top of the mountains, they came down into the valley, camped beside a river, and decided it was time to celebrate their accomplishment. A description of this event was duly recorded by John Fontaine, a member of the group. He wrote the following:

"We had a good dinner, and after we got the men together, and loaded all their arms, and we drank the King's health in champagne and fired a volley, and all the rest of the Royal Family and fired a volley — the Princess' health in Burgundy, and fired a volley, and all the rest of the Royal family in claret and fired a volley. We drank the Governor's health, and fired another volley. We had several sorts of liquors, viz., Virginia red wine and white, Irish usquebaugh, brandy, shrub, two sorts of rum, champagne, canary, cherry, punch, water, cider, etc."

Is it any wonder where Spotswood got his reputation for having a good time? Upon their return home, the governor presented each of his companions with a golden horseshoe "covered with valuable stones resembling heads of nails," and they all became known in history as the Knights of the Golden Horseshoe."

In his later years, Spotswood migrated to the Fredericksburg area. He lived in Germanna for a while, and owned considerable property in Spotsylvania, Orange and Culpeper counties. It is along here where the story gets a little — well —spotty. According to some accounts, including a 1931 edition of "Homes and Gardens in Virginia," and the 1930 publication of Margaret DuPont Lee's "Virginia Ghosts," Federal Hill either was built by or for the now ex-governor.

However, according to the third edition of the Virginia Landmarks Register, printed in 1987, Federal Hill "is a late 18th century architecturally formal dwelling which illustrates the dignity that could be achieved with wood-frame construction. It was built ca. 1795 for Robert Brooke, governor of Virginia 1794-96." Now if that is the case, Spotswood couldn't have lived, or even visited there, because he died in 1740! Maybe, if he didn't live there, he came back in spirit form because he liked the house and what went on in it.

In any event, it appears that Governor Brooke did buy the house at some point, whether it was built for him, Spotswood, or someone else, and he renamed it Federal Hill after the Federalist Party of which he was one of the founders. It is, nevertheless, a large, two-story frame house with walls of solid brick beneath the white clapboard. The interior has been described as "elegant," and contains "exquisitely carved woodwork of great dignity." The ballroom, occupying the entire north end of the first floor, has woodwork similar to that from the ballroom of Gadsby's Tavern in Alexandria, which is now displayed in the Metropolitan Museum of Art. A rare early summerhouse with louvered sides and ogee-domed roof (whatever that is) stands in the garden.

The legends of the reappearance of Spotswood at the house date back to early in the 20th century. Mrs. Henry Theodora Wight bought the property around 1910. According to at least one version, there were two sideboards in the dining room, because "in olden times huge hunt breakfasts were often given by Governor Spotswood and his lady." The smaller sideboard was used for the bowls of apple-toddy, eggnog, hot grog, etc., the customary drinks of the day.

It is here that a number of people through several generations have claimed to have seen the Governor. And the recollections of the sightings all have a strikingly similar ring, although many of those who witnessed the apparition were not aware that others had, too. The consensus is that Spotswood suddenly just appears, in front of the small sideboard, dressed in a pink coat and hunting breeches, "pleasantly engaged in mixing drinks."

In one fairly credible account, very early this century, Mrs. Wight had invited Mrs. Margaret Halsey Weir to dine with her at Federal Hill. But when she arrived, Mrs. Wight had to apologize that her cook and waitress had suddenly disappeared. She then explained that the cook's young daughter had told them she had seen "an old gentleman, with boy's pants, with a white plait down the back, tied with a black string" standing by the sideboard. The girl then said, "He had a silver cup histed (hoisted) to de picture of a old gentleman on wall." She then indicated that the gentleman she saw and the portrait on the wall were one and the same man. Mrs. Wight concluded that the child was too young to have invented such a story. Anyway, it was certain that the girl's mother and the waitress believed her, because they packed their belongings and left!

Mrs. Wight herself experienced the same phenomenon, although with somewhat different details, about a year later. She was drafting some business correspondence at her desk in the library about dusk one evening when the "same old gentleman" appeared to her, complete with boy's pants and pink coat and plait, but minus the silver cup. He lingered there a "long minute," she said, "and then faded gently into the twilight, much as though a curtain of gauze shut him from sight!"

In the intervening years, others have reported similar sensations in the dining room at Federal Hill. When the author first called Mrs. Lanier, the present owner, and asked her about the ghost stories associated with the house, she laughed a hearty laugh.

"If I did believe in ghosts, I guess I would be scared to death, because if there ever was a house that could be haunted this would be it." Mrs. Lanier and her late husband bought Federal Hill in 1947, and later began extensive renovations. "You wouldn't believe all the things we found here," she says. "We found great numbers of Civil War bullets, cannonballs, and hand-made nails." Indeed, the house was in the direct line of fire during the battle of Fredericksburg in 1862, and the old trenches still extend across the back lawn and terrace. It is said that Confederate general T. R. Cobb was killed in battle while facing the mansion, and a fragment of the shell can be seen beneath the northwest window of the drawing room that was turned into an operating room. "As I said," Mrs. Lanier noted, "if there were such things as ghosts, I'm sure they would be here."

Ironically, although Mrs. Lanier doesn't believe in haunting spirits, she and her husband had the house exorcized from ghosts in 1949, before they moved in! "We had some friends over to look at

Alexander Spotswood

the inside of the house while the repairs were being made," she says. It was a Captain and Mrs. Porter. Mrs. Porter had psychic sensitivities, and she and her husband had their house, Colby, on the Potomac near Alexandria, exorcized, because there supposedly was a ghost in residence there.

"I remember that the house was just a shell then," said Mrs. Lanier. "Everything had been stripped down in preparation for the renovations. We walked into the library and Mrs. Porter said she had a strong sensation that there was a 'presence' in the room. Because of this and the fact that there were so many stories associated with the house, she suggested that we have it 'done', too."

"So we talked to the minister at St. George's Church, and he said the bishop would be in town the following week." House exorcisms, it should be noted, are not taken lightly by the clergy. It helps, of course, to have a thorough understanding of what is involved, and the rites are performed in a very serious manner.

In this case, apparently nothing dramatic happened, as it did in the movie versions of "The Exorcist," and "The Amityville Horror," when priests were attacked, and in one instance killed. Mrs. Lanier says the bishop and the rector at St. George's came over one day, and as best she can recall they walked around on the first floor carrying prayer books and blessed the house. She doesn't remember them sprinkling any Holy water, or anything like that. She did say, however, that they didn't go upstairs, because it was in such "a shambles."

Mrs. Lee Langston Harrison, curator of the James Monroe museum, says that while the Laniers had the house exorcized, the upstairs and the attic definitely were not covered in the ministrations. She should know, because she lived in an attic room for a brief period when she first moved to Fredericksburg.

"It is a big, haunting house, there's no doubt about that," Mrs. Harrison says today. "When it was used as an army hospital during the Civil War, bodies had been stored in the basement, or ice house. I can remember hearing the story that one servant wouldn't go in the house until it had been exorcized because she told everyone who would listen that she wasn't going to 'be around no hants'.

"I moved into a 'turret' room — the house has lots of turrets and gables — in the late spring of 1986. Shortly after I had been there a few nights, I was awakened in the pre-dawn hours with a start. A table against one of the gables was banging against the wall. At first, I thought it might be noise made by one of the other tenants in the house. There was an aerobics instructor living downstairs.

But this specific banging kept occurring, always late at night, for two weeks straight," Mrs. Harrison says.

"I started sleeping with a hall light on. But every night I kept getting waked up out of a dead sleep about two or three in the morning. I started getting really scared. A young girl in the house who was really interested in psychic phenomena asked if she could sleep in my room one night, and she did, but nothing happened. Then one night I was roused at about 2:30 a.m., and the room was filled with what I can only describe as TV snow. You know, what it looks like when the cable goes out, or the station signs off for the night. The whole room was filled with this, and there was some sort of swooshing sound.

"I had a feeling of absolute terror. I sat up and screamed. And then I told the ghost, or whatever it was that was causing all this, if they would leave me alone I would be out of the house within a few days.

"Shortly after this, another young girl who had psychic sensitivities examined the room. She said she found much 'activity' all along one wall in the room, and that there was a spirit who was not malevolent in the closet behind my wall on the same floor as the attic. She said this area had been used as a surgery room during the War Between the States, and that many soldiers had died both from the surgery and from the lack of it. I certainly didn't doubt her, and I couldn't wait to get out of the house, which I did soon after."

Thus, it seems, colorful legends of a most mysterious nature abound at venerable old Federal Hill. Alexander Spotswood would have loved it. Undoubtedly, he would raise a glass to toast his haunting companions!

The Hauntings in 'Hooker's Houses'

e was one of the more colorful, if not successful, Union generals of the Civil War. He has been described as feisty, frank, manly and energetic, "but of somewhat less breadth of intellect than expected." He also was ambitious and was never reluctant to criticize his superior officers, especially generals George McClelland and Ambrose Burnside. In time he did reach his goal as commanding general of the Army of the Potomac, but his tenure was shortened by President Abraham Lincoln, who dismissed him and several field commanders for ineffectiveness.

This was Major General Joseph Hooker — "Fighting Joe" — as he was known.

Curiously, Hooker figures in two haunted houses. He made his headquarters in each of them in the days preceding and during the Battle of Fredericksburg.

The first house, Rose Hill, actually is located just across the Potomac River in southern Maryland, east north east of Fredericksburg. It was, in the late 18th century and early 19th, the home of Dr. Gustavus Brown, a well-respected physician who, it is said, attended George Washington at his death bed.

There was a long-standing legend at Rose Hill, dating back to Dr. Brown's era, or possibly even earlier, that a death in the family living in the house was always preceded by the baying of a "blue dog." No one knew the origin of the legend.

Some years after the doctor passed on, in 1801, the house was bequeathed to Miss Olivia Floyd, a woman known for her "intelligence and energy." She also showed uncommon courage, or perhaps craziness, in the face of danger. When the Union army came through the area and Hooker confiscated her house, she hid the family silver in the casket of the late Dr. Brown. And one day when the general was out and some of his staff aides were eyeing her fowl, she ran out of the house brandishing two pistols, one in each hand, and allegedly said: "Leave my chickens alone, you Yankees, or I'll put you in hell in five minutes."

If there was doubt by some that the blue dog's howling signaled an imminent death, it was forever dispelled, when the dog was heard yowling one night during the Civil War. This was followed shortly afterward by three sharp raps at the front door. Miss Floyd was then informed that her brother had just been killed in battle!

* * * * *

The second house that General Hooker used as a temporary headquarters preceding the fighting at Fredericksburg in December 1862, is called Locust Grove Farm. It is in Stafford County, about five miles north of Fredericksburg. The present owner is Joady Chaplin who has lived there since 1964. She says the land was originally part of a huge tract granted by King George of England to the Peyton family in the 18th century. Courthouse records indicate the house dates to about 1824. There are four large rooms downstairs and upstairs with a central hallway. The Chaplins added on a bedroom and a back deck, but took pains to maintain the integrity of the building. Hooker arrived here sometime late in 1862 when the Union army set up Camp Selvon, a huge area. Tens of thousands of Yankee troops camped in the vicinity.

The ghostly phenomena at Locust Grove began almost immediately after the Chaplin family moved in 36 years ago. The first to experience it was their youngest daughter, then four years old. "She came down one morning and said, 'who was visiting us last night'," Joady remembers. "We told her no one and said why do you ask. She replied, 'Well, then, who was that old man and woman who were in my bedroom?'

"We, of course, dismissed it at first, thinking it was the child's imagination. But both my daughters, the other one was six, said they saw the same couple several times. They said the man and woman were dressed in old clothes and the woman had buttons on her shoes. Then I began to get the feeling of a presence of some sort when I was alone in the house. I can't quite describe it, but it was like you knew someone else was in the room with you."

Joady continues: "One night I saw what appeared to be an old woman. It was a filmy, whitish apparitional figure. I couldn't make out any sharp features or clothing. It appeared at the bedroom door, came up to the foot of my bed and then just vanished. For some reason I wasn't at all afraid. Now my late husband was definitely not a believer in the supernatural. He said he had to see and feel something to believe it. One night he was sitting in the kitchen by himself when he looked up and he saw the image of an old man with gray hair and glasses. He started to say something to the man but he disappeared before his eyes. After that, my husband believed."

Other phenomena include a mystery guest on an upstairs bed and a little boy, about seven or eight years old. Joady's oldest daughter said she sometimes felt as if someone got into the bed with her, like the mattress would be pushed down and leave a visible depression. The boy was never seen in the house, but always romping about in the back yard.

"At first my daughters thought it was a neighbor's child named Jeffrey, but we called their house and Jeffrey was at home. The boy was dressed in clothes of another time, and he, too, would appear and then be gone in a flash."

Joady has not done any specific research to seek out who the apparitional couple and the little boy may have been. "But I did hear that sometime long ago the Peytons lost the house by gambling. There used to be an old horse racing track here and the Peytons apparently gambled heavily. The house was sold for taxes. if I had to guess, I would say that may be who the couple is . . . they must have loved the house and return to see that it's being taken care of. The little boy, I don't know. Maybe a Peyton child died a tragic death here."

Joady adds that she has not heard about the ghosts from any of the previous owners, but there is something strange about that. "I know Mrs. Widden well. She used to live here and I know she loved this house. But she would never come back to it. She has driven by the house many times but she would never stop and come inside. I don't know why.

"I will say, too, that this house has a 'hold' on you. You can't leave it. Since my husband died, friends have asked me why I don't sell it and move closer to town. There's no way I could ever sell Locust Grove."

Joady says hundreds of Civil War relics have been found in the grounds and woods surrounding the house. She personally has uncovered bullets, Union sardine cans and other artifacts.

One can only wonder if General Joe Hooker himself ever came face to face with either the blue dog of Rose Hill or the man, woman and little boy at Locust Grove Farm.

CHAPTER 8

The Horrifying Secret of the 'Lady in White'

(Northern Virginia)

(Author's note: This business of real ghost writing is getting more and more competitive. When I began this series of books back in 1983, there was virtually nothing on the subject available. Margaret DuPont Lee had written "Virginia Ghosts" in 1930, and it had been reprinted in 1966, but by this time it had been out of print for a few years. Today, there is a growing proliferation of material on the subject — both in book form and in the number of ghost tours around the commonwealth. Some of the volumes are pretty good, some so-so, and some are not so good.

mong the ones I found interesting is "Ghost Stories and Legends from the Old Confederacy," by Dr. Kenneth Stuart McAtee, a native of Berryville who now lives in Fairfax. A spry octogenarian, Dr. McAtee is a retired dentist who has specialized in research on his personal hero — John Singleton Mosby, the famous guerrilla fighter of the Civil War. However, the good doctor also has delved into the supernatural, and has published three books on regional ghosts in northern Virginia. He writes with a folksy, down-home style that is highly readable. And he is serious about his subject. He says he has a little psychic ability, his daughter has more, and his granddaughter absolutely sees things other people don't.

The following account, which I found intriguing, is from Dr. McAtee's second book, and is excerpted and adapted here with his permission. It involves a man and a woman who were born in the 19th century and the story is told by their grandson who has requested to remain anonymous. It occurred in a rural farm area in the general vicinity of Berryville.)

"Grandfather married well, and my grandmother was a pretty lady according to the pictures we have of her. They had two boys and three girls who all turned out well considering they only attended a one-room school.

"Come winter in the mid-twenties (1920s), my grandmother just dropped over dead in her kitchen in front of the youngest girl. She never said a word, and as she had always enjoyed good health, it was a complete surprise. Of course, all of the family was real upset, and my grandfather sent over to the county seat for the undertaker. Now that fellow had gone on vacation and there wasn't anyone else available. Folks in those days were a lot more self-reliant, and since there was no one else close, the neighbors went right to work.

"The women came in and washed my grandmother's body and dressed her in a white dress. She had always had real long beautiful hair, and they combed it and stuck in some artificial flowers. It being winter, they didn't have any real ones that time of year on the farm. The men got together and made a nice walnut casket that met grandfather's approval.

"They laid her out in the parlor, crossed her hands across her breast and had her holding a Bible, and cut a bunch of evergreens, pine branches that is, for decorations behind the casket. One of my aunts used to say that every time she smelled the scent of pine she always remembered her mother's funeral.

"There happened to be a preacher nearby, so they held funeral services the next day. They had to do this as she hadn't been embalmed, and they couldn't hold her body. The ground hadn't froze too hard for the neighboring men to dig a grave in the church-yard. The old church had been used as a hospital during the Civil War. She was buried the following day. It was a very sad occasion, especially because my grandmother was not given to sickness, in fact, she was up and going when everyone else was down.

"About a week after she was buried, a neighboring boy coming home near dark had a scare! He claimed his horse stopped in the road near where grandmother had been buried and wouldn't move, and as he was getting mad at the animal, a 'Lady in White' just floated across the road. He was scared to death, and said she had long flowing hair with flowers in it, and he swore it looked just like my grandmother who he had known for some years. Well, his family told him to shut up about the matter as they didn't want to cause my grandfather any more pain than he had already suffered.

"It wasn't long after that when two of the neighborhood men coming back from the county seat swore they saw the same thing! Of course, they had both been known to take a drink from time to time, and the whole affair was blamed on bad liquor.

"Although these stories got out, no one paid much attention to them until one day my aunt saw the Lady in White out of the kitchen window. She was terrified and they couldn't get the story out of her for a day or two. She finally said she was standing by the dishpan washing dishes, when grandmother, carrying a bouquet of flowers like she used to, walked right across the back yard. And she said the smell of pine was strong right there in the kitchen for a few minutes.

"Next thing, my younger uncle who as known to take a drink or two, was coming home in an open Model T Ford, and as he came up on the church there came the Lady in White floating towards him! He stopped the car and said she pointed her arm at him just like grandmother used to do when he got to drinking. Well now, he sobered up and wouldn't touch liquor at all except maybe a short nip at a wedding or something. He changed for the better and even got to be a deacon in the church in his later years. His wife used to say she wished he had seen that ghost about 20 years sooner for they would have had a better marriage and a lot more money.

"Over the years the smell of pine would suddenly appear in the parlor of the house, and any animals, cats and such, would high tail it out of the house when this happened. The family tried to hush these things up, but every so often someone would report seeing the Lady in White, usually in the cemetery.

"Now as grandfather got a little age on him, he used to read a lot and not spend so much time doing farm work. A magazine arrived that carried an advertisement for what were then new concrete burial vaults. The ad had a cutaway showing two caskets in the ground, one was full of water and the casket protected by the concrete vault was dry. The ad asked, 'Is seepage disturbing your loved ones?' It wasn't a very comforting ad, and grandfather got to studying on the issue.

"He finally went over to the county seat and told that undertaker he wanted him to get one of those concrete vaults for grandmother, and that fellow convinced him if they were going to dig her up that she ought to have a new metal casket. He told grandfather he would have to get authorization to dig her up and that might be a problem, but grandfather said he would take care of the matter.

"Grandfather went on along to the courthouse and saw that one-legged judge they used to have. He lost his leg in the Spanish-American War. Between the Civil War and the Spanish-American War, there wasn't much chance of a fellow getting elected to office if he hadn't lost an arm or leg or was crippled up. Later, this applied to World War I veterans, except if they had been gassed they couldn't look too healthy. Well, the judge just wrote out an authorization to open the grave for he knew grandfather had a lot of votes in the family and in the neighborhood. As long as the judge could have those votes, why I don't think he would have cared if grandfather would have had her dug up and had a taxidermist stuff her for display!

"So they set a date to install the new vault, and grandfather got my uncle to help dig open the grave. That concrete vault was heavy and the undertaker had some brothers who did logging and move heavy objects, come and erect a tripod with ropes and pulleys to handle it.

"Things went along pretty well and my uncles soon dug down to the box over the casket, which was pretty rotten and caved in. The casket was some better, but one end corner was gone. Well, grandfather said he didn't want to be there when they opened the casket, so he strolled off back of the cemetery. He was fooling around there when he heard one of my uncles exclaim something real loud and saw there was a lot of excitement over at the grave.

"When they opened the casket there wasn't much left but bones and hair and the dress that had stood up real well. But the thing was — grandmother's arms were no longer crossed on her breast, but were down along side her body, and her hands were full of hair!

"The poor woman had been buried alive!

"And when she came to she had reached up and pulled out all of her hair in terror!

"It was a horrible thing, and I think grandfather may have suffered a slight stroke right then. They couldn't do anything but re-bury her, and they did so right where she is today. Grandfather's health failed, and he didn't last long after that, and he always had feelings of guilt. Of course, a lot of the neighbors helped at the time, and they all believed she was dead then, so it wasn't really his fault.

"So that is a ghost story it is all right to tell now that so many of the people involved have passed on. The Lady in White who used

to be seen so often at the cemetery . . . . was seen no more. I guess the ghost just wanted to let people know what an awful thing had happened, and when they found out, why then she was at rest."

* * * * *

There was a happier ending to a somewhat similar situation more than 100 years ago in Bristol, in the far southwestern corner of the commonwealth. There was a severe thunderstorm early one morning in May 1883. An elderly lady went over to close a back window, and just as she did, a bolt of lightning struck a large tree only a few feet away. The jolt knocked the woman to the floor and when help arrived no pulse could be felt. Within a short period of time a nearby doctor was summoned and he pronounced her dead.

After the storm had passed, a close friend went to a local shop for a coffin, while other men were sent to the East Hill Cemetery to start digging a grave. (Apparently they didn't waste any time committing the recently departed to the ground in those days in Bristol.) Within hours the coffin was brought to the house.

Burial clothes were laid out and some neighbor ladies were giving the "corpse" a final bath, when, suddenly, the woman revived. She sat up and though dazed, asked those around her what was going on. There was no one to answer her. The petrified ladies had literally stampeded out the bedroom door!

Return to Windover Heights
(Vienna)

(Author's note: In "The Ghosts of Virginia, Volume II," (1994), I wrote a rather extensive chapter on a house in Vienna known as Windover Heights. Here, in synopsis, is part of what I said: "In the endless sea of look-alike condominiums, tract homes and townhouses which ring Washington, D.C., Windover Heights, virtually hidden on Walnut Lane in Vienna, stands like a lost beacon harkening back to an era of architectural elegance that belonged to another time. It has been described as having the appearance of a country manor, elegant in its grandeur, although by plantation standards, it is not a particularly large house. Depending upon whether or not you count the bathrooms (and walk-in closets), there are roughly 15 to 20 rooms, including a walled off area that conceals a secret passageway.

"The present house was built sometime between 1865 and 1869 (there are varying accounts) by a man named Captain Harmon L. Salisbury, who had commanded the 16th regiment of U.S. Colored Infantry during the Civil War. Windover Heights was built upon the foundations of a much earlier building, Huntington House, which was believed to have been destroyed by fire either during the Civil War or immediately afterward. A barn, a cupola (and a widow's walk) add further charisma to the property.

"In addition to the secret passageway inside, it is said that tunnels once ran from the basement to the barn. Whether these were dug in Salisbury's day, or date further back, is not clear, although the likelihood is that they may have been installed as an escape route from any invasion of Union soldiers. There is a report that the original Huntington House on the site was 'riddled with bullets' during the fighting in the 1860s before it was destroyed by fire.

"No one knows for sure just how many bodies are buried on the grounds. There are at least five: the wife of Captain Salisbury and two of their children; and a former slave and his daughter. It is not inconceivable that there may be a number of others, possibly former slaves and servants, and perhaps fallen soldiers from both the North and the South, unidentified victims of the fierce fighting that raged throughout the area.

"Beyond this, there are a number of suspected dark tragedies which took place either at Windover Heights, or its predecessor, Huntington House. There is no firm documentation on this — early records have been consumed or lost by fire — but it is strongly felt that there has been at least one murder-suicide here, possibly a second murder, and a terrible accident which killed another person.

"If ever a house was a prime candidate for the presence of supernatural spirits, this would be it.

"Consequently, over the past century and a quarter, Windover Heights has harbored a reputation as being haunted by as many as five or more ghosts! These may include: a benevolent female phantom, there to watch over resident children; a vindictive spirit, there to drive people away, especially those who attempt to renovate or change the house; victims of past tragedies seeking exposure of their ill-fated demise, and their attackers, seeking forgiveness; and an elderly former slave or servant, seeking to direct his 'lingering' daughter to the 'other side'."

The most active phenomena occurred in the 1960s, after a Mrs. Lucy Dickey and her five children moved into the house. The manifestations they experienced, over a period of years, included:

— Loud footsteps coming from a part of the wall that had been sealed up for decades. At one time this had been an entrance to a secret passageway which led to a narrow staircase going upstairs.

— The vision of a "shadowy" head which appeared to Mrs. Dickey one night. Later, after determining one of the spirits was named Martha, whose name was spelled out on an Ouija board, Mrs. Dickey said Martha later revealed to her that she was the "head" Mrs. Dickey had seen. She is believed to have been the daughter of Sarah Salisbury, wife of the Captain. She had shown herself to Mrs.

Dickey to alert her that one of her children had fallen out of bed.

— When Mrs. Dickey took some stones from the yard to help enlarge a terrace, all hell broke loose. Loud noises and midnight bangings occurred. Another session on the Ouija board indicated that Morgan, a name which was spelled out and believed to be the son of Mrs. Salisbury, was unhappy with the changes being made.

— A friend of the family, Nancy Camp, came to visit and the Ouija board spelled out the name Adam to her. He "said" he had been killed in the house and he "needed help." He then showed himself in apparitional form to Nancy. Terrified, she knocked Mrs. Dickey over backwards, the board went flying in the air, and Nancy ran from the room.

— One night in June 1967, Mrs. Dickey was awakened by the sounds of someone "crying, whimpering and moaning." She checked everyone in the house and they were all asleep, including the dogs. Then the phone rang. It was her 18-year-old daughter. She and one of her girl friends had been in a bad automobile accident and the other girl was serious hurt. Mrs. Dickey's daughter was "crying, whimpering and moaning."

— House guests and friends told of seeing and hearing: "a shadowy woman in white; the figure of a man walking about; and a slim dark-haired woman in a red robe." The Dickey children said they saw "grayish, wispy images."

— A friend of the family, Pat Hughes, came over one evening and she and Mrs. Dickey talked till about 3 a.m., when Mrs. Dickey went up to bed. An hour later Pat heard noises in the kitchen and thought Mrs. Dickey had got up for a snack. Pat heard footsteps pacing back and forth in the kitchen and told Mrs. Dickey to come on out. The apparition of a woman resembling Mrs. Dickey walked out from the kitchen. She was tall, thin, had long dark hair and was wearing a red robe with something like a shawl collar. When Pat realized what she was seeing she exclaimed, "My God, it's not Lucy! Who is it?" She turned around to see if anyone else was there, and when she turned back, the vision had dematerialized!

— One evening 11 people were in the house and they were having an Ouija board session, when all of a sudden they heard what clearly sounded like a "large horse" clomping across the front porch. They ran to the window, but saw nothing. Later, a maid told Mrs. Dickey that years earlier her uncle had ridden across the porch, his horse reared and threw him into a tree, killing him instantly!

— One of the Dickey children, Joyce, once saw a coat "swinging on its own" in the cellar. She opened a door and observed a man's "faint figure" walking away from her. Family members also said they had seen a "coiled head with mannish features" on the porch. They said the head looked like it was coiled in wires. No explanation was ever forthcoming about this phenomenon.

— The children told of several occasions where they felt sharp temperature drops in rooms, and sensed someone or something was there with them although they couldn't see anything.

— One child heard the sounds of water dripping. The drip slowly increased in intensity until it sounded like a waterfall was cascading at the back entrance to the house. Yet not a drop of moisture was found.

— In an effort to learn more about the "mysterious unknown residents" of Windover Heights, Mrs. Dickey held a seance one evening. This apparently greatly disturbed the spirits. There was loud banging in the kitchen and the sounds of something like a sack of potatoes being dragged across the basement floor. The dogs "went crazy."

Determined to find the cause of the "happenings," Mrs. Dickey, through a friend, invited the renowned parapsychologist, Dr. Hans Holzer, to come to the house and dispel the spirits. On May 11, 1968, he came. He listened to all the ethereal experiences Mrs. Dickey, her children, and others had had in the house, and afterward pronounced that he thought the encounters were genuine. There was a ghost, and perhaps several ghosts, at Windover Heights. Holzer said he would like to come back and bring a medium with him.

The ghostly activities continued in the interim. One night a group of the Dickey children' friends were at the house for a party. One young man went upstairs to a bathroom. He turned around to see a man staring at him. He said the man was dressed in a white, full-sleeved shirt, with baggy, knicker-type pants. Deeply shaken, the young man ran down the stairs to tell the others. He had no previous knowledge of the house's haunting reputation.

Holzer returned on April 10, 1969, with a medium. A few other guests were invited, including Dean and Jeanne Vanderhoff, who had owned the house prior to the Dickeys.

Now here is where a most curious coincidence comes into play. As I said, I wrote about this house in 1994, having done the research a year earlier. Five years later, on May 7, 1998, I was invited to give a talk about Virginia ghosts at the York River Circle of the King's Daughters annual book and author lunch in Gloucester. Two other authors were also to speak.

One of them was <u>Jeanne Vanderhoff!</u>

I was astounded. She had just written a whimsical book titled, "Gibbons in the Family Tree," about an unusual trip she had taken with her family, during which she had adopted two baby gibbons. During a chat before the luncheon she told me about the ghosts in her house — Windover Heights. She and her husband and their children had lived there for five years in the 1950s — a decade before the Dickeys had moved in. Here is what she told me:)

"The first time we noticed anything out of the ordinary was in 1954 when we started to remodel the house. We had bought the house from two elderly ladies and knew nothing of its background or history, and certainly nothing of its hauntings. I thought it was a very comfortable house with a warm feeling.

"Well, we had a very heavy double garage door. Every night for a week, at about 2 a.m., while we were asleep, that door would go up and down with a loud bang. We never could explain that.

"We then began to hear, at times, a woman's voice in the

kitchen, and once I heard what sounded like someone smashing all my china in the kitchen. Yet there wasn't even a tiny chip of broken glass or china. And each time we heard the woman and went to investigate, no one was there.

"One night we had a friend over for the evening and he was staying in a room behind the kitchen. In the darkness he heard a lot of racket in the kitchen and got up to see who it was. He nearly broke his neck. He fell over the kitchen table. Someone had moved it.

"That was about all we experienced during those years. We felt if there was something there, that maybe it had been satisfied with the way we had remodeled and was quiet after that.

"Some years later, after we had moved out and the Dickeys had moved in, Mrs. Dickey called me and asked if we had found anything strange there. I told her what had occurred, and she told me all sorts of things were happening to her and her children. She said she felt a 'terrible stillness' outside, that 'was trying to get into the house.' She also mentioned that a 'lovely lady' came in at night and covered her children up in bed. She added that there were a lot of inexplicable noises in the house — you know, footsteps, moans, sounds and so forth.

"She asked me if I thought she should have the house exorcized by a priest. I said it couldn't hurt, so she got a priest to come. Mrs. Dickey said someone told her there was an old tombstone out in the garden, and then I wondered if I had inadvertently disturbed it when I put in a terrace."

Jeanne continued: "About this time, my daughter got interested in an Ouija board and we began fooling around with it. One day, without our barely touching it, the planchette, or whatever they call it, began moving seemingly on its own. It spelled out the name "Nat." According to what the board then dictated, Nat had been a servant in the house long ago. He said he should have inherited Windover Heights, but apparently a past owner had reneged on a deal. He said that he and his daughter had died in the house, and he needed to get back to it so he could get his daughter out of there. We guessed that she was still there as a ghost and she wouldn't leave until he persuaded her to 'move on.'

"He said he needed me to get him back into the house and that I could do this by going up to the old widow's walk on the roof and calling out his name. He said he had been hunting for me for a long time because I had to take him back to this house, and I was the only one who could do it. He said he was happy when we were in the house but he didn't like the Dickeys. I asked him, on the Ouija board why he wasn't nice to them, and the board spelled out 'You have never lain at the top and tasted the unhappiness.' I said why are you causing these people all of this trouble? You never caused us any. He answered, 'I will misbehave because I will <u>drive them out!</u>'

"Then Mrs. Dickey invited me over when Hans Holzer brought in his medium. It was a very unnerving experience. When Holzer learned about our "conversations" with Nat on the board he asked that I go up to the widow's walk and call out for him. I felt foolish doing it but I did, and we felt his presence. Mrs. Dickey said there were a lot more manifestations after that.

"The medium began walking through the house and when she got through the hall to the dining room entrance she stopped. The room got real cold. She said she couldn't go through the entrance. She saw something hanging from the door. She said she saw a man leaning on a mantelpiece dressed in a costume of the 1700s. Windover Heights was not built until the mid-1800s, so this must have been in the earlier house. Windover Heights was built on the foundation of the older house.

"The medium sat down and went into a trance-like state. She said this man had murdered his friend. She began speaking in a masculine voice. He had murdered his friend and buried him by the barn. (Holzer and the medium felt this friend had been having an affair with the man's wife and that was the reason he had been killed.) The medium said the man was distraught and was going to kill himself before the murder was discovered and he was disgraced. He hanged himself in that entranceway and that was why the medium would not enter through it. As she was relaying this information, her face became extremely contorted, and her tongue turned coal black, as if she herself was experiencing the hanging. It was really scary. Holzer tried to convince the man that he had been dead for 200 years and it was time for him to go on to another world, but the man wouldn't accept that.

"That was about the extent of my involvement," Jeanne says. "But I can tell you this. I was terribly frightened by what happened on the Ouija board and I will never have another one of those in my house again."

The medium sensed several different spirits. One, she said, must have lived in the early 1800s because he related to her he believed Thomas Jefferson (1801-1809) was still President of the United States. She also claimed to have seen the "slim woman" that Pat Hughes had earlier observed. She also saw ghosts who had once been slaves or servants in the house, and that one of them had told her he had been buried in the yard. And she felt the presence of Nat — the one who had "communicated" to Mrs. Vanderhoff. She verified that he was there to "rescue" his daughter, and he said he was responsible for all the racket in the kitchen. It was his way of trying to scare Mrs. Dickey.

Holzer concluded that there was no rational explanation for the multiple manifestations. He believed that many things happened because Mrs. Dickey was sensitive to such phenomena; that the spirits could reveal themselves openly to her.

A year or so later, Holzer arranged for another medium, this time a man, to visit Windover Heights. He confirmed the first medium's findings. He said a man had killed his wife's lover in the passageway with an andiron and then hanged himself. He also sensed much violence in the fireplace area, possibly including another murder, and he believed all the mayhem which had taken place had put a curse on the site.

The Dickeys moved out of the house shortly after that. It was felt that by coaxing the spirits to "tell their stories," at least some of them had, at last, been put to rest.

CHAPTER 10

Apparitions from the Archives

(Alexandria)

(Author's note: In "The Ghosts of Virginia, Volume II," published in 1994, I included a brief selection of newspaper reports of ghostly activity gleaned from the Alexandria Gazette during the second half of the 19th century. T. Michael Miller, author, and director of the Lloyd House Library, compiled these for a Halloween project several years ago. Here, then, are a few more samples from that collection.)

HOLY COW!

September 2, 1869: "The residents of the neighborhood of the intersection of Water and Wilkes streets, the east end of the tunnel, were suddenly aroused and alarmed about four o'clock this morning by the shrieks and screams of a colored girl, who, while on her way to the pump there, saw a white cow which she mistook for a veritable ghost."

A HEADLESS SPECTER

January 18, 1886: "A headless ghost has recently been seen seated on the arch at the intersection of Royal and Wilkes streets. On Friday night last, two ladies who were passing that way were so much frightened by the ghost that they dropped a basket they were carrying and ran to the next corner where they told of what they had seen and asked some gentlemen who were standing there to go after their basket, which they did.

"A man some time ago had his head cut off at that place by being run over by the train."

ASCENDING INTO SPACE

May 31, 1889: "Officers Simpson and Sherwood say that while on duty last night they saw either a ghost or something that looked like what ghosts are said to resemble. They say that while on Franklin street between Lee and Fairfax, about 2 o'clock, during the storm, and when the night was very dark, their attention was attracted to rustling sounds, and that on looking back they saw a figure clothed in a white, flimsy material, which vanished immediately, the figure ascending into space."

A SHOCKING SIGHT

July 21, 1890: "A house at the extreme southern end of Alfred street has recently acquired the reputation of being haunted. Several months ago a lady died there under circumstances in no way remarkable, and recently the neighbors have been terrified by beholding the face of the deceased, peering through the window panes at them."

HAUNTING REVENGES

November 11, 1893: "Those occupying the same room in the city jail with Clarence Rone, the colored man who is charged with killing Edward Meade, say the alleged murderer is rendered uneasy every night by what he believes to be incorporeal visitations of his victim to the prison. Rone often declares he sees the murdered man peering through the wicket into the room and that at times the ghost enters and follows him. . . He has been undergoing a severe ordeal ever since he was arrested.

"Virginia Meade, who is also confined in the same institution, is said by her companions in prison to have the same experience after sundown. She, too, affirms that her late husband comes back to earth and exhibits himself gory and wounded unto death. Virginia Meade seems to have but little apprehension as to her fate and the only thing apparently that seems to ruffle her peace of mind is said to be the head of her late husband when it protrudes itself through the window at her!"

DON'T PLAGUE PHOEBE!

September 28, 1895: "More than 50 years ago there stood on the northeast corner of Pitt and Prince streets an old deserted building, which all the children of the town believed to be haunted, and none would pass it at night without fear and bated breath. Near the northwest corner there lived an old colored woman (named Phoebe) whose ears had been cut for petty larceny and whom the children all believed to be an old witch and they plagued and called her "old croppy" and "witch." The writer in passing loved to plague her. She would frequently say, 'I will fix you.'

"One day near about dark my father told me to go to market and get a beef steak and then call at the shoe makers and bring home a pair of boots. On his way near the market the writer saw old Phoebe and commenced to plague her. She replied as usual, 'I'll fix you.' On returning home, very dark and thick clouds overspread the heavens and it became very gloomy.

"When near the corner of Pitt and Prince streets, a vivid flash of lightning revealed to him one of the most horrible sights he ever witnessed — a white and headless swan! The writer quickened his pace to the opposite corner when another flash revealed to him this horrible object close to his side! When he arrived home he fell in the doorway as dead. On being revived and asked what was the matter, he stated that a ghost had chased him home."

A PARANORMAL PRACTICAL JOKE

August 5, 1898: "Some practical jokers on Wednesday night clothed the fire plug on Christ Church corner on Washington street in white for the purpose of making it look like a ghost. The perpetrators of the joke then secreted themselves for the purpose of witnessing the effect it would produce on certain individuals who would pass that way on their return home from an entertainment in the northern part of the city.

"The parties expected soon afterwards came along, and the antics of some of the belated individuals are said to have been amusing. A number of the party espied the object half a square away and took care to cross to the opposite side of the street. Others came close upon the plug before they noticed it, and went out into the street, passing around the supposed spook and at a convenient distance from it. None, it is said, had sufficient nerve to come in close enough proximity to examine the object, and most of those who saw it had blood-curdling stories to relate when they reached their homes."

I KNOW WHAT I SAW!

January 10, 1907: "A gentleman, who lives on Duke street near Royal, while on his way home a few nights since, at about 10 o'clock, was accosted in front of St. Paul's Church by a colored man who respectfully asked him if the church was open. The gentleman, becoming suspicious, immediately assumed the offensive and told the man that he knew the church was not open at that time of night. The colored man's manner became grave and the gentleman, seeing that he was in earnest, led him to the iron gates of the church and said, 'You see that the gates are locked; of course the church is not open.'

"The colored man then manifested fright and said, 'That gate is locked, sir, but as sure as I am standing here, I saw a woman, robed in white, with a train reaching almost to the sidewalk, enter that church door and disappear just as I reached this spot.' The man held to his story and could not be made to believe that he was mistaken. They then both left hurriedly for their respective homes."

CATCH ME IF YOU CAN!

August 16, 1909: "Last Saturday night at the witching hour when graveyards are said to yawn, two young men were proceeding along Hunting Creek road, a short distance south of this city, when, according to their statements, they saw a figure, supposed to be that of a woman, attired in immaculate white, but wearing a sable veil, walking ahead of them. They said they accelerated their footsteps, but the figure moved faster than its followers, either walking or gliding so fast that it was impossible to gain on it."

(Author's note: The following, from the Washington Chronicle and reprinted in the Alexandria Gazette, is my favorite.)

DON'T MESS WITH ME, GHOST!

April 19, 1875: "The last sensation in Alexandria was a ghost. It flitted about in white garments and chalked up houses and fences in the most reckless manner. On being investigated with a rolling-pin by a strong minded woman it endeavored to scare, the ghost proved to be an interesting widow with a taste for practical jokes. . . . She is now convalescing!"

CHAPTER 11

Glimpses Into Past Lives

(Author' s note: One of the joys of researching for this series of
books on Virginia's ghosts is in meeting some fascinating — and
charming — people. One of the most fascinating — and charming
— is a young woman named Barbara Lane of Alexandria. She is, in
a word, extraordinary. Barbara is a clinical hypnotherapist. She has
a PhD degree in meta-psychology and holds workshops and gives
lectures on a variety of metaphysical subjects. She does spirit
releasing work. If a ghost is lingering somewhere, she helps "move
it along" to where it should go — the other world or whatever.

But perhaps she is best known for her past-
life regressions. That is, through hypnotic
therapy, hypnosis, she is able to send people back to lives they may
have lived long ago. "I'm intuitive," she says, "and I can tap into
things like reincarnation."

She has, in fact, written a popular book whereby she regressed
a dozen or so Civil War reenactors back to when, in a past life, they
lived and fought in the 1860s. It is called "Echoes of the
Battlefield." Another book, "Echoes from Medieval Hall," involves
regressions into past lives during the Renaissance period. She is at
work on a third volume, "Sixteen Clues to Your Past Life," which
tells how and where a person can identity his or her past lives.

Of the Civil War book, Barbara says with the reenactors, it was
more than just a hobby. "They were all emotionally involved with
the war. It was something more." And, under hypnosis, the reenactors revealed a number of obscure facts they had no conscious
knowledge of — facts that were checked and confirmed later
through historical research!

One of the reenactors studied for the book was David Purschwitz, who lives near the Manassas battlefield. His great grandfather fought in the War Between the States. He told Barbara that when he once visited the site where his great grandfather had been wounded in action, "he shivered and relayed a strong gut feeling that the battlefield looked familiar. That same deja vu feeling would sweep over him every time he looked at pictures he had taken of the battle site."

During the regression, while under hypnosis, David recalled being in the Shenandoah Valley in the 1860s. He was then 20-years old, in the Union army, away from home for the first time . . . and scared. Further into the session, he tells of being in a battle, and as he is charging toward Confederate lines he is wounded, his arm is shattered, and he is captured. His left arm is amputated. Barbara noted that prior to this disclosure, David had been actively waving this arm during the regression, but after saying it had been removed, for the next 90 minutes, he never moved it again.

David recalled life in a southern prison camp, and then being released to return home. He described all of this in explicit detail, and later, after the regression, he was able to verify certain facts that he had related while under hypnosis — facts he had not known in a conscious state. He, like the other reenactors interviewed for the book, deeply believes he lived and fought in the Civil War. Barbara's book is an absorbing read, especially for reenactors.

I did a book signing with Barbara in 1997, chatted with her, and she told me she had once had her own ghostly encounter. It was some months later when I interviewed her. Here is what she said:)

"I went to the reenactment of the 135th anniversary of the great battle at Antietam in southern Maryland. There was going to be a fancy dress ball at the actual site of the battle, and I had a new evening gown. At the hotel where I was staying, one of the reenactors wanted to take a photo of me with one of his buddies. One of the photos had a kind of smeary light on it. On close examination, it appeared to be an apparitional form of a soldier with a gun. He had not been there when the photo was taken. Was he a creature from the past? I don't know.

"I then got in my car and drove over to the battle site for the ball that was to be held there. It was on the road from Hagerstown to Antietam. There seemed to be no one else on the road. It was about dusk and I remember how peaceful and quiet it was as I

passed by the scenic farmland.

"Then, suddenly, at the top of a hill, I saw a Civil War soldier on horseback. He came out of nowhere. He had on a blue uniform and a forage hat. At first I thought he might be a reenactor. But then I wondered, if he was, why was he so far out in the middle of nowhere. Why was he out here all alone, in uniform, and so many miles away from where the ball was to be held? And there was no campsite nearby. He looked real, but I don't think he was. There was something very strange about him. I passed by him in the car, and then he was gone. He rode off into the trees and vanished.

"Later, at the dance, I asked around, if anyone knew of such a reenactor who might be out alone on horseback. No one did. No one had heard of my phantom rider."

CHAPTER 1 2

A Crisis Apparition — With Proof!

(Reston)

(Author's note: Parapsychology experts say that, fairly often, when a loved one passes away, someone very close to that person, say a wife, husband, mother, father, sister or brother, may believe they see or sense the deceased at the moment of the death, even though they may be hundreds or thousands of miles away. There are, for example, numerous accounts of parents who say they saw an image of their son (or daughter) during wartime, at the precise instant they were killed. Is this an hallucination, or a case of what the professionals in the field call "crisis apparition?")

There are many theories. In the preface of G.N.M. Tyrrell's book, "Apparitions," H. H. Price writes: "In the so-called 'crisis-apparition' — it does seem pretty clear that the phenomenon is telepathic in origin. At or about the time when a person 'A' is undergoing some crisis (which may or may not be death), another person, 'B', usually a friend or relative, has a visual hallucination; and this may be so complete and lifelike that he (or she) at first believes 'A' to be physically present in the room, and is only undeceived when the apparition vanishes. It would seem that such 'telepathic phantasms' are just one of the many ways in which an unconsciously received telepathic impression may manifest itself to the recipient's consciousness."

The late D. Scott Rogo, parapsychologist, educator and writer, once said: "Crisis apparitions usually appear at the exact moment, or shortly after, that the agent has undergone an accident or death." One of the classic cases, frequently reported, concerned an English pilot named Eldred Bowyer-Bower, who was shot down during World War I while flying over France. The date was March 19, 1917. At about the same time he crashed, his half-sister, Mrs. Spearman, who was in India, said: "That morning I was sewing, and talking to baby. . . I had a great feeling I must turn around and did, to see Eldred; he looked so happy and had that dear mischievous look. I was so glad to see him I would just put baby in a safer place, then we could talk. 'Fancy coming out here,' I said, turning around again, and was just putting my hands out to give him a hug and a kiss, but Eldred had gone. I called and looked for him. I never saw him again." Two weeks later, Mrs. Spearman got word that her half-brother had been shot down — at the time she had "seen" him, and was missing in action.

In "The Ghosts of Virginia," Volume I (1993), I wrote about a celebrated instance of crisis apparition involving a sea captain named David Duncan. He was married and the father of two small children who lived in an apartment in Norfolk. On the evening of May 12, 1823, Duncan was anchored in his ship off the coast of Genoa, Italy. He was reading a book of poetry by the English author Edward Young. The book was titled "Thoughts on Life, Death, and Immortality." Suddenly, an apparitional fire flared up on the deck of the ship. Duncan raced to the deck and saw, clearly, in the raging flames, the image of his wife and two children. She was crying, "David, David, help us." Then the flames and the images disappeared.

It was several weeks before Duncan, fraught with anxiety, arrived back at his home port, Norfolk, to learn, to his horror, that, in fact, his wife and two children had died in a fire in their apartment on the night of May 12, 1823! And so, Duncan buried them in St. Paul's Cemetery in downtown Norfolk, and placed over their graves a headstone which read, "Insatiate archer, could not one suffice? Thy shaft flew thrice, and thrice my peace was slain." These were the exact words of poetry he had been reading when the apparitional fire appeared on the deck of his ship!

How can one ascertain if such a sighting, as Mrs. Spearman and Captain Duncan experienced, is an hallucination, or a real instance of crisis apparition? This is a tough question. Ask anyone who has experienced the presence of a loved one at the moment of death, and they will answer that they are convinced they actually saw the person who had just died.

But in some extreme, rare examples, there may be tangible "proof" of a crisis apparition. The following, well-known and documented case is what experts call a postmortem apparition. In this instance, a man's sister had died of cholera when she was 18 years old. Nine years later, while the man was in his hotel room in St.Joseph, Missouri, on a business trip, he suddenly became aware of a figure to the side of him. Glancing around, he was astonished to see the apparition of his long-deceased sister. What was peculiarly noteworthy about this ghost was that it was disfigured by a long red scratch on its cheek. Just as suddenly as it appeared, it vanished.

Upon returning to his home, the man reported this experience to his parents. When his mother heard about the scratch, she nearly collapsed. Upon recuperating, the woman admitted that when paying her last respects to the body of her daughter before burial, she had tried to 'touch up' the face and had accidentally scratched the girl's cheek. However, in an effort to hide the accident she had carefully concealed the scratch with makeup. No one but herself knew of the incident.

(All of the above serves as a "backgrounder prelude" to the following. It was told to me in December 1998 by a young lady named Sandra Ayoub, who works in my daughter Cindy's public relations office in Reston. Here is what she had to say:)

"I never believed in ghosts before. But all that has changed. On June 7, 1998, my father, Abrahim Ayoub, complained of stomach pains. He was just 50 years old and had been in perfect health. The pains were so severe, my uncle drove him to the hospital. He died in the hospital. It was totally unexpected. My uncle was so emotionally shaken, that he couldn't drive home, so he left the car and the car keys at the hospital. He said he would go back to get the car the next day.

"Friends and relatives came over to our house to comfort us. I couldn't sleep and neither could my sister, Julie. So we stayed up. We were in the den. It was about 4 a.m., when we both noticed that the room was getting freezing cold. It was the coldest air I had ever felt.

"And then, all of a sudden, my dad appeared. He was wearing the same clothes he had been wearing when he was driven to the hospital — a white shirt, khaki shorts and slippers. Julie and I both saw him clearly. We know we were not dreaming, because we were both wide awake. He looked at us, then walked over to the television set and put something on top of it. Then he went over to an easy chair and sat down. He kind of shook his head. I got the feeling that he somehow couldn't accept the fact that he was dead. It was the weirdest thing. And then he disappeared.

"Julie and I just looked at each other, like we couldn't believe what we had seen, but we knew we had seen it.

"We got up and looked on top of the TV set. There were the keys to the car my uncle had left at the hospital!"

CHAPTER 13

America's Most Haunted State Park?

(Southeastern Maryland)

oint Lookout State Park today is a popular resort site that is frequented weekly by hundreds of campers, picnickers, swimmers, crabbers, and fishermen and women. One reason they come is because of its ideal scenic location. It lies at the extreme southeastern tip of Maryland where the Potomac River meets the Chesapeake Bay. It is little more than a stone's throw from Walnut Point and Lewisetta on Virginia's northern neck. There are miles of pristine white sandy beaches.

It also may well be the most haunted spit of land on the entire east coast of the United States.

That is because it has a long history of tragedy and violence. Captain John Smith explored here in 1608. During the Revolutionary War, American colonists used the Point as an observation post, and in the War of 1812, British troops occupied the area, burning many of the then existing houses and buildings. In 1830 the Point Lookout lighthouse was constructed to warn passing ships. Still, the shallow waters offshore are littered with the wrecks of 19th century vessels and the scattered bones of drowned crewmen.

For a short time, in the 1850s, the site became a favorite summer resort for Virginians and Marylanders. Cottages sprang up and a fashionable hotel was erected. But the trade of tourists ended abruptly with the outbreak of the Civil War. The government bought the land and built the Hammond military hospital here in

1862 to treat wounded Union soldiers.

A year later, a decision was made which would lead to the Point's lingering reputation as a "place of hell," and as a region of substantial ghostly activity. It was decided, in 1863, to erect a prison camp here for Confederate soldiers. It was called Camp Hoffman.

Of all the unspeakable horrors of the War Between the States, none was more cruel and inhumane than the treatment of prisoners. Both sides, the North and the South, were equally guilty. The main reason for the deplorable conditions was not premeditated. It was the simple fact that neither side had foreseen the eventual enormous need for adequate prison facilities. Consequently, no one was prepared. This gross lack of anticipation directly led to the premature deaths and long-term suffering of tens of thousands of men.

When soldiers were captured they were herded, like cattle, into ramshackle buildings ill designed for the housing of humans. Worse, many were penned inside hastily installed barriers and were forced to try to survive in raggedy tents, sheds, lean-tos, or, literally, in holes in the ground. There was little food, pathetically insufficient medical supplies, and virtually no thought for the care of those unfortunate enough to be captured by the enemy. With few exceptions, healthy young men, those who lived, were reduced to disease-ridden, emaciated skeletons.

Some estimates were that more than one-third of all those incarcerated died. Rampant disease and malnutrition were the chief causes. There were uncontrolled epidemics of smallpox, diarrhea, dysentery, scurvy and hospital gangrene.

Historian Bruce Catton called such "life:" "A festering mass of corruption impregnating the entire atmosphere of the camps with pestilential odors." A slight scratch on the skin, even an insect bite, was likely to cause death by blood poisoning. Catton: "Hospitals were crowded with victims for the grave. Requisitions for medicines and supplies largely ignored."

Camp Hoffman was no exception to the grim tragedies which occurred in the early 1860s. It was totally unfit for such service. The ground was low, marshy, and infested with great hordes of insects, especially mosquitoes, and snakes. It was a haven for disease. The weather, too, was a killer. It was unbearably hot and humid in the summers and freezingly cold in the winters. Storms blowing in off the bay would at times inundate the grounds in high water.

The camp had been designed to hold 10,000 prisoners, but

Photo of an old photo: Confederate soldiers at the Point Lookout prison camp, circa 1860's.

more than twice that number were jammed into the wooded stockade, surrounded by a 12-foot-high fence. Inside the pen, 10 feet from the wall, was a fence called the "Dead Line." Any prisoner crossing this would be shot, no questions asked. There were no permanent barracks. As many as eight soldiers were jammed into makeshift tents. There was one blanket for every three men, consequently many froze to death during the harsh winters.

By a cruel twist of fate, black guards were stationed to watch over the Southern soldiers. In some cases, former slaves stood guard over their ex-masters. A number of prisoners were shot, murdered, indiscriminately. One was killed while looking through a peephole in the fence. Others were picked off at random for no apparent reason.

A sad irony was the fact that the prisoners could see, just across the Potomac, seven miles away, Virginia land. Many tried to escape, but most were swept out to sea by the strong currents and drowned. In two years, more than 3,200 Confederate soldiers died at Camp Hoffman! That was the official count. It is likely many more perished and their deaths went unrecorded.

The bodies were tossed onto a wagon and moved to the "Dead House" just outside the prison walls. They laid here for several days before being buried in mass graves. Identification was impossible because the graves were marked only with small crosses bearing no inscriptions. Often eight, nine or ten bodies were stacked in a single site.

Many graves were dug in swampy, marshy land only a few hundred feet from open water. Consequently, during storms and extreme high tides, the bodies were openly exposed. Bones were strewn everywhere. Eventually, a new burial ground was found further inland.

In 1910, an effort was made to exhume the bodies which had been left in the original graves near the water, but this job was badly botched, and even today it is not uncommon to come across an eerie skull or large bones following an intense storm.

On top of all this, there was a terrible shipwreck just off the Point on November 11, 1864. A Union gunboat, the U.S.S. Tulip, set off from Point Lookout to Washington, D.C. for repairs to one of its boilers. Worried that Confederate batteries along the Virginia shore might make his ship an easy target, Captain William Smith, against the advice of his engineers, ordered a second boiler fired up to make better time. It exploded, sending the Tulip to the bottom of the bay in less than two minutes, and killing 47 of the 57 men on board. Many bodies were never recovered, and most of those which washed up on shore were torn apart beyond recognition.

Is it thus any wonder that some of these once-proud soldiers may have lingered on, through the past 13-plus decades, as frail, starved, and emaciated ghosts? Such, apparently, is the case, for the reports of hauntings have persisted through the ages.

The manifestations have included sightings, unusual phenomena, and the ethereal wails of tormented souls crying out for help. In fact, the psychic activity at Point Lookout has become so prevalent that an annual Ghost Walk is held here every October, and dozens of parapsychology experts are drawn to the site to conduct serious investigations. What is particularly unusual about the supernatural happenings is the extraordinary number of witnesses who have experienced them. There are scores of people, ranging from tourists to park rangers to scientists, who swear they have seen or heard things of a totally unexplained nature — and at several different areas of the grounds.

The encounters have been well documented and appear in several books, including: Trish Gallagher's "Ghosts and Haunted Houses of Maryland;" Delores Riccio and Joan Bingham's "Haunted Houses, USA;" and "Sightings" based on the popular television series. The eminent parapsychologist, Dr. Hans Holzer, also has tracked the spirits of Point Lookout.

Following are some examples of the strange "goings on."

** For some unknown reason, campsites 137 and 139, located where a smallpox hospital stood during the Civil War, seem to harbor strong spirit activity. Park employee Carolyn Downey and her husband camped at 139 in June 1989. Here is what Carolyn reported: "I was asleep when I felt something touching my knee and shaking it until I woke up. My husband was sleeping with his back to me and it could not have been his hand that I felt." But there was no one else around.

** Ranger Donnie Hammett was in the same area a few years ago when he noticed a family was camping there. The parents seemed disturbed. Hammett asked them what was wrong. Reluctantly, they told him they had been in their cabin and it was locked. They woke up to see their three-year-old son outside at a picnic table. How he gotten out? He couldn't have reached the latch unlocking the cabin door. They said the boy seemed to be talking with someone they couldn't see. They asked him who it was, and he said the man in the gray uniform!

** April Haven, another park employee, told of a frightening experience she once had several years ago while patrolling the campgrounds late at night. "It was around three a.m.," she says, "and it was damp with a low lying fog. I noticed a chill in the air as I passed site number 145. As I walked along the road I felt as if someone was following me. As I neared the entrance to Conoy Circle, I heard a noise from behind. I turned around and saw a row of white, square-shaped tents in the middle of the road! Without a second look, I turned and ran for the camp office. Soaking with sweat, I commented out loud, 'There really are ghosts here.' When she and others returned to the site the tents had vanished.

** One of the most chilling experiences occurred to a Civil War reenactor one night at Fort Lincoln, one of the three earthen forts built to defend the prison. A reenactment was scheduled for the next day, so this volunteer decided to spend the night before in an old guard house. That evening he went outside to gather some firewood. He stooped down in front of the building and suddenly heard a bullet whiz overhead. The glass in the guard house window shattered. The petrified reenactor fled. The next day he walked back to the guard house. The window was not broken, nor was there a shard of glass out of place!

** At daybreak one morning four fishermen were driving through the park in a truck, heading for the beach. Out of nowhere, a man appeared directly in their path. The driver swerved hard, but it was too late. They all felt a perceptible thump. They had hit the man. All four fishermen leaped out of the truck, but to their astonishment, there was no one there. The mystery man had vanished in the morning mist.

** Several incidents have been experienced by ranger Donnie Hammett, who grew up in the area and has been a park ranger since 1977. Here he describes what happened on a March afternoon in 1977: "I was working the evening shift. Despite the beautiful warm weather, there were few park visitors. At about 4:30 p.m., I was on the Potomac River beach front gathering and recording weather data, when I noticed an elderly woman standing about 40 yards from me. She caught my attention because she was strangely shuffling slowly along looking toward her feet. I walked over to offer my assistance. She seemed very distant and our conversation was very brief. She said she did not need by assistance; that she lived up the beach 'aways;' and did I know where the gravestones were that used to be where we were standing. (I didn't.)

"I walked up the beach a few yards and when I looked back I noticed the lady was gone. I thought this was rather strange because there were no cars in the parking lot. Where could she have gone? I would have seen any cars entering or leaving the lot. Curious, I later asked park manager Gerry Sword if he knew anything about an old grave site. He told me that there had once been such a site where I had met the old lady. It was the Taylor family graveyard. Records show that one of the individuals buried in the lost cemetery was a woman named Elizabeth Taylor. Sometime afterward I searched the area thoroughly, but the lost grave has never been found. I have often wondered since if the odd woman I had met might have been the deceased Elizabeth Taylor looking for the rest of her family."

** Hammett and other park employees also tell of a sighting they have witnessed on a road that dissects the old Confederate cemetery near the water. "I guess I have seen it about a dozen times over the years," Hammett says. "It always appears in the rear view mirror of my vehicle as I pass along this stretch of road. I see a man in a gray uniform running out of the woods. He crosses the road and disappears where the old graveyard was. Each time I backed my vehicle up and got out where I saw him, but I never caught sight of him again. This is in an area that is thickly wooded, and there is no path or anything for anyone to follow. Who is he, and why does he appear here? I have asked myself this many times, but I don't know the answer. I do know that he appears out of the woods from where the old small pox hospital was located. And it is said Confederate soldiers would try to escape from that hospital. Is he still trying to free himself from the misery of prison confinement? Could be."

** Hammett was in the park office with ranger Tim Frania one day listening to tape recordings made during a ghost walk a few weeks earlier. Suddenly, Frania's face turned white. On the tape was what sounded like the voice of a man crying for help. The word help was drawn out like "h. . . e . . . l . . . p!" Frania said he was startled because he had heard that voice before. He said that one night while he was picking up some trash in a parking lot, he had heard the exact same voice calling for help several times over a half hour period. It seemed to be coming from the direction of the Chesapeake Bay. He searched the area but found nothing.

** The Franias — Tim and his wife, Joan — lived in a house near Point Lookout Park only a few feet from where the western wall of the Civil War prison once stood. Late one night Joan was asleep in bed alone, while Tim was working. She said she was awakened when she felt "the bedcovers rise off the bed and a draft of cold air blow under the covers." She felt the bed sink down on the other side and assumed Tim had gotten off work early and had come home. She reached over to put her arm around him — and there was nothing there!

Of all the eerie sites at Point Lookout, perhaps the most haunted is the lighthouse, which was built in 1830. There appears to be more psychic energy here, and more of a variety, than at any other single place in the area. Former park manager Gerry Sword seems to have been at the center of such occurrences. He lived in the 20-room lighthouse in the 1970s. At first, he attributed sounds such as doors opening and closing on their own, phantom footsteps, and crashing objects to his overactive imagination, combined with possible natural causes. But then things began to happen that he couldn't ignore, or, for that matter, explain.

** He began hearing "voices" in the house when he was there alone. At times there were "faint conversations." But he never could pinpoint the source. He also heard, on several occasions, the distinct sound of someone snoring somewhere behind the cupboards in his kitchen. Despite a thorough search, he could find nothing rational to account for it.

** One night a violent storm caused a power outage. Sword lit three identical candles in a candelabra in the living room. He went to the kitchen to fix his dinner and heard a loud sound coming from the room he had just left. He went back to look. One of the candles had burned about an inch, but a second one had burned nearly four inches. On the third candle, only about an inch of it remained, and a section of it was on the floor nearby. The wick on the candle on the floor had been lit but was now extinguished, yet the small piece of it in the candelabra was still aflame.

** One evening as Sword sat at the kitchen table, he said he felt at least six people pass him, coming from the kitchen door and going into another room. As each entity passed, he felt not only a "flow of air," but also the floor vibrating!

Point Lookout Lighthouse

** On another occasion, again while he was at the kitchen table, Sword said he got a strong feeling that he was being watched. He got up, walked to the door, and peered out the window. There, he saw the face of "a young man wearing a floppy cap and a sackcoat staring back at him through the window!" Most people might have retreated to the safety of a hiding place, but Sword's curiosity got the better of his fright and he opened the door. He said the apparition walked away from him and disappeared through the screens of the enclosed porch!

While most of the ghostly activity at Point Lookout is believed to be tied to the Civil War era, Sword thinks this particular sighting dates to a few years later. Through research, he learned that in 1878 a severe storm just north of the point caused the breakup and sinking of a large steamer. Thirty-one people drowned. One was a young man named Joseph Henry, whose body was washed up and buried nearby. The newspaper description of Henry and the fact that he had been wearing a sackcoat, matched precisely the vision Sword had seen. He became convinced he had seen the ghost of Joseph Henry!

** Tim Frania also has felt the presence of a spirit in the lighthouse. He once saw a "transparent lady standing at the top of the lighthouse stairs, wearing a long blue skirt and a white top." "She" dematerialized before his eyes. He has a feeling he somehow had a brief glimpse of Ann Davis, the first lighthouse keeper.

** Laura Berg and her husband, Eric, lived in the lighthouse before it became owned by the park. One night she was awakened from a sound sleep and saw "a circle of six lights" revolving on the ceiling over her head. She sat up and then smelled smoke. It seemed to be coming from the first floor. She raced downstairs and found her space heater on fire. Laura quickly extinguished it. Nothing could convince her that it wasn't the spirits of the lighthouse which, through the circles of light, had warned her of the impending danger. The spirits, she said, were her friends.

Through the years a number of psychic experts have examined the grounds and buildings at Point Lookout using highly sophisticated recording equipment. They applied a procedure known as electronic voice phenomenon, or EVP. This involves voices that can be heard on the tapes although nothing was audible during the recording process. In other words, the recording experts hear nothing while taping, but in playing back the tapes, sounds and voices are on them.

In 1980, the renowned ghost hunter and writer, Dr. Hans

Holzer, accompanied a group to Point Lookout. He was not disappointed in the findings. Holzer said of his visit that he found "intense psychic impressions" in several rooms in the lighthouse. He added that he could feel "pain and suffering" coming from a second floor bedroom.

During this visit, the experts recorded unexplained voices uttering such phrases as: "living in the lighthouse;" and "fire if they get too close to you." A woman's voice said "vaccine." Another female voice, possibly that of a nurse, said: "Let us take no objection to what they are doing." Are these in fact voices from the past? Such a theory was fortified when one recording had a steamboat whistle on it. Steamboats have not plied the adjacent waters for decades.

At one point, psychic Nancy Stallings, while touring the lighthouse with Holzer and others, felt an intense pain in her back. She believed someone in the past had been shot in the back there. Subsequent research revealed that a murder had taken place in the lighthouse in the 19th century, and that several Confederate prisoners had been shot in the back at the prison in the 1860s.

A trans-medium named Ms. Bradford said a spirit lurked in the lighthouse tower. She said it was of a man with blond hair and blue eyes, and that he, too, had been murdered over a jealous affair. She also sensed a feeling of someone being held in the building against his will. Dr. Holzer commented, "This place is haunted as hell!"

Another specialist who recorded unknown sounds was Lori Mellott-Bowles, director of Southern Maryland Psychic Investigations. She noted that voice phenomena can consist of many varieties of vocal effects, including singing, whispers, short phrases, and shouts. In the campground, she had one recording of a voice clearly saying, "You're in my home." There also was a frail plea that said, "Help me!"

Mike Humphries, an anthropologist and director of the St. Clement's Island Museum, has made more than 200 recordings of what he believes are "ghost voices." Many of these were at Point Lookout. Humphries says he feels most ghosts are "not hostile," although the ones he senses at the park "seem trapped." He adds that Point Lookout "seems evil . . . just unsettled." Some of his sounds there are screams. He says that once on a trip to the Point he became lost in the woods while looking for the entrance to one of the old Confederate graveyards. He played back his recorder, and a voice on it said, "to the right." It led to the way out of the woods.

Psychic expert Lynda Andrus conducted a seance at the lighthouse in 1985. She "received" the strong feeling of a male presence. All eight people at the session felt this. Lynda sensed the entity was wearing "a uniform light in color." It should be noted that this was her first visit to the park and she had not been told of any past ghostly activity.

Such experiences almost seem commonplace at Point Lookout. Most of those who have witnessed the sounds and sightings here believe they can be traced back to the 1860s when thousands of young men from the South lay suffering in the stench and filth of a polluted prison camp, their faint cries for help unheard . . . that is until more than a century later!

CHAPTER 14

The Most Haunted County in America?

(St. Mary's County, Maryland)

he fact is Point Lookout is only <u>one</u> haunted site in a county seemingly full of them. This is St. Mary's County, and it lies at the extreme southeastern tip of "mainland" Maryland (as opposed to the state's Eastern Shore.) St. Mary's, just 35 miles from Washington, D.C., is flanked by the Potomac and Patuxent Rivers on two sides, and by the Chesapeake Bay at its tip. The largest town in the county is Leonardtown which is about 20 miles directly east of Colonial Beach, Virginia. That's as the crow flies. To get to St. Mary's from Virginia one must cross the Potomac River bridge on highway 301, turn right (east) on Maryland 234, then take route 5 southeast. (If one keeps on, of course, to the end of the road he or she will wind up at Point Lookout.)

The county has been described in one college study as being "a haven for tales of the supernatural." It also is the oldest section of the state. St. Mary's City was the first capital of the Province of Maryland and the fourth permanent settlement in British North America. In 1634, 140 or so settlers, led by Governor Leonard Calvert, sailed across the Atlantic Ocean on two ships — the Ark and the Dove — and landed here.

Today, St. Mary's City, halfway between Leonardtown and Point Lookout, is recognized as one of America's best preserved archaeological sites and is a National Historic Landmark. It is to Maryland what Jamestown and Williamsburg are to Virginia.

Exhibits include the reconstructed state house of 1676, a tobacco plantation, an Indian hamlet, a replica of the square-rigged ship, the Dove, a 17th century town center, and St. Mary's Chapel, the site of the first English Catholic Church in the Americas. Several of the buildings here are reported to be ghost-ridden. Whether or not one will feel a presence here, it is, nevertheless, an interesting place to visit.

Herewith, then, are a few of the spirits of St. Marys:

** North of Leonardtown, off route 235, stands the Fenwick Inn, once owned by Dr. J. C. King. In the year 1905, Dr. King was out in the field with several of his hands, checking the tobacco crop, when two elderly ladies suddenly appeared before them walking down a path. They were dressed in what Dr. King described as "sun bonnets and clothes belonging to the colonial past." They appeared to be walking carefree and chatting, oblivious to anyone else around them. Just as quickly as they had appeared, they vanished before Dr. King's startled eyes. Neither he or any of his workers could offer a plausible explanation for the sighting. Eleven years later the doctor saw the two apparitional figures again. They glanced at him and evaporated. Dr. King's mother said that the wispy figure of an old lady dressed in black would occasionally appear by her side in the house and "follow her silently from room to room" before disappearing. The Kings had no ideas who the women were although they suspected they may have lived at Fenwick Inn a century or two earlier.

** There is a long-standing tradition that the woods on both sides of state route 249 leading into the hamlet of Valley Lee, again halfway between Leonardtown and Point Lookout, are haunted by a malevolent force. The forest here is so thick that the sun, even at high noon, doesn't penetrate the thickly massed foliage. Oldtimers here are not sure how the foreboding legend began, but it has endured for three centuries: according to the popular belief, if a traveler is caught in these woods during a storm, the road will disappear, the person will become lost and weary from searching for a way out, and will eventually die from thirst and hunger. It is said that such a fate occurred to three children many years ago. They became lost in the woods and perished. It is told that during terrible thunderstorms, their cries can still be heard between the thunder claps.

** Hollywood is a small village at the crossroads of 235 and 245 about five miles north of Leonardtown. It seems to have more than its share of psychic happenings. Take Sotterley Mansion, for example, which has a most colorful history. It was built in 1730, and the main building is 102 feet long, with a library wing at right angles and a detached kitchen. On the grounds are two brick garden houses, two gate lodges, a spinning house, custom house, and a brick warehouse which bears the date 1757.

According to Don Swann, Jr., the late renowned etchings artist and author of "Colonial & Historic Homes of Maryland," Sotterley's Great Hall "has been cited as one of the 100 most beautiful rooms in America." (The house is open to the public from June through September.) Key features include Chinese Chippendale mahogany stairs and a gallery on the second floor with a grooved hand rail and a "wonderfully wrought newel post." There also once was a secret passage which led from the cellar to some point on the grounds, presumably as an escape route during Indian attacks.

Sotterley "breathes romance and mystery," Swann says, and he points out that "long sessions at cards and gay parties once enlivened the countryside." In fact, one owner, George Plater, grandson of the governor, once lost the mansion "at dice" to a Colonel Somerville of Mulberry Fields. Swann adds that "Mistress Ann Rousby Plater, reputed to be one of the most beautiful women of Maryland, lived and died" at Sotterley, "and after her, 'The Rose of Sotterley,' daughter-in-law of the governor.

Swann also alludes to some highly intriguing phenomena at the site. "Ghostly figures took part in early morning duels," he notes, and "some say the muffled oarlocks of the funeral barge of Governor Plater, son of the builder, can be heard on the river on still nights." That should certainly whet one's interest.

** But the most famous Hollywood ghost legend centers around (or rather on and under) the old bridge on St. Andrew's Church Road, which crosses over a swampy area. The double tragedies which are alleged to have occurred here, and the subsequent ethereal activity that followed them, have been written and rewritten dozens of times in everything from local newspaper articles to national books. The hauntings have been investigated by several experts, including Lynda Andrus, founder of Andrus Phenomena Research Center in Lexington Park, Maryland, and one of the researchers at Point Lookout State Park.

Most of the sources agree that there are, indeed, two separate entities here. Citing local legend, one story involved a beautiful young slave who was cruelly sexually abused by her master in the years before the Civil War at a plantation site adjacent to where the bridge now stands.

The young slave woman was high spirited, and finally had enough. One night when the plantation owner entered her cabin she banged him over the head with an iron skillet and killed him. Terrified, she fled into the swamps, but the next morning a posse, led by a pack of bloodhounds tracked her down and she was slain.

It is her spirit, most hometowners believe, that sometimes, from nowhere, leaps out in front of motorists crossing the bridge at night, causing drivers to swerve sharply and slam on their brakes. This has happened on several occasions over the years, and there are skid marks on the road and scrapings of vehicle paint on the sides of the bridge to attest to it.

The second tradition is equally sad. It involves a young man and his wife who lived in the area in the early 1940s. He was called off to World War II while she was pregnant with their first child, a boy. Years later, on his return home, he called his wife from the town of Hollywood saying he was on his way to their rural home. Excited, she grabbed her son and started running down the road to meet him. Anxiously speeding, the young man rounded a danger-ous curve and slammed into his wife in the middle of the road. She was killed instantly, and the baby, according to the written reports, flew out of her arms and fell into the icy waters of the stream below the bridge.

Although an extensive search was conducted, the baby was never found!

Many Hollywoodians say that ever since that tragic time, on especially cold winter nights, the sounds of a baby crying can be heard by those crossing the bridge. In fact, the small dark stream which flows beneath the bridge is now known as "Cry Baby Creek."

** In the little town of California, Maryland, a few scant miles east of Leonardtown, Father J. E. Johnson served as pastor of the small St. John's Church for many years. He wrote a book of his experiences. It was titled, "The Story of a Country Pastor," and it included some mysterious incidents. One occurred late one night in his chapel. He had arrived there on a Saturday evening to pray and prepare for his service the next morning. He checked every window and every door in the building. They were all locked and he was alone. After he had retired and fallen asleep, at about one a.m., the bell in the steeple above the chapel rang sharply, sudden-ly awakening the pastor. It tolled seven times. Johnson could not sleep. He knew the bell was securely fastened and there was no way it could ring on its own.

He searched the chapel, but found nothing. He later wrote: "Could that bell have been tolled by the hand of some wayward soul lost in the shadows of darkness, and calling for prayers of relief? Could it have been the stroke of an intractable spirit seeking appeasement with its God? Could it have been a stroke of the bell by the wandering spirit of the poor dying man the pastor had visited and administered to at the beginning of that night? Alas, he knew not!"

But it had not been a dream. He was later told by several people in the neighborhood that they, too, had heard the inexplicable ringing of the church bell.

** Tudor Hall, just outside Leonardtown, is the ancestral home of the Key family, although its most famous member, Francis Scott Key, never visited there. The manor house was built in 1760 by Abraham Barnes. When he died in 1800 he specified that his 300 slaves be freed on the condition that they take his name, which may explain why there are so many blacks of that name in Maryland.

A study undertaken some years ago by county college students states that "ghost stories concerning Tudor Hall have made it an object of supernatural awe and mystery." The study cites local belief that one of the spirits is that of "Uncle Didon," a slave coachman of one the early Key residents. He supposedly reappears on certain dark nights "to answer the summons of his beloved master."

A second occurrence involved an old grandfather clock at Tudor Hall. It was said to stand silent for years at a time and strike only at the death of a member of the family. Here is what the students found in their research: "In the last day of Mrs. Key's life (it is not specified exactly when this took place), she suffered from a strange malady. Realizing the gravity of her illness, the family gathered at her bedside. A young servant was sent in haste to the nearby village of Leonardtown to procure the service of a doctor, and also to summon the old colored 'Mammy' who had so faithfully served 'Miss Maria' for many years.

"Returning through the darkness the two servants paused, listening and awe-struck, at the foot of the hill upon which the great house stood. Clear through the air of night sounded the sonorous toll of the old clock . . . one . . . two . . . three! Then the solemn stillness was broken only by the sobs of the old mammy who knew that her beloved mistress had passed forever from her care to the realm of the great Unknown."

And then there is this paragraph on Tudor Hall, taken from Don Swann, Jr.'s book on historic homes of Maryland: "Legend has it that on moonlit nights the ghost of Joseph Key is accustomed to take his ease on the porch in a rocking chair. Should one not be available, Mr. Key marches into the house and gets himself a rocker which he takes to the porch and sets down with a vindictive bang. Then he slowly seats himself and rocks serenely to and fro in the beauty of the night."

THE ENDURING CURSE OF MOLL DYER

f all the supernatural spirits which are said to roam about St. Mary's, from the northwest tip of the county to the dead end of the peninsula at Point Lookout, by far the most famous, or infamous, is the legendary Moll Dyer. Versions of her existence, both in life and afterwards, have been recorded in newspapers, magazines and books for more than a century. Consequently, there is some confusion about just who Moll was and when she lived. There are multiple versions.

One, published years ago in "Intimate Glimpses of Old Saint Mary's," by George Morgan Knight, Jr., contends that she was an Indian maiden who was seduced by a "handsome young paleface", left with his child, and then deserted. In this account, she took the baby to a secluded place in the woods near a stream, held the baby high over her head, and vowed vengeance on her departed lover while kneeling at a large rock. Knight wrote that "Mouldy" Dyer swore her oath so solemnly that she left the visible impression of her knee in the rock where she kneeled. "Despite the passing of the years, it (the impression) has been preserved. Some claim that the weeping of Mouldy Dyer can be heard on dark stormy nights when the run floods the highway, holding up traffic. According to the legend, it is flooded by the tears of the Indian maid who still weeps for her lover to return."

While that is a sad and romanticized rendition, it is not the most popular one. Most residents believe Moll Dyer was a native of England who came to America in the late 17th or 18th century for one of two or three reasons. Either she had once been privy to a life of luxury in her homeland and some ill fate descended upon her causing her to leave abruptly, or she was run out of England for some evil deed. Still another possibility is that some of her

ST. MARY'S COUNTY, MARYLAND

ancestors left for America to escape religious persecution, settled in St. Mary's County, and she was born there. No one really knows for sure.

What is believed is that Moll lived a strange and reclusive life in a hovel just outside Leonardtown, and her weird behavior — combined with a series of tragic events in the area — led to the commonly - held theory that she was indeed a witch.

Here's how Joseph Morgan, an authority on southern Maryland history and folklore, phrased it, in an article written in the St. Mary's Beacon more than a century ago: "Her history, no one knew, but there were stories told of her in another country where her lot was different and where she had all that was refined and beautiful waiting on her every step. Her tattered dress would at times reveal patches of an embroidered kerchief or a bit of faded lace, which might recall far off summers when the banquet hall rang with the music of her laughter and courtly men worshiped at the shrine of her loveliness. Great sorrow which crushed home and love out of her young life, came upon her, and with hate for her kind in her heart, she sought a distant shore to live out, alone and unloved, the remnants of her miserable existence."

Whatever, Moll lived in solitude. She would be seen traipsing through the woods, gathering mushrooms, berries, roots, nuts, and medicinal plants (for her incantations), but whenever anyone approached her she would retreat to her hut where she would remain for days at a time. Such odd behavior, of course, aroused the curiosity of the superstitious town's people. And when a series of misfortunes struck the community — crop failures, storm damage, illnesses, injuries, and the death of livestock and residents — Moll Dyer came under suspicion of being a witch. She, like her Virginia counterpart, Grace Sherwood, was blamed for casting an evil spell which caused every calamity imaginable. Such, of course, was not true, but that was the prevalent emotional atmosphere at the time.

In time, Moll was chastised and "encouraged to leave" the area. She steadfastly refused. Finally, when an epidemic of "unknown character" raged through the county, taking many lives, it was decided that the witch "had to go." So on what was described as the "coldest night of the winter," a group of town citizens marched out to Moll's shack in the woods and set fire to it. Moll barely escaped and disappeared into the woods.

Here is how Joseph Morgan recorded what happened next: "Nothing was heard of her for several days, until a boy, hunting for his cattle, espied her kneeling on a stone with one hand resting thereon and the other raised as if in prayer. Her life had gone out in the dark cold night, and she still rested in her suppliant position, frozen stiff . . . The story runs that she offered a prayer to be avenged on her persecutors . . . that a curse be put upon them and their lands."

And so, the legend of the curse was born. It was given added credence by the fact that the clear impressions of Moll's knee, where she knelt, and her hand, where she placed it, were <u>etched into the rock!</u>

Morgan added that: "Many times have belated travelers on this road seen the ghost of Moll Dyer making her midnight visitations to her accustomed haunts. It is told by those who have the courage and endurance to watch, that once in each year, on the coldest night of the winter, she may be seen wending her ghostly way from a point south of the run, where the remains of the hut can be faintly seen, to where the stone is, kneeling in the same attitude as on the fatal night, as if praying that her curse be continued.

"There are those who think that her prayer was heard . . . The country for several miles around the location of the hut is, to this day, with few exceptions, desolate and unproductive."

Moll Dyer's curse is a strong tradition that has survived into the present. There are still a few residents in the area who firmly believe their ancestors were, in fact, plagued by the supposed witch, and no amount of reason or logic can convince them otherwise.

Another cause for the legend's lasting endurance is the fact that articles and chapters about Moll continue to be written to this day, and invariably raise renewed interest. This was evidenced in 1974 when Baltimore Sun writer Philip Love wrote an article about Moll. He said he had searched extensively for the famous rock upon which Moll had knelt, but couldn't locate it. This roused a response from St. Mary's resident Woodrow Bennet. He told Love he knew exactly where the rock was and he would lead him to it.

Sometime later the two men led an expedition into the forest and came upon the rock. It is about two feet wide, three feet long, weighs nearly 900 pounds, and is shaped like a giant potato laying on its side. The indentations left by Moll's hand and knee are still clearly visible, and perhaps her curse is still active as well. Attempts to photograph the rock when it was discovered failed when cameras malfunctioned.

It was later decided, because of the widespread interest shown, to move the rock to the St. Mary's County Historical Society headquarters as a tourist attraction. Moll apparently didn't want it dislodged, however, because the move was delayed numerous times due to bad weather, a truck that wouldn't run, and illnesses which suddenly struck those involved in the rock's transference.

Today this rock has become almost as big an attraction as the beaches of the Chesapeake Bay a few miles down the road to the east. Children climb it and place their hands and knees in the indentations said to have been made by Moll so many generations ago. And the belief in the curse continues. It is told that nothing surrounding the spot where Moll's hovel existed will grow. The ground remains barren. . . and that many tourists who take pictures of the rock find to their dismay, that once their film is developed, it does not appear in the photographs!

The Mystery of the Missing Key

(Prince George's County, Maryland)

ust across the Potomac River, less than 20 miles east of Alexandria, Virginia, near Upper Marlboro, stands historic Mt. Airy. This is not to be confused with the Mt. Airy near Warsaw and Tappahannock in Virginia. Origins of this house date back to 1660, or perhaps even a few years earlier, when a hunting lodge was built by Charles Calvert, a prominent member of one of the founding fathers of Maryland. Over the years, the lodge became the center "around which the house spread out."

The first of countless disasters occurred here in 1752, when Mt. Airy burned to the ground. It was promptly rebuilt, and 22 years later George Washington came to attend the wedding of his stepson, John Park Custis. In fact, Washington apparently visited a number of times, often while enroute from his home at Mount Vernon to Annapolis (the house is just off highway 301.) Margaret DuPont Lee, in her 1932 book, "Virginia Ghosts and Others," called the mansion, "A rambling old structure hoary with age, the scene of merry-making and of wedding festivities and where the curtain has rung down at the end of many tragedies." Ms. Lee also noted that "Beneath can be found a cellar and entrance to a secret passageway leading through immensely wide old foundations and walls three feet thick, to an exit believed near the old bowling green.

The last of the Calverts to own Mt. Airy were Dr. Cecilius Calvert and his sister, Eleanora. After they died (Eleanora passed on in 1902), the house later was sold to a Mrs. Matilda Duvall. In 1931, Mt. Airy burned again, and, after the property was again sold, it was restored once more by Eleanor Patterson, then publisher of the Washington Times-Herald. It was here that she entertained such dignitaries as President Franklin D. Roosevelt and General Douglas MacArthur.

Mt. Airy was acquired by the Maryland State Department of Natural Resources in 1973 and became part of the Rosaryville State Park. In the 1980s the house itself was sold and converted into a fashionable restaurant.

Throughout most of Mt. Airy's long history, it has maintained a strong reputation for being haunted by a variety of phantoms. In fact, the spirit activity was at times so frequent, that nearly a century ago a group of experts from the world-renowned London Society of Psychical Research came to Maryland for a first-hand investigation of the phenomena. Among the suspected spirits are these:

** Elizabeth Brescoe Calvert, who inherited the estate from her

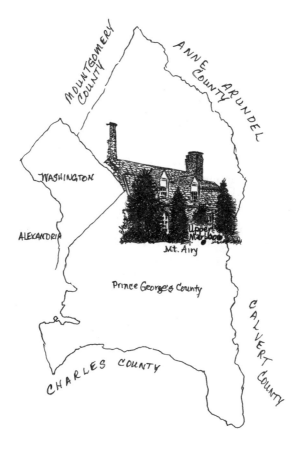

father, Benedict, in the late 18th century. She is said to still walk at night seeking a long-lost treasure that was supposedly hidden in the house and included both gold and jewels. It is perhaps Elizabeth who startled Mrs. Duvall one night in the 1920s by awakening her in the middle of the night, putting "cold fingers around her throat!" Mrs. Duvall, completely shaken by the experience, arose in bed to see only "the figure of a woman."

** Or could this apparitional woman have been, instead, Adriana Calvert? She was in love with a young man, but her father forbade the marriage. Adriana's health began to fail. As her father lay dying, his wife told Adriana she could marry her lover, but it was too late. As Ms. Lee put it, Adriana "awakened from the dream of life."

** There is one room in the mansion where, throughout the 19th century, no lamp would burn, and doors would open and shut "without cause."

** In the early 1900s, not long after the Duvall's bought Mt. Airy, they returned home one day after a long absence, and were "greeted" at the front door by a man "clad in ancient costume riding a horse! After a haughty stare, he vanished!"

** In more recent years, tradesmen during restoration work at the house have encountered several scary incidents including the sighting of a man "who wasn't there," and doorknobs which are turned and doors which are opened when there is no one there. Such occurrences so spooked one crew that they refused to work after dark.

** But possibly the most telling incident took place when the rather eccentric Eleanora Calvert died in 1902 at the age of 81. First, her death was yet another tragedy in the house. A lamp, presumably kerosene, exploded as she was carrying it from one room to another. Miss Calvert's body was placed in a coffin which was put in the front parlor of the house. Now, if the ghost of Eleanora was present at that time, it would have been greatly disturbed, because, in life, she did not like anyone using that parlor. And some believe that is the only plausible explanation — a ghostly presence — for what happened next.

When the coffin was put in the room the parlor door was locked and the key was laid on a table beside the door in the hall. The next day, when friends and relatives assembled for the funeral services, the key was missing. It could not be found anywhere. Finally, the lock on the parlor door was broken. Inside, astonished guests discovered the key lying on a table beside the coffin!

How did it get there? The mystery was never solved, but as Ms. Lee phrased it: "No mortal hand could possibly have placed it there."

CHAPTER 16

A Variety of Spectral Vignettes

The "Suffolk Miracle"

(Site Unknown)

(Author's note: In 1929 a book was published on "Traditional Ballads of Virginia," collected under the auspices of the Virginia Folklore Society. In it is an entry titled "The Suffolk Miracle," which was discovered by Cecil J. Sharp and a Miss Karpeles. One version of it was sung by Dol Small, at Nellysford in Nelson County on May 22, 1918. It is not clear where the story behind this ballad originated. It could have been in Virginia, or it could have been in the British Isles and was "imported" here by pioneering families. Nevertheless, it is a compelling legend, and, as most such traditions are, is supposedly based at least in part on facts.)

The ballad involves a young couple who fell in love — a young man and a farmer's daughter. No date is given, although the incident probably occurred 200 or more years ago. The girl's father did not approve of the blooming romance, and in an effort to discourage it, he sent his daughter off to his brother's place, 40 miles away, "to stay until she should change her mind."

Subsequently, the young man died — whether of a broken heart or of natural causes is not determined. A month after his passing, however, he, or rather his spirit, appeared at midnight at the girl's uncle's house. He was riding her father's horse and brought with him her mother's traveling gear. Since neither the girl nor her uncle were aware of his death, he and the girl were allowed to ride back to her father's house.

Along the way, the young man, "cold as clay," complained of a severe headache. The girl bound her handkerchief about his head. They rode on, and in two hours arrived at her father's house. The young man went to put up the horse, and the girl knocked on the front door. Her father was surprised to see her and even more astonished when she said her lover was with her — because her father knew that the young man had died!

So the father went to the stables to see for himself, but there was no one there. Yet the horse was found to be "all in a sweat."

To convince his daughter that her lover had, in fact, died, the father arranged to have the young man's body exhumed. "The grave was opened, and the kerchief (she had bound his head with) was found about the head of the mouldering body!"

This was told to the girl, and she died shortly after.

* * * * *

THE PHANTOM RIDER ON THE WHITE HORSE

lizabeth Hicks Corron, in her 1971 book, "Virginia's Golden Quadrangle," tells of a storied tradition about events which allegedly took place at the close of the Civil War, yet are still talked about by oldtimers in the area. They involve a man named Edwin Jordan, son of Colonel John Jordan, the owner in the early 1800s, of the Lucy Selina Iron Furnace at Longdale. Edwin became manager of the furnace in 1834, and built a large house known as "White Haven," with the help of slave labor. It was said to be surrounded by trees and was the "most elegant and impressive home in the area at that time." Author Corron said the vast estate covered 40,000 acres of land, and that the Jordans lived a "glamorous life. Some were openly envious and it seems as if there was little love lost between him (Jordan) and residents in the vicinity."

But then, Corron reports, "tragedy struck this family again and again," and Jordan "became a bitter and lonely man, and his closest friend seemed to be his white horse which he enjoyed riding at night as fast as he could fly."

Jordan was a staunch Confederate sympathizer, and "the story is told" that after he learned of Lee's surrender, and his slaves were freed, he hanged himself. Corron: "He was found hanging to a limb of an oak tree about 300 yards in front of his home. His faithful horse was standing under the tree pawing the ground, still by his master.

"Years after the death of Edwin Jordan, much truth mixed with folklore was connected with the Jordan property and an aura of tragedy surrounded the place. Several families occupied White Haven but did not live there long. They told of hearing 'things.' There were sounds of shuffling feet, the clanking of chains and pecking noises on the walls. Often the weeping of a woman and heavy pacing back and forth could be heard. No one would sleep in one of the bedrooms which had been the children's room. Because as soon as a person fell asleep, it seemed as if feverish hands lifted the covers off the bed and threw them to the floor. Those who tried to sleep in this bedroom told of being awakened by a cool hand placed on their brow and hearing someone tiptoe out of the room."

Corron concluded by saying, "the people in the vicinity of the Jordan estate were afraid to go out after dark, because residents swore they saw an apparition of a white horse with a phantom rider. Years passed and the story was still told of 'Ole Jordan' . . . who galloped over his plantation at night."

* * * * *

THE STORY THEY DON'T TELL AT COLVIN MILL RUN
(Great Falls)

Each Halloween, storytellers spin spooky yarns at the restored Colvin Mill in Great Falls, Virginia. This was a water-powered working mill for the production of flour which operated from 1811 until 1934. Today, it has been restored and educational tours are conducted to demonstrate how the historic milling process worked.

One sad story that isn't told during the Halloween events is that of a true account of the tragic death, and possible apparitional return of a young girl. According to local legend, the girl, sometime in the late 1800s, was sweeping ashes in front of the fireplace in the mill one night when her nightgown caught fire and she perished.

Colvin Run Mill

Several people, including visitors and employees, have said they have seen the vision of the girl appear, and when renovations were being done during the restoration work years ago, some of the craftsmen, for unspecified reasons, absolutely refused to go into the building after dark.

* * * * *

THE GHOST WHO SLEPT BY THE WINDOW
(Appomattox)

P am Smith, who lives in Stout Springs, between Appomattox and Lynchburg, believes she and members of her family may have psychic sensibilities. At least several of them have had haunting experiences. Pam herself has had such encounters in her house, which is only about seven years old. She says it was built on the site of an old sawmill, however, and there are hidden Indian burial grounds in the area.

Both she and her two and a half year old daughter, Katie, have seen the apparition of "a man in a funny hat." Katie says the man's feet stink, and he once tried to frighten her (successfully) by gritting his teeth and going "Grrrrrrr."

Pam's aunt Mattie lives nearby in a much older, two-story house. When she went to bed, upstairs, one night, she said someone or something pulled the covers off her. She yanked them back up, but the entity pulled them off again. This time she grabbed hold of the covers pulled them tightly around her neck. It was then she heard a strange voice say, "slide over, I always sleep by the window!"

Mattie leaped up out of the bed and replied, "you can sleep anywhere you like!" She ran downstairs and slept on the couch. Pam says to this day Mattie refuses to go upstairs anymore at night.

* * * * *

THE IMPATIENT BLACK STALLION

hosts of horses are fairly rare, at least in Virginia. There are a number of dog spirits, even cats, but few horses. There is however, one report of a prized white stallion owned by a farmer in Page County in the 1880s. He was killed by a Shenandoah Valley Railroad locomotive, and the farmer died soon afterward. According to one newspaper account, there were sightings for several years of the horse and its owner on the anniversary of the horse's death.

A better known legend involves a black stallion and a house called River Lawn, which dates back to the 18th century. It is located in Albemarle County, a few miles from Howardsville, near Charlottesville. The name of the house was applied in 1870 when, during a flood, the James River overflowed the Kanawha Canal and came up to the front lawn.

According to historian Elizabeth Rives Snead of Scottsville, the house was bought by a man named Booker sometime in the mid-1800s. He had two brothers who lived across the James River in Buckingham County. When Mr. Booker gave a party, he would signal across the river to his brothers. One of them would mount a large black stallion, swim the horse across the river, ride up to and inside the house and hitch the stallion to a newel post.

Long after the horse and the Booker brothers had departed this life, later residents would hear strange noises in the house. It sounded just like, they said, a horse pawing in impatience to go back home across the river.

* * * * *

THE VINDICATION OF NANCY HANKS
(Nottoway County)

he following is excerpted from a letter written by a "Mr. Watson" on August 6, 1916, which was originally published in a 1925 Bulletin of the Virginia State Library, and reprinted more than 50 years later in Walter Watson's book, "Notes on Southside Virginia."
It involves a house in Nottoway County known as 'Barebones,' in which, the writer believes, Nancy Hanks once lived. Nancy Hanks was the mother of Abraham Lincoln.

"Before the woods were cut, this place, "Barebones," on the south side at the falls of the creek, was one of the most sequestered and picturesque spots in the county. . . The isolation of Barebones and the silence of its woods attracted me in early life, and the place always seemed to me to have a mystic meaning, which I could not unravel.

"I can't let Barebones go without telling you a curious speculation I drifted into respecting this place. Some time back I saw in a Richmond bookstore a little book styled 'The True Nancy Hanks' by Caroline Hitchcock of New York. She was a lady of means connected with the Hanks family and sorely grieved at the damage tradition had done the reputation of the mother of Lincoln; and resolved to clear up the record of this lady of the wilderness.

"Turning its pages, I came across the statement that Nancy Hanks was born in Amelia County (Virginia) and emigrated with her father to Kentucky in 1785. The next time I went to Amelia Court House I got the old deed books and looked up her father's moderate realty holdings. . . The only land owned by him seemed to be immediately on Barebone Creek (then Amelia now Nottoway).

"If personal association may invest material things with spiritual life, why may it not be that the memory of Nancy Hanks — the vicissitudes of fortune which came to her after life and to that of her son - is the spirit which still broods over the wild waste of Barebones?"

THE 'MAN IN THE PENNY'

uane Snyder, a native Virginian now living in Florida, tells of some interesting occurrences which happened to him and his parents when he was a small child living in an old house in Charlottesville. "My mother always said it was haunted, and I believe her," he says. My father once was awakened in the middle of the night and saw the apparitions of three small children dressed in long flowing white nightgowns, standing at the foot of his bed. He rubbed his eyes and asked what we were doing up at that hour, thinking it was his own children. But it was not. He got up and the visions vanished. He then went into our bedrooms and saw that we all were sound asleep. He never could understand that.

"My mother believed it may have been some children that might have died in the house long before we moved into it. I was just a small child and sometimes I slept alone in a room that had once been a large pantry. I saw an apparition myself one night, but I didn't know how to describe it, so I told my mother I had seen the 'man in the penny.' At first she didn't know what I meant, but finally it dawned on her that I must have seen an old man with a beard, since Abraham Lincoln's likeness was on the penny. I told her that was what I had seen."

* * * * *

LEAVE OUR GHOST ALONE!
(Hardy)

(Author's note: In "The Ghost of Virginia, Volume III, published in 1996, I included a chapter called "A Ghost Named Frankie." It concerned the ethereal experiences Jim and Becky Ellis had at a house in Edinburg, halfway between Harrisonburg and Winchester. The Ellises ran a restaurant there until they sold it in 1984. The manifestations, which included sounds and a sighting, were believed by Becky to be caused by a young boy. She later learned that a nine-year-old lad had been tragically killed in an accident in the early 1900s.

In May 1998 I ran into the Ellises again, this time at the Heart of

Virginia Festival in Farmville. Jim said they were now running a bed and breakfast at a place called "Over Home." It is located in Hardy, Virginia, a few miles southeast of Roanoke on route 116. It, too, apparently, has a spirit.)

Over Home is a pre-Civil War house which features spacious rooms with tall ceilings and great windows that overlook the more than 100 acres that surround it. All rooms, says Jim, are decorated with antiques and collectibles, and have working fireplaces. The Ellises serve a large country breakfast, with "a wonderful surprise" every morning.

The house is on property that once belonged to Confederate General Jubal Early. He was born only a mile away. Both he and his horse, "Tar River," lie in eternal rest in the family cemetery near here. Coincidentally, there are reports in the area of the ghost of Jubal Early's brother. William Early's nocturnal ventures manifest themselves as a strange light in the mountain foothills; a light that has been seen but never explained by hundreds of area witnesses over several generations. They say it is the golden light of Early's lantern, as he wanders restlessly from tombstone to tombstone in an isolated cemetery where he was interred, searching for a cache of money lost when he died. (See "The Ghosts of Virginia, Volume II.")

In the late 1800s Robert Lovelace bought the estate and he and his wife, Sallie, reared nine children. The oldest child was Sallie Lovelace. The youngest was Mamie Lovelace. She was the mother of Jim Ellis! Thus Jim and Becky have restored the house with loving and painstaking care, "while capturing the elegance and traditions of the past."

They also have reason to believe that one or more of Jim's ancestors may still be in residence. "You know me," Jim declares. "I have a hard time believing in all that, but still there are things that happen here that I can't logically explain. We had a lady guest once who came in to spend the night, and immediately announced, 'they're here!' She was talking about spirits. From her description of what she felt, it sounded like Aunt Sallie. She rolled up the sleeves of her dress and all the hair on her arm was standing straight up. That was a little unsettling."

Jim said a reporter for the Roanoker Magazine came out to the house after he heard about the possibility of ghosts, and when he entered Over Home, he immediately introduced himself to the spirits.

Jim adds that another lady guest came to the house and that evening she flipped out a crystal ball on a long silver chain and began to twirl it around. "I asked her what she was doing," Jim says, "and she explained she was going to dispel the spirits in the house.

"I said, 'wait a minute!' They're our spirits, and we like them here. Leave them alone!"

* * * * *

THE BANGING ON THE SWINGING DOORS

rom a newspaper dispatch, October 9, 1939: "A few miles south of Coeburn (Wise County), stands the Flat Woods Methodist Church. Due to crowded school facilities it has now become necessary that a part of the students of that section have their classes in the church.

"Several days ago, as the children were preparing to bid their lessons adieu for the day, a loud thumping was heard at the front door. Investigation, much to the dismay of teacher and students, revealed no one there. Then, both doors (a double door type) started mysteriously swinging in and out. Meanwhile, the thumping grew louder. After several minutes, as the children looked on, open-mouthed and bewildered, the doors abruptly stopped their antics and the pounding subsided.

"Charles Hillman, principal, who had been away at the time, put in his appearance. Everyone, jabbering excitedly, tried to relate the strange happenings. If Mr. Hillman, a veteran of many years teaching in Wise County, had any doubts, they soon vanished, for before the very eyes of the teachers and students, the doors again started their swinging in and out, in and out, and once again the loud thumping sound accompanied the swinging, this time louder than before.

"Still a little skeptical, Hillman carefully examined all the space under, behind and in front of the doors. His search revealed nothing. Gradually the swinging subsided and the loud hammering died away.

"Professor Hillman said that it couldn't possibly have been the wind for no breeze was blowing at the time, and then, what about the heavy knocking, almost as if someone had a hammer beating on the wall?

"Fairy tale? Definitely not, said the teachers, and they'll stake their reputations on it."

* * * * *

THE LEGEND OF TWO SCOTTISH LASSES
(Staunton)

Do the spirits of two young Scottish lasses, who died tragically more than 350 years ago, still linger in the twin mountains guarding Staunton which were named for them? Many area residents believe so, and incoming freshmen class coeds are told that indeed, the mysterious lights sometimes seen on the mountain slopes are being carried by the ghosts of Betsy Bell and Mary Gray.

The legend of how these peaks were so named had its origins in Scotland in the year 1645. Betsy and Mary were the daughters of wealthy land owners, and were the best of friends. Both were said to be beautiful, charming, vivacious, and full of life. And both were in love with the same young man.

That year, however, the dreaded bubonic plague was sweeping through Europe causing widespread death wherever it surfaced. When victims began to fall in the town near where the two girls lived, one of their fathers sent them to an isolated shelter on the far outskirts of his estate, to quarantine them so to speak. Bored and restless, the girls welcomed their young man friend to visit their remote cottage, and thus, in time, contracted the dread and deadly disease. They were buried side by side near a river, and the sad story of their demise was passed along by the Scots, generation to generation, until it evolved into a folk legend.

During the horrible years of religious persecution, many left their native Scotland and settled in County Tyronne, Ireland, for there the land was similar to their own native hills and broad valleys. There were two small mountains ringing the Irish town of Omagh, and they were given the names Betsy Bell and Mary Gray.

Then, in the middle of the 18th century, colonies of Scotch-Irish left their homelands and came to America to help settle the new land. As families descended down the Shenandoah Valley, many were struck with the beauty of the land in and around Staunton. It was strikingly similar to their native regions in Scotland and Ireland. And so a settlement was started in Augusta County.

Flanking Staunton were two small mountains, remindful of the ones around Omagh.

And so these, too, were named Betsy Bell and Mary Gray. The legend continues.

* * * * *

SOMETHING THAT 'SWOOSHED' AT CHIPPOKES
(Surry County)

o they or don't they . . . have any ghosts at the old mansion at Chippokes State Park, on the south side of the James River about halfway between the towns of Smithfield on the east, and Surry on the west?

Maybe they do, maybe they don't. It depends on who you speak to. The park manager and chief ranger decline to talk about any unusual psychic activity there, but other employees and visitors say some strange things have happened to them while on the grounds.

Either way, Chippokes — the park and the house — are both scenic and historic, and well worth a tour. Just down the road from the more famous (and more haunted) Bacon's Castle, ("The Ghosts of Virginia, Volume I," 1993) the property here was first occupied in 1612. By 1616, a land grant had been given to Captain William Powell, and he chose the name "Choupocke," a friendly Indian chief in the area at that time. Ironically, Powell was killed in the great Indian massacre of 1622. (Whether or not Choupocke was one of those who became unfriendly is not known.)

Chippokes has been a working farm for more than 350 years. Corn, grain, tobacco and apples were the main crops in the 17th and 18th centuries; peanuts and tobacco in the 19th century; and a variety of crops as well as livestock in the 20th.

The mansion itself was built about 1854 in the plain Greek revival style. Several early outbuildings and farm structures, stretched along a lane, preserve the plantation atmosphere. According to "The Virginia Guide," written more than 50 years ago, the main house "was built to conform with the early pattern that involved a river view, beaded weatherboarding and chimneys and dormers. On the grounds are slave houses that bear testimony, in their comfortable and well-designed simplicity, to the 'ante-bellum' prosperity of the plantation."

Another author has written that Chippokes "commands a magnificent panoramic view of the lower James . . . and radiates the charming atmosphere of years of long ago . . . But the highlight of the estate is the five-mile drive over fertile fields, through shadowy woods, down to the sandy beach at the river's edge.

Such a view is enjoyed by thousands of visitors each year, and every July an annual "Pork, Peanut and Pine" festival is held here, including live entertainment (country and gospel music), craft demonstrations, and mouth-watering barbecue and peanut pies.

Chippokes was given to the commonwealth in 1967 by Mrs. Victor Stewart "to serve as a learning center for the history of Virginia agriculture." She and her husband had purchased the estate in 1917. Some believe it may be Mrs. Stewart who has made her presence known at Chippokes long after she had departed this earth.

One who does is Jo-An Miller, a volunteer tour guide at the park. She was in the mansion on a rainy day in 1997 when there were no tourists around. She got out some sewing. All of a sudden the front door sprang open by itself, a coldness enveloped the room, and "something" swooshed by her, "whirling like a dervish." "I saw only hair and fabric," she recalls, "but not the face or real form of a human being." It swished by her toward the double glass doors inside the hallway and then went through the unopened doors.

Jo-An thinks it well have been the spirit of Mrs. Stewart. "They had been doing extensive renovations to the house, and maybe she didn't like what they were doing," she says. Chief ranger and curator Catherine Correll says a number of tourists have reported strange sounds and sightings in the house and on the grounds, but she is reluctant to pass them on.

A receptionist at Chippokes did say that a local young lady had a rather frightening experience a few years ago. She had come to the mansion after it had closed for the day, and was sitting on the front steps when she heard footsteps behind coming down toward her. She assumed it was a park employee. As the steps neared her she looked around. There was no one there. She ran to her car as fast as she could and drove away.

So there may well be spirits about at Chippokes, worth a visit either way, even if the officials there don't want to talk about them.

THE GHOST WHO (MAY HAVE) INDUCED LABOR

(Author's note: You just never know when or where the next ghostly legend is going to surface. In November 1998, some men came to my house to lay some television cable lines. One of the young men, Ron Holmes, had read a couple of my books and said he, or rather his mother, had an encounter, and it may, or may not, have had an indirect effect on his birth, in June 1962. Ron and his mother, Ann, live in Hampton, Virginia. I talked to both of them and some of the exact details are blurred by the passage of time, but this essentially is what they told me.)

hortly before Ron was born, Ann got up early one morning in an old house (she was then living in North Carolina.) As she looked down the long hallway toward the kitchen, she caught a glimpse of a strange and unexpected sight. She saw, or thought she saw, the figure of a man standing by the sink, dressed in military green-fatigues. He seemed to be drinking a glass of water. At first, she assumed it was her husband, who was in the Air Force at the time, but then the sudden realization struck her — she had left her husband sleeping in bed!

The Holmes' apartment in the house had only one entrance. How could someone have gotten into the kitchen? Then, before Ann's eyes, the figure turned around, looked at her, and then faded away. "At least, that is what I think happened," she recalls. "I really don't know if it was a ghost or not. It happened so fast. I don't really know what it was that I saw. It is difficult to explain. I have felt the presence of my father at times, long after he had passed away, but this was the first time I saw anything."

Understandably, Ann screamed, then ran back toward the bedroom, and fell. Her husband immediately got up. She told him what had happened. He checked the kitchen and there was no one there. But, curiously, the water from the tap was running, and there was a half-full glass of water on the counter!

Ron says a neighbor later told them that a young man, a military man, (that might explain the fatigues) had killed himself in the attic of the house some years before the Holmes moved in.

And shortly after the incident, Ron was born. He speculates

that the ghost, or whatever it was, may have helped induce his mother's labor.

* * * * *

RECREATION OF A BRUTAL MURDER

In Blackstone, Virginia, 40 miles south of Richmond, near Fort Pickett and the Nottoway County Court House, is an old house still harboring a haunting memory of long ago. In his book, "Old Homes and Families in Nottoway," (1932), author W. R. Turner says this house became a tavern in the late 1700s operated by a German named John A. Schwartz.

Sometime later, according to Turner, a man lived in the house. He had a beautiful daughter who fell in love with a young man. However, her father disapproved of him and forbade his daughter to see him. The couple decided to elope. About midnight one evening she started down the stairs to meet her lover. She was wearing her best silk dress, and the rustling of the dress and the creaking of the stairs awakened her father.

He raced down the stairs and attacked the startled young man, stabbing him to death. The father was brought to trial, but was acquitted, claiming self defense.

Turner wrote: "Be that as it may, it is said that often now around midnight one can hear the rustling of a silk dress and the creaking of the stairs, followed by blows, and then groans, as the awful scene is being reenacted."

* * * * *

THE UNSEEN, UNHEARD, UNFELT 'PRESENCE'
(Reedville)

(Author's note: Small world department. A year or so ago I learned that the Book Cellar, a delightful shop in the downtown mall in Charlottesville, had a new owner. His name was Tom Tiede. I was excited. Thirty-odd years ago, when I was a public information officer for NASA at the Kennedy Space Center, I gave a tour of Cape Canaveral to a young Tom Tiede. He was then a fledgling columnist for Scripps-Howard. I had read some of his work and I liked his writing. He has a flair and a style for telling a story succinctly and poignantly.

As the years passed, I read more of Tom's work. He sent back some of the most heart-warming (and tear-jerking) dispatches from Vietnam. Many called him the Ernie Pyle of Vietnam. Pyle was the beloved journalist who captured the human side of World War II. For three decades Tom wrote his columns from all corners of the world. He covered four different wars, traveled more than two million miles, and toured 130 countries. He also has written "about 15 books," and was on several of Larry King's shows. At one time, Tom's column was published in 750 newspapers, worldwide.

In April 1998, Tom dropped me a note telling me about his book store. He carries my books. Then he piqued my interest with a notation at the bottom of his letter. He said, "By the way, I used to have a beach place on the northern neck of Virginia. When you are older, I will tell you of the only time in my life . . . that I have ever been truly frightened, jogging past a house so haunted that I was on a first name basis with the ghost."

Seven months later I drove over to Lynchburg to do a book signing at the River Ridge Mall, so I called Tom and asked him if I could drop by on the way back to Williamsburg. He said fine. This is what he told me.)

"Back in the early 1980s I had a beach house in Reedville. I used to jog there at night. I'll never forget the smell. They used to have some medhaden plants around there on the water, and the odor was pretty strong to say the least. Still, I loved to run South Point, about a three-mile jaunt. I would go out about midnight when all was quiet. About halfway through the run I would pass an ominous old house. It was abandoned, and it must have been at least 100 years old. Someone said an old sea captain owned it at one time. It was the type house they might have been used for a horror movie. It had a widow's walk and all. And there was a local tradition that a man had once been murdered there. I never did verify that, however.

"Well, there was something about that house. I don't quite know how to describe it. I guess you could just say it was spooky. Everytime I would pass it, I would get a bad feeling, like there was something evil there. Once in a while, the leaves would rustle as I ran by, and every now and then I thought I would see lights flickering in the house. It was probably just my imagination. But you know I am not an 'afraid' person. Listen, I've been through just about everything you can think of, wars, pestilence, whatever. But this old house just struck a chord of fear in me. It got so bad that I wouldn't run by it anymore

"Yet, there was something compelling about the house. It was like a magnet drawing me to it. I had to go inside. So one night, about midnight, I went up to it. I walked around back and went through a window. I had a flashlight with me.

"I didn't see a dead body or anything. In fact, I didn't see anything at all. There were no sounds, no footsteps. But there was something! I got an overpowering feeling of evil. It was repulsive to me. I couldn't stand it. I'm not sure there is such a thing as a presence, but if there is, it was there, and it was overwhelming. I had to get out of there."

Tom said that for the rest of the time he owned that cottage and jogged at night, he was never able to run past the house again!

* * * * *

THE GHOSTLY LOVER WHO RETURNED
(Lexington)

When Colonel and Mrs. Paul Welles bought the house known as "Old Morningsides" some years ago, Mrs. Welles commented that it actually "looked like it was haunted." She said the ironwork railing which encloses the open porches at the first and second floors was "almost strangled in wisteria," and the grass and shrubbery seemed to have been uncut for years. In fact, the house, part of which dates to 1850 and part decades earlier, had long held a reputation for its spookiness. Friends even warned the Welles not to purchase it because they "would have trouble hiring servants."

Previous owners had reported strange sounds which included doors opening by themselves and mysterious footsteps. One resident was once "awakened by a presence, and saw a 'woman' silhouetted between her and a window. No servant would stay in the house after dark.

Research into the history of Old Morningsides revealed that during the War Between the States, the Paxton family lived here. A daughter, Madge, was engaged to a young Confederate officer.

According to legend, one night Madge was in her room at the front of the house which overlooks the large, second floor porch, when a servant knocked at her door and told her that her lover was downstairs, home from the fighting.

Mrs. Welles continues the account: "Overjoyed, she put down her things and hurried down the first eight steps to the turn, where there is a little platform, and looked down. There, at the foot of the steps, was her beloved, in his uniform except for his cap, waiting for her with outstretched arms."

She raced down the stairs, but just as she reached out for him he vaporized. Her arms encircled nothing!

A few days later the family received word that the young man had been killed in battle. He had died at the exact instant Madge Paxton had tried to embrace him!

Madge, grief stricken, never married, perhaps because it was said that her fiancée's spirit was seen from time to time in the halls of the old house. Mrs. Welles added that, "She lived to be an old lady, and after she died, Miss Madge, young and lovely, could be seen with him."

* * * * *

"WATCH OUT FOR 'WILD SALLY!'
(Westmoreland County)

On state road 622 between Montross and Stratford Hall (the birthplace of Robert E. Lee) is a darkened swamp bottom surrounded by a deep forest of maples, white oaks and beech trees. There is a local legend that this particular stretch of ground has long been haunted by the ghost of an eccentric woman known in these parts as "Wild Sally." She lived, it is believed, in the late 19th century, and according to the legend she went into the swamp one night long ago to search for her missing dog. She was never seen again, at least in mortal form.

Oldtimers in the area say her spirit is occasionally glimpsed still wading through the swampland, lantern held high, looking for her dog. The scare factor she has created has been strong enough to encourage scores of local teenagers to drive out of the swamp late at night and conduct their own investigation. (The tradition is Wild Sally bounds out of the woods to frighten those brave enough to venture there after dark.) Consequently, most of the young people have returned wide-eyed and open-mouthed, after they probably experienced the nocturnal sounds of a barred owl, rather than the sloshing of Wild Sally.

Richmond Times Dispatch staff writer Lawrence Latanè, III, is one who had a scare. It was in October 1997, when he drove out to the swamp one night seeking a good Halloween column for his paper. He said as he rounded a curve down a dark country road, his headlights caught the frightening glare of two red eyes. For a "startling second," he said, he thought he had encountered Wild Sally herself.

It turned out to be a startled opossum!

* * * * *

THE DOG THAT WARNED FROM HEAVEN

atty Summers of Evington, a few miles due south of Lynchburg, is an "Animal Communicator," and is the author of "Talking with the Animals." In a newspaper column published in March 1999, she tells of an extraordinary incident related to her by an unidentified woman she called "Dorothy." Dorothy had a white toy poodle which died 20 years ago.

Recently, Dorothy had an unusual dream in which she saw the poodle tied to a rope atop a pile of wood. Then someone struck a match and lit the wood. Horrified, Dorothy screamed, then ran and snatched the dog from the blazing fire. Amazingly, the poodle was unharmed. Not even a single hair was singed. As Dorothy stroked her former pet, she noticed a singular buzzing in her ears.

She awoke from her dream, but still heard the buzzing. She roused her husband, and when they got up and opened the bedroom door to enter the hallway, they found their home filled with smoke. The wood stove had become "blocked up."

Dorothy told Patty Summers that if she had not had the dream she and her husband "would not be here today!"

Oh yes. Her late poodle's name . . . was Angel!

CHAPTER 17

What Evil Secrets Lurk in Crystal Caverns

(Shenandoah County, near Strasburg)

henandoah County, roughly 30 miles south of Winchester, wrote historian Henry Howe in 1845, "was settled by Germans from Pennsylvania, a plain, frugal, and industrious people." Howe quoted another author, who in the 1750s, penned: "The low grounds upon the banks of the Shenandoah are very rich and fertile. They are chiefly settled by Germans . . . I could not but reflect with pleasure on the situation of these people; and think, if there is such a thing as happiness in this life, they enjoy it. Far from the bustle of the world, they live in the most delightful climate and richest soil imaginable.

"They are everywhere surrounded with beautiful prospects and sylvan scenes — lofty mountains, transparent streams, falls of water, rich valleys, and majestic woods; the whole interspersed with an infinite variety of flowering shrubs, constitute the landscape surrounding them. They are subject to few diseases, are generally robust, and live in perfect liberty. They are ignorant of want, and are acquainted with but few vices. Their inexperience of the elegances of life, precludes any regret that they have not the means of enjoying them; but they possess what many princes would give half their dominions for — health, contentment, and tranquility of mind."

One might wonder, in such a peaceful area, among such a contented populace, why would there be reason for ghostly activity. Possibly, because tragedy struck even here, most notably in atroci-

Crystal Caverns

ties committed by Indians on the settlers, dating back more than 200 years.

A reason for haunting? Consider the following, written by the acknowledged "Historian of the Valley," Samuel Kercheval, in the 1830s: "In the year 1758, a party of about 50 Indians and four Frenchmen penetrated into the Mill Creek neighborhood, about nine miles south of Woodstock, and committed some murders, and carried off 48 prisoners. Among them was a young lad of the name of Fisher, about 13 years of age.

"After six days' travel they reached their villages west of the Alleghany mountains, where they held a council, and determined to sacrifice their helpless prisoner, Jacob Fisher. They first ordered him to collect a quantity of dry wood. The poor little fellow shuddered, burst into tears, and told his father they intended to burn him. His father replied, 'I hope not;' and advised him to obey. When he had collected a sufficient quantity of wood to answer their purpose, they cleared and smoothed a ring around a sapling, to which they tied him by one hand, then formed a trail of wood around the tree, and set it on fire.

"The poor boy was then compelled to run round in this ring of fire until his rope wound him up to the sapling, and then back, until he came in contact with the flame, while his infernal tormentors were drinking, singing, and dancing around him, with 'horrid joy.'

"This was continued for several hours; during which time the savage men became beastly drunk, and as they fell prostrate to the ground, the squaws would keep up the fire. With long sharp poles, prepared for the purpose, they would pierce the body of their victim whenever he flagged, until the poor and helpless boy fell, and expired with the most excruciating torments, while his father and brothers, who were also prisoners, were compelled to be witnesses of the heart-rending tragedy."

Reason enough? But there are no reports of the boy's ghost returning.

Kercheval did, however, write about one supernatural experience which occurred to a man at Shaffer's Cave, near Mt. Jackson, southwest of Front Royal. "A large human skeleton was many years ago found in this cavern, the skull bone of which a neighboring man had the curiosity to take to his dwelling house. This aroused the ghost of the dead man, who, not being pleased with the removal of his head, very soon appeared to the depredator and harassed him until he became glad to return the skull to its former habitation. The ghost then became appeased and ceased his visits. It is said there are many persons to this day (1830s) in the neighborhood, who most religiously believe that the ghost did really and truly compel the offender to return the skull."

Are there ghosts still active in Shenandoah County? A number of residents believe there are, and perhaps one of the most haunted sites in the area is Crystal Caverns. The legends are so strong here, in fact, that during Halloween week in 1998, throngs of curious visitors descended in the caverns to partake in a ghost walk. "We were booked solid," says chief curator Bob Denton. "We had to turn people away." Some of the traditions recounted are folklorian in nature and can be traced back to the 1700s.

Denton: "If one follows Route 11, the 'Old Valley Pike,' northeast from Strasburg, the road climbs steadily up a large, skinhole-pocked hill lying between the town and Cedar Creek. Beneath the hill's verdant surface exists one of the lower valley's truly hidden treasures." It is today known as Crystal Caverns at Hupp's Hill. According to Denton, the cave was used as a campsite and shelter by ancient native Americans for countless centuries. Artifacts found in or near the cave's entrance can be traced back at least 3,000 years, and "it is suspected that human habitation of the site may extend back to the end of the last Ice Age."

Hupp family members were among the hundreds of German settlers moving south from Pennsylvania and arriving in this area in the early 1700s. It was in 1755 that one of the Hupps first discovered the cave near the crest of a large hill (hence the name.) Kercheval wrote: ". . . there is one (a cave) on the land of George F. Hupp Esq., near Strasburg. This is said to be pretty extensive with much stalactitic matter."

For years the Hupps and others used the cave, with its year-round temperature of 54 degrees, as a "natural refrigerator" to store perishable foods such as milk, butter and meat. It is believed that during the Civil War the cave served two purposes: one, it was used as a stop on the underground railroad, sheltering escaped slaves making their way north to free states. Two, it was used as a hideout by deserters from both sides.

Crystal Caverns was first opened as a tourist attraction by a Hupp descendent in 1922. By torch and candlelight, visitors viewed such underground formations and rooms as "Giant's Coffin," "Brontosaurus," "The Ballroom," and "Crystal Pool." In ensuing years large crowds gathered on the grounds to tour a small zoo and an historic museum. Concerts were also held, featuring such legendary band leaders as Count Basie, Duke Ellington and Cab Calloway.

In time, tourism waned and the cave became largely neglected and in disuse. Crystal Caverns reopened in June 1998, adjacent to the new Stonewall Jackson Museum. The site is now open year-round Monday through Saturday from 10 a.m. to 5 p.m., and Sundays from noon to 5 p.m.

As to the haunting legends here, Denton says, "In the earliest days the cave was said to be the home of a spectral 'Black Dog.' This widespread denizen of the Appalachian mountain region was almost always a monstrous, feral hound with 'burning red eyes,' and 'fangs dripping with gore,' that wreaked bloody vengeance on the wicked and unrighteous. More than likely, these tales were the exaggerations of the observations of early settlers in the Strasburg area, who recounted that the cave was a den site for wolves. In support of this, wolf scat and gnawed bones have been found in the drier, less visited recesses of the cave."

Denton continues: "It is also said that Indians used the cave to dump the bodies of enemies killed in raiding parties, however, it is doubtful that they would have wanted to dwell for any length of time in a burying place, thus invoking the vengeance of the dead."

Of the Civil War era, Denton notes that there is a long-standing local legend that one of the escaping slaves died within the cave, "and his spirit still dwells within the dark limestone passages!" Denton adds that "Perhaps the most compelling story is of a Confederate soldier who staggered, wounded and bleeding, into the depths of the cave at the end of the Battle of Cedar Creek, on October 19, 1864. This young man was trying to escape being captured by Yankee cavalry patrols, and in his fear and desperation, ended up lying alone and in the darkness deep within the cavern in what is now referred to as 'the Ballroom.' Weakened by blood loss, he died a few hours later.

"His identity is unknown, but strangely, marked in the cave's ceiling near the spot, is a set of initials 'T H' and 'C S.' Are they the soldier's desperate attempt to leave some identifier behind, with the 'C S' indicating Confederate States?'

"It's uncertain, but to this day, the spot where the soldier's spirit left his body is marked by a strangely perfect and unearthly cross in the rock of the cave's ceiling. It is the same room that spectral 'vapors' have been seen, especially in the crevice-like passage that lies above the 'crystal pool,' a limpid green underground lake. These misty vapors have no rational explanation, and seem to disappear when the curious draw close. Yet they have been seen by countless visitors, and continue to mystify and perplex all who observe them. The crypt-like atmosphere of 'the Ballroom,' lying at the lowest point of the caverns, only tends to amplify the feelings of a spectral presence."

And, finally, Denton says, "The cave was the favorite 'haunt' of the famed psychic and astrologer Jeanne Dixon, who visited often and found it a pleasant place to meditate, saying it 'enhanced her psychic abilities.' She felt it was a place of great power, a sort of 'focal point' for supernatural energies coursing through great underground channels in the Shenandoah Valley. Many 'sensitives' who have been to the cave have verified Ms.

Dixon's observations."

Whether or not a visitor today will encounter the spirit of a vengeful Indian, a runaway slave, or a bloodied Confederate soldier - or hear the guttural growl of a supernatural (or real-life) beast, is speculative at best. The natural wonders of Crystal Caverns merit a tour nevertheless.

CHAPTER 18

The Ghost Who Loved Good Times

(Culpeper)

(Author's note: How do you get rid of ghosts? How do you move them on to whatever next plane or plateau exists, if there is such a thing? I have been asked that on occasion. One lady in Fredericksburg once called me and said she had a ghost in her house and she wanted to sell the house and was afraid the spirit would adversely affect the selling price, what should she do? The only thing I knew is what others had told me - they had said just have a heart-to-heart talk with the ghost, and that seemed to work to some degree. At least in most cases the phenomena quieted after such a conversation.

But with the fraternity house at Randolph Macon, and the following case, there may be another, although terribly more drastic way to extinguish a haunter. That is if the house burns down! Obviously, I don't recommend that!)

Certainly one of the friendliest ghosts written about in Virginia was a young woman named Alice Grimes. Her manifestations were recorded in Margaret DuPont Lee's classic book, "Virginia Ghosts," published in 1930.

It is not specified when Alice lived and died, what she died of, at what age, or precisely when she came back in ghostly form. An educated guess would be that she was from the era of the second half of the 19th century. The house she and her family lived in is described only as being "flanked on either side by immense chimneys with dormer windows in the high-pitched roof." It probably burned in the late 1800s or early 1900s. Nearby is a small graveyard where a tombstone, "guarded by five tall cedars," is inscribed to the memory of Alice.

Mrs. Lee either interviewed or more likely corresponded with a woman named Elizabeth Daingerfield, who lived in the house after the Grimes. She and other members of her household all told the story of Alice's reappearances in the house. She was, they all agreed, a most friendly spirit who lingered not to frighten, but rather to seek the companionship of those still living.

According to Elizabeth, she first saw the ghost 25 years earlier. (That would put the date at about 1905 or earlier.) "I never pass a clump of cedars without thinking of her. She was very real and very vivid and I was never in the least afraid of her," Elizabeth said. "Even today I should like to see her again. Jule saw her first in the parlor. I recollect Jule was a very practical unemotional girl. She walked the entire length of the parlor, thinking the girl sitting at the piano was Mary Heneberger, and said, 'Sing 'When I remember'.' The ghost turned a lovely face to her, with a sort of reminiscent, questioning smile. The choice of the song was strange, for the last verse goes —

'When I remember something promised me
But which I never had nor can have now,
In that the promiser we no more see
In country which accords with earthly vow.'

"It was in early spring, quite early in the evening, about six, and there was nothing alarming even when she saw her no more, and knew her for a ghost."

One of the Daingerfield women reportedly saw the apparition many times. Once she was walking in the yard in front of the house with a young man from the village. The vision of Alice appeared just before them. Ms. Daingerfield told her companion to follow Alice and speak to her. He first walked, then ran, but he couldn't catch up. Then he lost sight of her among the five cedars surrounding her grave.

Mrs. Lee wrote: "In the late afternoon one day Mrs. Daingerfield, Elizabeth's mother, saw Alice as she came into the drawing-room. The girl, her back turned, was sitting at the window looking out into the yard towards the little group of cedars. Mrs. Daingerfield went up to her and spoke. Alice turned. There was the same wistful smile, the same gentleness, the same regret —

and then, as with the others who saw her, she was no more."

"There were a number of times," Elizabeth said, "when a number of us saw her at the same time. This was apt to be when we were happiest, planning a party. We rarely saw her at night. Never suddenly or in unsuspected corners. Often when alone I have wished she would come and stand near me. There is no explanation other than we saw her. Often when we were sitting together, often when alone, she was there. She was gentle, she was beautiful, always smiling just before she went away.

"Once I remember going out of my room into the long hall upstairs, and this figure being just in front of me in the hall light, I called, thinking it was a friend staying with me: 'Mary, wait, our ghost may join me,' and I followed one step behind down the long stairs into the lighted hall below, where the figure turned and a far more lovely face than Mary's laughed into mine and faded."

Elizabeth continued: "Again when a young doctor, a most matter-of-fact soul, walked with me one brilliant moonlight night, laughed at my stories of my ghost, and when I said 'She is right in front of us now,' he looked scornfully (at the figure) and said 'nonsense.' Reaching out to touch her, his hand went <u>through</u> (her) — there was no substance!

"Alice Grimes was very real and grew to be rather an omen of good times. One evening Jule followed her into the parlor, we all seeing the figure lead the way and sit down by the piano. One of us strolling up threw an arm around her shoulder — but only the vision was there."

Elizabeth said after the house burned, "we never saw Alice Grimes again."

CHAPTER 19

Multiple 'Hants' in Madison County

inety seven miles north-northwest of Richmond, 25 miles or so north of Charlottesville, and a few miles west of Culpeper, lies Madison County, of which author Henry Howe said in 1845, "commands a beautiful and picturesque view of the Blue Ridge and neighboring mountains." At that time the town of Madison "contained four mercantile stores, one Baptist and one Episcopal church, and about 50 dwellings." There are considerably more today, churches and dwellings, yet the county retains a rustic charm that has prevailed since it was formed in 1792.

Where else will one find such colorfully-named towns as Banco, Criglersville, Hood, and Wolftown. Criglersville, named for a German emigrant named Jacob Crigler, has a particularly interesting background. He and a band of Germans sailed for Pennsylvania in 1717, but a storm blew them to the Virginia coast where they were sold as servants by the ship's captain to pay for their trip. After serving seven years of indentured servitude, Crigler, and presumably some followers, settled in what would become Madison County, hence the name of the town. Wolftown, a stone's throw south of Madison once was a popular stagecoach stop on the route between Alexandria and Charlottesville, but it is unclear how it got the name. Also a mystery is how Banco and Hood came to be known as such, although one will find an antique car museum in Hood.

Whatever, there apparently are a goodly number of haunted houses in the county, as evidenced by the fact that nightly ghost tours are offered at various times during the year. (For specifics, call the Madison Chamber of Commerce (540-948-2988). There also have been several written references to these rural spirits — in newspaper articles, especially around Halloween, and in books. One of the best volumes is a beautiful coffee table edition titled "Madison County Homes - A Collection of Pre-Civil War Homes and Family Heritages." It was written, photographed and privately published in 1975 by Vee Dove. You won't find this in bookstores, but some libraries have it in their Virginiana section.

Following are some excerpts culled from the above sources. Most of these accounts are, however, brief in nature and some lack details as to the exact times of their occurrences. Still, they present a colorful glimpse at part of the county's storied lore.

NEARLY GONE BUT NOT FORGOTTEN!

Maple Hill is a Dutch colonial-style house which overlooks Criglersville, believed to have been built in the early 1800s. The name probably was taken from a 200-plus-year-old maple tree in the yard. Among the features in the house are six fireplaces. It is interesting to note that most of the original hardware here was sold in the 1930s to the Williamsburg Restoration Society. Maple Hill owners then needed a new roof and repair on the chimneys. It was during the Depression and times were hard, so a deal was struck.

There is no ghost here, but there almost could have been. Sometime back in the 1800s, when a family named Wilhoit lived in the house, one of the daughters took sick and was thought to be dead. In those times, in such a country region, there were no undertakers. Funerals generally were held a day after a person died, and the custom here was for the women to sit in the room with the "body" and the men were in the yard, while the preacher stood in the front doorway and preached the service.

In this instance, the coffin was carried into the yard and opened for all who wanted a final look at the young lady. The last person to pass by noticed an eyelid move, and realized the girl was not dead! A doctor was hastily summoned, the Wilhoit girl recovered, and actually lived to be an old lady!

A SIGHT FOR HER EYES ONLY

The old John Fishback House, on route 29 a mile east of the town of Madison, was built in the 1790s. John was a wheelwright, and it is said that most of the covered wagons which ventured west from this region were made by him. John and his immediate descendants raised large families. John and his wife had 13 children, another John and his wife had 12, and so on down the genealogical line. During the Civil War Union soldiers camped out on the grounds and ate every Fishback chicken they could catch, although the family was able to bury and thus save their valuables.

Sometime after the war, the wife of Robert Edward Lee Fishback, (obviously named for the general) kept seeing a ghost of an old man in the house. No one else saw him. It must have made a vivid impression on her because she described the man in explicit detail to her husband, and he said she had presented a spitting image of his father, Staunton Fishback!

THE SOLDIER WHO <u>REALLY</u> LOST HIS HEAD!

A mile north of the Locust Dale Post Office, on route 614, stands Lovell, a lovely old plantation built in 1840. The legend here is that during the Civil War several Union soldiers came to the old kitchen at Lovell and demanded food. The cook told them she had none, that other troops had been through and confiscated everything. All but one soldier left. He had spotted a loose flagstone in the kitchen floor and discovered hidden food beneath it. As he was lifting out a ham, the hefty cook beheaded him with a meat cleaver. She then dragged him outside and buried him under the coffee trees in the yard.

Ever since, "when the moon is right and the wind is howling," his apparition appears on the observation platform located atop Lovell, "waving his arms and seeming to search the surrounding lawn for his missing head."

THE RETURN OF MRS. BLANKENBAKER

A mile or so from the village of Haywood, on route 609, is the Richard Blankenbaker home, built in the early 1800s. It commands a beautiful view of the surrounding valley, enjoyed not only by residents over the years, but, perhaps by a ghost as well. This figure has been seen walking across the yard wearing a gray dress with a deep ruffle.

The family cook, on her way to the hen house one day to prepare chickens for dinner, heard the back gate open and the latch close. She saw no one, thought it was the wind, and went on with her chores. A few minutes later she heard a chair on the porch gently rocking, and when she looked, she gasped. There, in the chair, was Sarah Ann Blankenbaker. The only problem was, Sarah had died long years before. The vision quickly vanished, as did the cook.

Another house resident saw only the shoes of the ghost. She said she had twice seen the shoes of someone coming from the bathroom into the dining room. The shoes were described as being of an earlier era. They were of "soft black leather with buttons!"

THE LIGHT THAT SIGNALED DEATH

Near Banco, on route 721 is the Weaver home, known locally as White Oak Hill Farm, built in 1859. There is a well-known county folktale which allegedly involved a young slave boy named Jim Towles. He was told to pick up some wood chips one day, and when he arrived at the woodpile, a man-slave told him to put his hand on the chopping block. Jim did, and the man cruelly, and for no unspecified reason, lopped off half his fingers. There is a semi-happy ending, however. Despite his handicap, Jim Towles grew up to become an accomplished fiddler.

The psychic phenomenon here involves a mysterious light which is said to have appeared in an old graveyard on the grounds the night before someone died.

OF CRYING BABIES AND A HEADLESS HORSE!

Thoroughfare Mountain Farm, near Leon on route 631, is believed to have been built in the 1830s. Once visible here, but long since vanished, were the headstones of Confederate soldiers killed at the Battle of Cedar Mountain.

There is a long-standing tradition at this home of a family who neglected their young child to the point of starvation. For years after its death, "the cries of a baby" could be heard in the cellar. Even stranger is the encounter of an old farmer on the property. He swore he once saw a headless horse race past him and disappear into a gulley near the home. All the farm's horses were then inventoried and accounted for. Some believed it may have been a horse killed in the Civil War battle.

A SHADOWY FIGURE ON THE WALL, OR . . . ?

On route 621 is Glen Oak, formerly known as Golden Rock, once the home of the Lillard family. It originally was a slave cabin, but was added onto and enhanced over the years. In pre-Civil War days, the story is told of a frightening experience which happened to a slave. He spent the night in the home's old bedroom so he could get up early the next morning to help during "hog-killing time."

Before daylight the next day, the owner got up and was lighting a fire when he heard loud banging and thumping noises coming down the back stairway. When he got the door open, there was the slave, his eyes as large as saucers. He said he had seen "old lady Lucy" rocking in a chair in his room. Lucy Collins Richards, a previous resident, had been dead for several years. The owners suspected a shadow from the fire outside might have caused unusual shapes on the bedroom wall, but this did nothing to convince the slave who had "seen what he had seen." He never again would spend another night in the house!

THE SPIRIT WITH THE PEGGED LEG

The George Leitch home on Main Street in the town of Madison dates to the early 1800s. It features two brick chimneys and an English basement. According to author Vee Dove, "an amusing story is told about this home when Dr. and Mrs. Powell were in residence. It seems, shortly after they moved in, noises in the night kept them awake. Sounding like something walking down the hall, the noise would stop just outside the master bedroom door. The Powells had been told the house had a ghost, that of Terle Taylor, who supposedly had a wooden leg, and, some said, walked the halls making a banging noise with his leg."

Hardy Glassner is a young lady who is a resident of Hood, Virginia, in the county. She has collected local ghost legends and runs periodic ghost tours, which, she says, are based on "fact, speculation, and some fiction." She has a haunting audio tape of her tales. The tape includes the peg-legged ghost, however, Glassner says there is a logical and non-supernatural explanation for the eerie noise in the house. One night Mrs. Powell was looking out her dining room window when she was startled to see a large turkey jump onto the fence and fly to her roof. More turkeys followed. They belonged to the Powell's neighbor, Lela Blankenbaker, and they made the same sound as had been heard in the house by the suspected ghost.

A SIGNAL OF IMPENDING DEATH

Glassner says there are more inexplicable happenings at the historic Hunton House, built in 1800. It was used as a hotel in the 1850s and more recently was the home of Sarah Frances Johnston, the long time mayor of Madison. Some of the current residents have said they see an apparitional lady walking whenever there is a family crisis or when the house is about to be sold. The image walks from the second floor porch, opens a door, and then proceeds to the back hall. But the more bizarre phenomenon centers around an old chest of drawers dating back to the building's hotel days. It was said that this chest would "crack like a pistol shot" just before a resident family member died. The chest was taken to a local furniture store for examination, but no earthly reason for the death knell sound could be found.

THE GHOST AND THE GOLD COIN

Glassner also tells of the spirit of a young lady who lived at Oak Hill, a house three miles south of the town of Madison, in the middle of the 18th century. She was the daughter of Joseph Early. Allegedly, a young colonel George Washington lodged there one night, and upon his departure the next day, he gave the young woman a gold coin. She was so enamored with Washington that she had the coin made into a breast pin which she wore everywhere.

According to long-standing tradition, Early's daughter eventually married a prominent local lawyer and they moved to Kentucky. There, the couple must have suffered through some terrible marital strife, because the husband supposedly ordered two of his slaves to choke his wife to death with a silk stocking. For this, he was tried, convicted and hanged. But, Glassner says, some Madison residents have reported seeing the young woman roaming about the county at night, with the shiny gold coin flashing in the moonlight. It is as if she has come back hoping George Washington will return.

LOSING ONE'S HEAD OVER A HEADLESS HORSEMAN!

Another of Glassner's accounts centers on a strange phenomenon near Aroda, a few miles southeast of the town of Madison. Here, along a certain stretch of road on route 230, there has been a disproportionate number of motor vehicle accidents over the years. What is particularly unusual about this is the fact that there are no dangerous curves along this corridor and visibility is excellent.

Glassner offers a possible explanation. She says many years ago a worker was walking to his job one morning early, when, through a haze, he saw a rider on horseback approaching him. At first he didn't think much about this, because many people still used horses as transportation in those times. The worker then suddenly froze. The rider had no head! The frightened man then ran hell-bent to the nearest house to report what he had seen. His story gained credence when, over time, others reported seeing the same apparition. It is conjectured that the sighting of a headless horseback rider may well be the cause for so many otherwise unaccountable accidents on route 230!

A LOUD DEPARTURE TO ANOTHER WORLD

South of the community of Brighwood, on route 629, is the Carpenter House, dating to the mid-1800s. Here, the ghost of Mrs. Marc Wayland once appeared in a most bizarre manner. According to witnesses, she had gone to Roanoke to live with her children. Sometime later, residents heard a "terrible noise" on the second floor of the house. It was the sound of a walking cane rubbing first across the floor, and then it became more violent. The cane began banging on the roof shingles, becoming louder and louder. The noise appeared to rise up through the roof and then was never heard again.

The night the eerie sounds were heard, Mrs. Wayland died, more than 125 miles away!

A SIGN OF 'DIVINE WRATH AND DISPLEASURE'

The Eagle House in Madison County, circa 19th century, once served as a tavern and later as a schoolhouse. It was here, the date is unspecified, that a tragic incident occurred, still remembered throughout the area as the "Carpenter-Clore episode." A Mr. Carpenter whipped the son of Edmund Clore for some offense at school. Clore became "uncontrollably angry" at this act, came into town, and shot Carpenter dead. He then hid under the Episcopal Church, but was discovered, arrested, tried, and sentenced to be hanged.

A newspaper account told what happened next: "On the day set for the execution, a vast throng of persons began to assemble to witness the final scene — a thing that was common everywhere in those days. Men and women, boys and girls, old and young, white and black, filled the village of Madison Courthouse and overflowed far beyond its bounds. Many were walking; some were on horseback; many were in huge wagons. People came from great distances, even from the Valley of Virginia. It was a huge festival, though the people were solemn. Hawkers and peddlers shouted their wares. Of course, persons of refinement were not there."

Then a most strange thing happened. It was said that an unusual phenomenon took place the day of the hanging. "As the hour of the execution approached, a thick darkness settled upon the area. Hens went to roost, cows came up to be milked and farm hands found it too dark to remain in the fields. People were much alarmed."

When the prisoner was led from the jail, complete silence fell upon the multitude. The execution took place.

Some said it was "a sign of divine wrath and displeasure!"

CHAPTER 20

Scary Scenes at Stonewall Cottage

(Harrisonburg)

(Author's note: I am indebted to attorney Joseph B. Yount III of Waynesboro, who wrote a paper in 1979 about his family and its associated history with Stonewall Cottage in Rockingham County, and was gracious enough to share a copy of it with me. The paper is titled "Ghosts and Frights at Stonewall Cottage," and Mr. Yount says, "All of these events happened before I was born. I have done my best to recount them exactly as they were often told me by my late father, Joseph Bryon Yount, Jr. I have tried not to exaggerate . . . I have tried to be as accurate as possible. Some of my kinsmen may think it ridiculous to record these stories. In doing so I do not intend to dishonor the dead . . . The various stories about Stonewall Cottage and its haunts . . . have been a part of my family folklore all my life. Truth is stranger than fiction, they say, and I have no reason to believe that any of this is untrue.")

Some downright scary things have happened over the years at Stonewall Cottage on the Valley turnpike just north of Harrisonburg. Some of the occurrences remain inexplicable and are linked with the supernatural, while others have been caused by quite natural and rational, if unusual, means. Yet the effect has been much the same — spine-tingling chills! Take the case of the reburial of Uncle Joseph Dovel, for example. This, "ghostly excitement at Stonewall Cottage is not

118

really extra-terrestrial, but must have been equally hair-raising," writes Yount. It seems that in 1938, several family graves were to be moved from the land at Stonewall Cottage to lots in Woodbine Cemetery at Harrisonburg. Among those to be moved was Captain Joseph M. Dovel, "the young lawyer who had joined the Confederate Army and become a captain of the celebrated Valley Rangers of the Stonewall Brigade, only to become injured and ill with camp fever and to return home to die in 1863 at age 23." The undertaker hired a crew of black laborers to exhume the bodies. They found Captain Dovel buried in a cast iron, bullet-shaped coffin with a glass window over his face. The hinged coffin was held shut by two large bolts.

"Aunt Bettie Post and my father were present when the iron casket was raised. The men dusted off the window, and there was Captain Dovel, looking as if he were merely asleep," says Yount. "He was buried in his Confederate uniform, with a crimson sash for decoration. Aunt Bettie asked the undertaker if he would open the casket for a moment, to enable her to see her uncle 'in full regalia.' The men unscrewed the screws and lifted the top." As soon as the air hit inside, there was a mild, soundless implosion. The body disintegrated instantly into dust before their eyes. Yount adds that some of the men ran off in all directions, Aunt Bettie rushed back to the house, "and my father had yet another terrifying time at Stonewall Cottage to remember."

Yount's father was the sole witness to another of the "colorful after effects" of the haunted stories that circulated about the cottage. This occurred in 1934, when Aunt Laura died sitting up in her chair one night. She had apparently suffered a fatal attack during the evening, before coming upstairs to bed, and her body was not discovered until the next morning. Aunt Laura had left instructions that she wanted to be buried in a shroud, and this request proved to be somewhat difficult to fulfill. Yount's father went from store to store in Harrisonburg "trying to locate the old-fashioned, long out-of-date garment. He could not find one, and one of the neighbors commissioned a nearby Mennonite lady to make one.

"The undertaker had prepared the body in the coffin and placed it, as was the custom, in the front parlor. The house was dark, the shutters still closed in the front, seldom-used rooms. My father went around to the rear where the family and friends were gathered. After a while, Aunt Sallie asked my father to go over to the parlor to get her something from behind the organ. He had to pass through several rooms and the hall to get to the parlor. It had been the aunts' custom to carry keys and lock the doors behind them as they went from room to room at Stonewall Cottage.

"My father always said he wasn't afraid of anyone living, but didn't like to fool with the dead. Nervously, he entered the parlor. . . (he) glanced at Aunt Laura, her eyes closed, her form lying stiffly in the coffin. He walked past to the end of the room and reached behind the organ. Suddenly, he heard a loud snap, which he always described as sounding like a 'rat' trap going off. He looked around and saw Aunt Laura in the coffin, her eyes opened and apparently staring at him, her head turned in his direction, her false teeth half out of her opened mouth.

"My father claimed he was so much in shock that it took what

Stonewall Cottage – 1895. Left to right, Laura Belle Stephens, 1862-1934; Martha Josephine Stephens, 1856-1899; Mary Elizabeth Dovel Stephens, 1829-1902; Sallie Georgiana Stephens, 1870-1938.

seemed an hour for him to walk past the coffin and leave the parlor. He called out the front door to the undertaker, who came immediately. What had happened? Because of the delay in discovering the   body, staying as it was in a sitting position all night long, rigor mortis had set in. The undertaker had braced her mouth shut with a brace under her chin, obscured by the high collar of the shroud. My father apparently jarred it loose as he walked across the creaky floor. The brace slipped, throwing the head ajar . . . My mother remembered well how white and pale he looked when he returned to the Stonewall Cottage kitchen."

Yount says one of the unexplained psychic manifestations concerned an old lady who always sat by the fireplace smoking a clay pipe. "After her death, others in the house could still hear her knocking out her clay pipe against the fireplace after everyone else had gone to bed for the night. This story, often told me by my father, is verified by his sisters, who are still living today (1979). They all said without question that the lady knocking out her pipe was Martha Burnsides Stevens Cowan (1806-1895)." Yount says, however, he is not sure whether this phenomenon actually took place at Stonewall Cottage or at a house near Lacey Springs, five or six miles to the north.

Under a heading called "Restless Spirits That Wander," Yount writes: "I now come to what I believe to be the true ghost story of Stonewall Cottage. It happened in 1902. For its accuracy I have virtually identical oral accounts from two people, namely (1) my father, who was five and 1/2 years old at the time and present at the occasion, and (2) his first cousin, Addie Yount Wood, who was 15 years old at the time . . . Addie was a favorite niece of my grandfather, Joseph B. Yount, who also witnessed the events of 1902. She lived on a farm near Waynesboro, Virginia, neighboring his, and she well remembers the excitement caused when he came home from Stonewall Cottage in 1902 and related this story. She says he told it to her many times, and, as she puts it, 'I know that Uncle Joe wouldn't have made up something like that.'

"(I might add that my father's younger sisters have tended to discredit the story. Even while he was living, they tended to discredit it as largely the account of an exaggerated imagination. It seems to embarrass them to think about their grandmother as a ghostly presence. My father always cut them short when they talked that way, insisting that he knew what he had seen. My father was a colorful, educated man, an active practicing attorney for 47 years; he had a keen memory and could imitate voices of long-dead people; he loved to tell stories of old timers. I have no reason whatsoever to believe that he fabricated any part of this story, especially since his account agreed in virtually every detail with what Addie Wood remembers her Uncle Joe telling her in 1902.)

"Stonewall Cottage in 1902 was the home of Mary Dovel Stephens, 72, and her two daughters, Laura, 40, and Sallie, 32. . . Brother Will, who had disappointed the family by his marked lack of responsibility and unwillingness to take over the farm operation, was living in Winchester, Virginia. . . The Stephens family of Stonewall Cottage was well-to-do, but it was very burdensome work for the three women to operate the big farm with often undependable hired farm labor.

"One late summer day in 1902, Mary Dovel Stephens, while eating a hearty dinner, remarked to her daughters that there was some very important business that she needed to tend to at once. (Some speculated that she intended to write a will that would eliminate her son from sharing in any part of her share of the farm.) . . . Immediately after the dinner at which she had made these remarks, Mary Dovel Stephens lay down to rest on a fainting couch and without warning died instantly of an apparent heart attack. She was buried in the family cemetery south of the house near the orchard. A week of so after the funeral, Sallie and Laura asked their brother-in-law, Joseph B. Yount, to come to Stonewall Cottage for several days to help them with business affairs in connection with the settlement of the estate. Joe brought his 5 1/2-year-old son, Byron, my father, along with him.

"The first night of their visit, Joe and his young son went to bed in the front upstairs bedroom, a room in which an old rocking chair was located. Sallie and Laura were supposedly asleep in the upstairs bedrooms to the rear of the house. Shortly after they went to bed, Joe and his son heard the distinct sound of the front door being opened and the tread of footsteps lightly ascending the main stairs. Suddenly, the door to their bedroom seemed to blow open, and the rocking chair began to rock as if some ghostly figure were sitting in it. Grandfather attributed these strange happenings to the wind, arose from bed, and closed the door. He and his son fell asleep. When they awoke, the bedroom door was open again, with no indication that it had been opened by anyone else in the house.

"Grandfather said nothing, not wanting to alarm the recently bereaved sisters-in-law. The next night, perhaps out of caution, he pulled a side chair against the inside of the bedroom door to insure that the wind could not blow it open. He and his son were nearly asleep when, again, they heard the front door open and close, the sound of footsteps ascending the stairs, and then, to their amazement, the door was pushed open, as if by some invisible force, sliding the side chair back against the wall, and then the rocking chair began to rock.

"This was too much for my grandfather. He abruptly arose, hurriedly dressed, took my father by the hand, and walked down to the rear of the house, where Sallie and Laura were supposed to be sleeping. To his surprise, he found them both awake, each with a frightened look. The expression on his face caused them to say, 'Well, you have heard it, too! It has happened every night since mother was buried. We thought we were losing our minds. If it continues, we will have to move away from here.'

"The next day my grandfather took Sallie and Laura to see their minister and told him of the apparent poltergeist. He was the minister who served the nearby Melrose Church of the Brethren, where the dead woman had also belonged. He contacted one or two fellow pastors . . . That night at Stonewall Cottage the ministers joined Sallie and Laura, my grandfather and father, for prayers. The ministers read appropriate words from the Bible and led the group in prayer. I have never looked in the Bible for the text, but my father described it as some verse about 'restless spirits who wander' or 'troubled spirits who wander.'

"The prayers and readings were enough to summon the spirits, and the mysterious footsteps were soon heard. They said further prayers, and one of the ministers exhorted the spirit, 'In the name of God, what do you want?' These words were repeated, and when there was no response the ministers then said, 'In the name of God, be at rest.' The prayers and exhortations were effective. Never again during the remaining 36 years of family occupancy did the restless spirit wander the halls of Stonewall Cottage.

"My father always professed to believe that it had been the ghost of Mary Dovel Stephens, who had died before attending to her important business and who could not rest. . . All I can promise the readers of this account is that I have not exaggerated it one iota. I have written it as it was told to me by one who was there."

CHAPTER 21

The Ghost That Got the Last Laugh

(Western Virginia)

(Author's note: I love to browse in old book stores. In April 1998 I was poking around in "Too Many Books," a shop in Roanoke, and came across a dog-eared copy of "Tales and Lore of the Mountaineers," by William B. Price. I believe it was originally published in 1963. Price, a self-professed "collector, story teller and teacher," was born in Preston County, West Virginia.

It is not noted exactly where this episode took place, likely in the extreme western portion of Virginia, or somewhere in West Virginia. It was told to Price by a man named Clint Brown. The time, too, is uncertain, although it probably was in the second half of the 19th century. Brown was a farmer.)

It was late on an October evening when Brown was out in his barn milking one of his brindle cows. It was raining. Above the sound of the rain he heard "a strange wild laughter." At first, he wasn't sure the sound was real. He stood up. It came again, "ha! ha! ha! ha-a-a-a!" ha-ha-a-a! It sounded human. It definitely wasn't an owl, or any other creature. He walked to the barn door and looked out. He couldn't see anything in the darkness, and then walked back to the farm house.

Just as the Browns were sitting down to their supper, there was a sharp rap at the front door. Mrs. Brown opened the door.

There, soaked to the skin by the rain, stood the figure of a tall, gaunt man. Brown said, "I looked into the black eyes shining beneath the dripping brim of his old felt hat and knew the laughter I had heard had been borne from the lips of the man who stood before us."

The Browns welcomed the stranger in, brought him some dry clothes and fed him. Brown asked him if he was the one laughing that he had heard. He nodded, and roared with laughter, "ha-ha-

ha!" He ate heartily — pot-roasted coon and cabbage, corn dodgers and cold buttermilk. Brown asked him where his horse was and he laughed again, saying he didn't have one. The Browns were surprised at the deep, throaty voice stemming from such a thin, wan man. After dinner the man told him he was trying to get to Fort Henry (near Wheeling), and that he had come from the east. He said he was an inventor of sorts and he wanted to build a boat that would run by its own power - a steamboat.

The man said his boat would travel on land as well as water. The Browns looked at each other. Brown said, "I saw his eyes burning with madness or fancy or some strange fever of the mind." He then noticed that the man, who wouldn't give him his name, took a big silver watch out of his pocket and wound it with a key attached to a heavy silver chain. The Browns then invited the man to spend the night.

In the middle of the night, Brown said, "there seemed to be a light and moving sound of laughter riding on the night's increasing wind. Mrs. Brown awakened her husband at 6 a.m. He got up to start a fire and noticed the stranger's boots were gone, but his old felt hat was still hanging on a peg. He had gone. Brown said to himself, "Lord, let thy strong arms bear our Laughing Stranger safely home."

Mrs. Brown added, "We'll never see that pore soul again. She then told her husband that while he slept the previous night she heard the sound of laughter around midnight. She heard someone walking about on the kitchen floor and then the squeaky hinges of the kitchen door opening. Brown said he thought it "strange indeed that any man would set out across country without protection for his head."

Mrs. Brown urged her mate to round up some neighbors and go out looking for the man. A mile from their house, on the bank of the Yarrowbone Creek, they found his boots. Down stream, they found the body of the stranger lodged in the branches of a tree that had fallen into the stream. The men carried it back to Brown's barn and prepared it for burial. There were three silver dollars in the man's pockets, but no silver watch and chain.

Brown: "That night, as the clock struck twelve, we heard a sound upstairs, like someone walking barefooted across the creaking floor. The kitchen door then opened and shut very gently. Later we heard a ghostly laughter coming from the woods near the mill race rapids!"

They buried the man the next day in the graveyard on a hill

overlooking the creek.

A year later, to the day, the Browns went to a night church service. As they reached the Yarrowbone ford — they heard "that horrible laugh roar out over our heads." The horses broke into a gallop and the Browns were shaken to the core. They hurried home. That evening, again at midnight, they heard the "soft thudding of bare feet upon the upstairs floor." The sounds went through the kitchen and the door softly opened and closed.

Brown: "We held our breath and listened. Then a mournful laughter drifted up from the woods along the creek: 'Ha-ha-ha! Ha-ha-a-a!'" The Browns didn't sleep much that night.

In an epilogue, author Price wrote: "For 50 years the sturdy house stood, and for more than half of them, it was empty after Clint and Mary Brown passed to their reward. The house was considered famous for the ghost of the Laughing Stranger. Passersby reported that laughter frequently sounded through its dusty rooms; and a lean shadow, some said, went in and out of the doorway when October's rains came pouring down. Sometimes, some claimed, a death's head looked out from an upstairs window.

"Then one September day a farmer, who had bought the house, plowed up a big silver watch to which was attached a heavy silver chain. After that nothing more disturbed the abandoned house. The ghost of the Laughing Stranger was laid and now at rest."

The Mystery of the Missing Coat

(Eastern West Virginia)

(Author's note: One of the most repeated folklorian legends, which has been reported in Virginia and several other southern states, concerns a ghostly hitchhiker. There are many variations, but most often they involve a young woman who is seen usually at midnight or thereafter on the side of the road seeking a ride. Some of these phantom women are dressed in a party gown, and one report included a wedding gown. But the story line is much the same: the young lady was out at a dance, wedding, or whatever, had a fight with her boy friend, and left him, or he left her. Often it is raining, or there is a storm brewing.

hen a driver stops and picks her up, she tells them what happened and where she lives. But when they get to the house, the girl has disappeared. Shaken, the drivers go up to the house and are generally greeted by an older woman, usually the girl's mother. She tells them her daughter died tragically in an accident years earlier at the site where she was seen on the side of the road.

Several people have sworn such an experience has happened to them. The following encounter is yet another version of the ghostly manifestation — with an unusual twist. It has been passed down for generations in the mountains of eastern West Virginia and has been recorded in newspaper articles and in James Gay

Jones' book, "Appalachian Ghost Stories and Other Tales." Here, essentially, is what happened.)

This incident involved a man named Hugh Nelson, but the actual date of it is undetermined. It probably was several decades ago because it was said the roads were in very poor condition at the time. He had been called and asked to be in Marlinton early the next morning for a business deal. He left his office in Morgantown in the afternoon and by the time he arrived in the Alleghenies, it was dark and he was caught in the midst of a torrential thunderstorm. Nelson said the combination of the storm and the mountains created an eerie sensation. Lightning was flashing all around him, high winds were blowing tree limbs and other debris across the road, and the rain was so hard he had difficulty seeing. But there was no nearby shelter because there were no houses within miles.

As he rounded a sharp curve he was astonished to see what appeared to be a young woman standing off on the side of the road waving at him to stop. She was dressed in a bride's gown and was soaking wet. Nelson stopped. He said the woman appeared to be in a state of shock; her eyes were "dark and piercing" and her skin was extremely pale.

She then told him that she had just walked up from the valley below where a flash flood had washed out the bridge and that her girl companion had drowned. She warned him not to take the road into the valley, but to go down the mountain by an alternate route. She said she lived on this other route and asked him if he could drop her off at her house.

The girl was shaking from the cold, and Nelson took off his coat and put it around her shoulders. They then drove down a narrow, graveled road winding into the countryside. The girl told Nelson that her name was Janet Grey and that she lived about five miles away. Curiously, Nelson did not question her about why she was wearing a wedding gown. They rode in silence. It took nearly half an hour to travel over the rough, rain-soaked roads to reach her house, and when they arrived there, she thanked Nelson for the ride, hurried up the steps to the porch and then disappeared inside without even glancing back.

Nelson drove on to his appointment in Marlinton, realizing later that he had left his coat with Janet. Since it was now late at night, he decided to return to her house the next morning to retrieve it. In town that evening he was told that a flash flood had washed out the bridge Janet had told him about, and that a man

had drowned when he hadn't seen the bridge was gone. But there was no mention of any young lady drowning. Odd, Nelson thought. It piqued his curiosity.

The next morning he drove back up the old country road to the house where he had dropped Janet off. He was greeted at the front door by a white-haired elderly lady. He told her what had happened the night before. The lady shook her head and told him he must be mistaken, because she had a daughter named Janet, but she had died five years ago!

She said Janet was to have been married in a church on the other side of the valley. On the night before the wedding, while on the way to the church for a rehearsal, Janet and a friend who was to be a bridesmaid, drove into the river during a storm and both were drowned!

When Nelson looked at the woman in disbelief, she said, "come on, I'll show you her grave. She's buried on a little knoll in back of the house." As they walked, Janet's mother said, "it was so near her wedding day, we decided to bury her in her wedding gown." This shook Nelson to the core, because he had not mentioned to her how Janet had been dressed when he picked her up. As they approached the grave, they both stopped and stood stunned.

In front of them, draped over the headstone on Janet Grey's grave . . . . was Nelson's coat!

C H A P T E R   2 3

The Ghost that (May Have) Committed Murder

(West Virginia)

an a ghost cause physical harm to the living?

Parapsychology experts say possibly, but in extremely rare cases. The most celebrated example, unquestionably, would be the famous Bell Witch of Tennessee, who, in the first half of the 19th century wreaked havoc on the Bell family, which the witch contended had cheated her out of property in life. After death, she came back to haunt individual members of the family, in particular Betsy Bell, a young teenager at the time. Before eye-witnesses, on numerous occasions, it appeared that Betsy would be slapped and pinched repeatedly by unseen hands. Red spots and welts would be raised on various parts of her body with no apparent cause. Scores of witnesses, including some professional psychic investigators, attested to the harmful manifestations. The witch also was accused of almost choking Betsy's father to death.

At Aquia Church north of Fredericksburg (see "The Ghosts of Fredericksburg," 1991), there is an account of a woman who entered the allegedly haunted church with two ghost busters, and was immediately slapped by something or someone invisible to human sight. The blow was so sharp it left a deep red hand imprint on the woman's cheek.

There are also many instances of poltergeist activity whereby objects, sometimes very heavy objects, are moved about seemingly

132

on their own. Books, dishes, glass and ceramic ashtrays, and other items have sailed across rooms and crashed into walls. Sometimes they strike people. One of the most startling occurrences of such activity took place on a farm house in Augusta County in 1825 (see next separate chapter). Here, fist-sized rocks flew dangerously both inside and outside the house. Again, there was no visible cause for the sensation.

Some experts attribute such phenomena not to ghosts or poltergeists, but rather to what they call psycho-kinetic activity. That is, they believe moving and flying objects are caused by a living person rather than a spirit, usually an emotionally-upset adolescent child. But the debate goes on. No one really knows.

One of the most intriguing cases of serious harm, in this instance death, possibly caused by a ghost occurred in Logan, West Virginia, in 1917, and has been investigated and written about extensively. There, a young man named Jim Daniel joined the armed services during World War I, and was sent to fight in France and Germany. He left behind his girlfriend and bride-to-be, Darlene Mastin. The two lovers corresponded regularly, but after several months, Jim's letters stopped arriving.

Meanwhile, Jim's older brother, Will, tried to persuade Darlene that she should marry him. She steadfastly refused, saying she was waiting for Jim to return. Connivingly, Will concocted a despicable scheme. He had a fake telegram delivered to Darlene saying Jim had been killed in action. Distraught and heart-broken, she finally yielded to Will's incessant appeals and married him.

On December 24, 1917 — Christmas Eve — Darlene was in the kitchen when she heard a loud voice coming from the living room. It was Jim's voice! He was shouting at his brother, Will, saying words to the effect that, "I know what you've done and you're not going to get away with it!"

Then there was the loud report of a pistol shot. Darlene raced into the living room. There lay Will on the floor, a bullet hole in his forehead. He was dead! There was no one else in the room, or in the entire house for that matter, and the doors were locked from the inside.

Darlene knelt over her husband's body in utter shock. Minutes later there was a knock at the front door. In a daze, she opened the door. It was a telegraph messenger. He handed her an official telegram. It read that Jim Daniel had been killed in action in Germany on December 21, 1917!

A thorough investigation followed. There were no clues or

leads as to the assailant. There were no footprints outside the house and no broken or open windows or doors inside. No gun was ever found. In fact, Will didn't even own a gun. The case was never solved.

Darlene, however, remained convinced, to her dying day, that the ghost of Jim had somehow returned from a grave thousands of miles away to effect revenge on the brother who had stolen the one he loved.

Stone Showers
From Hell — Part II

(Augusta County)

(Author's note: Of the hundreds of ghostly encounters I have
written about over the past 17 years, one of the most bizarre, most
unusual, and most frightening, would have to be a chapter entitled
"Stone Showers from Hell," in the first volume of "The Ghosts of
Virginia," published in 1993. The phenomena occurred at an isolated farmhouse known as Greenwood about a mile north of the village of Newport, roughly halfway between Staunton and
Lexington in Augusta County. The date was 1825. Here lived a
highly respected physician, Dr. John McChesney, and his family; a
wife and four children, one an infant.

*T*hey were staunchly religious, God-fearing
people. Reasonably prosperous, they owned
a large farm of several hundred acres, and lived in a spacious
house situated miles from the nearest neighbor. The McChesneys
also owned a number of slaves who tended the farm. Among them
was a young girl, about 10 or 12 years old, named Maria.

The supernatural terror which was to reign down upon the
McChesneys, causing stark fear, and, eventually, tragedy, began
sometime in 1825, and centered around Maria. It began one spring
afternoon when the slave girl came screaming into the house
claiming that she had been beaten up by an old lady witch. There
were welts and bruises all over Maria, but she was so hysterical the

family could make little sense out of her protestations.

That was when the manifestations began.

* That same day, Mrs. McChesney heard the "tinkling of glasses" coming from the dining room. She went to investigate and found a tray containing a decanter, wine bottles, and glasses teetering over the edge of the sideboard, with only the rim of the tray resting on the board. It appeared to be hanging in mid-air defying every natural law. She shoved the tray back onto the sideboard and left the room. The tinkling continued. She went back into the dining room and there was the tray again suspended in air.

* Over the following weeks a "steady barrage of clods of mud and rocks hurled through the house and in the yard. Sometimes they came from <u>inside the house</u>, sometimes from the outside, yet no one could determine where they came from and they followed no directional pattern. Often the rocks were hot and actually singed the spots where they fell, and they left great dents in the walls, mantel and furniture. This went on, sporadically, for a period of months. One writer said, "sometimes the rocks came thickly, like a burst of gunfire, sometimes only one at a time, and hours apart. It is said the stones averaged 'the size of a man's fist,' and some of them were 'too large to be thrown by a person of ordinary strength'." Not once, during any of these incidents, was anyone seen hurling stones at the house.

Once, a large rock was thrown into a pitcher which had a long, narrow neck — impossibly small for a rock of that size to pass through without shattering it. On another occasion, a group of church elders came to the house for dinner. As one of them reached for a biscuit, a sharp black stone flew from a corner of the ceiling across the room and sliced the biscuit in half!

* Maria was the special target for abuse. Frequently, the girl would go into convulsive screaming fits crying that she was being beaten. The sounds of heavy slaps and blows could be heard distinctly above her cries, and, before the eyes of the members of the family, great welts would appear on her body.

* One day Maria was making a nuisance of herself in the kitchen and the cook shoved her out the door onto the porch. As she stood there, crying, she was suddenly pelted with large floppy objects that appeared to be soggy, oversized pancakes. This episode was witnessed by family members and slaves.

* The infant McChesney son began to have strange and frightening seizures. Lying in his crib one day, he went into a screaming fit, and what appeared to be tiny bloody pinpricks spread rapidly

McChesney House

across his body. It was not unlike the red welts raised on the body of the young girl in the movie, "The Exorcist."

As the weeks and months passed, the manifestations intensified. Yet despite all the unexplained activity, Dr. McChesney steadfastly refused to believe it was caused by anything out of the ordinary. He is alleged to have said, "no intelligent person could believe for a minute that his home had been invaded by ghosts." His wife, however, felt otherwise. She had noted that whenever the psychic occurrences surfaced, Maria always seemed to be around.

Mrs. McChesney convinced her husband to send Maria away. So the slave girl went to the house of a brother-in-law. As she arrived a great clatter was heard inside the house although no one was in the house at the time. It sounded like a "stampede." When the in-laws rushed inside, they found that every stick of furniture and all the knickknacks in the parlor had been piled in the middle of the floor. While they stared in disbelief, clods and rocks began to sail through the room and crash into the furniture. They immediately sent Maria back to Greenwood!

Despite the medical skills of Dr. McChesney, the baby died in the convulsive throes of a screaming fit, his tiny body flamed with the bloody pinpricks. When the family returned to the house after the funeral, the rocks began flying again. One hit a cousin in the forehead, causing a deep gash. Thomas Steele, an in-law, then cursed the invisible rock thrower, and became himself a target, "pelted with clods of sod and earth, until he was almost covered with them."

Dr. McChesney, for safety, sent his children to their grandmother's house near Midway. Maria went, too, and the disturbances continued there. Stones flew, and the furniture in the kitchen "moved of its own accord." Bottles turned upside down and "danced" with no one near them.

Finally, Mrs. McChesney told her husband that she would leave him if they didn't move from the house. Reluctantly, he agreed. He sold Maria and her parents, sending them away forever, and he and his family subsequently moved to Staunton.

That, in essence, is a summary of the incredible happenings at Greenwood 175 years ago. It is still talked about in the area to this day. And an argument still rages. Was it a real poltergeist who wreaked such havoc on the McChesney family? Was Maria possessed of "demonic spirits?" Or was it a case of what parapsychologists call psycho-kinesis? This is a phenomenon known as Recurrent Spontaneous Psycho-kinesis. Some believe such eruptive activity as occurred at the McChesney house may, in fact, be sparked by an individual who is at the center of the disturbances, in this case, Maria. Paranormal scientists contend such disturbances may be caused by tension or certain neurological features.

So the debate continues. A descendent of the McChesneys wrote some years ago that whatever it was that occurred at Greenwood in 1825, "It was real and it was evil, and no one will ever know exactly what it was."

*   *   *   *   *

On a personal note, I should add that when I originally wrote about the McChesney ghost, poltergeist, psycho-kinetic agent, or whatever, I drove to Augusta County to photograph the house. I had a difficult time finding it. My understanding was no one was living in the house at the time, but the farm was still tended. Finally, two miles off the nearest main road, I rounded a curve and saw the place in the distance. There were many animals in the fields surrounding it, but there was an eerie sense of isolation about the house itself.

I must admit, as I drove up, walked up on the porch and knocked on the front door, I felt a certain uneasiness. I didn't see or hear anything, but still I was a little uncomfortable. No one answered, so I took my photos and left without tarrying.

That was in 1991. Seven years later, in May 1998, I was signing ghost books at the Pungo Strawberry Festival in Virginia Beach. A young man named James Lutman approached me, and said he grew up in a house adjacent to the McChesney farm. It was a house Dr. McChesney had built for his son, James. James Lutman said a lot of strange things had happened in this house, including the possible return presence of the <u>ghost of Maria (!)</u>, and that I should talk to his mother, Peg Davis, who was then living in Florida. I interviewed Peg on November 30, 1998, and here is what she told me:)

THE SPECTRAL RETURN OF MARIA

"Dr. McChesney had log homes built for several of his sons, all in the area of Greenwood, the family ancestral home. My ex-husband, George, and I bought one of these and a farm of 155 acres in 1977. It is about two or three miles from the McChesney House. We had been told that our house was haunted, but we hadn't thought too much about it. It was a beautiful farm and we were thrilled to get it. There were scenic vistas in all directions, and we loved animals.

"Actually, we had been told that more than one of the McChesney sons' houses was haunted. No one would stay longer than a few months in one of them. Oldtimers in the area said something about blood would keep seeping up from the floor and no one could get rid of it. The house remodeled several times, would go vacant for long periods of time.

"Now I knew a little about Greenwood, the McChesney main house. I had toured through it and I had seen the mantel where the scars from the rocks are still evident. I saw Maria's bed which was still in one of the old slave quarters on the property.

"Yet, none of this was on my mind when we moved in. We had been told that Maria, the little slave girl, had been sent here once after being dismissed from Greenwood. She had been allowed to sleep in a certain place behind an upstairs bedroom which led to the attic.

"Well, I changed my mind about the house, and its possible spirit or spirits, the first night I was there! I went in to take a shower that evening. I shut the bathroom door and locked it. Then I lit a little log fire — it was chilly in the house — and I turned on the shower.

"Suddenly, I could feel the hair on the back of my neck raise up. I felt there was a presence. It got colder in the room, and I looked behind me. The door which I had locked was open! Now it had been locked from the inside! How did someone open it? I got really spooked. I didn't see anything, but it was like electricity in that room.

"And then I turned and looked in the mirror. There, clearly drawn in the steam on the glass was the stick figure of a little girl — and the name Maria! The letters were dripping, so I knew that it had been freshly done. No one had done it earlier to scare me and then the steam had brought it out. This had just been done! You can't imagine how frightened I was. There was definitely some kind of presence there.

"All of us, myself, George, and the our children, would come to the realization, over the next 10 years, that there was a ghost in the house, and it all pointed to being that of Maria. It was never a malicious spirit, but it was often mischievous. It would pull all sorts of pranks.

"For example, before our washer and dryer arrived, I would hang up clothes out in the yard. One day, when I was alone, I went out to do this, and when I went back, the screen door was locked. It locks from the inside, so how did this happen? This occurred a number of times.

"Maria, if that was who or what it was, was very active. We all would experience 'things.' Like whenever we would go into the root cellar and reach to turn on the light switch, before we could do it, we would see the switch be turned on by unseen hands. You could actually see the switch being moved.

"Doors would lock and unlock on their own. Cabinets would open in front of us. Pictures would be moved around when no one was home. Objects would disappear and then mysteriously reappear. George loved pretzels. There would be a bag of pretzels on top of the refrigerator - high enough so the children couldn't reach it. The pretzels would disappear, and neither George or I had touched them.

"At the time, I was teaching high school in Crozet, near Charlottesville. It was quite a little commute. One night I went to a banquet and it was late when I drove home. As I crested the hill leading down into the little hollow where the house stood, I was elated to see that every light in the house was on. I said to myself, 'oh, good, they've stayed up for me.' Then I was distracted by the glow of a reddish light which was going from the house to the barn. I thought at first it might be George going out to check on an animal, but then I saw our big German Shepard. The hair on its neck was standing straight up, as he seemed to be following the glow. That dog wasn't afraid of anything, but he was cowering. I got scared. Then I turned toward the house — and all the lights were out! It was pitch black. I couldn't understand what was going on. I called out and I whistled, and I can whistle loud, with four fingers in my mouth. There was no response. I went into the house and found everyone sound asleep. How do you explain that?

"One day my brother Jim was over, and we were telling him about the ghostly episodes. He scoffed and started teasing us, saying we were crazy. Just as he said this, there was a loud booming sound coming from the back of the house. Bam! Bam! Bam! We all ran out on the back porch. We had seven hams hanging up on large hooks, curing. All seven of them were swinging wildly against the back wall, as if someone were pushing them. There was no wind. They were banging and banging. What caused that?

"Then one morning, my son James came down from upstairs — he had been sleeping in the room where Maria reportedly had slept — to go out to the school bus. I have to admit that all of us felt a little uncomfortable in that room. It's hard to describe. It was just a feeling, but it was very real. It just always gave us the willies. Anyway, it was cold out that morning and James was only wearing a flannel shirt. I told him to go back upstairs and put on a jacket. He went back up, and in a minute or two came back running down the stairs screaming. He was terrified. He collapsed halfway down the stairs. I ran to him and asked what was the matter. He said that when he had gone back into the bedroom he saw a little girl standing in the corner. At first, he thought it was his sister. But then he realized the girl was <u>black!</u> He said he distinctly saw her. James still won't talk about it to this day, but he said he would never forget it.

"These are just a few of the many things that happened to us in that house for a period of about 10 years. I decided to do some research. I learned a little more about Maria from people whose families had lived in the vicinity for generations. Some were direct descendants of slaves who had worked at Greenwood. They knew all about the McChesney ghost incidents. They said that when Maria was finally sold and moved away, she had been taken to the Mississippi River and 'sent across the water.' I came to learn that this expression meant Maria had been put to death either as the river was crossed, or just after the crossing. It had been felt that the devil had possessed her body and could not be driven out, so she was 'sent across the water.'

"In time, I began going to the little Oak Hill Baptist Church, which is near our house and the McChesney House. It had been abandoned for years, but had recently reopened. I talked to a lot of the people there, and especially to the Reverend Icky Woodson. I told him about all the activity in our house and that we thought it was the spirit of Maria. He told me to have a 'talk' with her.

"So that night the children and I sat down on the steps and told Maria that we knew she was there and that we all loved her and knew that she had had a hard life. We understood all that and we accepted her — that she was welcome in our house as long as she wanted.

"As we did that, I could feel that something was happening.

"We have not felt her presence in the house since."

So, hopefully, Maria's spirit is, at last, at rest.

CHAPTER 25

When the Dead Came to Say Goodbye

(Staunton)

(Author's note: P.M.H. Atwater, Lh.D., says, "I am an international researcher of the near-death experiences and spiritual transformations." She is uniquely qualified for such a profession, since she herself has had three near-death experiences. Atwater is the author of such books as "Coming Back to Life — the After-effects of the Near-Death Experience," and "Beyond the Light — What Isn't Being Said about Near-Death Experience."

I corresponded with her a few years ago after I had written about a Civil War soldier ghost in a house known as Selma in Staunton. Atwater, who lives and works in Charlottesville, was able to "move that spirit on to where it should go." Today she is one of the world's leading authorities on the Near-Death phenomenon. She has interviewed hundreds of people who have been declared clinically dead or were believed to be dead, and somehow, miraculously, revived. Over the past 20 years or so there have been scores of popular books on this subject.

In reading her book, "Beyond the Light," I came across a most fascinating case study involving a woman named Sandra H. Brock of Staunton. It was in a chapter titled, "Unpleasant and/or Hell-like Experience." I have to admit that I never realized there was such a thing. In everything I had read, the Near-Death accounts mostly involved pleasant encounters. I had also interviewed Dr.

Raymond Moody about 20 years ago for a magazine article when he was at the University of Virginia. His 1975 book, "Life After Life," revolutionized study on this topic. I was of the mistaken impression that most people who had such experiences — saw an intense, brilliant, and often beautiful light, a tunnel, perhaps long-dead relatives, etc. Atwater thus opened my eyes to this rarer "dark side."

With the gracious permission of the author and of the publisher, Birch Lane Press Books, I include excerpts from the study of Sandra Brock.)

In 1980, Sandra had a more-or-less routine operation, which included having her spleen removed. Complications arose, however, and she hemorrhaged on the operating table. Three times over the next 24 hours she nearly died. The day after the operation, during a blood transfusion, she said she "started feeling really weird." Just after a nurse had left her room, Sandra says, "I started being pulled through a tunnel. It was a terrible experience because all I could see were people from my past, people who were already dead, who had done or said something to me that had hurt me in one way or another. They were laughing and screaming, until I thought I could not stand it. I begged and begged that I be allowed to go back. I could see a light at the end of the tunnel, but I never got close to it. All of a sudden I was back in my bed, just thankful I had not died."

Atwater wrote that Sandra actually had several near-death-type experiences scattered over a long life. She had once stopped breathing when she was but a few weeks old. She survived "numerous" near-fatal accidents as a child. Atwater: "She displayed the typical aftereffects of the near-death phenomenon, including stunningly accurate psychic abilities, extended perceptual range, and heightened faculties." Sandra told Atwater "she has been visited by the dead, 'advised' of pending deaths, and has known the exact moment individuals died." Atwater says Sandra "has been haunted throughout her life, and not just by the deceased who grabbed at her in death's tunnel." She also revealed memories of "frightening creatures crawling into her bed when she was young and making her scream and cry," and "adult misunderstandings and distressing dreams."

Three years after Sandra's 1980 operation, her husband committed suicide. It was then that she had a most extraordinary ghostly encounter. Atwater wrote: "At that time, her father and son, long since dead, and her recently deceased husband, physically and in broad daylight, drove up to her front door in an old Cadillac, honked the horn, and called out, 'We're together now and we're okay. We just wanted you to know.'

"With that said, the group, car and all, disappeared."

CHAPTER 26

The Ghost Who Loved Debussy

(Louisa County)

When Don and Nancy Tucker decided to retire, they looked around for a peaceful place in a rural setting, but within easy reach of the amenities that a city could offer. When they came to the small town of Trevilians, about five miles west of Louisa, and not far from Charlottesville, they knew this was the place. Artistically driven people, the Tuckers wanted to open an up-scale antique shop; not one of those ramshackle places where unsold flea market items are housed, but a class place.

When they then discovered that the old Trevilians Methodist Church was up for sale, it seemed perfect for the setting they wished to produce. They bought it in 1992, when it was virtually "rotting in the ground." It had been abandoned for some time. They knew little of its history when they purchased it, and nothing of its hauntings. They were soon to learn.

The church had been built in 1916, and they found the story behind its founding fascinating. It seems at that time a young woman named Lennie Roberts, probably no more than 20 years old, was a devout member of the Lasley Methodist Church a few miles down the road. "Miss Lennie," as she was known, fell in love with the preacher at Lasley, but the budding romance soured. No one remembers the exact details. Anyway, Miss Lennie felt it difficult to continue attending the church and set her mind to developing a new one.

With uncommon energy and an apparent charismatic touch, since she had no money of her own, she convinced some of the Louisa area's well-healed residents to back her project. Land was donated and she solicited enough funds to build the new church, which, to everyone living in the region, is still fondly known as "Miss Lennie's Church." Although the young lady died long ago, she still seems to "make appearances" in the church sanctuary more than 80 years after it was dedicated.

The Tuckers, meanwhile, have slowly built up their business. "We sell a general range of antique furniture. Most of our pieces are more than 100 years old," says Don. "We have a fine collection of glassware and concentrate on artwork, old engravings, original prints and the like. The walls of the sanctuary make a fine display area." Don also does custom framing for rare papers and art, including a document signed by President James Madison. Some of the frames are made out of cherry wood, curly maple, and some out of hard pine taken from old church pews.

Clients arrive from Richmond, Charlottesville and northern Virginia. "Old Church Antiques" is located at the intersection of Route 22 from Shadwell and Charlottesville, and from Route 33 coming from Harrisonburg. It is accessible from interstates 64 and 95. The area is historic in that the largest cavalry battle of the Civil War was fought here. With 5,500 men, Confederate generals Fitzhugh Lee and Wade Hampton defeated a Union Army force of 8,500.

Not long after the Tuckers moved in, "things" began to happen. "I was a skeptic when it comes to ghosts," Don says. "I will admit sometimes it was a little strange, what happened, but I developed alternative theories for most of the incidents at first. Noises, I attributed to creaking boards and floors in the old building. Or maybe a train was passing by and rattled things. We sometimes heard voices in the sanctuary. Well, maybe someone had their car radio turned up loud when they stopped at the stop sign at the intersection outside. We would see shadows, and I thought maybe clouds were passing over the moon. We thought our imaginations might be running wild at times. Things like that. But after a while it became more and more of a stretch to explain all the phenomena. Especially when our daughter and my mother-in-law also reported unexplained events."

What did the manifestations include?

"Nancy and I both enjoy playing the piano. One evening I was playing in the sanctuary when I had the distinct feeling that a presence of someone or something was standing over me. I saw a shadow. I thought Nancy had come in, but when I turned around there was no one there." Over the years this has happened to Don on five separate occasions, and to Nancy twice. And it has only occurred while they were in the sanctuary playing "Clair de Lune," or "Reverie." Both pieces were written by the great composer Claude Debussy!

"We both felt the same sensation each time," Don recalls. "Nancy, too, sensed a presence and turned to see if it was me. It wasn't and no one else was there. We both described it, not as frightening in any way, but as a 'warm, friendly presence.' We did some research and found that Miss Lennie had been in the choir at the old church and loved music. We made the assumption that Debussy must have been her favorite composer, because the presence only appeared when his music was played. I confess that I was still a bit of a skeptic, but I didn't have a rational explanation for these phenomena."

Sometime in 1995 the Tuckers daughter, Melanie, came to visit, along with her four young boys. Don and Nancy had not told her about the happenings. Melanie and her children slept in the sanctuary. At three a.m. one morning Melanie rushed to the other section of the building, awoke her parents, and complained that there were sounds of people in the room and she couldn't sleep.

Although she appeared genuinely frightened, Don assured her that there was no one in the sanctuary, that all the doors and windows in it were securely locked, and convinced Melanie it must he her imagination. She went back to bed. Two hours later, she, and her boys were back. They said they heard the distinct sounds of feet scraping on the floor and the "murmuring of voices" throughout the night. A car radio blaring at the intersection wouldn't explain this. Melanie said, "Dad, the entire congregation is coming in." The daughter and the grandchildren would no longer sleep in the sanctuary.

Even at this point, Don was reluctant to admit anything out of the realm of the ordinary. But the next event, six months later, convinced him otherwise. His mother-in-law, Thelma, came to the old church for visit. Although she was then 87 years old, Don said she was as sharp as a tack. One morning at breakfast, Nancy asked her mother how she had slept. Not well, she replied.

She then reported that she had heard voices in the sanctuary and "two big thumping noises." She also felt "vibrations." When Don said it probably was just a car outside with teenagers and their loud speakers. Thelma said that with all the windows, she would have seen car lights. She didn't. Don asked her when all this had occurred and she said at 3 a.m. He said how do you know it was 3 a.m.? She said the clock had struck three times.

It was then that Don's skepticism crumbled.

"That was a mechanical impossibility," he says. "It couldn't be true. That clock had not run for three years. We had personally turned the device off with a key. There was no physical way the clock could run."

Later that day, Don and Nancy entered the sanctuary to see for themselves. They were shocked to find the pendulum not only swinging, but the clock was keeping the correct time! They checked the room. All the doors and windows were locked. Unnerved, they turned the clock off again. It has not run since.

There is one other "coincidence." When Don was a small boy, his first grade teacher read to him from the book, "Mrs. Wiggs of the Cabbage Patch." He loved it and never forgot it. Sixty years later a friend of his came to the antique shop and gave him a book as a present. It was the same book! The inscription inside read: "December 1902, To my son William Scott Danne." Danne was a son of a Mosby Ranger from the Civil War. Colonel John S. Mosby was a Confederate legend during the war, who wreaked much destruction on Union forces, and came to be known as "The Gray Ghost." His son, it turned out, was buried in an old cemetery across the street. Don thought this to be especially strange.

All these incidents, particularly the striking clock that had been turned off, have convinced Don and Nancy that some things just cannot be satisfactorily explained.

"We like to think it is Miss Lennie and she approves of our restoration work at the church," Don muses. "She also must love Debussy. Sometimes Nancy and I get teary-eyed when we talk about it. Like I say, I have not been afraid, but I have had goose bumps at times. I really can't explain the voices and the footsteps in the sanctuary. Are they members of the old congregation returning for another sermon? And the clock. Your guess is as good as mine. But we now believe it's something real. Come on by and maybe you will see for yourself. We're open from April through December. We'd love to show you around."

CHAPTER 27

The Mysterious "Ladies" at Recess–Bremo

(Fluvanna County)

e was a Virginian, well-known in his time, but all but forgotten today. His name was John Hartwell Cocke. He was born in 1780 and died in 1866. An enthusiastic advocate of education, he helped Thomas Jefferson found the University of Virginia, and served as chairman of the building committee. Cocke, says "A Guide to the Old Dominion," "thoroughly denounced slavery as 'the great cause of all the great evils of our lands,' educated his own Negroes to useful trades, and then emancipated those who seemed fit for citizenship. He also was a "teetotaler" and was elected first president of the American Temperance Union, organized in 1836.

Cocke built three impressive mansions in the early 1800s on or near the James River in Fluvanna County, about 15 miles from Palmyra. The first two, Lower Bremo and Bremo-Recess were styled after historic Bacon's Castle in Surry County. Cocke was a native of Surry. The Cockes lived in the Recess house until a larger home, Upper Bremo, was completed in 1820. Jefferson himself participated in its design.

Margaret DuPont Lee, author of "Virginia Ghosts," published in 1930, wrote about Bremo-Recess, calling it "by no means large, but picturesque and quaint." She also wrote of the "first" ghost there. And herein lies a puzzle. In her account, she wrote a cryptic sentence which is left unexplained: "It comes to us, a mysterious green dress lies in a trunk upstairs." Curious.

Ms. Lee says that in March 1930, a festive dinner was held at the old Willard Hotel in Washington. The purpose of this occasion was to raise money for the purchase and restoration of Stratford, the magnificent plantation in which Robert E. Lee was born in 1807. One of the guests at the dinner was Dr. Lewis Greene, and that evening, at his table, the subject of the supernatural was raised.

Dr. Greene then told his dinner partners of a highly unusual experience he had once had at Bremo-Recess 20 years earlier. He then was a guest at the house. One evening the family went out to a party, leaving him alone. He placed a bottle of wine and some crackers on the dining room table as refreshments for the family when they returned. Then he settled down in a comfortable chair in an adjacent room and began reading a book.

He told Ms. Lee that after reading for awhile, he saw a shadow pass over his book. He looked up. There stood a woman wearing a green skirt. "Astonished, he followed her into the dining room, but there she was not!"

Sometime later, the family returned to the house. The doctor led them into the dining room. The bottle of wine had disappeared. "Why, I put the bottle there," the perplexed doctor said. "The ghost must have taken it." Ms. Lee wrote that as Dr. Greene said this, one member of the family nearly fainted.

It was never determined who the ghostly lady might have been. However, it could be reasonably speculated that since the home's founder, John Hartwell Cocke, was such a die-hard advocate of temperance, it might have been his wife.

The second "lady" of Bremo-Recess was described to the author at a book signing in Chantilly, Virginia, in November 1998. A young man said that descendants of John Cocke long employed a woman to nurse and help raise their children. She was so well thought of that when she died (date unknown), she was buried in the little family graveyard. One year a large piece of her tombstone broke off. It was then that the apparition of the woman appeared to members of the family then living in the house. The visions continued over a period of time. That is, until the broken stone was repaired.

"She" was never seen again after that.

The Psychic Proffitts
of Lovingston

(Author's note: I get a considerable amount of mail during the year. Some have called or written and said they had previously been afraid to speak about ghostly occurrences for fear that people would think them crazy. From the always-interesting correspondence, I have, through the years, gleaned some entertaining stories for inclusion in this series of books.)

uch was the case when a young lady named Nancy Connor sent a check for a copy of one of my books, and enclosed a succinct, yet intriguing note. It said, simply, "My mother lived in the Proffitt House in Lovingston. 'Helen' still lives there." I was hooked. I tracked Nancy down to her home in Tampa, Florida, and she led me onto a number of other sources who, like her, contributed to the following chapter.)

Can an entire family clan be psychic? There are many cases on file where the psychic "gift" apparently has been handed down from parent to child, sometimes covering centuries. In other instances those "born to see" may skip a generation or two. The Proffitts of Lovingston — the town about halfway between Charlottesville and Lynchburg on Route 29 must surely fit somewhere in one of these categories, because several members of the family have been either on the "giving" or the "receiving" end of spectral manifestations over a lengthy period dating back to the earliest days of the 20th century and perhaps beyond.

The Proffitts are virtually as prominent and as prolific in the area as are the Lovings — the family from which Lovingston took its name. In fact, there still is a Proffitt House on Main Street — a large, three-story structure that likely was built sometime between 1810 and 1815, say Michael and Kay Crabill, the present owners. "Some people believe the house was first constructed in the late 1700s and was a tavern," Kay says, "but all our research indicates that it probably was built shortly after the auction." This is a reference to an event the Lovings staged in 1809. To build up the town they auctioned off parcels of land at dirt-cheap prices to anyone who promised to put up at least a 12 foot by 12 foot structure on the property within three years.

"Some people have told us the ground floor part of the house was constructed first, but we believe the house was all built at one time," Kay says. "The ground floor has a cook-in fireplace and then there are two upper floors. There are only two bedrooms on the third floor, but they are huge rooms, as was the custom at the time it was planned." There also is a wrap-around porch, which runs around three quarters of the house.

"My father bought the house from Grafton Tucker, I think sometime in the 1920s," says Mary Proffitt Walker, now (1992) a still spry and lucid 85-years-old and living in Port Charlotte, Florida. "We lived there for years and years." Mrs. Walker tells of the time, after she had married and moved to Washington, D.C., when a boarder in her house there told of seeing a gentleman in her room standing at the foot of her bed. Then the woman noticed a photograph of Mrs. Walker's father, which had just been reframed, and declared that was the man she saw in her room — John Fletcher Proffitt. Mrs. Walker told her boarder that her father was dead, but that when he had visited her in Washington he always stayed in that same bedroom.

Mary Walker's father and her mother, Verdie Teresa Tyree Proffitt, who lived on a farm at "the Cove," were said to have had a number of scary psychic encounters in and around Mountain Cove church and cemetery. Mrs. Walker and her sister, Estelle Stevens, who stills lives adjacent to the church, both say that their mother was a great story-teller and sometimes told some pretty wild tales.

"But she swore they were true," Mrs. Walker says. "It was quite a colorful era," adds Nancy Connor, Mrs. Walker's daughter. "There was a hanging tree, and my grandfather was involved with the Ku Klux Klan." According to Mrs. Walker and Mrs. Stevens, their parents met up with all sorts of haunts near the church and

Proffitt House

cemetery, always late at night.

"I can remember my mother telling me that once she and my father were coming from the Cove to Lovingston in a one-horse buggy, carrying a load of fresh eggs to sell to merchants," Mrs. Walker recalls. "As they passed the graveyard, something spooked the horse and it reared up, the buckboard turned over, and all the eggs were broken.

"Another time my mother said they were passing by in the same area when a man ran out of the cemetery with a white sheet over his face. He grabbed the reins and said 'you're not going anywhere.' She said it scared both of them, but that right before their eyes, the man vanished." Mrs. Stevens says still another time, as they were stopped once again passing the churchyard, a man jumped out in front of them with a shawl over his head. He appeared in the shadows to be "Uncle Riley Proffitt" — a member of the family who had been killed in World War I!

Nancy Connor vividly remembers Verdie Proffitt, her grandmother, telling her about one time when Verdie and her husband were passing by Mountain Cove and their horse stopped dead in ins tracks and refused to move. "She said John finally got out of the buggy and put a blanket over the eyes of the horse. Only then, would it start up. Something had shaken it to the marrow," Nancy says. "Grandmother then said, that as they got a few yards away, they both turned back to look, and they saw a headless horseman! She said she was not making up a story, that it actually happened. It should be noted that a number of old timers in the Mountain Cove area have also attested that they have witnessed strange apparitions in and around the church grounds.

Arthur Stevens, Estelle's husband, has heard the stories, too. He grew up in the area and his relatives are dotted throughout the valley community. His ancestors have lived here since the mid-1700s. "I never saw a ghost myself," he says. "I did hear some strange moaning one night by the cemetery, and it gave me a creepy feeling. A lot of slaves are buried there, too, though their graves are unmarked. They used to just put a plain stone on them, but most of them are long gone. Well, the moaning turned out to be a crow sitting up in a tree.

"One time when I was a young man, I came by that old cemetery after I had had a lot to drink. I decided to rest a little, so I laid down in a sunken grave. I wondered later what might have happened if someone had come along and I raised up out of that grave," Arthur laughs. "I reckon they would have thought they had seen a spirit all right!"

Estelle Stevens has had a series of separate ghostly visitations herself in more recent years. She was married earlier to William Byrd and they lived in Roseland, south of Lovingston in the Piney River area. William, allegedly, was a carouser who liked to go out at night looking for action at the nearest watering hole. Estelle sometimes would go out looking for him.

One night William got into a scrape over a woman in some tavern, and he and another man got into a fight that resulted in the man shooting and killing William. There was a lot of conflicting testimony at the subsequent trial, and the man pleaded self defense and got off.

It wasn't long afterwards that William began to return, in spirit form, to visit Estelle. "I would wake up to see him either at the foot of my bed or sitting where he always sat in the room, over in the corner in a chair by the stove," Estelle says. "I would always ask him how he got in the house, and he would say, 'just like I always did,' through the window. Many times I would get up out of bed and walk over to where he was sitting and try to touch him, but whenever I did, he just vanished. He wasn't frightening or anything, but I really didn't know what to do. I wondered if I was going crazy or something. So I finally went to my minister and I told him about William's visits and I asked him what to do. The minister said to tell William that everything was okay, and that I didn't need him any more and he could go on to where he was supposed to go. So I did that the next time he came into the house, and I never saw him or heard from him again."

Of all the associations of the Proffitts with psychic phenomena in the area, however, undoubtedly the most tragic involved a four-year-old girl named Helen Loving. She was the daughter of Dora Proffitt Loving, and they lived in the Proffitt House. At the time there were some boarders who lived there also. They packed peaches in the county.

One day in September 1932, little Helen, found some matches in the boarders' room and crawled under the bed and started striking them. Her dress caught fire, and in her terror, Helen ran down the stairs, screaming and then ran outside, running all around the wraparound porch. The flames spread quickly and by the time others reached her, she had been burned so badly that she died some days later in a Lynchburg hospital.

"Oh, she was something special," says Mrs. Walker. "She was so bright and so pleasant, just a joy to be around. We all loved her so much. Everyone in Lovingston loved the ground that child walked on. We just knew something was going to happen to her."

Fifty years later, Maureen and Joe Boles were living in Proffitt House. "It was a total derelict when we bought it," remembers Maureen, now living in St. Augustine, Florida. "Of course, at the time, we didn't know anything about the house or its past history, or the fact that Helen Loving had been burned there and subsequently died.

"Well, there were a couple of things that we couldn't explain. We had a couple of guests once and they stayed in one of the upstairs bedrooms. They said they had heard a child playing in the room that night, in the corner of the room. They got up, but they couldn't see anything. They said they couldn't stay there anymore, and they left the house.

"There were plenty of other times when you felt like there was sort of a 'presence' in the house. I mean you wouldn't directly see or feel anything, but you still felt kind of uneasy. I can't really explain it, but maybe you know what I mean," Maureen continues.

"And then one day I was down at the base of the stairs when our dog stiffened and began barking. I had a funny feeling. Something told me to look up, and when I did I saw a little girl.

She must have been about four years old. My impression is that she was in a long gown, like a night gown. It was an old one, and she looked like she was standing over the steps on her tiptoes and peeping over the bannister at me. She was only there for a second. It was a fleeting glance, but there was no mistaking that she was a little girl. And then she vanished. I checked upstairs, but there was no one there. I never saw her again, just that once."

(Author's note: The description Maureen Boles gave of the little girl she saw matched Helen Loving perfectly. Yet, strangely, Maureen did not know who the girl was, until I informed her of the tragic fire incident during an interview with her in January 1992. Present owners Michael and Kay Crabill say they have not been visited by Helen during their time in the house. They theorize that the little girl must be satisfied that Proffitt House is being well taken care of.)

CHAPTER 29

The Most Awesome 'Presence' of Thomas Jefferson

(Monticello and Poplar Forest)

(Author's note: I have written extensively about Thomas Jefferson in past editions in this series on Virginia ghosts. In "The Ghosts of Charlottesville and Lynchburg," (1992), and repeated in "The Ghosts of Virginia, Volume I," (1993), I said: "Some staff members at Monticello say that on occasion, after the mansion is closed for the day, they have heard the sound of a man humming a cheerful tune when there is no living mortal around. Jefferson's overseer, Edmund Bacon, once wrote that Jefferson 'was nearly always humming some tune or singing in a low tone to himself'."

n "The Ghosts of Virginia, Volume II," (1994), I told of a phone call I have received from Jennifer Wilson who lives in Fairfax. She said that in the summer of 1992, while visiting Monticello, she had a haunting experience at the little "honeymoon cottage" near the main house. She felt a frigid chill although it was a warm day. "I had the strangest feeling there was a presence there," she said. "A little later I walked down to Jefferson's grave site and the feeling of a presence was so overwhelming there, I had to leave."

A little over a year later, Jennifer revisited Monticello, this time

Poplar Forest

with her mother. She again felt the strong sensation of a presence. She then walked the grounds alone and returned to find her mother sitting on the edge of the terrace. She appeared visibly shaken. "She had felt the same sensation I had," Jennifer said. "She wanted to leave immediately."

Was there a reason for this? "I have done some genealogy work and it may be that Alex Garrett is one of my ancestors," Jennifer noted. Garrett was Jefferson's lawyer!

And in "The Ghosts of Virginia, Volume III," (1996), I wrote a chapter on a little boy ghost at Poplar Forest, Jefferson's "getaway home" near the Peaks of Otter in Bedford County. Actually, the ghostly experiences occurred at a house in a development just outside the Poplar Forest property, but it may have involved the apparition of a former slave child who lived in Jefferson's time. He appeared frequently to a young lady named Cindy Holt. Through a psychic, Cindy learned that the "boy" liked her because she reminded him of one of Jefferson's nieces, who used to visit their famous uncle at Poplar Forest. The psychic later found an old picture of a Jefferson niece one day while researching in the library.

It was the spitting image of Cindy Holt!

And so it was, when in the process of writing this book, I

became excited with two new, previously unrecorded instances in which the "presence" of Jefferson may have surfaced. The first one involved a newspaper article about the renovations underway at Poplar Forest. It was published in May 1998, and mentioned that Jefferson's spirit had been "looking over the shoulders of the craftsmen working at the site."

The second incident was related to me in July 1998 while I was signing books at the annual Hanover Tomato Festival in Mechanicsville. A young lady who had worked as a researcher at Monticello for five years told me of a most intriguing encounter she had experienced there in 1992.

Both occurrences dealt with a "presence." What exactly is that? It is not an actual sighting, and it is not any other physical activity that is sensed, such as footsteps or other sounds, the feeling of a cold spot, or any specific smell or odor. The number six definition of presence in Webster's Dictionary says it is "something (as a spirit) felt or believed to be present." Curiously, just below this entry in the dictionary is the definition of a "presence chamber." And that is, "the room where a great personage receives those entitled to come into his presence."

This led me to wonder . . . can the presence of a spirit, the same spirit, be felt in two different places — 75 miles or so apart? Perhaps it can if the presence involved is that of so towering and dominant a figure as Thomas Jefferson. But judge for yourself.)

THE HOME AWAY FROM HOME

Jefferson loved Poplar Forest. It was his special hideaway; a rural retreat in the scenic shadows of the Peaks of Otter where he could get away from the constant procession of well-intentioned guests who descended upon his home at Monticello. Although he was a gracious host, there were times when he cherished his privacy and needed time by himself to write, to think, and even to relax. That is why he chose to build Poplar Forest — just far enough away to satisfy these needs. After his long service as a public servant, including his two terms as the third President of the United States, he would come here three or four times a year and stay for periods up to two months. It would refresh him.

Poplar Forest, so named for the many trees which surrounded it, is an octagonal brick house with a formal portico featuring four slender Roman Doric columns. In the design of the house, Jefferson incorporated many of the architectural ideas he had collected through years of study and travels in France and Italy. The interior is divided into four rooms around a central hall 20 feet square. Opposite the entrance passage is a drawing room which opens through French windows onto a portico that overlooks the garden. In the bedrooms, as at Monticello, Jefferson placed the beds in alcoves. And there is a 16-foot-long skylight, the largest of its time in America. Once completed, Jefferson praised the house for its "tranquility and retirement much adapted to my age and indolence." Here, he said, he enjoyed the "solitude of a hermit."

In 1812, Jefferson wrote: "When finished, it will be the best dwelling house in the state, except that of Monticello; perhaps preferable to that, as more proportioned to the faculties of a private citizen."

In recent years, however, Poplar Forest lapsed into a state of deterioration. A fire in 1845 had destroyed the roof and damaged the interior. Years of neglect followed while the house was in private hands.

Then in 1984, a nonprofit corporation raised enough funds to buy the house and 500 acres of surrounding land, and the renovations began. It was a massive project that was to take 14 years and more than $14 million to complete. It is now, however, open to the public from April 1 to late December each year, from 10 a.m. to 4:30 p.m.

During his lifetime Jefferson wrote of Poplar Forest over 1,500 times, including many references to his directives during the original construction. Researchers spent several years carefully studying every document to authenticate their restructuring work. The house, in fact, was taken apart, brick by brick, "to unravel the mystery," according to Travis McDonald who headed the restoration. "We peeled back the layers of time," he said.

Craftsmen used the same materials and many of the same techniques that Jefferson's workers had employed nearly 200 years ago "to understand what the founding father went through to build it." This even included the use of handsaws and chisels, hand-wrought nails, and mortar mixed in a large wooden tub. Chief craftsman Doug Rideout said, "It gives you a taste of the genius of Jefferson."

McDonald, Rideout, Eliza Thomas, a member of the board overseeing the renovation, and others intimately involved in the project — all say that it could not have been done without the presence of Jefferson himself!

"His spirit was looking over the shoulders of the volunteers and craftsmen every day," Thomas says. "Everyone who has worked here the past 14 years has been deeply influenced by Thomas Jefferson. He was here for every step of the renovation. We couldn't have done it without him!"

McDonald added that, "The big thing we've learned about the house is how autobiographical it was. People say they feel Jefferson more in this house than in Monticello." "You come here," concludes Eliza Thomas, "and you will feel his presence the minute you walk in the door."

A SPECTRAL REUNION AT MONTICELLO

Shelly Willis today is a high school teacher (drama) at Hanover High School, but for five years, from 1989 to 1994, she worked at Monticello as a researcher and an occasional historical interpreter.

"A lot of people who work there, even today, won't openly talk about it, but privately they will tell you they believe Thomas Jefferson's spirit is still in the house, big time," Shelly says. "I know that's the way I felt from the first day I went there. I never felt alone in that house, even when I was alone in it. Sometimes I would work late at night there after everyone had gone home, no tourists, no workers, and the security guards were not in the house. But I never felt like I was alone. Some houses when you walk in them, you immediately feel alone. Never here. I felt it was like my second home. And it was a warm feeling, never a scary one.

"I have walked by Jefferson's burial site at night with no one else around, and even here, I never felt alone, never scared. It was a very comforting feeling, like there's a friend here. I talked to others who worked there and they all felt a sense of belonging at Monticello. I still miss it, and I get a wonderful feeling everytime I think about it."

Shelly says there have been a few specific incidents which fortify the feeling of a supernatural presence. For example, a security guard told her that one night he was walking through the all-weather passageway underneath the house, when he said he saw a strange light approaching him. He said it passed by and then "ran up" through the holes cut in the floor beneath the entrance hall to accommodate the cannon ball weights of the large clock above. The guard went straight upstairs to see what was causing the light. There was no one there, all the doors were securely locked, and a plausible explanation was never found.

"Others have had similar experiences," Shelly says. "There is a particularly strong sensation of 'him' in the parlor and in the west end of the house. 'He' liked to look out onto the west lawn."

The incident that convinced Shelly that Jefferson's presence remains occurred in 1992 when there was a special reunion at Monticello for Jefferson's descendants. It was held in the evening, after tourist hours, and there were about 1,200 people there. Shelly and other employees were positioned throughout the house. She was in the dome room on the third floor — a section not opened to the public because of the size of the stairs up to it. The stairway is only 24 inches wide, but on this occasion it was open to the descendants.

After touring the house, the descendants gathered on the west lawn for a photograph. Shelly remained in the dome room. "I opened a door to a little room outside the dome room, shaped like a triangle, and used for storage. There is a little window there overlooking the west lawn and I wanted to see the descendants getting their picture taken. I was alone on the third floor. No one else was around.

"Just as the photographer flashed his camera outside, I heard a low noise behind me in the small room. It sounded like a soft voice although I couldn't make out what was said. There was a very strong sense that there was someone in that room with me at that moment. I felt it was Jefferson and that he, too, was looking out the window, admiring his 'family.' He was such a patriarch. He loved his family, and it seemed like he was so pleased that all his descendants had come back together. It was a real intimate feeling. I looked around but there was no one in sight.

"Then the door to the little room closed by itself. The door doesn't swing. You have to forcibly open and close it. I thought at first one of my friends might be trying to play a trick on me, but when I opened it and looked, there was no one there. And I would have heard any mortal being if someone had been there, because the floors are wood and you can hear them creak when a person walks on them."

Shelly adds: "I was convinced it was the presence of Jefferson and he was pleased. It was like a proud grandfather looking down upon his grandchildren. I know it was one of the warmest experiences I have ever had, and I will never forget it."

The Frozen Ghost at Lime Kiln Bridge

(Lexington)

n 1845, historian Henry Howe wrote of Lexington: "It is beautifully situated, 146 miles from Richmond, on the west bank of the North River, one of the main branches of the James. . . . The town, as a settlement, has many attractions. It is surrounded by beauty, and stands at the head of a valley flowing with milk and honey . . . . Flowers and gardens are more prized here than in most places."

Lexington also is the home of Washington and Lee University and Virginia Military Institute. Robert E. Lee spent his last five years here. Stonewall Jackson is buried here. One of the world's most scenic wonders, Natural Bridge, is but a few miles up the road, as are the Blue Ridge Mountains.

And, apparently, the area also has its share of spirits of the past. In fact, local author Anne McCorkle Knox wrote a book about supernatural happenings in and around Lexington. It is titled, "the Gentle Ghosts." In her lead paragraph, she said: "When the oak leaves rattle, and winter's chilly fingers creep along the spine, Lexington ghosts come out of their hiding. Some are gay and charming, some are hideous specters . . . "

One that might well qualify for the latter description could be the eyeless body of l8-year-old World War I veteran Aubrey Tyree, the victim of perhaps the most notorious murder in Rockbridge County history, certainly in the 20th century. The case went on for more than three years and labored through four separate trials of

the accused murderer. It essentially remained unsolved, although in most residents' minds there was little doubt of who the actual killer was. And possibly because there was no final resolution of the matter, it is widely believed by many locals that the victim's ghost still can be seen on freezing cold winter nights at the spot where his lifeless body was discarded 80 years ago.

Here is what is known: Aubrey Tyree was a handsome strapping lad who, at 16, lied about his age and joined the army. Two years later, in 1919, he mustered out and returned to his home at Kerr's Creek, near Lexington, where his father was the blacksmith. It was then that he began courting a childhood sweetheart, Jessie Chaplin. But there was a complication. In Aubrey's absence while he was overseas, Jessie had been seeing an older man, an eccentric farmer named Addison Mohler. He was sort of a country recluse who kept to himself mostly, but he adored Jessie who was 20-odd years or so younger than he. Although they had not been formerly engaged, Addison felt that Jessie, more or less, belonged to him. Thus when Aubrey came home and began see her, he and Addison seemed to be on a collision course.

It was an odd situation. Addison was a wiry, small man about five feet four, and less than 120 pounds, but Jessie was attracted to him, maybe because he owned hundreds of acres of land and several farmhouses. Whatever, when Jessie began seeing Aubrey, Addison became incensed. The two men had words. On December

27, 1919, Aubrey Tyree left his house at about five in the afternoon enroute to see his sweetheart.

He was never seen alive again.

On the morning of March 9, 1920, his body was found washed up on the bank of the North River in a secluded spot near Brown's Hole, about a mile from Lexington. Where the body's eyes had been, there were only sunken sockets, and the skin was black and swollen. Identification was difficult, but when a scar was found on the left cheek, one that Aubrey had gotten as a child when a dog bit him, it was determined that this was the body of the young Tyree.

An autopsy was performed, and the county coroner revealed that Aubrey had not died of drowning in the river. He had been dead before he had entered the river. There was no water in his lungs, but there were hard clots of blood on the back of the head, indicating he had received a severe blow or blows. There was a four inch crack in his skull!

On March 25, the Rockbridge County News reported that Addison Mohler had been arrested "on a warrant charging him with being under suspicion of having caused the death by violence of Aubrey Tyree." A subsequent search warrant was issued contending that Addison "had concealed in his house or on his premises certain articles of clothing belonging to Tyree, feloniously taken."

The arrest was based, in part, on what Jessie had told authorities, including Addison's jealousy and the fact that the two men had argued vehemently. When police investigated Addison's house they found nothing incriminating. But when they went to search a log cabin a half mile away, near an old sawmill where Aubrey had last been seen, Addison objected. He said the place was locked and he had lost the key. Officials entered through the windows.

Although the cabin had not been lived in for several years, there were suspicious signs of recent occupancy. It appeared that a large fire had been built in the fireplace at least within the past two or three months. Floor boards had been taken up and replaced. The original boards were found and had "red splotches" on them, possibly blood. Other red spots were found upstairs, and on rocks beneath the floor boards, especially near the fire place.

Observers surmised, from all the signs, that a violent struggle had taken place in the cabin.

There was also a curious expression Addison had used a few

days earlier in a letter to Jessie. He said, "Sorrow is now shadowing around me." Some interpreted this to be a veiled confession. Although the evidence was circumstantial, it led to the arrest of Addison. (Does all this sound strikingly familiar to a 1990s murder case set in Los Angeles, California? Read on!)

Authorities had a problem, though. If he had killed Aubrey, as they suspected, near Hogback Mountain, how did the body get to an isolated site on the North River, nearly 10 miles away? Since Addison was a much smaller man, how could he have conveyed the corpse across that distance without being detected?

A possible solution was offered in the testimony of two brothers, Henry and Edward Kirkpatrick, of Alone Mills. They had been traveling from their home two or three days after Christmas 1919, and were passing over the Lime Kiln Bridge, when they happened to look down into the frozen North River and noticed something singularly strange. There was a hole in the ice that appeared to be "freshly broken." It was large enough for a human body to pass through.

It was then speculated that Addison, or someone, had transported Aubrey's body to the bridge and tossed it down into the river. The body then, once the ice had thawed nearly two and a half months later, washed down stream a mile and a half to the spot where it was discovered. This was a much more plausible hypothesis to what actually happened.

Addison Mohler's trial began on November 8, 1920, more than 10 months after Aubrey had disappeared. Witnesses testified that Addison had not pulled up the floor boards in his log cabin until after Aubrey's body had been found. At one point commonwealth attorney R. R. Ruff dramatically shook his finger at Addison and shouted, "You beady-eyed little murderer, confess! You know you did it!" But defense attorneys put up a passionate plea, suggesting that how could a man so slight in physical stature have committed such a vicious deed. Addison himself was convincing in his self-proclaimed innocence when he took the stand. The jury seemed confused and became hopelessly hung. A mistrial was declared.

Prosecutors sought a new trial and this time, on February 18, 1921, the jury found Addison "guilty of murder in the second degree, and (we) fix his punishment at twelve years in the penitentiary." The defense lawyers appealed and were granted a third trial. Like the first one, this, too, ended with a hung jury. Consequently, and unbelievably, a fourth trial commenced in May 1923, over three years after Aubrey's body had been discovered on the banks of the river. Again, the jury could not agree on a verdict, and the judge freed Addison. He was, in the opinion of many, "not convicted but not exonerated."

One of the first things Addison did upon reaching home was to board up what had become known as "the death cabin." He lived out his life in what one reporter called "desolate solitude."

When Aubrey Tyree's body had been found in March 1920, it was said it was wrapped in white sheets. Author Knox says that for the past eight decades, "when gray mist rises to hide the clear water" at the Lime Kiln Bridge near Lexington, an impressive number of witnesses say "they have seen the body of the murdered man wrapped in his white shroud, lying still on the moving current."

Apparitions Aplenty at Longwood College

(Farmville)

(Author's note: For years, I had heard about the ghosts at Longwood College, but I could never quite pin down enough information to write about them. Everyone would tell me that the school was haunted by multiple spirits, but no one knew the details. Students mentioned the apparition of Dr. Joseph Jarman, long-time president of Longwood. They said they still hear him walking with a cane through the buildings at night. Others told of a professor named Edith Stevens who was killed in a fire years ago, yet still wanders a certain walkway between buildings. Fires, in fact, appear to be involved in several of the incidents. Co-eds said each Halloween a candlelight "ritual" is held whereby members of the freshmen class are told of the hauntings. "It's pretty scary," one young lady said. "If the aim is to frighten us, it works.")

I n May of 1998 I participated in the annual "Heart of Virginia" festival in Farmville. From interviews with students there, from information gathered later, and from a Halloween newspaper article in the Farmville Herald, written by Marge Swayne, I have been able to piece together some of the supernatural occurrences in and around Longwood. Here goes.)

Edith Stevens, it seems, was a professor at the college and head of the Natural Science Department in the 1920s and 1930s. There

Confederate Monument

was an explosion and fire in one of the laboratories, and Edith is credited with saving several students' lives. She, however, was badly burned and died a short time later. Apparently, she returns on occasion to scold gardeners near the site where the fire occurred.

This legend is related by Dr. James Jordan, currently a professor of anthropology. He notes that Edith Stevens had a close friend named Leola Wheeler, and when Leola died, a marker was placed at the site, which, coincidentally, is near where the fire occurred. Jordan says whenever this marker is neglected and becomes overgrown with weeds, the ghost of Edith vents its wrath, appearing as a "ball of fire" in the attic of the Stevens Building. This is more than enough for the workmen to clear away the site post-haste.

As to Dr. Jarman, whenever there is a theatrical production in Jarman Hall, a red rose and a play program are placed in a prominent position, respecting the ghost of the former president.
According to local resident William Lynn, whenever the ritual forgotten, Dr. Jarman's spirit acts up. He says the electricity, the sound board and the theater's lights "don't work right."

At Tabb Hall, the screaming of an unseen hysterical young woman is heard on occasion. This may be tied to past fires. One occurred in 1927, destroying the dining hall, laundry, pantry, servants' quarters and a number of the students' rooms. In 1949 there was another fire. Dr. Jordan thinks these past tragedies may be the cause for the ghostly shrieks, usually late at night. It is believed that the screams are a warning of impending danger. Once, for instance, when the wailings were heard, students rushed to a window and saw a co-ed being attacked outside. At other times, small fires have been discovered in time to avert serious consequences.

There is a rich tradition, too, associated with a familiar landmark in Farmville — the statue to Confederate heroes of the Civil War, which was dedicated October 11, 1900. It is directly across the street from the college, in front of the Methodist Church. According to Mrs. Lucy Lancaster, who ran a gift shop on High Street for many years, if one goes down to the statue at night and looks across the street to the college, the glow of street lights behind the statue will cast a shadow on the building — when all is right with the world.

But sometimes the shadow will not be there! It is then that one must be careful. For Mrs. Lancaster said that when she was a child, in the early 1900s, she was told that when the shadow could be seen on the wall of the college building, it meant "the soldier" was in the statue and all was well. But when the shadow could not be seen, "the soldier" was out roaming about the town with his rifle and trouble was afoot. Dr. Jordan says that one night there was a fire on Main Street and several buildings were burned. The shadow could not be seen that evening.

In the newspaper article, writer Marge Swayne says, "Another mystery on the campus is the too-thick wall that joins one college building built in 1839 with an addition constructed in 1884." Dr. Jordan relates that "the wall is about four feet thick — wide enough for a man's body. People say there are things inside the wall we don't even want to think about."

Another source for the hauntings in Farmville is the Reverend William Thompson, pastor of College Church. He was once called in to do an exorcism on a building known as "The Alamo." It, too, was consumed years ago by a fire. Before that, however, co-eds reported seeing the apparition of a "blond woman" in their room at night. After the reverend visited, the sightings stopped.

One reason for the many hauntings at Longwood, some residents speculate, is the fact that a family cemetery apparently has been "lost" somewhere on the grounds of the college. Surveys dating to 1836 indicate that the burial grounds for the Josiah Chambers family were located in the heart of current campus grounds, but no one today knows where. According to Dr. Jordan there is yet another old cemetery near Longwood House. All the headstones, markers and the wrought-iron fence have long since disappeared, but "all the bodies are still there, 22 of them," Dr. Jordan says.

Reverend Thompson tells of another cemetery tradition — This one at College Church on the grounds of Hampden-Sydney College. "This concerns a Betty Dickerson who died in her teenaged years shortly after the Civil War," he says. "Someone in the family rode to Farmville to send the death telegram to her kin." Her brother was then in Texas. He wired back not to bury her until he arrived. He wanted to see his sister's "sweet face" once again. This presented a problem. This was before the days of embalming, so how were they to preserve the body?

Thompson says they got a local coffin maker to build a two-layered coffin. The corpse was placed in the top and beneath it was a lined metal container. Friends, relatives and neighbors donated ice to be put in the bottom. But after three days they ran out of ice, so the funeral was scheduled for a Tuesday afternoon. The brother arrived that morning. He went into the parlor where his sister was laid out. She was wearing a black dress with a red flower tucked into the bodice.

Reverend Thompson: "He bent over to kiss his sister and felt the flower move!" A doctor was called in and checked her pulse. He found none, but at the brother's insistence, a stimulant was applied. "In two or three minutes, Betty sat up, opened her eyes, and started talking to people."

The reverend adds that, "Miss Betty Dickerson lived to be 96 years old, and every day of her life, she wore a red flower!"

THE GHOSTLY MUSIC CRITIC AT COLE HALL
(Bridgewater)

Over the years a number of students have been terrified by haunting sounds and other manifestations in Cole Hall on the campus of Bridgewater College. Some of these may be supernatural and some may not. Back in the 1980s drama professor Ralph MacPhail, an avowed skeptic, said he couldn't resist the temptation to make "spooky noises" in the building at night when he knew someone else was in the area, but unaware of his presence. That may explain some of the alleged phenomena, but not all.

Others have experienced sensations as yet unexplained. They say there is a real ghost in Cole Hall, and he most often makes his presence known when piano music is played. He doesn't like piano music, but does seem to appreciate organ music and male quartets and quintets.

The "appearances" began in 1960, when students began seeing the apparition of "an old man." Organ students, practicing in the hall, claimed they often felt as if someone was listening as they rehearsed. One night a quintet was rehearsing, when one of the students looked up and saw an "older man sitting in the top section of the balcony, listening intently." He said the man suddenly vanished.

In 1974, Steve Mason, assistant dean of student development, was in Cole Hall, and after rehearsals for a play were over and everyone else left, or at least Mason thought they had left, he decided to play the grand piano. He said he began to feel nervous, then glanced over his shoulder and saw "two glowing, unblinking eyes starting at him from the recesses of the darkened balcony . . . with obvious displeasure. Mason left the building abruptly.

Four years later, a student was in the hall practicing a dance for her drama class. The tape she was using had a piano introduction. Without any apparent cause, the tape stopped. The student glanced toward the balcony. There, she saw an old man standing — "his arm extended and his bony finger pointed directly at her." She, too, left quickly.

It was never learned who the apparitional figure was, or why he haunted the hall. But he was around for a number of years. Many heard his footsteps at night when the building was supposedly empty, and some reported windows that would open and close by themselves . . . even the ones that were nailed shut!

Letters from the Author's Mailbag

(Author's note: I get some of the most interesting letters! Here is a selection:)

THE FIGURE IN THE ROTUNDA

(Author's note:) In "The Ghosts of Charlottesville and Lynchburg," (1992) I wrote a brief note about the rotunda at the University of Virginia in Charlottesville. "There was a report, years ago, that a 'Phantom of the Rotunda' haunted the great domed building. According to one newspaper account, this ethereal being disappeared with all the books when the university's library was moved to the new Alderman building in 1938." Then I added, somewhat whimsically, "it must have been a literary ghost."
In January 1998, I received the following from E. R. Conner, III, of Catharpin, Virginia:)

"**I** am not sure but I may have seen a ghost in the Rotunda during my first year at the University, 1967-1968. I <u>did</u> see something unusual. The Seven Society was the best known of the secret societies at the University at that time. I don't know much about the society, but I have always heard that the group had only seven members at any one time. I do know that the only way in which the general public learns that someone has belonged to the Seven is through the publication of a strange symbol along with a member's obituary.

"Anyway, the society received its mail in envelopes deposited at the statue of Jefferson inside the rotunda. I believe that the envelopes were placed on a small table or stand rather than on the base of the statue itself. The method of mail delivery was common knowledge, while the method of pickup was unknown.

"One evening about dusk I decided to visit the rotunda. Out of curiosity, I walked over to the statue, which stood on the left side of the main floor as one entered the building from University Avenue. I looked to see whether the Seven had received any mail. That evening an envelope indeed was there. For some reason that I cannot explain fully, I extended my hand and touched the envelope for a few seconds. Perhaps I thought this action would bring me good luck on forthcoming exams, although I did not and still do not consider myself a particularly superstitious person.

"Turning to leave, I caught sight of a <u>form</u> on the upper balcony on the opposite side of the interior. There were two tiers of balconies in the building, and this form, or figure, as it proved to be, was standing on the top balcony. Visible above the balcony rail were the head and shoulders of a young man . . . with short dark hair and a dark jacket. He was looking at me blankly. When my eyes met his, he seemed to step back toward the wall behind the balcony rail.

"I saw this figure for no more than about two seconds. I initially assumed that either a fellow student or a young faculty member had been watching me. But what struck me was I did not hear any footsteps when the figure withdrew from sight, and as I remember, the acoustics in the rotunda were quite good. The figure did not speak, nod, or acknowledge my presence in any way except to retreat as quickly as possible from my gaze.

"It seemed especially strange that the figure did not speak. In those days, students, faculty members, and even maintenance workers at the university normally said at least 'good evening' in a situation such as this. During their indoctrination into university traditions, first-year students in fact were told that etiquette demanded spoken greetings.

"The overall impression given by the figure that I saw was one of extreme shyness, or even furtiveness. After 30 years, I have not determined who, or what, this figure was."

*   *   *   *   *

(Author's note: Mr. Conner also wrote about a couple of other ghostly encounters he had heard about.)

"Stover's Mill, still standing when I was a child in the early 1950s, was located on Trap Branch, off Route 628, just south of Route 55, in Fauquier County. Built of stone, it later burned. The community near Stover's Mill was known as 'Little Georgetown.' Older folks there told the tale of how the miller's wife dreamed of a child in a white dress shortly before her little daughter drowned in the mill race. In the version I heard, the girl fell from a window of the mill into the race, and was buried in the dress that her mother saw in her dream."

* * * * *

"I'll close with a bit of unsolicited material. About two and a half miles northwest of Beverley's Mill, between Broad Run Station and The Plains, in Fauquier County, is a farm called 'Avenel.' The private lane leading to this farm extends in a northeasterly direction from Route 55, and this private road crosses the railroad line now owned by Norfolk Southern, within sight of the highway.

"Many of my family and friends worked for the Southern Railway, which previously operated this line. I have heard stories to the effect that the 'White Lady' of Avenel (see 'The Ghosts of Fredericksburg,' 1991) was seen not only by residents and visitors there, but also by crews of trains passing by, beginning in the steam engine days and extending into the diesel era.

"According to some of these accounts, engineers applied their air brakes and stopped their trains when they saw the 'White Lady,' which they initially took for a human being, on the tracks. The lady, of course, would vanish.

"Not long ago I took an auto ride with retired Southern Railway trainman and conductor Martin R. Runaldue of Manassas. As we passed the entrance to Avenel he began to talk about strange experiences that some of his former co-workers, now deceased, had had in that area. Mr. Runaldue stated that one day, a diesel-powered freight train was going west when the engineer noticed a carriage overturned on the embankment near the private crossing.

"Surprised to see a carriage, not to mention one that had been wrecked, the engineer used his radio to call the flagman on the caboose and instructed him to take a close look when the rear end of the train passed the crossing. When the caboose reached the place, the carriage was gone!

THE MYSTERY LADY OF THE GHOST TOUR

From Kathy B. Heer of Fairfax: "My husband and I were in Williamsburg March 26-28th (1998)) for a little get away while grandma watched our two kids. We did not have ghosts on our minds, but we had an eerie experience that you might be interested in.

"We made a reservation to go on the ghost walk tour (based on the author's book, 'The Ghosts of Williamsburg.'). The weather was balmy, warm, and it was a beautiful night. An older woman was our guide. About three-quarters into the tour my husband and I were standing on the outer perimeter of the group listening to the guide. I remember we were standing at the end of a tall boxwood hedge that the guide pointed out as being 200 years old. She had just told us about the house where the first Christmas tree in America was erected. Our tour group was all alone at this point on the street.

"Suddenly my husband nudged me and said, 'Look at that statue,' and pointed to a spot on the side of the Christmas tree house in the shadows on the edge of a pale circle of light put off by a flood light high in a tree. I saw a small woman all dressed in black, her dark hair in a bun, with her arms crossed underneath a shawl. Her face was unusually pale. As we stood mesmerized, she moved one pale arm from under her shawl, and put her hand on her cheek, as if worried.

"She was looking off into the distance, not seeming to notice our group in the street off to the left of her. The rest of the tour group had their backs to her. The hair was standing up on the back of our necks as we stared at this strange figure for what seemed like a few minutes, but probably wasn't.

"Suddenly, she just _faded_ into the shadows!

"My husband and I turned back to the group but no one else seemed to have noticed anything. We didn't know what to think. My first thought was that we'd seen some sort of prop for the ghost walk, and I kept waiting for the guide to say something about the woman in black. What she did talk about next was the woman in white appearing at the foot of a bed in the house next door to the one where we had seen our lady. (The Peyton-Randolph House in Colonial Williamsburg).

"My husband and I did not talk about it until we were back in our car. Our shared opinion was that it had really been very strange, and why would a young woman wearing what appeared to be Civil War-era clothes be standing there at nine o'clock at night? If someone wanted to scare the tourists on the ghost walk, why didn't they do something more to attract attention?

"The scariest thing came out a little later when my husband, who works for the National Imagery and Mapping Agency, and analyzes photos and images from satellites, pointed out that while the evening was breezy and the trees were moving gently, and our guide had to continually push her hair out of her eyes, nothing was moving on the woman. Her hair was in a bun, but her skirt was full and her shawl appeared to be fringed. The breeze was moving nothing on her. I would never have picked up such an inconsistency but my husband has a trained eye.

"We are not assuming that this was anything supernatural, but it has given us pause. We are still talking about it. . . . I know this sounds a little crazy, to have taken place while on a ghost walk, but we are credible people and the occurrence seemed very odd to us. I've never seen anything that struck me so eerily. I am a psychologist by profession and well grounded in science but I do believe there are things we cannot explain. Did we have one of those experiences in Williamsburg? I truly wonder."

(Author's note: The ghost tour people from Maximum Guided Tours say they know nothing of such a woman in black!)

GHOSTLY HANDS STOP A CLOCK

From Sharon Morris of Goochland: "I would like to tell you of my family's ghost story. My aunt and uncle, Howard and Beth Rock, live in my grandfather's old home place in Goochland (near Richmond). It is located on Stokes Station Road in Rock Castle. It seems in years long ago, my (late) grandfather, Charles Boutelle Rock, hated to hear the clocks running. He would always stop them in the house. Well, my aunt and uncle have an old clock hanging in their kitchen, and it has a latch type hook to keep it closed. I have opened it myself and it is very snug and you must push hard to open it. On many occasions my aunt and uncle will be having breakfast and look up to see the clock has been opened and stopped — again and again!

"Also, last summer my mother and stepfather were attending an annual party that my aunt and uncle have at their home. This is an outside affair, and everyone was sitting on the patio. At the top of the patio is a gate that you must enter to get onto the patio. This gate is heavy and it has a spring closure on it. This spring is tight and is hard to open. It was a hot summer evening and no wind was blowing at the time. My mother says she caught a glimpse of the gate slowly opening and then closing very slowly and quietly. Two other people saw this happen. There is no way a wind could open the gate nor would it have closed so quietly. Weird!"

THE PROTRUDING HEAD

From Marc Harvey, Yorktown: "On several occasions I have entered the garden adjacent to the Nelson House here in Yorktown (see "The Ghosts of Williamsburg and Nearby Environs," 1983). Each time I enter, I experience an odd sort of cold feeling. The sensation increases as I near the back wall. Unfortunately, I suffer from vertigo and find myself far too disoriented to remain in the area for long.

"The last time I went into the garden my good friend, Kate, was with me. Surprisingly, I had no feelings of dread, nor did I experience vertigo. However, as we reached a bench at the far wall, I saw a head protruding from a plaque on the wall. It slowly rose to the top of the bench and then disintegrated like a cloud of smoke before our very eyes. Simultaneously, Kate and I ran from the garden and into the street. Once we felt safe in the comfort of my home, we came to discuss exactly what we had seen. To my surprise, she said she saw the exact thing I saw. Immediately, I became dizzy and my vertigo kicked in."

JOIN THE CLUB

From Allison Monette of Crozet: "I am affiliated with the International Ghost Hunters' Society based in Warren, Oregon. I started my own local club called the Central Virginia Ghost Hunters' Society." (Anyone interested may contact Allison at: 1367 Orchard Drive, Crozet, VA, 22932.)

WE'VE BEEN HERE BEFORE!

From Rick Taylor, Stuart's Draft, came a 20-year-old newspaper clipping about 150-year-old house in a community called Ladd, near Staunton. It is located on Virginia Route 632 beside the South River. According to the article at least two families experienced a variety of psychic events in the house in the 1960s and 1970s. Mrs. Jo Ann Griggs, for example, often heard voices upstairs in the house when no one was there. The sounds ranged from soft whispers to occasional "hollering." Each time the premises were searched, but no source was ever found.

Pat and Bonnie Tallent moved into the two-story frame structure after the Griggs. They, too, heard the mysterious sounds, which included: footsteps walking across an upstairs bedroom floor; a "thumping" noise in the living room which caused the family cat's fur to stand straight up; the voices of an unseen man and woman; and kitchen cabinets apparently opening and closing by themselves.

The chilliest encounter occurred one night when Mrs. Tallent awoke to see a strange looking man and woman standing over her bed. She said they were dressed like Dunkards, a sect of 19th century German Baptists who came to this area for religious freedom. The man had blue eyes and a beard. He wore a hat and his coat had no lapels. The woman wore a close-fitting cap or bonnet with straps tied beneath her chin.

Mrs. Tallent had enough presence of mind, under such scary conditions, to ask the couple how they got into the house. The man replied: "We've been here." With this, the apparitional couple turned and walked through a wall at the opposite side of the bed. A door had once been where they passed but had long been sealed up.

One of Rick Taylor's co-workers bought the house in the 1980s. Rick asked him if he had found anything out of the ordinary, and he said, "No, because we had the house exorcized when we moved in."

NOT EXACTLY A GHOST — BUT . . .

D. S. Carr of Montpelier sent a November 1997 clipping from the Richmond Times Dispatch. It was about the unearthing of ten 150-year-old caskets in Roanoke to make way for a new building site. The graves were being moved for reburial in Roanoke County's Mountain View Cemetery.

In the digging, archaeologists found an "elaborate cast-iron coffin that looked as though it encased a mummy." When they broke its seal and looked inside, they were stunned. "There lay the well-preserved body of a man with a thick black beard. He was clad in a blue shirt, and on his chest lay flowers, their leaves still green. Waxy flesh covered his face and hands and his dull yellow teeth were intact." It was believed these were the mortal remains of a man known as Yelverton Oliver, head of one of the Roanoke area's most prominent families a century and a half ago.

A SPIRIT CAPTURED ON FILM?

Nancy Jenkins of Covina, California, sent a, well, strange pho-

tograph. It was taken on the campus of the College of William and Mary in front of the Brafferton Building. In "The Ghosts of Williamsburg," I wrote about the spirit of a young Indian boy who, in the 18th century, was forced to go to a special school and was housed at Brafferton. To escape his sad confinement, he would slip out at night and run through the wee hours of the morning. He ran, it was said, like a deer. The boy died well before his time, and to this day, students at the college swear they see, in the early morning mist, the image of the Indian lad striding across the campus.

Nancy Jenkins took the Ghosts of Williamsburg nightly tour when she came to visit the town a couple of years ago. On the darkened front lawn of the campus, her son took a photo, which, upon development, shows some sort of filmy apparitional image. Nancy and her son are convinced it is the image of the Indian boy.

WHEN OUTDOOR PLUMBING WAS DOWNRIGHT SCARY!

From Bob Bailey, Bristol, Virginia: "My mother was raised in Washington County in the first two decades of the century. Her father, John William Short, was an engineer on the narrow-gage railroad known locally as the 'Virginia Creeper,' and was absent from home sometimes for days at a time. My grandmother, Caroline (Combs) Short, was at home with my aunts, my uncle, and my mother, Georgie, who was five-years-old at the time.

"Of course, there was no indoor plumbing in those mountains in 1908. My grandmother would take the girls outside and let them back up under the house. After the girls had been under there, my grandmother took her turn. My Aunt Nell, about seven then, suddenly screamed at her, 'Run!' My grandmother, momentarily frozen in confusion, stood there until the second scream of 'Run!' then broke from her trance, dashed out from under the house, and hustled the girls into the house.

My Aunt Nell explained to me later that she saw a 'shadowy figure' approaching her mother with his (or its) hands raised as if to encircle her mother's throat. No one ever figured out who or what that figure was."

"AS OF SOMEONE GENTLY RAPPING . . . "

From Valerie Brady-Andersen of Warrenton: "I would like to share a story with you that took place here in Fauquier County. Somewhere between Marshall and Middleburg there is an abandoned house that has quite a bit of folklore to its credit. Apparently some time ago a woman from Pennsylvania was found dead inside the house. The story goes that she was visiting friends in the area and had gone out for a drive. Her car was found in front of the house with the ignition still in the 'on' position. It was ruled that she had a heart attack, odd since she was in her late 30s and had never had any serious health problems. Prior to this, the house had been labeled haunted and her mysterious death only fueled the fire.

"I had my own 'experience' there not more than four or five years ago. I was dating a guy and he took me to see the 'haunted house.' We were parked outside when we both heard a very distinct tapping on the glass of the rear window of the car. I dismissed it as an animal or something explainable, but it was very distinct and I began to feel very strange. We were out of there faster than you could say 'gone!'

"Sometime later we took a different car and tried it again. Same tapping on the rear window. This happened four different times with four different cars. I assure you everybody's hands were accounted for and the tapping (like fingernails) was not coming from the inside of the car.

"Why the rear window? Why tapping? We never saw anything unusual, but we all <u>felt</u> something unusual. I still wonder what it was. It was as if somebody or something was trying to get our attention. The tapping had a desperate or urgent kind of rhythm to it. Who knows?"

CHAPTER 33

The Ghost That Scratches

(Covington)

(Author's note: During a book signing at the Mountain Book Store in Covington in 1997, I met a young lady named Laura Lemons, who said she knew of a friend of hers who had a ghost in her house. Laura gave me her number and said to call. A year or so later, I did. Not only did her friend have a ghost, but Laura, too, told me of an account that surely falls into one of those "how do you explain this" categories.

Seems a number of years ago, back when heavily traveled Todd's Lane in Newport News was still a dirt road, Laura shared a house with a young man named Alan Wyatt. A number of "common" manifestations, if there is such a thing, surfaced in the house. "I would like hear footsteps upstairs when I was alone in the house," Laura recalls. "And when I would get up enough courage to go upstairs and look around, I wouldn't see anything, but the air would be frigid. I would get goose bumps and shiver all over. The lights in the house would go on and off without cause.

"But the thing that got both of us, Alan and me, occurred one day when we went upstairs together. Alan had put a large empty cardboard box in the middle of the room. He was going to pack some things in it. When we walked into that room — and no one else had been in the house, it had been locked — the box was turned upside down and a child's tea set was neatly laid out on top of it. Now Alan had no children and there were no toys in the house. Where did that tea set come from? Had there been a girl who had died in the house years before? I don't know.

"Anyway," Laura concluded, "call my friend, Barbara Fitzgerald, and get her to tell you about her spirit. Barbara lives in an area called Moss Run, which is about eight miles west of Covington. Here is what she said:)

"Our house really isn't old at all. We built it about eight years ago, so I really don't know why 'she' bothers us. It started with the sounds. We would hear someone walking downstairs when we had gone to bed. But each time we looked, there was nothing there. I'll never forget one night. I fell asleep on the couch. When I woke up, I got up and started to go up to the bedroom, when something grabbed my nightgown, and for a few seconds I couldn't move. It scared me to death. There was something right in my face. I could hear and smell breathing!

"It affected all of us in the house at one time or another. I remember one night my mother was sleeping in a guest room, and suddenly she started screaming as loud as she could. I ran to her room. She was hysterical. I asked her what was the matter, and it took quite some time before she calmed down enough to answer me where I could understand her. She said she was lying in bed and something squeezed her around the waist. She said it felt like a man's arm. She would never sleep in that room again.

"Before he died, my father lived in the house for a couple of years, and he said he used to talk to the ghost. This was before the phenomenon occurred to us, and we just laughed at him. But he said our house 'was hainted.' Turned out he was right.

"The activity seemed to center around my teenage daughter, Wanda. A rocking chair would rock in her room with no one in it, or at least no one she could see. Sometimes she could see something making an depression on her bed, like someone lying down. But it was the scratches that worried both of us. Remember the red welts that appeared on that girl in the movie, 'The Exorcist.' It was sort of like that. She would wake up sometimes with long red scratches running all around her waist and down her back. Now we knew she hadn't done this to herself, because she didn't have any fingernails to speak of. She chewed her fingernails down to the core. So how do you explain that?

"The ghost, or whatever it is, also bothered our dog, Hannah. She is a golden retriever. Sometimes she would bark and bark, uncontrollably, while staring at something. And she would snap, like she was trying to bite someone's leg. Then she would jump up in bed and just tremble all over. She definitely sensed something.

"I never did see an apparition or anything," Barbara says, "but once I did see some images dancing on a wall. It looked like shadows of people moving about. But it was mostly sounds. Someone walking — upstairs if we were downstairs and downstairs if we were upstairs, or on the stairs.

"I'm pretty sure it's a female ghost, and I'll tell you why. One night I felt a chilling breeze go past me, and I heard this voice say, 'I am Magma.' It was the most beautiful woman's voice I think I ever heard. Somehow I have a feeling like Magma is an Indian. I think I may have scared <u>her</u> one night! She kept waking me up, and I finally got tired of it. I jumped up and told her to leave me alone and get out of here. She hasn't been as active since then.

"Because this is a relatively new house, people have asked me whether there is an old cemetery or an Indian burial ground around here. I asked some long-time residents, and I did find out that our house is built on a site where an old tavern once stood. Taverns in this part of the state back 100 or 200 years ago were pretty rough places. There were a lot of fights and killings weren't uncommon. I wonder if Magma might have been involved in some sort of tragedy back then. Maybe someday she'll let us know."

'Doc' Pinkard's
Dark Secret

(Roanoke)

hat is it about Doc Pinkard's old house that sets one ill at ease? There is an eerie feeling here at 4347 Franklin Road in Roanoke in a converted house that was built in the 1920s. Today it is an art and antique gallery, but there is an unpleasant aura that seems to linger from bygone days. Customers notice it while browsing in the shop, and some old time neighbors steadfastly refuse to enter the place today, even in the daylight.

Why?

Some of the long-time residents are convinced the house is haunted. And there are a number of reported manifestations seen by several witnesses to back up such a claim. Tom Davis says he first heard about it when he bought the house in 1972. He says an old man walked up to him one day outside the building and told him, "I'm standing as close to it as I'll ever come to it. It's haunted. I've heard the awfullest moaning coming from it." Then the old man walked off.

"Older people down here wouldn't come in here," adds George Ferguson, who bought the art and antique shop from Davis. "They'd stand outside and talk to you, but they wouldn't come inside. They said I was crazy for coming in here." Ferguson says he has heard strange and unaccountable noises inside the house; noises he has investigated and found no rational source for.

Others, too, have had weird experiences in the house-shop.

There is, for example, the instance of the disappearing customer. Davis says that when he ran the business he saw a man enter the gallery many times, but when he would turn to help him, the man was gone. He has no idea where he went. Ferguson has had the same thing happen to him.

Customers speak of unnatural "vibes" coming from the upstairs section, and once a man told Davis he had seen another customer literally evaporate as he stared at him! According to Davis, the man said, "that man didn't move forward or backward. He just went poof." Davis added that the man had goose bumps all up and down his arms. "I don't believe in ghosts," says Davis. "I was probably just not being observant enough, but I don't know how you explain things like that."

Roanoke Times staff writer Christina Nickols wrote a Halloween article on the house in October 1997. For background material, she talked to Loyd Aurbach, director of the Office of Paranormal Investigations in San Francisco. He told her, based on what she had uncovered in her interviews, that the house may not be actually haunted. He said "real" spirits tend to be a "lot more rambunctious" than the passive apparitions that have been sighted at the gallery. Instead, he believed what customers have seen are "imprints" of past events and people that can still be experienced today. "It's more like a recording," he said.

He told Nickols that such imprints often occur in areas with a high magnetic field, and the fact that iron ore was once mined in the region is a clue that such a field could exist.

But if the entities heard and seen are imprints, ghosts, or whatever, who and what are they and why are they there? Old timers in the area all deeply believe they are associated with the first resident of the house, a charismatic man named John Henry Pinkard, and known as "Doc" Pinkard.

In the 1920s and early 1930s, (he died in 1934), Doc operated a flourishing herbal medicine business in the house. Whether or not he was a certified doctor is not known, but it is believed that many Roanoke natives, from all walks of life, sought Pinkard out for treatments. He had a house full of jugs of alcohol, which he mixed with herbs to sell as a remedy for everything from the common cold to asthma. Doc was black, but many of his most frequent "patients" were white. In fact, all of the apparitions seen in the gallery in recent years were white.

Perhaps adding to the eerie atmosphere of the house was the fact that Doc Pinkard was, in a word, well — strange. It is said that he once constructed a fence of hollow ceramic jugs, which, when the wind blew, made an "awesome howl." Some believed he did this to frighten neighborhood children who climbed into his apple trees in season and made off with the fruit. But others think Doc did this just to scare off curious onlookers who tried to peer in his windows and see what kind of concoctions he was brewing.

Who are the apparitions, or imprints, that have remained behind at the old house-turned-gallery? "We hear a lot of footsteps here at times when we know no one else is in the house," says Ferguson. "We always say, 'that's just old Doc Pinkard'." But since the sightings are of "white" visions, not black, this doesn't add up.

Rather, long time residents say, it is likely the house is haunted by former customers of Pinkard. They say some of these people went in the house . . . and never came out! One man told Tom Davis when he bought the house in 1972, that patients who died while being treated by Doc . . . were buried in his basement!

The Ghost Guardian
of the Payroll

(Grayson County)

(Author's note: I like to sign books at craft shows across the commonwealth. Not only do I sell a few books, but I also get some good leads for ghostly legends from the thousands of Virginians who attend these events. At the 1998 Heart of Virginia Festival in Farmville, I was set up in a "literary corner" next to Gary Walker of Roanoke. Gary has written several books about the Civil War, including "The War in Southwest Virginia, 1861-1865," which has received critical acclaim. Gary came in a Confederate gray uniform. In one of his books, "Civil War Tales," he had a chapter about a well-known ghost in Grayson County, down in the "toe" of the state, south of Wytheville. He graciously has allowed me to "retell" it. Gary said he heard this account from members of several families, but some of the specific details are hazy.)

E veryone agreed that the incidents occurred toward the end of the war on Chesterfield Mountain in the county, and that it involved a man and his wife and an army payroll. Gary believes it was a Confederate payroll since the husband and wife were living in the south. Some believed the payroll was in gold, but Gary thinks it more likely was in paper money, since there was little gold left in the southern banks at that time, and soldiers were generally paid with bills. He also contends that it was not the Yankees, but more probably a band of "bushwhackers and deserters" who tried to steal the money. Gary reasons that many deserters fled to the rough mountains along the Virginia-North Carolina border to avoid capture and a firing squad. These desperadoes preyed on civilians, mostly women on rural farms, their husbands off fighting. "Assault, thievery and brutality were their trademarks."

Here is what Gary believes is the "most likely scenario: A young man was in charge of the Confederate payroll and he was somewhere on Chesterfield Mountain when he got word that a gang of deserters was enroute to steal it. He buried the money in a secret hiding place.

The deserters captured him and when he refused to reveal where the payroll was hidden, they began to beat him. Still, he wouldn't talk, figuring if he did tell them where the money was, they would kill him anyway. This only incensed the men and they continued pummelling him. Finally, he lost consciousness, and died.

The men then sat down to think. Surely, they felt, the payroll master wouldn't have buried the money without telling someone else where it was located. Who could a man trust more than his wife? They knew where their victim lived, so they saddled up and rode to his house.

She was an attractive young woman with flowing blonde hair, and all the interviewees agreed she had on a long white dress that day. The pursuers caught her and demanded to know where the payroll had been buried. Whether or not she knew this is in dispute, but in either case, she, too, refused to respond. They told her they had killed her husband and they would kill her, too.

They stripped the dress from her body and tortured her. They slapped her, whipped her with a bull-whip, and burned her on various parts of her body. This time they were more methodical, fearing she would die, as her husband did, before she could reveal the secret. She suffered for hours before she lapsed into "merciful death." Gary wrote: "For their acts (the bushwhackers) received nothing on this earth; but they did reserve a place in the lake of fire that burns forever on the other side.

"The story does not end here . . . From the end of the war until the present day, a woman dressed in white with long flowing blonde hair has been seen many times on the mountain. Most unexplained sightings of ghosts occur at late night or in low light. Ghosts are only seen for a fraction of a second in a haze or shadow; but this woman's appearance is always in full light, and she remains for some time. She never speaks, but locals believe that she wishes to."

Over the past 130 years, she has approached a number of people on the mountain. Gary says that although many have seen her, most were reluctant to talk about the experience, and those few who would, asked to remain anonymous. One man told Gary he had lived in the area all of his life and had heard the stories about the Lady in White since his youth. He said one day he was walking up the mountain following an old logging road. He then walked into the woods and sat down. He was dressed in brown clothing and shielded himself with underbrush. He was there to hunt squirrels.

As if from nowhere, he saw a woman walking on the logging road. She had long blonde hair and wore a white dress. He said, "I knew who she was right away. I knew she could not see me from the road because I was well hidden in the trees." She walked up the road until she was exactly parallel with the hunter. She turned from the road and started up the hill toward him. She looked the hunter straight in the eye. The man was frozen with fear. He wasn't sure if she was walking or floating, but she didn't appear to be a translucent figure, she looked like a flesh and blood woman.

As she drew close, she made no sound, although branches, twigs and dried leaves covered the ground. When she was within 10 feet of the terrified hunter, he leaped up from where he had been sitting and ran as fast as he could. He ran until he was out of breath. When he finally looked back, she was not there.

Gary said a more recent witness was a woman on the mountain who was washing dishes when she looked through the kitchen window toward the garden. She saw the same vision, and asked herself, 'what's that woman doing in the garden?' She went out the back door, and said the woman in the white dress was staring directly into her eyes. She added that there was "something unnatural" about her eyes which frightened her and she raced back into the house. She again looked out the window, but the figure had vanished. She knew the woman couldn't have run out of sight because she could see far across the fields. The vision had simply just disappeared.

Another hunter encountered the entity in a clearing in the forest. He said she was lying on the ground and her blonde hair was "radiating out from her head in an almost circular pattern." She stared directly into his eyes. Although he had a rifle in his hands, he also ran away as fast as he could.

More recently, Gary notes, a boy and his girl friend drove to a secluded spot on the mountain, and "from out of nowhere, a woman with blonde hair and a white dress rode past the car on a fast-moving horse. Then the woman turned around and stopped directly in front of the car. She stared into the boy's eyes. He immediately reached for his keys to start the car, but before he could move an inch, the woman had dematerialized.

Gary says the locals at Jim Lloyd's barber shop in Rural Retreat, Virginia, also tell of another startling incident. They said a country musical band from Taylor Valley drove into the mountains one day to take some publicity photos in a natural setting. They used trees, undergrowth and streams as background. While photographing they saw nothing out of the ordinary. Yet when the pictures were developed, on one of them there was a lady in white, with long blonde hair sitting near the band beside a stream!

Gary says most of the witnesses agree that they believe the woman is the wife of the payroll master who has come back to, at last, relinquish her long-held secret of where the money is buried. Gary added a postscript: "There are those who say that some people's souls get stuck between Heaven and Hell. Because they have something they must accomplish on this earth, something that they didn't accomplish while alive, they must remain until their destiny is fulfilled.

"If that is so, let us hope that her next appearance will be her last: that someone will ask 'where is the money?' so this woman can at last find peace in death."

A SECOND 'LADY IN WHITE'
(Albemarle County)

(Author's note: There is a very similar account of a ghost lady dressed in white who confronted a mountain man in the dawning years of the 20th century in western Albemarle County. The legend was recorded by oral historian George Foss in 1941. He interviewed a man named Robert Shiflett in Brown's Cove, Virginia, who said he had heard it from an uncle when he was a child. I estimate the time frame to be about 1915.)

"Many folks from this side of the mountain went over in season to work for the big farmers in the valley. These mountain people used to go over into the valley in the fall of that year at harvest time in late summer to harvest the wheat. They'd go back in autumn to harvest the corn crops. Everything was done by hand in those days, that is, as far as cuttin' corn. And then after the corn was in, they would cut wood for the winter for these big farmers over there.

"And so, as my uncle related, he had started out — in those days you didn't work by the clock, you worked by the sun — he started out just before daylight so he could get to his work. He had started that morning up the hollow, up to the woods, a hollow called Lewis's Run. Most hollows had a stream in them; a stream was a run. And he said it was a dreary looking, spooky looking place. And he said the farther he got, the worse he felt. He felt cold chills.

"And he said he looked up the hollow and he saw a woman in old-time attire like his mother used to wear. And he said he didn't think anyone lived up there, so he asked himself, 'well, why would a woman be way up in this mountain this early in the morning, a wild looking place like this.'

"He said he kept walking and she kept coming. And said when she got near him the clothes in particular didn't look natural, and he noticed she never batted an eye, she never blinked an eye just like she was looking through him and walked right by him and said he felt a chill and turned around. . . . There was nobody there.

"And he said he went on up until he got to a good place to cut the wood and said the more he worked, the more apprehension he felt about being up there, and he started out. And said when he got back to the same self-same spot that he had met this woman coming down, he saw her coming back again. And he said his heart stood still then. And he had always heard, if you were confronted with any-thing supernatural or anyone from the grave, to ask them in the name of the Lord what they wanted.

"And he said when she got up in front of him that time, she didn't attempt to pass. She stopped right in front of him. And said it just para-lyzed him, everything but his tongue, and he said he did manage to get out, 'What in the name of the Lord do you want?' And he said she pointed to a cliff on another mountain and said, 'You see those rocks over there?' She said, "For 100 years my bones been laying in a cave under those rocks. . . I was murdered 100 years ago, and my body was hid there, and if you will go get my bones and give them a Christian burial you'll be greatly rewarded for it.

"And he said she just disappeared.

"He come out and he told these people in the community what he thought he saw, and he tried to get someone to go with him, and they laughed him to scorn. Naturally, the experience he'd had the first time had unnerved him enough he wasn't going to take a chance of meeting her again in a remote place, so he didn't go.

"But I heard him swear in my father's house that that was absolutely true."

C H A P T E R   3 6

The Photogenic Wraith at the Bedrock Inn

(Pounding Mill)

(Author's note: In February 1997, I received a letter from a lady named Sloane Hunter of Pounding Mill, Virginia. I have to confess I had no idea where this was. I looked it up. It's in Tazewell County in the southwestern part of the commonwealth, a few miles below the town of Tazewell, and 20-plus miles north of Abingdon and Marion. "I have an inn about 45 minutes from Abingdon (true, because the roads are very mountainous) on route 19-460," Sloane wrote. "It is unique in that it is my husband's family's home and also it is in their rock quarry." Intriguing. "This part of Virginia has been somewhat overlooked," she continued, "and I would like to invite you to this area with accommodations at the Bedrock Inn, in hopes that you will include us in your next publication. If you are interested in our ghost story, please contact us." Very intriguing. "PS - a picture of our ghost is enclosed." Extremely intriguing! How could I resist.

nd so it was, when I was invited to speak at the Marion Library in August 1998, I decided to make a swing through that part of the country and include an overnight stop at Sloane's inn. I did some research and found that there may in fact be more than one haunt in Pounding Mill. Several years ago a native of the area, Charlotte Deskins told of a psychic experience she had. "Our region," she said, "tends to

Bedrock Inn

have a lot of supernatural events connected to it. The real magic lies in the mountains of Virginia."

Charlotte said she and her family moved into a house that was "a pretty one with a long, high porch, a deep, cool basement, and a stand of fruit trees nearby." She was then 12-years-old. "We had only been living there a short while when I was awakened one morning by the sound of breakfast being prepared," she noted. "A kitchen door slammed. Dishes were being rattled in the cupboard as if someone were setting the table. There was the familiar creak of the oven door, and then the sounds and smells of bacon frying and coffee brewing. Yet it was not yet light outside my bedroom window."

Charlotte donned her robe and went down to the kitchen. It was dark, and no one was there. "The kitchen stood silent. No food was cooking and all the dishes rested quietly on the shelves." She ran to her parents' room to tell them about it. This phenomenon occurred a number of times over the next few months. "Oddly enough, none of us were afraid. Being brought up in a spiritual mountain family, we knew there was little to fear from such a thing. However, it soon became annoying, for we were all being awakened."

One morning Charlotte's father had had enough. "When the

pre-dawn breakfast preparations began," she said, "he leapt out of bed and ran into the kitchen. 'Whoever you are, go away!' he shouted. 'You don't live here anymore! We do, and we're tired of getting up every morning at daybreak. So get out and leave us alone!'

"My father's temper must have gotten the best of that ghost, for it never returned. Perhaps it found a more pleasant place in which to have an early breakfast."

And now, on to Sloane Hunter's spirit.)

Background on the Bedrock Inn: The grandfather of Sloane's husband, (Mike is her husband) came to the Pounding Mill area in 1913 to direct work in the huge rock quarry which fronts route 19. This was one of only three large quarries in the state at the time.

The rock is crushed into stone and used as road beds and along railroad tracks. The grandfather, C. M. Hunter, also built a house next to the quarry (hence the name Bedrock Inn). After C. M. Hunter and his wife, Rebecca, died, the house stood vacant for about 20 years.

In the early 1980s, after Sloane and Mike were married, they began looking for a house near the quarry, where Mike continued the family efforts at the quarry. They looked at the old house Mike's grandfather had built and although it was in a run down condition, Sloane fell in love with it. They began extensive renovations. "After we began the restorations process," Sloane says, smiling, "there were many times when we felt that we would have been better off to have bulldozed the place and started over from square one. In retrospect, however, I know that we did the right thing in restoring the old home. There are some things in life that have meaning beyond boards and nails and bricks and mortar. Retaining the presence and aura of this old home has meant more to Mike and his sons than most people would dare to understand. I think the peg floors and pine board walls were cut from trees on the place and milled right on the site.

"Although I don't know how to accurately describe the difference in an old dwelling versus a new one, I do feel that maybe character and strength built in an old house resembles the character and backbone of the type of people it took to settle and develop this wonderful part of our country. Over time, strength and the proper structure reveal itself in buildings, and, more importantly, in people. This strength and this heritage is enjoyed now by a fourth generation of Hunters who have lived in this house."

Sometime later, Sloane and Mike decided to make the home

into an inn. "We offer an elegant setting for private parties, business conferences, or just a peaceful weekend getaway for those who do not have time to travel very far," Sloane says, adding that future plans could include a restaurant.

"I have always believed that houses are like people in the sense that most are worth saving. It is a truly wonderful feeling to know that you have brought laughter, love, and living back to a broken dwelling, and that this Pounding Mill house in particular will be standing another 80 years at least. We hope the Bedrock Inn will represent the perfect setting to nurture your spirit and that you will leave feeling refreshed and at peace with the world."

(Author's note: I arrived at the inn at about 4 p.m. on Friday, July 31, 1998, after driving through the mountains from Big Stone Gap. No one was home at the time but there was a note to come on inside. I did. I sat down in the large, comfortable den and picked up a book on the history of Tazewell County. As I have said many times before, I have never experienced any ghostly manifestations, but I must admit, as I sat there alone, I heard some inexplicable sounds coming from an adjacent bedroom. At first I thought someone may have sneaked in the back of the house and was playing a trick on me. I got up and went to look. There was no one there. I sat back down, and heard the noises again. I don't know what was causing them. I did feel a little funny. Pretty soon, Judy Shelton, the Hunters' inn keeper showed up, and later Sloane and Mike arrived.)

"This is a very spooky place at night," Judy offered. "It's so isolated, off the road. There are no other houses around." She is a native of Doran, in Baker Hollow, in the county, about 25 minutes away. She has been at Bedrock for about two years. What has she experienced herself? "Things get moved around. You know, stuff will be in different places from where I put it. The lady who was here before me said she heard things, especially in the attic. I once heard a baby crying when there were no infants in the house." Anything else? "I was in the kitchen one day," Judy continues, "when something or someone breezed by me. I was alone in the place. And sometimes when I am sitting in the den I get the feeling that someone is behind me. So one day, out of frustration, I just said, 'If you're here, I'm here, too, and I've got a job to do. I know that may sound silly, but . . .

"I like this place, but I've never stayed here at night, and I'm not going to stay here at night by myself!"

When Sloane came in, she told me that she personally has not experienced any strange happenings other than one. "We have four dogs and we give them water in number 10 wash tubs," she said. Sometimes, within a few minutes, all the water will be gone, and we know the dogs couldn't have drank it. We just say the ghost must be thirsty today."

Sloane believes the ghost at Bedrock may well be Rebecca Hunter, Mike's grandmother. "She loved this house, and I feel her soul just couldn't release from it. Before she died, she had crippling arthritis and they gave her heavy doses of morphine. I haven't heard her in the house, but Mike and some of our guests have." She died in 1962.

Mike has experienced her presence. "Back about 25 years ago, long before I was married, we used to bring dates here and party," he says. "Late at night while we would be in the den, we would hear footsteps coming down the long hallway from the back of the house right up to the den. Then they would stop. We never did see anything. There was nothing unfriendly about it, but it still was a strange thing. Now, when Sloane isn't here and I'm by myself, I bring in the Labs to be with me. I have heard that same sound, all in the original part of the house, many times.

One of the long-time guests at the inn, Dennis DePriest, also has been "visited" by the ghost. One night he carefully folded his clothes and left them in neat piles on his bed. Later, when he reen-

Ghostly image in the den at the Bedrock Inn

tered his room, the clothes were strewn all over the floor. It gave him a chill.

And, finally, there is the photograph. Sloane says a newspaper photographer came about three years ago to do an article on the new bed and breakfast. He took a few shots in the den. When his pictures were developed there is a large apparitional figure looming in the center of one photo before a roaring fire. It appears even though the Hunters had an informal exorcism, a "house blessing," performed in 1990. No one has a rational explanation for the appearance of the figure.

(Author's footnote: I slept in the bedroom, number four, nearest the end of the hall and the den. I listened carefully, but I did not hear any phantom footsteps. But I was tired and maybe the spirit realized this and tread very lightly that evening!)

CHAPTER 37

The Haunting Legend of Lovers' Leap

(Southwest Virginia)

he eminent 19th century orator and states-
man, William Jennings Bryan, called it "The
Eighth Wonder of the World." It was formed more than a million
years ago when water dissolved limestone and bedrock. It is a
giant passageway carved over the millenia by the running waters
of Stock Creek through Purcell Ridge in the Allegheny mountains.
This is Virginia's famous Natural Tunnel. It is located in Scott
County in the extreme "toe" of the commonwealth — approximately 350 miles southwest of Richmond, 40 miles west of
Abingdon, and 12 miles west of Estillville. This marvel of nature,
through which freight and coal trains have passed for most of the
past century, is 100 to 300 feet high and 900 feet long.

Writing about the tunnel in 1832, a Lt. Colonel Long of the U.S.
Army, said: "To form an adequate idea of this remarkable and truly
sublime object, we have only to imagine the creek, to which it gives
a passage, meandering through a deep narrow valley, here and
there bounded on both sides by walls rising to the height of two or
three hundred feet above the stream; and that a portion of one of
these chasms, instead of presenting an open thorough cut from the
summit to the base of the high grounds, is intercepted by a continuous unbroken ridge more than 300 feet high, extending entirely
across the valley, and perforated transversely at its base, after the
manner of an artificial tunnel, and thus affording a spacious subterranean channel for the passage of the stream.

"The entrance to the natural tunnel, on the upper side of the ridge, is imposing and picturesque, in a high degree; but on the lower side, the grandeur of the scene is greatly heightened by the superior magnitude of the cliffs, which exceed in loftiness, and which rise perpendicularly — and in some instances in an impending manner — more than 300 feet; and by which the entrance on this side is almost environed, as it were, by an amphitheater of rude and frightful precipices.

"The width of the tunnel varies from 50 to 150 feet; its course is that of a continuous curve, resembling the letter S — first winding to the right as we enter on the upper side, then to the left, again to the right, and then again to the left. Such is its peculiar form, that an observer standing at a point about midway of its subterranean course, is completely excluded from a view of either entrance."

Historian Henry Howe, in his classic 1845 book, "Historical Collections of Virginia," writes: "In the view of the lower entrance to the Natural Tunnel, there is represented an occurrence which took place many years since. At this point the deep gorge, through which the creek passes, is bounded on three sides by a perpendicular wall of rock over 300 feet in height, the fourth side being open to allow the passage of the creek after leaving the mouth of the tunnel.

"The rocks at this place have several small caves, or fissures, in which the nitrous earth from which saltpeter is extracted has been found. One or more of these are in the sides of the tunnel itself. A gentleman informed us that the first time he visited the tunnel, some persons were inside extracting saltpeter, and that the smoke belching forth from its mouth and curling up the gorge, enhanced the natural gloom and hideousness of the scene."

Howe also told of a daring, and hair-raising feat attempted at the site by a man named George Dotson. He was lowered from a 300 foot cliff by a rope to an open cavern that had never before been explored. Howe: "The rope not being sufficiently long, the last length, which was tied around his waist, was made of the bark of leatherwood. When down to the level of the fissure, he was still 12 or 14 feet from it horizontally, being thrown so by the overhanging of the wall of rock. With a long pole, to which was attached a hook, he attempted to pull himself to the fissure. He had nearly succeeded, when the hook slipped, and he swung out into the middle of the ravine, pendulum-like, on a rope of perhaps 150 feet in length. Returning on his fearful vibration, he but managed to ward himself off with his pole from being dashed against the rock, when away he swung again. One of his companions stationed on the opposite side of the ravine to give directions, instinctively drew back, for it appeared to him that he was slung at him across the abyss. At length the vibration ceased.

"At that juncture Dotson heard something crack above his head; he looked, and saw that a strand of his bark rope had parted. Grasping, with both hands, the rope immediately above the spot, he cried out hastily "Pull! for _____ sake pull!' On reaching the top he fainted.

"On another occasion, the bark rope being replaced by a hempen one, he went down again and explored the cave. His only reward was the satisfaction of his curiosity. The hole extended only a few feet."

It is little wonder thus that legends seem to abound in and around Natural Tunnel. The most prevalent of these, passed down generation to generation for the past two or three centuries, is known simply as Lover's Leap. There are places all over the world called by this name, but oldtimers in the area insist this was the original one. It predates the arrival of Virginia pioneers in the 18th century by a considerable period of time.

It was then that Sac and Fox Indians lived within the shadows of the tunnel and the cliffs surrounding it. Their chief was called Black Hawk. He had a daughter named Winnoa. From childhood, she had adored a young boy known as Swift-Foot, as he had her. They were inseparable, but often their meetings from an early age through their teens had to be made in secret. For some unaccountable reason, Black Hawk despised the boy, and separated the couple whenever he could.

In time, Swift-Foot became a strapping and outstanding brave, and Winnoa blossomed into a beautiful young woman. They vowed their love for each other. Still, although Swift-Foot became an honored hunter and warrior, the chief would not relent. The tribal custom for a young man to wed a chosen mate was for him to give a worthy present to the girl's father. Swift-Foot had caught a beautiful black stallion which he knew Black Hawk had long admired. He presented the horse to the chief, but Black Hawk would not accept it. Swift-Foot was despondent. He felt if he could not marry Winnoa he would never wed.

In his distraught state, he joined some other braves who went out on a warring party to drive off some Cree Indians who had invaded their hunting grounds. As they camped one night, the Crees attacked, outnumbering the braves by four to one. Several of Swift-Foot's companions were killed, but a few escaped. Swift-Foot got away but broke his leg as he leaped from a ledge. His prized horse had been stolen. He hid himself beneath a rock outcropping.

Swift-Foot had a pet wolf which he had raised when it was a pup. It was well trained, and he directed it to go back to his village for help. A day or two later, as he lapsed in and out of consciousness, Winnoa arrived and they managed to get back home.

While recuperating, Swift-Foot's mother told him the reason Black Hawk hated him and refused his plea to marry Winnoa. She said that when she had been a young squaw Black Hawk had asked her father's permission to marry her, but he was denied. He had nursed the grudge ever since.

Nevertheless, once healed, Swift-Foot returned to reason with Black Hawk. He was refused again, vehemently. He stalked off. Winnoa followed him. He climbed straight up to the highest cliff near the entrance to the tunnel, where they had often played together as children.

He looked down at the stream flowing more than 100 feet below. Before his beloved could reach him, he leaped. When Winnoa reached the peak, without hesitation, she, too, jumped to her death. And so, the original legend of Lover's Leap was created.

It has some ghostly overtones. There are those in this colorful region who swear that if you are at the bottom of the cliff on certain still evenings at dusk, you can sometimes see the silhouettes of first one, then two shadowy figures plunging in rapid succession from the top of the cliff into the surging waters of the creek far below! There are no screams, just silence, eerie silence.

Bountiful Legends in Big Stone Gap

(Wise County)

(Author's note: In past volumes in this series on Virginia ghosts, I have drawn extensively on the haunting stories uncovered by Works Progress Administration writers who fanned out in the hills and hollows of Southwest Virginia in the 1930s and 1940s recording oral histories of area folklore. (Another segment of these colorful historic heirlooms is included in this book.) In re-reviewing this material, it became evident that a large percentage of these stories originated in Wise County, far down in the "toe" of the commonwealth in the heart of the Appalachian Mountains.

Here lie the towns of Big Stone Gap, Norton, Wise, Appalachia, Coeburn, and Pound. Here lie some of the most legendary characters of Virginiana:

* The notorious "Red Fox of the Cumberlands," Dr. Marshall Taylor, preacher, medicine man, lawman, and murderer, who was hanged for his part in one of the most infamous ambushes in American history. (See "The Ghosts of Virginia, Volume I.")

* John Fox, Jr., the brilliant, Harvard-educated author who wrote so poignantly about mountain life in this part of the state, including his classic, "The Trail of the Lonesome Pine."

* James Taylor Adams, the prolific author of hundreds of folklorian articles on the mountain people and their customs.

Among the ghost tales from this region are such intriguing gems as: "The Cryin' Baby of Big Stone Gap;" "The Singin' Rocks of Highway 23;" "The Haunted Horseshoes;" "The Man They

Killed Twice;" "Chased by a Dead Horse;" and "The Cat that Wouldn't Stay Dead."

hus, when I was invited to speak at the Marion, Virginia, Library in the summer of 1998, I accepted immediately, because it would give me a chance to tour through the southwest part of the state and to retrace the sites in Wise County that Fox, Adams and others so eloquently wrote about so many years ago.

It was a fantastic trip. To get to Wise County, I drove up highway 23 and first visited Natural Tunnel State Park. I toured the Southwest Virginia Museum, the John Fox, Jr., Museum, the Meador Coal Museum, and other sites. I interviewed Ramond Burgin, a professor at Mountain Empire Community College and an expert on regional folklore. I talked with several other county residents who graciously shared their memories and recollections with me.

Interestingly, I found that a lot of the traditions of ghost lore recorded by the WPA writers six decades ago had been lost in time, and few current citizens remembered them. I did, however, find some new versions, but the problem was they more or less were just "snippets" of lore. Details were difficult to track down. Nevertheless, herewith is a sampling of what I found.)

Karen Newton, who works at the Southwest Virginia Museum, tells of a long-standing supernatural legend at a place called Watertank Curve near the old Stonega Coal Camp, about four miles outside the village of Appalachia. "When you go into the hollow there," she relates, "there is a real bad curve near where the watertank is. The story goes that about 50 or 60 years ago a coal truck came around the curve and struck a young girl standing in the road, killing her. On dark nights, as you round the curve, her apparition jumps out in front of your vehicle. A number of people have said this has happened to them, including my uncle. He said he rounded the curve one night and there was the girl right in front of him. He hit her, or at least he thought he did. He stopped his car and got out, but there was no one there!"

This seems to be a popular story with several variations. According to professor Ramond Burgin there is another dangerous stretch of road, called "Dead Man's Curve," near Dunbar between Appalachia and Norton. It is said that it was here, in the 1920s, that a man and a woman were involved in a terrible auto accident on a rainy, foggy night. The woman was decapitated. Some long-timers in the area have said that on certain stormy nights, motorists rounding this curve have seen, in their rear-view mirrors, the wispy image of a headless woman sitting in the back seat. As they near town, the figure disappears.

A student in Burgin's folklore class told him about an incident that occurred late in the 19th century at High Knob, near Norton. It was when the railroad was coming through the area building tracks during the coal boom. They had rights to go through the property of a feisty mountaineer, but everytime they approached, he fended them off with his rifle, declaring they would never come that way as long as he was alive. Under mysterious circumstances, his house burned down one night with him in it. The railroad came through. But for years afterward, as the trains came to this patch of tracks, engineers, firemen, and others swore they saw the apparition of the old man cursing and waving his rifle at them.

Burgin tells of an old cabin on Cliff Mountain, near Duffield, built on the site of an ancient battle between warring Indians two or three centuries ago. "People spending the night there have had their sleep disturbed by the sound of tom-toms and the rhythmic thump of dancing feet," he says. And outside the cabin, a phantom Indian has been sighted hurling a ghostly tomahawk and then galloping down the ridge. Burgin adds that this particular cabin "is also home to an invisible 'knocking spirit,' or poltergeist, with a really terrible disposition. It has been said to throw large stones from the hearth and fireplace at intruders, most of whom follow the spirit's suggestion and get out rapidly."

THE TRAIL OF THE LONESOME PINE

hen John Fox, Jr., wrote "The Trail of the Lonesome Pine," early in the 20th century, he made Big Stone Gap and the surrounding mountainous area famous. His novel about love between a native country girl and a "furriner" who came in during the coal boom; feuding families; and colorful characters — was based, in part, on fact. The central roles in his book — those of June Tolliver, Devil John Tolliver, and the Red Fox — were drawn from real people. Devil John Tolliver was actually a man called Devil John Wright, whom Fox had known. The Red Fox was Dr. Marshall Taylor. And June Tolliver, daughter of Devil John Tolliver, was in reality a teenage girl named

Elizabeth Morris.

In the book, the young man who came to the coal fields (actually a geologist from Boston named Jimmy Hodge) finds June Tolliver, they fall in love, and live happily ever after. Fact: Hodge did meet the real Elizabeth Morris who was described as being "appealing, intelligent and attractive," and he really did persuade her parents to let her come to town (Big Stone Gap), stay in a boarding house, and get an education. But the real June Tolliver (Elizabeth) didn't fall in love, etc. She got terribly homesick and went back to her mountain home after three months in the town.

The house she stayed in is now called the Tolliver House (formerly the Duff House.) It is in the downtown area next to the Lone Pine Playhouse, where, during the summer months, Fox's novel is staged as an outdoor drama.

There is some evidence that the Tolliver House may be haunted by a feminine ghost. Whether or not it is June Tolliver/Elizabeth Morris is not known. In 1964, a woman named Becky Arnott, of Kingsport, Tennessee, and her brother, Dr. Nick Botts, were visiting Big Stone Gap. Botts took a photo of the Tolliver House, although it was locked and closed to the public that day. There was no one inside.

After the film was developed, Botts showed the photos to his mother. She pointed out that there appeared to be a woman standing in an upstairs window holding something in her hands. Botts had the picture blown up. The figure remained in the window. Becky Arnott did some research and learned that there was a persistent rumor about the house. One of the families who previously lived there said they had seen the apparition of a woman wearing a long gown and carrying a candle, come out of an upstairs closet and walk over to the window. Becky declared, in a subsequent newspaper article, that "this ghost picture is authentic."

And then, there is the John Fox, Jr. Home in the center of Big Stone Gap. Fox was born in Stony Point, Kentucky, in December 1862, and his family moved to Big Stone Gap when he was a young man. He did much of his writing in this rambling big house, which today is a museum open to the public. In all, he published a dozen or so novels and more than 500 short stories. Conversant in several languages including Latin, Greek, French, Italian, and English, Fox was equally comfortable in the high society circles of New York City or in the backwoods, dirt floor log cabins of Virginia mountaineers. His own lifestyle was as adventuresome, or more so as was that of the charismatic heroes and villains he wrote about. Fox died in 1919 of pneumonia at the age of 56.

Two of his sisters lived in the house for a number of years after that. Today the house, built in 1888, is a Virginia Historical Landmark, and is filled with furnishings and mementoes of the family. Folklorist Ramond Burgin says that a few years ago when workmen were making repairs on the building they reported hearing "phantom footsteps" when no one else was around. Burgin wonders if John Fox, Jr., the man who wrote about so many legends and traditions in the history of southwestern Virginia, still lingers along the halls and rooms of the old house he loved so well in life.

(Author's note: Of course, no section about ghosts in southwest Virginia would be complete without a legend or two concerning haunted coal mines, since such mines so dominated the area in the late 19th and early 20th centuries. And there were so many tragedies associated with such dangerous work. While on my trip through Big Stone Gap and the surrounding area, I learned of a couple of such traditions.)

One involved a mine in Harlan, Kentucky, just across the state line. In 1931 a terrible explosion ripped through the underground tunnels killing five men and creating such rubble that the mine was closed for more than a decade. It was reopened during the second World War when coal was in such short supply. Almost immediately, workers reported seeing the apparitional images of the dead miners. One man, working in a side tunnel, came running out of the mine one day after seeing a "shadowy figure" carrying an "old fashioned lamp."

He said the figure had only "empty sockets where his eyes should have been!"

Others had similar experiences. One day two miners were outside eating their lunches when they saw "something shadow-like" come out of the main tunnel entrance. It appeared to be the transparent image of a man, so real looking that they invited him to sit down with them. He vanished in thin air.

Several miners, in fact, were so numbed by such encounters that they quit their jobs.

A GHOSTLY WARNING SYSTEM

he second occurrence, also in the shadows of the surrounding Cumberland Mountains, took place in 1914 when three men died during a tunnel cave-in. After this accident this particular shaft was sealed off. Several nights later some men were working in an adjoining chamber when, suddenly, three balls of pale light appeared in front of them, moving up and down. There was no rational explanation for the phenomenon, but the miners, most of whom were superstitious by nature anyway, read it as a bad omen. They scurried out of the mine. No sooner had they cleared the area when the entire roof in that section collapsed!

Several weeks later, a crew started to go down into a shaft on an elevator. The three strange lights appeared again and darted about the surprised workers. By now the word had spread about this manifestation and all the men got off the elevator immediately. Just as they exited, the elevator plunged several hundred feet to the bottom of the shaft!

The lights were seen a number of other times. Once, a miner was in an abandoned tunnel when the entrance gave way, filling the exit with debris. There seemed to be no way out and the man's oxygen was running dangerously low, when the three lights appeared and began "dancing off one of the walls." The man looked there and found a small crevice through which he crawled to safety via an adjacent tunnel.

Another time, a foreman was inspecting a section of steel rails on which the coal cars ran. The three lights materialized and "directed" him to one side of the track. Just as he stepped aside to that spot, a runaway coal car that had broken loose zipped past him.

It was documented — officials kept records — that the lights appeared exactly 20 times over the period from 1914 to 1934, and each time one or more lives were saved. The mystery was never satisfactorily explained.

CHAPTER 39

A Winged Ghostly Revenge?

(Wise County)

I n the late 1800s in the mountains of south-west Virginia, there were three notorious gunmen who compare favorably (or rather unfavorably) with such infamous outlaws of the old west at Jesse James, Billy the Kid, and Doc Holiday. They included: the legendary Marshall (Doc) Taylor, perhaps most noted for his ambush at Killing Rock, near Pound, Virginia, in which he and his henchmen shot several members of the moonshining Mullins family; and Devil John Wright, whom author John Fox, Jr., portrayed as "Devil John Tolliver" in his classic book, "The Trail of the Lonesome Pine." Wright was credited with having killed 27 men. How many of these were murdered is not known.

The third member of this trio of flamboyant desperadoes was a man named Talton Hall, described by one writer as a "clansman, feudist, and killer." The estimates on how many men Hall shot and killed during his years in the hills ranged from eight or ten, all the way up to 99. (The former figures are more likely closer to the truth.)

All three men were feared far and wide in the lawless years in the Cumberland area in the years between the end of the Civil War and the beginning of the 20th century. In the words of historian Roy Sturgill, Taylor, Wright and Hall, "inaugurated a rein of terror in the mountains." Murders were the daily amusement of the gang, and although they were frequently arrested, the terror of which they inspired assured their acquittal when brought to trial.

Hall may have presented the most frightening image. According to writer Henry Scalf, Hall, after shooting one of his victims: "climbed a fence, flapped his arms and crowed like a rooster, and shouted, 'After this I'm going to be called Bad Talt Hall'!" To emphasize how terrifying Hall's reputation became, Sturgill reported: "Hall was acquitted of the cold blooded murder of Henry Maggard in 1866. He killed Don Pridemore in 1875 and was acquitted; a cowardly jury acquitted him of Mat Baker's murder in 1881, and he went free when he murdered his brother-in-law, Henry Houk, in 1883. In 1885 he killed his cousin, Mark Hall, and laughed at the sheriff, who tried to arrest him."

On July 25, 1891, Hall committed what has been described as "one of the most atrocious murders ever perpetrated in this section." On that day Enos Hylton, a special policeman from Norton, had apprehended "a desperate character of the region" named Miles Bates for stealing a watch and pistol. As Hylton was bringing the prisoner in, Hall came out of the woods and ordered Bates' release. Hylton refused. Hall then pulled out his 38 caliber pistol and shot him, killing him instantly.

There are at least two strong theories which have persisted through the years that Hall had planned to slay Hylton for reasons other than releasing Bates. One was that Hall had fallen in love with a woman married to a man named Sayler. By coincidence, the woman happened to be Hylton's sister-in-law. When Sayler was murdered soonafter Hall had courted his wife, everyone believed Hall was the assassin. Hylton had openly sworn that he would kill the man who had shot his brother-in-law, and Hall had undoubtedly heard this.

The second theory, also often mentioned, was that lawman Hylton had become too much of a hindrance to the outlaws and bootleggers in the area, and a price was put on his head. Perhaps Hall collected such a bounty, for when he was apprehended for killing Hylton, a few months later he had several hundred dollars on him.

Hall was finally convicted and was hanged in Wise County on September 2, 1892. A short time before the execution, Talt Hall gave an interview to a newspaper correspondent, in which he revealed a curious psychic experience he said that had haunted him from the time he shot Hylton. Here is what Hall said:

"After killing Hylton, I fled to the woods and traveled through the wilderness in the direction of Coeburn, brooding over the course I should pursue to get away. I was surrounded and overshadowed by a thousand little birds that screamed incessantly and fluttered about me, and darted at my hands and face with their sharp bills, trying to peck my eyes out. It was with great difficulty that I fought them away with a bush, for they seemed eager to do me harm.

"The singing and chirping of these birds rang in my ears for several days. After I fled to Memphis, and took up my abode in that city, the sounds ceased to haunt me, until a few days before my arrest, when I again began to hear the birds as distinctly as when they attacked me in the woods of Wise County. I heard nothing more of them, and had quite forgotten the cruel sound until quite recently when they began again, and are now annoying me greatly."

Hall, the reporter said, was convinced this phenomenon was a "punishment" for the crime he had committed.

CHAPTER 40

More 'Treasures' From the James Adams Collection

(Southwest Virginia)

(Author's note: In volumes II, III, and IV of this series on Virginia ghosts, I included selections from what is known as the James Taylor Adams collection. During the Great Depression, the Works Progress Administration funded a program whereby writers were sent out into the mountains and valleys, hills and hollows of rural areas in the commonwealth to collect oral histories on Virginia folklore. One of the most prolific chroniclers was a man named James Taylor Adams. Among his papers are more than 200 ghost legends, dating back a century and more. Taylor and others conducted the interviews. These "new" accounts are part of our rich heritage, and are reprinted here with the permission and courtesy of Clinch Valley College and the Blue Ridge Institute.)

THE SPECTRAL RETURN OF COUSIN OLIVER

Mrs. Caroline Peters of Norton, Virginia, interviewed by Emory Hamilton, October 2, 1940.

"hen John Shepherd lived on the High Knob I used to go up there sometimes and every time anything would get wrong with any of them they'd send after me. One time they sent after me when one of their children was sick. I went and the child had pneumonia. . . Me and Mary (John's wife) went out in the yard. It was pretty and the moon was shining. All at once a man come up beside me and started whispering in my ear, 'pssssssssst.' I never could understand what he was saying. It just sounded like somebody whispering, 'pssssssssst.' He had on black shoes and I could see the crease in his pants. He went away and in a few seconds he come back again. I hit the porch and went in the house as hard as I could go. Mary never did see it. I saw it again in the hall as I went in. . .

"I never thought of a haunt when I first saw this because I don't believe in haunts. The first thing I thought about was a cousin of mine that had disappeared a long time before this. Way back yonder my father had a cousin, Oliver Vermillion. Oliver had raised some cattle and drove them from Scott County through here to sell them. This place was a swamp and laurel thicket then. Just a house or two where Norton now is.

"Oliver had sold his cattle and got a right smart of money out of them. He had it in his pocket and had started back across the mountain home. He looked back and saw an old man that used to live here in Norton following him. Well, Oliver never was seen anymore after that. When the man come and whispered in my ear, the first thing I thought of was Oliver Vermillion, but I never saw him in my life before."

A MESSAGE FROM THE DEAD

iss Virginia Owens, Norton, interviewed by Emory Hamilton, October 30, 1940 (the day before Halloween!)

"I have a friend who is an undertaker. After he finished school he entered an establishment in Cincinnati, or Chicago, I'm not sure which. He said once they brought in a fellow who had got killed accidentally and that he didn't have anything on him to establish his identity. They held him the required time and were getting ready to bury him in the Potter's field, but he and some of the other workers asked that he be held a while longer. The owner of the establishment granted their request and they searched further for information that would lead to his identity, but with no success.

"Their time was up and they had to do something. They were talking about how they hated to bury him unknown, because they felt that he was from some prominent family or had some people that would be anxious to know about him. Finally, he said that one of the other undertakers, or possibly the owner of the mortuary told them that he could find out where his people were, but he disliked to do it. They begged him to do so and he eventually consented.

"The dead man was laying on the marble slab and he (the undertaker) got a piece of paper and a pencil and laid it down on the slab beside the dead man and told them all to stand back. They stood back and he stood beside the dead man, but he didn't touch him, the slab, or the paper and pencil, dropped his head and mumbled something under his breath.

"In a second the pencil raised up and started walking over on the paper and started writing just like some invisible hand was guiding it. It wrote something and then dropped down. The fellow (undertaker) raised his hand, but didn't look at what was written and turned to the fellows and said there is his address, and hurried from the room shutting the door behind him.

"They went to the piece of paper and written on it was a street address and telephone number in Portsmouth or Cleveland, Ohio. They called the address and it was the fellow's sister. She and her brother were the only two living members of a wealthy family. They had been separated and hadn't heard from each other for five years. She came immediately to claim the body."

THE GHOST IN THE BARREL

 rch Mefford of Wise, interviewed by James Hylton, September 16, 1941.

"I recollect a time a few years ago that I was visitin' down at the old stompin' ground at Ramsey and night come on and as I'se with a Jones feller I knowed and of course I went and stayed all night with him as it was in the cold winter and much wind a blowin' everywheres and the snow was thick and fast. I eat supper with the family of seven, bein' five kids besides him and his wife and we set 'round the fire and talked of ole times that night till late. Then we all went to bed.

"Well, sir, 'long about midnight I guess, I was waked up by something howlin' 'round by the corner of the house by my bed, and as I'se with Clem. Clem Jones was my friend I'se stayin's with and I noticed he'd woke up too. I ask him what that was and he said in a shaky voice that he guessed it was the ghost of Lillian comin' back. I thought that's mighty funny and ask him what he meant by that. He said as I recollected then that he's had a little girl years fore that fell in a rain barrel and drownded there at that corner. She'd been playing in the yard with her brothers and sisters and leaned over the barrel which was about half full of rain water they'd caught to wash clothes with and she'd somehow lost her balance and fell in and fore any of the others knowed where she was at she'd drownded.

"It'd hurt them purty bad at the time and I'd forgot 'bout it till then. Anyway, a long wailin' howl rent the air and it made a feller's hair stan' up on his head, "I'll tell you. It kepp up and I got up and put some more coal on the fire and took a chew of tobaccer to agg up my nerves. Most everybody in the house was awake by then and they all seemed to know what it was 'sposed to be and looked right pitiful outten their eyes. They all huddled together in thir beds and set up part of the time and said it'd do that in the winter time 'bout the time of year Lillian had fell in there and drownded.

"After some time it stopped and they all went to sleep, but I never. I stayed awake the rest of the night thinkin' 'bout them takin' it the way they did and the look in their eyes when they was talkin' to me 'bout it that night. Well, the next mornin' they wasn't nothin' more I wanted to say and hurt their feelins but I asked the old man Clem 'bout it after we'd got on the road away from the house, what did he think 'bout it and he said it was the ghost of his little Lillian comin' back to them and that I ought to hear it sometimes when she'd holler loud and all night long.

"Well, I had noticed the rain barrel as I went outta the house that morning and I saw it was a plain barrel with the side bung knocked out and that was why it was a half full when she got drownded, it wouldn't hold no more'n that and the water run out when it got to that hole. Well, the wind had blowed hard that night I recollect and I thought it was the wind blowin' in that hole in the barrel, and I told Clem, but he looked hurt at me and said that didn't have anything to do with it, as he'd been tole by his parents fore him that when a little girl child got drownded in a rain barrel it would come back and bother you in your sleep until you moved the barrel. Well, they needed the old barrel to get rain water in to wash and hadn't moved it for that reason. He said every winter night when the wind blowed she'd come back to them.

"It did sound like a little girl cryin' I have to admit that much, whatever anybody thinks."

THE GHOST THAT WAS ALWAYS ON TIME

Logan Tonker of Big Stone Gap, interviewed by James Hylton, January 14, 1942. Hylton prefaced his article with this: "He (Tonker) says this experience happened to him in Big Stone Gap and in an old red brick building that stands on Shawnee Avenue in the western end of town. It has fallen away somewhat and is showing its years. It has been vacant now for many years. The men of the lower ebb and flow of life used to play poker there in the past years and about 40 years ago a man was killed in an upper room on the back side. It had been passed around from mouth to mouth that the house was 'hanted'." Here is the interview with Tonker:

"I'd always heard that the Baker Building in Big Stone was hanted as I'd lived there most of my life. I 'lowed to see fer myself what it was all 'bout. I'd heard that at 8:25 p.m., that iffen you'd go there upstairs, you'd see this feller come in through the wall and make a move as iffen to set down and make motions with his hands as if dealin' cards. I'd got purty full one night and some fellers was talkin' 'bout it and I decided to see for myself, so 'round to the buildin' I went. I set there about a half hour when I heard the L & H (train) comin' down from Norton and I knowed I's on time, for it runs and is due here at 8:30 on time so I waited and looked to see what I could see.

"Well, it weren't long for the first thing I knowed I was lookin' at the light like the shape of a man and it'd come right through the wall, too. It stood there while the train was passin' and then at once it got smaller like somebody settin' down and iffen I'd not been full of wine I'd never stayed there like I did anyway.

"Well, it set down as I say and it looked like a man settin' there dealin' cards over the table and I figured as I'd seen enuff 'bout then and skeedadled outta there fast as I'd ever run before in my life I know. Later I told it 'round town and some others tried it and found out the same as I did. The house is still there and you can try it for yore self some time iffen you give yourself the hankerin' to do it. I've seen and heard lots of stuff, but that beats me I'm a tellin' you right now, yes siree!"

Writer Hylton added this footnote: "I have investigated this and some say that it is true that you can see this sight when you wish at 8:25 each night. Others say that it is the train passing over a railroad bridge in the distance and casting the flickering light on the wall, and that since the train has been discontinued, it can't be seen. But others say that you can see it for yourself now as you could for many years. At any rate, they never play poker there in the night time anyway."

A VISION OF A COFFIN

rs. Mary Carter, Glamorgan, Virginia, interviewed by James Taylor Adams, March 26, 1941.

"I've heard Ma tell that one time before her little brother Ira Roberts died that grandpa stepped out in the yard one night and in a minute called to his wife to come out there. She axed him what he wanted and he said he seed somethin' over on the hill across the holler just like a little coffin. He tried to show it to her, but she couldn't see it. He would say, 'Look right there. Don't you see it? Why I even see the handles on it.' She couldn't see a thing.

"He went to it, but when he got thar thar wasn't anything thar. But when he got back to the house thar it was jes as plain as ever. He went to it again, but didn't find a thing, but when he got back he could see it.

"He said somethin' was goin't to happen and shore enough his baby, little Ira, took brain fever in just a few days and died. When they brought the coffin in the house, grandpa looked at it and said, 'Thar's the coffin I seed 'tother night'!"

(A related incident was told to James Taylor Adams by Mrs. Betty Adams of Big Laurel on the same date, March 26, 1941.)

"I've heard Ma (her grandmother) tell that one time way back yonder that two young men was coming up a creek home one night when they looked on ahead and saw something white on the corner of a rail fence. They didn't know what it was, but they eased up a little and saw it looked just like a small coffin. A child had died in the neighborhood a few days before this, and it looked exactly like the baby's coffin. (Whether or not it was the same coffin Mrs. Carter told about is not known.)

"They started to go around it and all at once it just seemed to dissolve into air and a big something that looked like a sheep ran right across the road in front of them and into the bushes. They never found out what it was."

IT ROSE UP OUT OF THE GROUND

en Schoolcraft of Wise, interviewed by James Taylor Adams, August 28, 1941.

"It was in 1914. I'd been courtin' up on Cox Hollow. Been up to Floyd Cox's, goin' to see one of his girls. Was coming back up Indian Creek about midnight. Got right there below where the convict camp was. Old road then. Coming round that point. Kept seein' something movin' up on the point above the road. I sort of rubbed my eyes. Said to myself, hit hain't nothin'. You're jes imaginin' you see somethin'. I wasn't afraid of nothin'. But I heard somethin' walkin' in the dry leaves then.

"There was a great ol' big stump above the road and all at once it jes started stringin' out right above that stump. Seemed to be comin' right up out of the ground and liftin' right up over me. Man, I can't tell you what it looked like. Had the form of a man, but it was white like white steam or smoke and was, oh, five times as big as any man ever was. My first thought was to take a whack at it. I grabbed my gun. Then I thought it might jes be somebody doing that to scare me, knowin' I'd be along there that night. . .

"So I said to myself, I'll not shoot. Might kill some feller that I'd allus be sorry about. So I jes hit out up the road. Got up there to the swamp. Everybody said there was a ball of fire to be seed there coming across the swamp. I couldn't help lookin'. I didn't see no ball of fire, but there comin' right across the swamp and towards me was that same thing. I didn't fool around but hit out up the road to Dan Collins. They told me there was an old graveyard on the hill jes above there. First time I had heard about that. They also told me things had been seed there lots of times."

THE 'SAD CINDERELLA' WHO CAME BACK TO HAUNT

ay Horton of Hurricane, Virginia, interviewed by James Hylton, September 23, 1941. Of this session, Hylton wrote: "He (Horton) reminds the writer that his folks were children of early folks in this part of the country and believed almost devoutly in a 'Hant' or 'Belief" tale of any kind, along with signs and omens of all sorts. He says that it was only natural for them to believe in them after their old parents before them did so so strongly. That his mother and father both

221

had lots of experiences in life that made them believe more so in them and they both died believing in them, too. His father told him this tale before he died."

Horton: "Old man Davenport that used to live next to us out on the old homeplace, had a girl that was about half foolish and they made her do all the hard and dirty work 'round the house and all sech as that. She never went anywhars though and minded every thing they said for her to do and worked hard all they said for her to do. If she'd be washin' clothes out in the yard and drop a piece of cloth or soap, they'd lash her with a limb. Neighbors talked about it sumpin' awful for a long time and then, like all other things, it died down a little and nobody paid any more 'tention to it I guess.

"Anyway, her mind must a went plumb blank when it happened, I guess fer they'd been so mean to her, I guess she'd stood all she could. Well, one night about bed time they's all around a big fireplace and she was over in a far corner like they made her set most of the time, and she was cold and shiverin' a lot, and all at once I heard them say later, she looked right funny outta her eyes and jumped up and run to the front door and out into the night air. They run after her to see what in the world was wrong, but she run towards a high rock out in the back of the place a few hundred yards, and where a lotta rock was below it.

"She never stopped and I guess she's already outta breath when she reached it for she fell over the edge and onto the rocks below and cracked her skull. Well, after folks got lanterns and went and carried her back to the house and scoldin' her all along, she had to be washed all over she was so bloody. She died soon later that night talkin' outta her head kinda and said something about comin' back to them some time later and doin' her work. She still had work in her mind I guess 'cause that was all they ever let her do. Well, nobody seemed to care much about her dyin' and in a few days every thing was the same again.

"But later, when some of the boys was out on the cliff huntin' winter wood, they heard somebody moanin' and groanin' sorta like somebody was hurt down below, and they looked all over but couldn't see nobody nowheres. They went to the house and told the others about it and the next day all of them went and looked, but couldn't see anything.

"But that night they all was around the fire as that was the night Eppie, for that's the girl's name that died, run outta the room. They all heard an awful noise, just like when they went and brought Eppie back to the house. They all recollected the sound, too, and it started comin' home to them right then and there, too. Every night in that winter it bothered them and finally one of the younger boys let it out among his pals and they told it and it got started all over the Hurricane (the town), and people started talkin' 'bout how mean they'd been to the poor girl and said it's good 'nuff for them.

"You can go to the place right now and on any night you go you can hear that wailin' and moanin' like somebody in awful pain. I do know that later some of the older folks like to went crazy theirselves over it and wanted to move. It wasn't long after that that the old man and woman both died, and after that the boys could hear the noise. You can go and see and hear for yourself when you like, and you'll hear it, too!"

THE DEATH SIGN OF THE DOG

 lbert Mullins of Roaring Fork, Virginia, interviewed by James Hylton, April 11, 1941. Said Hylton: "This was told to me at his residence on what is called the Cane Patch, a section of woods between Kent Junction and Roaring Fork that has been the home of the older Mullins before him, who paid a good deal of attention to folk tales and lore."

Mullins: "My mother always had a lot of faith in signs and I have had more than one person to ask me about the time the Warf boy was killed at the shop at Roaring Fork. We was sittin' 'round the fire at home one night and we heard a dog from a hillside up above the house and the barn, and we knew it wasn't our dog for we didn't have one at the time. It didn't sound like it had treed anything, but was wailing like you know and it wasn't a bark and it wasn't a howl either. I don't know what you would call it, but it was making an awful racket and it bothered us all the night.

"But when I mentioned it to Ma, she told me it was a bad sign and that before night fell the next day, somebody near or at the Fork would come into bad trouble of some kine. She said that when the dogs made a noise like that that somethin' sure awful bad was in the future and was close at hand at that.

"Well, anyway, it howled or whatever you call it all night and we didn't get two minutes sleep. Next day a Warf boy by the name of Rand who lived with his parents in the camp of Roaring Fork was standing by the forge in the shop with some powder and caps in his pockets, and he forgot to remember the dynamite and leaned over a little too far, and it exploded. Well, everybody there knows what followed. He was tore to bits and they had to pick the poor boy up in pieces from a great distance between the store and the shop. It was the worst accident that ever happened to anybody at Roaring Fork and I don't guess it will ever be forgotten.

"Well, I thought about what Ma said the night before when the dog was making that awful noise on the hill above our house. . . Next day when I went home, Ma asked me if I remembered seeing any dogs around the place where the accident happened, and when I come to think of it they was several along in the crowd when they carried the body down to the ambulance.

"Well, sir, I don't know about it but that night they say a dog howled above the store where the boy was blowed to pieces, all night. But it never howled any more after the night of the accident. I don't know whether it was the same dog or not, but Ma said she'd bet a pretty if the truth was knowed that it was the same dog."

RETURN OF A CIVIL WAR SPIRIT

Mrs. Polly Johnson of Wise, interviewed by Emory Hamilton, September 23, 1940.

"John Moore, my brother-in-law's brother, during the Civil War was laying out from the Yankees. They lived on Laurel Ridge. He wasn't strong . . . (he was) little and pale. He had consumption, I reckon. The Yankees was out hunting him and run upon him. He fell down behind a log and they shot him. He begged them not to shoot him anymore. He said 'this shot will kill me. Don't shoot me anymore, let me go home and see my wife and little children once more.' They said, 'Yes, you can see your wife and children once more,' and bang! They shot him twice more.

"Such things can be so, for he wanted to see his wife and children so bad. It tormented him because he couldn't see them. His spirit or something could have come back, because he wanted to see them so bad.

"After this, something got to bothering around Uncle Aaron's house (presumably where the Confederate soldier's wife and children lived). They couldn't keep the door shut. They lived in an old-time log house. In them days they had latches for the doors with a string run through a hole to the outside. You could pull the string down on the outside and it lifted the latch on the inside. Well, they just couldn't keep the door latched.

"My daddy could talk to spirits, and they sent after him to come and see what he could do. Daddy went. They didn't have any lights them days, but pine torches. Caroline (possibly the wife) walked around the table and the door flew open and hit her in the back. She said, 'Oh that hurt!' She shut it back, but they couldn't keep the door shut. It'd fly open every time they shut it. After supper they talked a little while and then it was way in the night. Uncle Aaron said he was going to bed and they all went to bed.

"Daddy was going to set up and watch. They had left the door stand open. Daddy had prepared him some little pine splinters, to make him a quick light. Daddy was going to lay down before the fire. . . He shut the door and stuck his splinters in the fire to make a good light.

"The door flew open and he kept his eyes on the door. The splinters lit up and there in the door stood a man with no head on. Daddy aimed to speak in the three highest names, but he said it shore did frighten him and he said the man stood there with no head in his white shirt sleeves and his hands in his pockets. (Daddy) said, 'What in the hell are you doing there?' And in just a jump or two Daddy was in the bed. He lit right in behind Uncle Aaron.

"He said when he asked that, the man stepped backwards, off the steps, and was never seen nor heard anymore."

MAN'S BEST FRIEND TO THE END

Mrs. Jennie Renfro of Wise, interviewed by James Hylton, March 25, 1941.

"When my son-in-law, Janis Taylor, bought Little Teenie, a little white and black dog of the terrier breed, he thought very much of him. The little fellow was smart and easily caught on to the many tricks they tried to teach him. The dog grew and would go meet Janis every night when he came home from work. He was a salesman and was away through the week and the little fellow would go about the house and whine all the time that he was gone. Then when he could come in over the weekend, the little fellow would cut a shine that was a sight to see.

"Well, it was about two years after that that Janis took very sick and it was necessary to take him to the Coeburn hospital at once. . . He remained there until his death several weeks later. His wife and I sent to visit him which was nearly every day. He was mindful of everything going on around him and was conscious up and until death took him.

"Anyway, after about the third day we went to see him, he said he saw Teenie come into the door of his room and jump up on his bed, but when he reached out to pet him, he vanished. We only laughed and thought that he had been dreaming, but it continued that way nearly every day until about two days before he died. The first day he mentioned it to us again and said that the little dog had come into the room the night before and put his front feet upon and bed and whined and whined. That evening late, he said the same thing, and the next day before he died, that night he saw the dog again, and told us to pick him up and put him on the bed where he could reach him and pet him some. We tried to pass it off, as we thought then that he was out of his head, but we were advised by the doctors that he was wholly as himself. He said the dog was with him on the side of the bed just a few hours before he died, and stoutly maintained it for some minutes while he talked to us.

"There was no dog that I could see in the room, and, of course, I knew we had left the little dog at home when we left!"

CHAPTER 41

A Supertitious Custom That Solved a Crime

(Southwest Virginia)

(Author's note: In "The Ghosts of Virginia, Volume IV," (1998), I included a chapter called the "Ordeal of Touch." In colonial times there was a superstitious belief that if someone had been murdered and the murderer touched the wounds, the victim would bleed afresh, thus exposing the killer. And there are documented cases of where such a ritual was practiced in the commonwealth in the 17th century.

Here then, is another instance where this quaint custom was used, or rather threatened to be used, and such a threat was so feared that it caused a murderer's confession. It was told to interviewer James M. Hylton by Mrs. Polly Johnson in Wise, Virginia, in November 1941. Hylton was one of the writers employed by the Works Progress Administration to gather regional folklore. For clarification, I have edited Mrs. Johnson's testimony.)

"bout 100 years ago (probably the 1830s or 1840s), two men slipped up behind a widder (widow) woman and kilt her while she was nursing a young baby child. My Pa told me about it. He said a big feller by the name of De Lapp, and a feller named McCullin, a little runt of a man, got together in uh bad way tuh start with. That they met one time when thuh big feller was hidin' uh body under uh bridge. (McCullin saw this, became afraid, and started to run, but De Lapp caught him, threatened to kill him if he ever told of what he had witnessed, and thereafter bullied him into other crimes.)

"One time at a place not far from Pa's house these same two robbed uh feller later and kilt him and was hidin' his body under uh little wood bridge when uh woman comin' down thuh road seed them. They caught her an started to do her in too, but she begged and prayed tuh them that her children was home with nuthin tuh eat and she'd been tuh beg some meal for tuh make some hoe-cakes for them, which wuz thuh truth. She'd been left uh widder and uh little child'd been born since then. She had several other little ones besides at home too. Thuh fact was thuh woman had had uh awful hard time rearin' her little ones since her husband had died, and all the folks wuz glad tuh do what they could tuh help her. (At this point McCullin 'sided with her," and pleaded with De Lapp to spare her life. De Lapp finally reluctantly agreed, and the woman went home. But later, De Lapp changed his mind, and fearful the woman would expose them, forced McCullin to go to her house.)

"That night early she put them (the children) tuh bed and went tuh bed herself as usual with thuh little baby that was nursin' from her breast. (The two men) went to thuh house and slipped up outside in thuh cold deep snow and thuh big one made thuh little feller put the barrel uh his gun through uh chimney pit and shoot. He never wanted tuh to it, but thuh big De Lapp feller put uh pistol tuh his head and swore and bedamned he'd blow his head off iffen he didn't do it. So thuh little feller closed his eyes and shot and they slipped off in thuh dark.

"Well, uh neighbor, three days later, noticed no smoke comin' from thuh chimney and thought they might need wood or coal and went tuh see if they needed help when they found thuh dead woman shot through thuh back, so's thuh bullet went through her heart and had kilt her dead. Then officers wuz called and a investigation started and thuh tracks in the snow found. They found thet thuh little children had got up in thuh two mornin's as ever and played about thuh house and then went back tuh bed at night thinkin' their mother was sick or asleep. (Miraculously, the baby had somehow survived and was taken to a hospital.) Well thuh kids had played about thuh room and all thuh time blood run down from thuh bed and they'd tramped through it and their little tracks wuz all over thuh house.

"Tuh sheriff wuz a awful good man and knowed he wuz stumped. So he called in uh hired detective tuh help him and it wasn't long till they'd simmered thuh suspects down tuh about eight fellers, and De Lapp and McCullin wuz two uh them, too. Thuh body hadn't been moved yit, and they got all these men in thuh house and thuh sheriff said, 'They's uh sayin' thet iffin a man murders, and iffen he touches thuh person he murders, thuh blood will flow from thuh wounds. So I want yuh men tuh go one at a time and put yore finger on that bullet hole on her breast and see what happens.'

"Well, six uh thuh men gladly went forward and nothin' happened. So thet left only thuh other two, McCullin and De Lapp. So they stood there but thuh sheriff wuz not easy tuh fool, so he said tuh thuh little feller, 'Go ahead McCullin.' But thuh little runt drawed back from thuh bed and put his hands over his eyes. He said he couldn't do it, and then admitted tuh what him and De Lapp had done. De Lapp started tuh run out, but they caught him 'fore he got through thuh door. They tuck them tuh thuh jail in town and thuh detective went tuh work of 'em with questions.

"Then McCullin tole how De Lapp had forced him intuh uh life uh bad crimes and tole thuh whole story. De Lapp, though, wouldn't budge uh inch and jest set thar an cussed 'em all. Anyway they sentenced them both tuh be hung, and in a short time they wuz all ready fer 'em too. Everybody had been worked up over thuh killin' uh thuh good woman and wuz ready tuh see that jestice wuz done. In them days, they stood 'em up in uh wagon and placed uh rope 'round their necks and then pulled thuh wagon way from 'em, and I guess jest choked 'em tuh death.

"Anyway, McCullin wuz hung first, as they thought De Lapp would break too, but he didn't. And McCullin hung and twisted us few minutes and then his people got him and galloped off down thuh road with him. They say tuh this day he come to and lived uh better life. But they done different with De Lapp. They let him hang uh few minutes and then drove thuh wagon back in under him and let him rest uh while. And so in uh few minutes they's pull it out from under him and left him choke uh little more. For one hour they done this till finally he died by sufferin'. And everybody thought he'd deserved it.

"That wuz one time everybody said that uh folk belief, or superstition, solved uh crime, with thuh help uf uh good, honest sheriff uh thuh mountains, and uh honest detective too."

CHAPTER 42

The Living Legend of John Henry

"John Henry was a li'l baby, sittin' on his mama's knee,
Said 'de Big Bend Tunnel on de C & O road gonna cause the death of me.
Lawd, Lawd, is gonna be the death of me."

Who was John Henry?
Was he a real person known throughout southwest Virginia and eastern West Virginia as "the steel driving man?" Was he a myth perpetuated by decades of embellished folklore handed down generation to generation? Or was the truth behind one of America's most popular legends somewhere in between? Likely.

In any event, John Henry's story was told and retold with awe and revered admiration in coal mining camps and along road construction sites for more than a century. He became a true American hero in the style of a Paul Bunyon or Casey Jones. It has only been in recent years, in the high-tech, computerized, electronic era, that his name has faded virtually into oblivion.Few school children today have ever heard of him.

Who was John Henry? He was a steel driver. Steel drivers swung heavy mauls (sledge hammers) down onto steel drills to bore into rock. The resulting holes were filled with explosives and then blasted so tunnel openings could be made through mountains to lay railroad track.

It took a powerful man of extraordinary strength to wield these

10 to 20 pound mauls. And John Henry was said to be the strongest of the strong.

> "John Henry was hammerin' on de mountain,
> An' his hammer was strikin' fire."

Who was John Henry? In the late 1920s, Louis W. Chappell, then an associate professor of English at West Virginia University, tracked down the hundreds of rumors, myths and legends of Henry and wrote a book. He deduced, after interviewing scores of old timers, that the real John Henry was a black man who plied his strenuous trade in the mountain area separating western Virginia and eastern West Virginia. He believed Henry to be in his early 30s, about six feet tall, and weighing around 200 pounds, all of which appeared to be muscle.

Although Henry already had earned a widespread reputation as being the best steel driver in the land, it was an incident that occurred sometime around 1870 which made him internationally famous. It was then that an automatic steam drill was brought to the Big Bend Tunnel in what is now the green hills of West Virginia. Henry had been driving steel at Big Bend.

According to Chappell, Henry rejected the new-fangled invention and "everything it was apt to stand for, rose up in his integrity and announced that he could sink more steel than the drill." A contest was arranged. The foreman brought John Henry two 20 pound hammers, one for each hand. The steam drill was set up on the right, and Henry on the left. The entire work gang crowded around man and machine, "in a grunting, cheering throng."

> "John Henry tol' his cap'n, lightnin' was in his eye;
> 'Cap'n bet yo las' red cent on me,
> Fo' I'll beat it to de bottom or I'll die,
> Lord, Lord, I'll beat it to de bottom or I'll die!"

A signal was given and the race was on. Here, it appears, fact and fiction co-mingle. Some said the contest lasted only a few minutes. Others said it was hours. Chappell believed the test was over in under an hour . . . "The great Negro, with a 20 pound hammer in each hand, slung them down, one after the other, on the steel, driving it into the rock."

Sweat glistened from the granite hard body of Henry in the dusty heat of the tunnel. According to Chappell, in the midst of the excitement, the steam drill got hung in the seam of the rock and lost some time. When it was over — however long it lasted — the steam drill had bored one hole nine feet deep.

John Henry had drilled two holes — each seven feet deep, for a total of 14 feet! The work gang roared its approval.

What happened next is also subject to wide interpretation. The alleged eye-witness accounts differ greatly.

"He drove so hard till he broke his pore heart,
And he lied down his hammer an' he died,
Lawd, Lawd, he lied down his hammer an' he died."

The majority of those interviewed by Chappell agreed that he did not die that night from a burst blood vessel in his head, although this has long been a popular version, and may have helped inspire the songs written about him. Some said Henry continued his work in the tunnel. Others held that he was killed in a blast of rock and buried under the big fill at the east end of the tunnel. The truth is probably lost in the sands of time.

"Carried John Henry to the graveyard,
    They looked at him good and long;
Very last words his wife said to him;
    'My husband he is dead an' gone,
    My husband he is dead an' gone'."

Chappell wrote that the marks of John Henry's hammers were said to have remained until the tunnel was double tracked many years later.

John Henry had become a folk hero. One writer penned: "His super strength, his grit, his endurance, and his martyrdom appeal to something fundamental in the heart of the common man. Working men idolize brute strength." It was also reported that Henry's wife had engraved on his tombstone - "Here lies a steel driving man."

His legend flourished for more than a century. Perhaps it was perpetuated, in part, by what old timers in the Big Bend Tunnel area have said for years . . . That on a calm still night, if one listens closely at the east entrance to the tunnel, one can still hear the clanking sharp ringing of 20 pound hammers striking steel in a steady, rhythmic beat!

CHAPTER 43

Bury My Bones — Again!
(Southeastern Kentucky)

(Author's note: In past volumes in this series, I have written about instances where ghostly figures appear to mortal beings and make it known that they had died and not been properly buried, and that their spirit cannot rest until their bodies have been reinterred. Here is another chilling example of this phenomenon. The account has been reported in area newspapers, often repeated at Halloween, and was told by, among others, the late folklorian, Michael Paul Henson, in his book, "More Kentucky Ghost Stories.")

This particular incident occurred more than 70 years ago to the family of James Franklin in the town of Somerset, Kentucky. At the time, Franklin was in the Navy and stationed in Virginia, presumably at Norfork, and he would travel across the commonwealth, cross the Cumberland Mountains, and return home every chance he got. The Franklins had just moved into an old house, and while James was back at his base, his wife became disturbed by "things" happening that she didn't understand.

While in bed one night, she heard the sound of a child's rattle. It went from one side of her bed to the other, as if something was trying to gain her attention. She turned the light on and searched the room, but there was nothing there. She turned the light back off. Then she heard the distinct sounds of the patter of a child's feet, and of a baby crying. She looked again. Nothing. Understandably, she didn't sleep much that night.

The same thing happened the next evening, and the next and the next. It continued nightly — the rattle, footsteps, the sobbing, and also short, scary gasps and heavy breathing. A careful inspection of that room and others revealed no source. After a week or so or such recurring manifestations, the Franklin's maid abruptly quit and neighbors, at first friendly, found ways to avoid the house.

Mrs. Franklin's nerves were shattered. She called her husband and urged him to take leave and come home. She told him she thought she was going to have a nervous breakdown. He was a skeptic, but after he arrived and heard the same sounds, he launched a thorough investigation. He determined that the noise actually was centered around a small attic room directly above the bedroom. Two nights later, he sat up at night in an effort to pinpoint the origin.

In the hallway he saw a small girl wearing a long-flowing gown that obviously was from another time period. As he watched in stunned silence, the apparitional figure slowly climbed up the staircase that led to the attic. He followed it, and, in the dark, heard sobs beyond the door to the little room above the bedroom. He flicked on a flashlight and looked around but didn't see anything.

The next morning, in daylight, he climbed back up the stairs and searched once more. He saw a crude patch on one wall. He ripped it off the wall, and behind it found a tiny space about four feet wide and three feet high. It had been covered over years or even decades before.

In this small recess he saw, curled in an open, partially decayed box, the skeleton of a small child! She had on a long white dress, and clutched in one bony hand was a broken rattle! Later, the Franklins learned that such a child was remembered to have lived in the house perhaps a half century before. No one knew what had happened to her.

The skeletal remains were removed and a proper burial was arranged. The sounds and the sightings of the little girl were never heard or seen again.

WHOSE BONES ARE THESE?

A few months after the end of the Civil War, hundreds of Confederate veterans and others volunteered to help in a cleanup campaign at Hollywood Cemetery in Richmond. While walking through the area where

Union soldiers were buried, some of the veterans noticed two Confederate grave sites. One headstone read: "Lieutenant A. W. Latimer, Forty-nine Georgia regiment, died May 29, 1865." The other read: "Rebel; died June 15, 1865."

When word of this discovery spread, many men volunteered to dig up these graves and transfer the bodies to the section where southern soldiers were interred. Several Virginia Military Institute cadets began digging, but were halted when cemetery superintendent James O'Keefe arrived on the scene and ordered the work stopped. He told the men that the bodies in question "were not Confederate soldiers, but were buried under that name for reasons which he was not at liberty to divulge."

The workmen ignored his plea, kept digging, and opened the coffins. In Lt. Latimer's, they found a gray Confederate jacket with infantry buttons and a pair of blue pants lying on top of a blanket-enclosed body. The second coffin also contained Confederate clothing. The two bodies were reburied in the southern soldiers' section.

But the mystery of who they really were has never been solved.

CHAPTER 44

Some Indian Legend and Lore

(Statewide)

(Author's note: Following are some passages, gleaned from a wide variety of sources, relating as to how Virginia Indians viewed ghostly themes.)

THE "GHOST DANCE"

rom Henry Davenport Northrop's book, "Indian Horrors, or Massacres by the Red Men," published in 1899: "The Indian, more than any other man, seems to have a belief in the supernatural . . . He had always talked of the great spirit and of the Happy Hunting Grounds. His surroundings, his education, the traditions of the past, all lead to the conviction that there are supernatural powers and wonders."

In his book, Northrop wrote of a most curious custom, called "The Ghost Dance." He noted that some wise chiefs used this dance, and other prevalent superstitions, to their advantage. In the Ghost Dance, "warriors and braves fasted for 24 hours. Then, at sunrise, each brave goes through the 'rite of purification.' This is done by the fanatics going through what is called a 'sweat-lodge' (where water is poured on hot rocks inside a tent, creating a sauna-like effect, which) cleanses and purifies. The braves then paint their faces with dark blue, and a red cross on each cheek. At high noon, the braves form a circle, joining hands. At a signal,

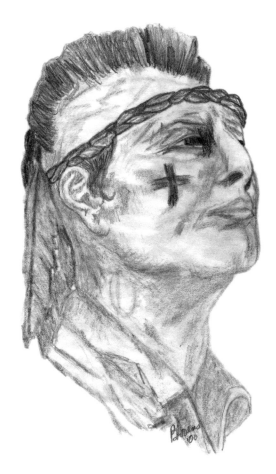

every brave looks down on the ground and they then begin to circle around, singing a weird and mournful dirge. (This lasts about an hour.) They get dizzy, and, aided by hunger, sweating and the quick change from darkness to light, become ecstatic and faint, and are then considered fit to receive the Holy Spirit."

SOME STRANGE FUNERAL CUSTOMS

ccording to Helen Rountree, author of "The Powhatan Indians of Virginia," with "ordinary" Indians, the body was wrapped with its jewelry in skins and mats and laid in a stake-lined grave. The body might be "flexed or extended," lying on its back, face or side. After such a burial, female relatives remained at home, mourning loudly and with their faces painted black. Wailing for the dead could also be done by men.

In burials given to "high-status" people, the body was wrapped in a mat and laid on a scaffold about three or four yards high. Sometimes relatives threw beads to the poor, and a "jolly feast" followed. During these funerals, other bodies, previously placed on scaffolds, were examined, and "any that had been reduced to bones were taken down, wrapped in a new mat, and hung in the houses of their relatives, where they remained . . . until the houses were abandoned."

BELIEFS OF AN AFTERLIFE

aptain John Smith, among others, said that Virginia Indians told him that when they died, "their souls traveled westward until they reached the setting sun." There, they found: "most pleasant fields, growndes, and pastures, where yt shall doe no labour, but stuck fynely with feathers and paynted with oyle and Pocones rest in all quiet and peace, and eate delicious fruicts, and haue store of Copper, beades and hatchetts, sing, daunce, and haue all variety of delights and merryments till that (soul) waxe ould there as the body did on earth, and then yt shall dissolue and dye, and come into a womans womb againe, and so be a new borne vnto the world."

But this was not the only belief. Others said that "souls traveled eastward to an undisclosed destination." Some believed that the "souls of wicked men . . . hung betweene Heaven and earth." One chief told that "a soul first went treetop high, where it saw a broad, flat, easily traveled path with many edible berries and fruits growing on either side." This soul, after being so nourished, would travel on to find its forefathers, "living in great pleasure in a goodly feild, where they doe nothing but daunce and sing and feed on delicious fruicts." These souls, however, would age, become "starke old men," die and then "reenter the Powhatan world."

DO NOT DISTURB THE DEAD!

 he following legend was told to James Taylor Adams, a Works Progress

Administration writer, by Elbert Bond, on May 26, 1941. It typifies many traditions about unexplained psychic phenomena which seems to occur when Indian graves sites are disturbed.

"I've heard the old people say that the best and only way to keep a gun from being 'spelled' was to mix Indian bone filings with your power. They used to say that the old timers would hunt everywhere for an Indian grave and dig up the bones and file or scrape them to get the dust for their gunpowder. That was a long time ago. Guess they hain't any Indian bones left now, and if they was, people wouldn't use 'em. Some would, too, for I've heard people say right here lately they believed their gun was spelled.

"One time they say that an old man went up on the hill above where Willie Kilgore lives to dig in an Indian grave, and the first lick he struck, the whole earth all 'round him started to tremble and shake and he heard a rumblin' down under him jes' like thunder. He tried again and it done the same way. So he got scared and run off and they never could git him back thar anymore."

A MYSTICAL INVOCATION

 rom the book, "By-Ways of Virginia History," by R. H. Early, published is 1907, comes the following:

"A very touching legend concerns two lovers whose story came to an untimely termination by the death of the lady-love. Her body was interred upon the top of a solitary hillock overlooking a beautiful valley, their former trysting place; and here the bereft one came bringing his flute every night and morning and essayed to console himself for the separation, with a love-song composed to her memory.

"At the end of a year, a bone from one of her arms appeared above the mound. Accepting this as a token of remembrance from his dear one, he discarded his reed and, converting the limb into a musical instrument ever afterwards, substituted this novel flute for the less sacred one.

"Tradition asserts that the souls of the twain, now united, still haunt the burial spot, and that at sunrise and sunset may be heard the zephyrs of Dawn and Dusk, the strains of the mystical invocation."

A **REAL** DESCENT INTO THE MAELSTROM

(Author's note: One of Edgar Allan Poe's most thrilling short stories — to me — is "A Descent into the Maelstrom." It is about the incredible experience of an old Norwegian fisherman, who tells of being sucked into the swirling vortex of a huge whirlpool off the coast of Norway. Poe wrote: "The edge of the whirl was represented by a broad belt of gleaming spray; but no particle of this slipped into the mouth of the terrific funnel, whose interior, as far as the eye could fathom it, was a smooth, shining and jet-black wall of water, inclined to the horizon at an angle of some 45 degrees, speeding dizzily round and round with a swaying and sweltering motion and sending forth to the wind an appalling voice, half-shriek, half-roar, such as not even the mighty cataract of Niagara ever lifts up in its agony to heaven. . . Accounts of this vortex . . . cannot impart the faintest conception either of the magnificence, or the horror of the scene.")

arge boats, giant fir trees, and even whales caught up in this boiling, hissing watery pit, were never to be seen again. The fisherman tells of the time he and his brother were themselves embroiled in the whirlpool. "We rushed headlong into the abyss . . . Never shall I forget the sensations of awe, horror and admiration . . . The boat appeared to be hanging, as if by magic, midway down, upon the interior surface of a funnel, vast in circumference, prodigious in depth . . . My gaze fell instinctively downward. In this direction I was able to obtain an unobstructed view . . . Round and round we swept, in dizzying swings and jerks . . . I perceived that our boat was not the only object in the embrace of the whirl. Both above and below us were visible fragments of vessels, large masses of building timber, and trunks of trees, broken boxes and staves."

The fisherman leaves his boat and clings to a barrel. He sees his brother vacuumed past him, circling madly, heading to the bottom of the vast chasm. Miraculously, the fisherman is hurled <u>upward</u>, and thrown out into the storm-tossed ocean. He is rescued by the crew of a passing ship, and is speechless from the memory of his terrorizing experience.

He later says, "Those who drew me on board were my old mates and daily companions, but they knew me no more than they would have known a traveler from the spirit-land. My hair, which had been raven-black the day before, was as white as you see it now."

Poe's mesmerizing tale is strikingly similar to an alleged real-life account of being drawn down into a surging, violent whirlpool at a site some miles south of the extreme southern border of Virginia. It happened to two Cherokee Indians at the mouth of a river in an area known as "The Suck," and was reported by author James Mooney in his book on "The History, Myths, and Sacred Formulas of the Cherokees." Mooney called the episode "The Haunted Whirlpool," and described it this way:

"It happened once that two men, going down the river in a canoe, as they came near this place saw the water circling rapidly ahead of them. They pulled up to the bank to wait until it became smooth again, but the whirlpool seemed to approach with wider and wider circles, until they were drawn into the vortex.

"They were thrown out of the canoe and carried down under the water, where one man was seized by a great fish and was never seen again. The other was taken round and round down to the very lowest center of the whirlpool, when another circle caught him and bore him outward and upward until he was finally thrown up again to the surface and floated out into the shallow water, whence he made his escape to shore.

"He told afterwards that when he reached the narrowest circle of the maelstrom, the water seemed to open below him and he could look down as through the roof beams of a house . . . and there on the bottom of the river <u>he had seen a great company of people, who looked up and beckoned to him to join them,</u> but as they put up their hands to seize him the swift current caught him and took him out of their reach!"

THE GHOSTLY LIGHT IN THE JAMES RIVER

(Williamsburg)

(Author's note: There is a rather colorful legend sometimes told at the historic Carter's Grove mansion near Williamsburg. It is highly folklorian in nature, and the authenticity of the event is sketchy at best. However, it is an intriguing tale which possibly had some basis in truth at one time. Today, it is sometimes told around Halloween by descendents of Indian tribes which once roamed both sides of the James River in this area.)

merica's first colonists had a hard enough time surviving as it was. To start with, they were ill-equipped to begin a new colony in the wilderness. Many were "gentlemen" who had little or no knowledge of manual labor. There were precious few craftsmen or farmers who knew anything about building houses or seeding fields. Consequently, a great number of the original settlers died during the first year or two of the settlement at Jamestown.

Eventually, however, men with the needed skills arrived and the foothole colony began to survive — and expand. Plantations began to spring up both east and west of Jamestown.

One of the principal reasons for the success was the fact that — thanks largely to the artful diplomacy and negotiating skills of Captain John Smith — the colonists were not, with few exceptions, accosted by the native Indians in the area. Actually, by providing corn and game, the Indians had helped the English make it through what became known as "the starving time." Had the Indians attacked the settlers with full force in their first years of existence, it is highly doubtful if the colony would have survived.

The Indian chief largely responsible for peaceful relations was the powerful Powhatan. After he died in 1618, he was succeeded by Opechancanough. For four years he built the strength of the regional tribes. Opechancanough had never been at ease with the colonists. He feared they would increase in number to the extent where the Indians would be driven from their homelands entirely.

This fear festered, until it grew into an unabated hatred, and Opechancanough began to plot an all-out attack on the white "enemy." It was easy to whip up strong sentiment among his people, for they were slowly but surely being driven from their favorite hunting and fishing grounds.

The trigger for the attack occurred in March 1622 when two settlers murdered an Indian named Nemattanew. Opechancanough was ready. On the morning of March 22, 1622, members of the Powhatan Confederacy and the Chickahominy tribe entered the colonists's homes and settlements along a seven mile stretch from Jamestown on both sides of the river. The unsuspecting colonists were totally unaware of impending danger, for these Indians worked side by side with them in the fields, and daily traded with them.

The Indians "came to work" without their weapons. But once they had arrived, they grabbed axes, hatchets, knives, hoes, poles

and whatever they could find, and began fiercely attacking the colonists — men, women, and children. It was a dreadful slaughter. Within hours, more than 350 settlers had been killed.

One survivor later wrote: "They fell upon the English and basely and barbarously murdered them, not sparing age or sex, man, woman or child. Being at their several works in the house and in the fields, planting corn and tobacco, gardening, making brick, building, sawing and other kinds of husbandry, so sudden was the cruel execution that few or none discerned the weapon or the blow that brought them to destruction."

Plantations at Appomattox, Flower de Hundred, Macock, Westover, Powell's Brook and Martin-Brandon, among others, were destroyed. No life was spared.

The entire colony might well have been wiped out except for a single Indian named Chanco who warned his benevolent "master." A colonist wrote of this incident: "That God had put it into the heart of the converted Indian to reveal the conspiracy by which means Jamestown and many colonists were preserved from their treacheries, was regarded as the most exquisite incident in the life of the colony. For more than 300 of ours died by these pagan infidels, yet thousands of ours were saved by means of one of them alone which was made a Christian. Blessed be God forever Whose mercy endureth forever. Blessed be God Whose mercy is above His justice and far above His works; Who brought this deliverance whereby their souls escaped even as a bird out of the snare of the fowler."

Perhaps nowhere was the massacre as devastating as at Martin's Hundred, a fledgling settlement several miles east of Jamestown, on the James River at a site where the Carter's Grove mansion now stands. Here, 73 settlers were unmercifully killed — and herein is where the legend begins.

It is said that one of the English women at Martin's Hundred was so breathtakingly beautiful that even the Indians were struck with admiration for her. She had long black hair which she tied up with blue and white ribbons. Still, she was not spared in the assault. She was struck down as she stood in the doorway of her cabin. Somehow, bloodied, she managed to crawl to the edge of the woods and tried to hide, but the vengeful Indians caught her again. She was scalped, her precious hair and ribbons torn from her skull. She was left for dead.

Incredibly, the woman again crawled, this time to a trash heap where she remained until the Indians left. She lived till the next day, then died. But her courageousness, and beauty, has long survived in Indian tradition.

For it is told, till this day, that sometimes, when the fog and mist arise on the river on still nights, the faint moans and screams of the slaughtered colonists at Martin's Hundred can still be heard wafting across the area where a thriving settlement once existed over 375 years ago!

And on clear moonlit evenings, the story is told that a tiny spot of light can be seen dancing in the river. It is, some say, the reflection of the moon on the bare white skull of the beautiful woman who wore blue and white ribbons in her hair and was scalped during the terrible Indian raid of 1622!

CHAPTER 45

A Potpourri of Psychic Encounters

(Various Sites)

(Author's note: Some people have all the luck! Here I've been tracking Virginia ghosts for the better part of the last two decades, and I have never experienced, yet alone seen a single apparition. While in December 1998, I learned of a young lady who lives in Kenbridge, Virginia, (Lunenburg County), who not only has had her own otherworldly encounters, but she seems to run into a good ghost tale everywhere she goes.

I was signing books at the annual Bizarre Bazaar Christmas craft show in Richmond when another young lady, Patricia McGetrick, rushed up to me practically breathless. She handed me some papers and a couple of photos, and told me all about Karen Lynch (the one from Lunenburg County.) "You have to call her," Patricia exclaimed. "She knows about all sorts of ghosts! There's the screaming statue, the ghost of the old lady who froze in a snow storm and only reappears when there is a tragedy in the house. And what about the photo of the dog? Isn't that an apparition surrounding it?"

Patricia went on, excitedly. I couldn't scribble fast enough, and I got confused. So a couple of weeks later I called Karen to see if she could straighten things out for me. Here is what I learned:)

THE FROZEN GHOST

 s a child, Karen lived with her parents in a house in Gladys, Virginia, between

Brookneal and Rustburg, and near Appomattox. It was built in 1954. Karen says the house is on the site of an older plantation home; that a slave cemetery is located between her parents' home and the older structure; and that a mill race is behind the house - a ditch dug to run water to a mill to grind corn or grain.

Karen's grandparents told her of a long-standing legend of a lady who lived in the plantation home in the 1800. She got caught out in one of the worst blizzards of the 19th century. It is said the snowdrifts were six to seven feet deep. The woman froze to death. It is her ghost, Karen believes, who periodically returned to the house in which Karen grew up.

"I saw her when I was nine years old," she says. "I was heading toward the kitchen one night when I looked up and saw someone sitting at the kitchen table. It was a woman with her back turned to me. I didn't recognize her. Then she turned to look at me. It was just a casual glance, but when I saw her I was scared so bad I couldn't move. I was paralyzed. The woman had no facial features! There was a head, with a little bonnet on it, and she was wearing a Victorian-style dress, but there was nothing where the face was supposed to be! It was like a shadowy blackness, no form at all.

"Both my mother, Clara, and my grandmother, Ressie, also saw the woman on different occasions. My mother said the vision appeared to her whenever I had gotten into trouble as a sort of rebellious teenager, or when I was sick. She also appeared when my grandmother died. And one night, I had a friend over and we were sleeping on the pull-out sofa in the living room. All of a sudden I awoke to hear my girlfriend talking to someone standing beside her. She thought it was me. When I answered her, from the other side of the bed, she freaked. She said she had had seen the form of a woman standing close beside the bed.

"Sometime later, the back porch was closed in and made into an extra room. My sister-in-law was sitting in that room one night when she said she had the sensation that someone or something was sitting on her legs. There was a definite pressure, like a large cat or something. She had heard our accounts of the frozen lady ghost, and I guess it all was too much for her. She got up and left and refused to come back into the house.

"I think it's a little unusual," Karen continues, "that the apparition has been seen periodically for so long. It has appeared over a number of years. She is no longer scary, in fact, in a way she is comforting. There has never been anything vindictive or destructive about her. Perhaps she just enjoys the comfort of a warm house."

THE SCREAMING STATUE

Karen attended Sweet Briar College, and while there heard of another strange, and tragic, legend. "I can't verify the facts, but this is what I learned. There is a large statue on the campus of a girl or young woman. I was told that the gentleman who founded the college had a teenage daughter. When she was about 14 or 15, she was raped and became pregnant. She died in childbirth. Her father then had the statue erected. It is massive, maybe about 15 feet high. Rumor were that she was entombed upright inside the statue.

"Sweet Briar, of course, was a women's college for a long time, but a few years ago, men were allowed to attend. Once that happened, on the anniversary of the girl's death, I believe sometime in April, there are many witnesses who swear the head of the statue moves, and a scream, like a scream uttered during childbirth, is heard. I've had several girls I went to college with there swear to me they have experienced this phenomenon. One of my friends, a girl with a high sensitivity to psychic phenomena, swears to all things she holds dear, that she has seen and heard the statue. I haven't myself, but I plan to visit there next April and see for myself."

MUFFIN'S GHOST

In the early 1980s, Karen lived in a rented house in South Hill that had once been a doctor's office and residence. She thinks some of the doctor's patients may have died in the building. "Nothing really happened out of the ordinary to us while we lived there," Karen says. "But I think our dog, Muffin, may have sensed something there that we didn't. She would go to the foot of the stairs, for instance, and bark looking up the stairs, like someone might be there. And sometimes Muffin's eyes would follow something, like it was walking across the floor of a room. We never saw anything, but I think Muffin did. We never could explain what happened to the photos we took of the dog. There would always be a mist-like form hanging around Muffin." (Karen's friend, Patricia, gave the author one of these photos.)

Muffin

THE SCRATCHING ON THE WALL

K aren had a friend, a biology professor (now deceased) at Lynchburg Community College. He lived in an old house across the street and a few doors down from Point of Honor, a historic house on Cabell Street, off Rivermont. Karen said the professor told her that there had been a terrible tragedy in the house where he lived, which he believed occurred in the 1880s. At the time a prominent family lived there. One of the sons then, apparently was mad, or either went temporarily berserk, because he killed his sister one night, and perhaps another family member, the professor wasn't sure of the details. At any rate, the family allegedly had the matter hushed up and somehow managed to keep the son from standing trial.

Rather than sending him to an institution, they decided to lock him up in a small room upstairs. The family kept him imprisoned in that room for the next 20 years, until he died. They must have fed him through a slot in the door or something, because it appeared no one ever entered the son's room. Long after he died, workmen while renovating the house, broke into the secret room and were appalled at the decades of filth which had accumulated.

"I went to see the professor one day," Karen recalls. "His room was next to the one in which the son had been kept. Now I like to go on ghost hunts. I think it's fun. But let me tell you, when I went into that house and into the professor's room, I had the most horrible feeling of an evil presence. I had the strongest feeling of terrible, terrible sadness. That is one place where I never wanted to go back to.

"I asked the professor about it. He said he had not seen anything unusual in the house, but the thing that bothered him, was each night when he went to bed, he would hear this scratching sound, like someone's fingernails clawing the wall of the room opposite his — the room where the son had been locked in all those years."

Karen says the professor died in the house of a massive heart attack when he was only 35. "I have often wondered if he was frightened to death!"

CHAPTER 46

The Wreck of Old 97 — Part II

(Danville)

(Author's note: In "The Ghosts of Virginia, Volume II" (1994), I included a chapter on the historic train wreck of "Old 97" just outside the city limits of Danville. It occurred on September 27, 1903. The state historical marker at the site says, "The southbound mail express train on the Southern Railroad left the tracks on a trestle and plunged into the ravine below. Nine persons were killed and seven injured, one of the worst train wrecks in Virginia history."

Steve Broady was a substitute engineer on this run and was unfamiliar with the fact that there was a long and treacherous stretch of track, curvy and with a sharp descent, as the train approached Danville. Instead of slowing down, Broady, who was trying to make up time lost earlier on the run, ran into this dangerous section at full speed. As Broady hit the first part of the down grade he realized his error and tried to brake, but the air pressure was gone. It was too late. One writer recalled the scene this way: "The engine struck the first rails of the curve, wavered and swayed for a moment . . . then continued straight ahead. With a sickening lurch, the stampeding locomotive left the track and bounded onto the trestle, bounding and skipping along the crossties while wood splinters flew in every direction. The mail car behind the tender left the rails, then the second car, the third and the fourth.

"The runaway express rolled to the right, leaped above the yawning chasm, and fell toward the bottom. With a thud and roar never before heard in Danville, the engine's left side struck the creek bed; she half-buried herself in the mud, the drive-wheels continuing to turn slowly. As steam spewed in every direction, the four cars tumbled and shattered almost on top of the overturned locomotive, seemingly exacting revenge for their fate. The last car struck the pile of debris; its wheel bounded off; and it came to rest with one end pointing to the sky, as if gasping for air.

"For a long moment the awful silence of death hovered over the scene." It was soon broken by "the frantic shouts of rescuers, and the shrill songs of hundreds of freed canaries flying wildly overhead."

I concluded that chapter with this: "It has been told by Danvillians for nearly a century now that if one stands still on an autumn afternoon at a little past two, at the foot of that three mile down grade and listens closely, 'Old 97,' with (engineer) Steve Broady at the throttle, echoes yet through the Valley of the Dan."

When I published volume IV in this series, I sent a copy to Kay

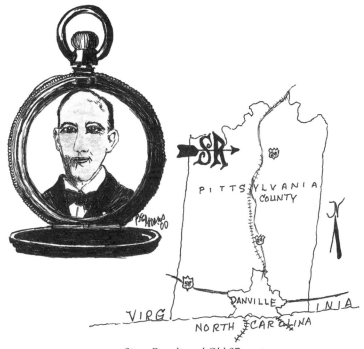

Steve Broady and Old 97

Ragland Boyd of Manakin Sabot, Virginia. I had reprinted a couple of Kay's articles in the Crewe newspaper in IV, which she had so graciously sent me. One chapter was titled, "The Ghost Train at Lomax Crossing. After she had received the book, she called me and asked if I would be interested in another version of the Wreck of Old 97. She had, some years earlier, interviewed a man who said he was an eye and ear witness of the train's ghosts. Here, excerpted, is what Kay wrote.)

"This story does not deal with historical data, but with the paranormal aspects of the tragedy. The locale was a fitting one for a disaster. The skeleton-like railroad trestle loomed above the rock strewn ravine through which Stillhouse Creek cut a jagged watercourse. The right of way has long since been rerouted, but according to eye witness accounts, 97 continued to make its run for years after the wreck.

"The late Edward J. Enoch related the following about the now famous train disaster. The Enoch family lived on a tract of land adjoining the forbidding Stillhouse Branch area. Edward was awakened one night by the sound of a train rumbling its way along a disused section of track near his home. Startled by the approaching train, he ran to a window. To his astonishment, he saw the headlight of an engine and lights visible in several coaches. Then the red lamp of the last coach came into view and the noise of the train receded, followed by a melodic whistle in the distance.

"Edward knew about Old 97, having heard detailed accounts from his father, a railroad employee stationed at Danville. He had not been told of a spectral train rumbling over a section of track that led nowhere.

"Next morning he questioned his father and mother and to his surprise he intercepted a startled look between them. His mother said, 'E. J., you have seen Old 97. We've both seen it and heard it, too.'

"His father added, 'Steve Broady is still trying to bring his run in and he means to keep trying. We never know when the train will be visible.'

"Young Edward questioned his father excitedly. 'But Pa, you told me that 97 wrecked in the afternoon. I saw it at night. His father replied: "Time don't mean anything to Steve. I never knew of 97 coming by except at night. You may never see it again, son. Steve don't have to keep to no schedule now.'

"For a week the young man kept watch in his room, but to his disappointment, no ghost train came in sight. At last his patience was rewarded. First there was a distant hollow roar, as though an engine and cars were crossing the trestle. It came nearer with the familiar rumble that he knew so well.

"Out of the darkness a headlight beam pointed a bright finger of radiance. By the moonlight he could see a plume of smoke, dark against the sky and lights in two or three coaches behind the engine. When the red light of the last car passed on to the north, he heard the whistle blow 'two short, two long,' indicating a crossing.

"E. J. was fascinated by the mystery. He told no one, but went quietly out the next night and hid in the scrub growth near the abandoned track. He continued his vigil until at last he saw the spectral engine and car moving toward him over a partially dismantled track. The splintered and missing cross ties could not possibly have supported a train.

"The young man was so close to the old right of way that he could see the shadowy figure of a man in the engine cab. He was also aware that the cars behind the engine were express rather than passenger coaches. The ghostly train moved on and the whistle reverberated through the stillness.

"Suddenly, a new sound caught his attention. He heard birds singing and chirping in the wake of the phantom train. His fragmented thoughts turned to something his father had told him about Old 97 on its last run. One of the express cars had carried a large shipment of canary birds bound for Atlanta, Georgia. The crates had broken open in the wreck and many of the birds escaped.

"The added realism of the song birds caused young E.J. to beat a hasty retreat. He avoided the area where he had seen the 'ghost of Old 97' for days, until his curiosity bolstered his courage and he again visited the site — but in daylight.

"Prior to his next investigation, there had been a week of heavy rain, and Stillhouse Creek was higher than usual. E.J. slipped and foundered along the bank of the stream and stopped below the support timber of the old trestle. His footing was uncertain and he clutched at a bush to prevent a fall.

"The roots parted from the sodden earth and the young man saw what appeared to be a fragment of cloth. He pulled it from the muddy leaf mold and discovered his find was a piece of canvas. The lettering could still be read: 'U.S. MAIL.' No doubt it was tangible evidence that he had located the exact spot of some of the wreckage of 97, and he carried the souvenir home. (The writer, Kay Ragland Boyd, was shown this bag by E.J. when she interviewed him.)

"A number of times the Enochs and other residents of the area heard or saw the arrival of Old 97 late at night. On one occasion, as E.J. waited, the now familiar pattern varied.

"Suddenly, the frightful shriek of a steam locomotive whistle shattered the silence. He saw a great out-pouring of steam and heard the splintering sound of tortured metal. The ground under his feet trembled and the quiet night became a volume of horrible crashes that seemed to continue for an inestimable time.

"E.J. hastily withdrew to his home, discovered that his parents were awake, the house was lighted, and they had experienced at least a part of his own terrifying encounter with the ghost train.

"No one could provide a plausible explanation. Only E.J. had seen the apparition, although his family had heard the awful crash. The young man suddenly asked his father, 'What's today's date?'

"Mr. Enoch looked at his railroad watch. After a moment's hesitation, he replied, 'Son, it's 3:15 a.m., and the date is September 27th'!"

That was the anniversary of the crash. Kay Boyd concluded her article by asking, "Does Engineer Steve Broady still try to make the curve onto the trestle in North Danville? Does he yet strive to complete his run and 'put her into Spencer (N.C.) on time'?"

A CHIRPING FOOTNOTE

When Old 97 went hurdling into space after leaving the tracks, the first thing noticed by horrified witnesses was the deafening noise of the crash itself. The grinding, crunching sound was said to have carried for miles about. It was then followed, for a few seconds at least, by what was described as an eerie, unreal silence. After this came the groans and cries of victims, curiously mingled with the excited chirping of hundreds of canaries.

There were, in fact, six crates of canaries on board, bound for Atlanta. The crates were partially destroyed by the impact. One writer reported: "Eyewitnesses said that the hundreds of yellow creatures singing and fluttering amid the dark splintered wreck and the moans of the victims lent a particularly macabre touch to the scene." Some said the birds remained in the area for many years afterward — a living visual reminder of the tragedy.

Especially in the 19th century, canaries in cages were taken into coal mines in Virginia and other southeastern states when miners went to work underground. If they stopped singing or collapsed, it meant there were poisonous gases in the mines that might either suffocate the miners or explode; the delicate birds would react faster than the men. Thus the phrase "the canary in the coal-mine" came to refer to anything that portends disaster.

CHAPTER 47

A Trilogy of Mecklenburg Mysteries

(Clarksville Area)

(Author's note: The following two interesting accounts were brought to my attention by a gentleman at the July 1998 Lake Festival held annually in Clarksville. He said that when his father was 12-years-old, in 1899, he was told about the death of a man who was a well-recognized fiddle player in Goochland County. As was the custom in those days, there was a wake — a "sitting up with the dead," where relatives and close friends would sit in the parlor with the deceased in his coffin, through the night. It was winter time and there were several inches of fresh snow outside.

About midnight, the drowsy "sitters" were suddenly awakened by a loud banging at the front door, followed by the door latch being jiggled. Assuming it was a friend arriving late, they went to the door and opened it. There was no one there or in sight, and there were no human footprints in the snow. This particular phenomenon occurred three times during the night.

Sometime after the last incident, all present clearly heard a bow scrape across fiddle strings in the loft, where the dead man's fiddle had been placed. No one dared to go upstairs and investigate. Instead they all huddled together and prayed for the dawn to hurry.

The second area haunting was recorded in a Mecklenburg Sun newspaper column by James N. Sheppard, and is excerpted as follows:)

 "Iron Gate Road (just outside Clarksville) is just down the road from the Russell Stover candy plant. The drive leads to a beautiful old home called 'Sutherland,' currently owned by Harriette and Jesse Overstreet."

It is not specified exactly when the original part of the house was built by Robert Greenwood, although it probably was in the late 18th or early 19th century. Greenwood died in 1833. The strange manifestations associated with Sutherland began sometime after 1870, when an Englishman named Washington Dodge bought the house. He is said to have had the first horse drawn mower in the county.

But there was a certain area of ground where the mower would break down everytime it crossed it. Nothing would grow on this patch of land, and a frustrated Dodge finally cordoned it off with tobacco sticks.

A later owner was a rather eccentric woman named Mrs. Lucy Gooch. She bought the house in 1914 after her husband, Wayne, had just divorced her for a young woman. Despite the desertion, however, she kept a life-size portrait of her husband in the living room. And for some odd reason, ghostly or otherwise, she refused to stay in the house alone. She would hire boys or young men to stay in the house with her. One such tenant was ordered by Mrs. Gooch to sleep in her room — with a pistol under his pillow. Exactly what she was afraid of was never made known. Incidentally, Mrs. Gooch died in 1944 after tripping over her dog and breaking her hip.

The Overstreets bought Sutherland in 1978. Columnist Sheppard says here is what has happened in recent years:

— The previous owner (1974) told them that his mother-in-law had spent one night in the back bedroom on the first floor, and went home saying she would never spend another night there.

— The Overstreet's daughter's dog was afraid to go to sleep in that room and paced the floor all night with his fur standing straight up.

— Harriette Overstreet's cat refused to go in that room.

— The Overstreets heard furniture being moved upstairs" when no one else was in the house.

— There is one other weird thing: Washington Dodge was said to have been buried with his horse in the same grave by a road near the house. Yet when this part of the road was rebuilt and widened a few years ago, no bones were turned up!

Who it is, or was, that haunts stately old Sutherland has never been determined.

WHO HAUNTS ANGIE'S BRIDGE?

o complete this trilogy, Patricia McGetrick, of South Hill, Virginia, gave me a newspaper clipping of a long-standing legend in east Mecklenburg County. It was written by reporter Donna C. Gregory, and published Halloween week 1998, in the South Hill Enterprise. Patricia added some details, as did long-time area residents. The facts, however, are sketchy, and the variations of the tradition are considerable.

This much is known. Sixty years ago there was a bridge which spanned the Meherrin River at a point which separates Mecklenburg and Lunenburg Counties. It was destroyed in a sweeping flood in 1940, and was replaced by a modern structure on High Bridge Road. To many in that region of the commonwealth, the spans, both old and new, are known as "Angie's Bridge."

Angie, supposedly, was a young college student from a well-to-do Lunenburg family. She came home for a long weekend with her boyfriend, but it rained for three days straight. As Angie and the young man began the return trip to school in Richmond, they drove over the wet-slick roads in a 1930s model Ford sedan.

South Hill resident Charles H. Crowder, Jr., remembers the incident. Floods caused by the incessant rains washed away the bridge's steel superstructure. Road workers built a temporary wooden bridge to allow traffic to pass until a more permanent span could be constructed. However, unbeknownst to Angie and her friend, recent torrents had washed away the underpinnings of the temporary bridge.

According to Crowder, the upper part of the bridge collapsed as the Ford passed over it, sending the car plunging down into the angry, swirling waters below. Angie's friend, realizing what was happening, opened Angie's door and pushed her out of the car as it sank. She was swept several hundred yards downstream, and finally, near exhaustion, managed to swim to shore. By the time help arrived at the scene, it was dark, and still raining. Rescue efforts were in vain.

The next day, the car was found upside down, 50 feet below the bridge, but the young man was not in it. Crowder, who was a teenager at the time, says, "I was there when they dragged the car up to road level. The top of the car was mashed flat onto the dashboard and over the transom over the back seat.

"No one ever knew what happened to that young man. He's never been seen or heard from that moment to this. It's fairly rare that someone just so completely disappears. There was never any trace of him," Crowder says.

On hearing of this incident, reporter Gregory did some extensive research. In the September 21, 1940, issue of the South Hill Enterprise, she found an account of the actual accident. The problem is, rather than answers, it raises more questions. For example, for the past six decades, everyone has called it Angie's Bridge, assuming the girl involved was named Angie. But the newspaper article says her name was Lessie Deel. Then who is, or was, Angie?

The young man was named Oscar Feitig, 24, of Richmond. Search parties combed the river for five days and found Feitig's overcoat, but not his body. The article stated: "A wire net has been strung across the river at Union Mill and people have walked up and down both banks to make sure that Feitig did not die there from exposure and injuries. Besides the dragging, the river has been dynamited in hopes of forcing the body to the surface."

Sadly, in another article published a month later, Feitig's father pleaded for anyone who might have information about his missing son to come forward. He held out the scant hope that Oscar might still be alive somewhere and "suffering from memory loss."

While no word of young Feitig, either dead or alive, ever surfaced, there are scores of people, on both sides of the county line, who swear they have heard ghostly sounds emanating from the spot where the car hurtled into the flood waters so long ago. And here, the variations come into play. Some stoutly contend they have heard the screams of the young couple. Others have heard a woman crying for her lost friend. A few have reported hearing a male voice shouting "Angie." There have even been accounts of strange sightings: unexplained shadows dancing on the river banks; and a white scarf, believed to be the girl's, still floating in the water.

Was there a real "Angie" who preceded the tragedy of 1940? There are those who will tell you "she" plunged into the river when a buggy turned over on the old bridge, perhaps 100 years ago. And her body was never found.

So is it Angie's ghost who haunts, or is it the spirit of Lessie Deel. . . or that of Oscar Feitig. . . or all of them? There does seem to be one consensus: eerie sounds from someone are heard in the area of the old bridge.

Beyond that, the mystery may never be unraveled.

CHAPTER 48

The Matching Faces of a Distressed Woman

(Franklin)

(Author's note: I love the letters I get from people all over the commonwealth. I particularly liked the one I got in February 1998, from a young woman named Leslie Bell-Stanton of Smithfield. She is a psychologist with the Franklin City Public Schools. She began by saying, "I am a lover of history and ghost stories and have truly enjoyed reading your stories more than others because of the historical tone that you take and the details that you provide. . . . Also, I would like to talk with you about a very intriguing ghost story I have been involved with. I have what I feel to be a really neat tale. . . . I was not the primary person, but I have spoken with her and she has agreed to talk with you about it. Her name is Earlene Sprouse and she lives in Surry. She is the educational diagnostician and speech pathologist with the Franklin City Public Schools.")

ranklin is about as far south as you can go and still be in Virginia. It is just nine miles above the North Carolina line, and hour of so south of Virginia Beach, and a few miles southwest of Suffolk. To get there, one passes through rural vistas that have changed little over the past 200 years. Situated on the western side of the Blackwater River, Franklin was a small town in the days leading up to the Civil War. When the Seaboard and Roanoke Railroad crossed the river sometime later, enabling the emergence of the timber and paper industries, Franklin grew. Today paper plants still dominate the area's skyline.

Near the courthouse is a tall Confederate monument topped by the erect statue of a soldier facing north. Carved in stone are these lines:

"With shouts above the cannon's roar
They joined the legions gone before
They bravely fought, they bravely fell
They wore the gray, and wore it well."

But Franklin may be better known for a notorious slave insurrection which took place near here in 1831 and was immortalized by Virginia author William Styron's book, "The Confessions of Nat Turner." A chapter on Turner is included in "The Ghosts of Virginia, Volume I," (1993).

Leslie Bell-Stanton said her ghost story began when part of the education department moved from trailers to a central office building. Actually, it was a former private residence whose rooms had been converted to offices. It was known as the Pace Mansion, after W. T. and Meta Pace, who had the huge house built in 1905. Mr. Pace, a logging tycoon, at one time owned a great deal of land in and around Franklin. After the Paces departed, (several are said to have died in the house) it became the Franklin Public Library for a while.

Leslie continues: "Prior to our arrival we had been told of the 'ghosts' that resided there, and I fondly recall being told about hearing the trapeze noises coming from the attic. 'It's just the Pace children playing in the attic' which is so large, I was told, that trapezes were used there. I tended to work late at night and so I prepared myself for the event."

It wasn't long before the education staff began experiencing "things." There were unexplained noises, mostly coming from the attic area. There seemed to be an aura of spookiness prevalent in the old manor home. Leslie's office was a "cold spot." Some employees refused to stay in the house after dark. Others would never enter the attic. One day Leslie was sitting at her computer when, without any apparent reason, or from any known source, several books "flew" off her bookshelf and crashed to the floor. Leslie got up from her work, said "you can have it," and promptly left the building.

But it is the ethereal experience of Earlene Sprouse that still has everyone talking. It is best told in her own words:

"We had just returned to work coming off a Memorial Day holiday, and when we entered the building there was a terrible stench, a dreadful smell. We thought a cat or some other animal may have crawled under the house and died. So we asked the maintenance man to go down into the cellar and to look under the house to see if he could find out what was causing it. Well, he got down in the basement and began banging real loud on the foundation. He made a heck of a racket. You could hear it all through the old house.

"I was in my office when I looked up and there was a lady standing at the door. She appeared confused and distressed. She was an elderly lady with thin lips and a prominent nose, and she was wearing wire rimmed glasses. She had the most startling blue eyes. They were robin's egg blue. She was dressed in an old fashioned brown outfit with tortoise shell buttons and a lace collar. And she had on these old fashioned type shoes. She looked very distraught. Then, she just disappeared. I went out the door and asked my secretary if she had seen her. She said she had, but no one else in the building did. I asked all around, and they all started kidding me, like I had seen a ghost or something. But I didn't think I had because she appeared to be flesh and blood. You couldn't see through her.

"I don't know why, but I became quite concerned. Who was this woman and why did she look so concerned. It began to worry me. So I sat down and drew a picture of the woman, you know, a sketch. I took that around and asked if anyone had seen her. No one had.

"Well, about a week or so later a lady named Ann Williams came into the office. She was related to the Pace family. I think it was her great grandparents who built the house. She saw the drawing I had made and seemed surprised. She came back a few days later and had an old faded black and white photo with her. She had gone home and gone through some old albums.

"She laid the photo down next to the sketch, and they <u>matched perfectly!</u> It was the same woman! Ann called her "Aunt Nanny," and said she had been one of Meta Pace's daughters. She had died in the house decades ago. When I saw the two pictures together — the same face, the same hair, and especially the same eyes, although the woman in the photo wasn't wearing glasses — I could feel the hair on my head standing straight up! Ann had also brought in a pair of old shoes, and they were virtually identical to the ones I had seen the woman wearing when she appeared at the door.

"I had seen a ghost after all!"

"I know I am not crazy. I saw what I saw and it was a real woman. I'm Hungarian, and we are supposed to have a second sight. But she didn't look scary at all. She just looked distressed. I think maybe the maintenance man banging around in the basement might have disturbed her and she appeared to see what was happening to her house. That's the only thing I can think of. How else do you explain it?"

Earlene says she only saw her once (and that was enough for her), but she adds that some of the cleaning ladies later claimed they saw the same woman and they steadfastly refused to go near the attic after that.

Scary Return To Cold Harbor

(Near Richmond)

(Author's note: In my book, "Civil War Ghosts of Virginia," (1995), I wrote a chapter about the alleged ghostly activity at Cold Harbor, near Richmond, site of one of the bloodiest battles of the entire American Civil War. The fighting took place on June 3, 1864. Here is part of what I said.

"According to many, the battle here was a dreadful and tragic mistake from the start. For example, Major General Martin T. McMahon of the Union forces, wrote: 'In the opinion of a majority of the survivors, the battle of Cold Harbor never should have been fought. There was no military reason to justify it.' Union commanding General U. S. Grant said in his memoirs: 'I have always regretted that the last assault at Cold Harbor was ever made.

"Although Grant was still licking his wounds suffered recently at the Battle of the Wilderness near Fredericksburg, he was anxious to launch an all-out assault, come Hell or high water, to bring the war to a quick close. Many historians feel Grant committed a monumental blunder by ordering a no-holds-barred frontal assault on Lee at Cold Harbor. First, his troops were exhausted after the hard battles to the north and then the long march toward Richmond. They were described as being 'dirt-caked and worn out.'

"Second, the Union officers did not know the land.

Inexplicably, neither Grant nor General George Meade had ordered anyone to make a detailed survey of the ground. Thus when the charge came, their infantrymen ran into dense thickets, impassable briar patches, and swampy bogs which slowed their advance to a crawl and exposed them to enemy fire. And third, as historian Bruce Catton put it: 'The hard fact was that by 1864, good troops using rifles and standing in well-built trenches, and provided with suitable artillery support, simply could not be dislodged by any frontal assault whatever." He cited General George Pickett's ill-fated charge at Gettysburg as an example.

"The battle that ensued was one of the most disastrous debacles of the war. One survivor later described the action by saying the Southern riflemen opened fire with one long, rolling volley — 'A sheet of flame, sudden as lightning, red as blood, and so near, it seemed to singe the men's faces.'

"Major General E. M. Law, C.S.A., summed it up this way: 'I could see more plainly the terrible havoc made in the ranks of the assaulting column. I had seen the dreadful carnage in front of Marye's Hill in Fredericksburg, and on the old railroad cut which (Stonewall) Jackson's men held at the second Manassas; but I had seen nothing to exceed this. It was not war; it was murder!'

"It is estimated that 7,000 Union soldiers died in one half hour period, and more than 13,000 were lost overall, compared to 1,700 dead Confederates. There is also this chilling note. As the two armies moved out of Cold Harbor, they left a ghastly scene behind. Scattered in the trenches, across the open area, and in the woods were hundreds of corpses. Some apparently laid there for years afterward! A traveler visiting the site in 1869 - five years later - recalled seeing partially exposed skeletons 'all over the field'."

As I said in 1995, "ample justification for ghostly phenomena?"

To this, I added, "Over the years there have been many reports of strange sounds and sights across this desolate battlefield. There have been Civil War reenactments here, and some of the reenactors have told of ethereal encounters . . . mysterious cold spots in the torrid heat of the summer . . . fleeting glimpses of phantom soldiers scurrying for cover . . . the muffled sounds of moans and cries and weeping . . . and of cocking muskets."

One of those who has experienced such phenomena at Cold Harbor is a young woman named Ann Bailey who lives in Richmond. In 1992, she and her husband, Charles, were camping out at the site during a reenactment. She was awakened in the middle of the night and peered directly into the grizzled, apparitional face of a bearded Union soldier. She said it definitely was not a reenactor. Although it was all quiet on the battlefield, she said she also heard "distant musket fire, military drum beats, and the sounds of bodies being dragged across the ground."

Charlottesville author and psychic Nanette Morrison took a photo of a tree when she once visited the battlefield. She said she had been "compelled" to take the picture. When it was developed, she added, she could see the face of a Union soldier in the print. In a newspaper article reenactor Tim Fredrickson told of sensing strange pains when he walked across the battlefield. The pains would instantly dispel when he left the site. On one occasion he said he saw the ghostly image of a soldier running toward him. He added that the image "passed through his body as he stood stunned," and that it felt "like a wave of emotions washing over me." Fredrickson believes he fought at Cold Harbor in a past life.

I also quoted Robin Reed, executive director of the Museum of the Confederacy in Richmond, who said: "There's no question that you can go to certain battlefields and feel a sense of foreboding . . . There's something strange about this site (Cold Harbor.)"

All of this serves as a prelude to the following, which was told to me by a man named John Williams at the Newport News Fall Festival in October 1997. Here is what he had to say:)

"I was at Cold Harbor on a night 27 years ago with my cousin and two friends and their dates. We were all crammed into a Mustang. In those days you could drive through the battlefield at night. It was a good place to take girls, you know. We stopped and parked. It was about two in the morning. It was as quiet as a graveyard. All of a sudden, everyone on the passenger side of the car began screaming and shouting for us to get out of there. I didn't see anything, but they were going crazy banging on me to move.

"I started up and as we went around a bend I looked up and there was a Civil War soldier on horseback right in front of me. He was staring right at me! It scared the hell out of me. I slammed down on the accelerator and we got out of there quick.

"Later, I asked the others what they had been screaming about. They all said they had seen a mass of spectral figures rising up from the trenches! They all swore to it, and they swear by it to this day!"

CHAPTER 50

Caught in a Civil War Time Warp

(Richmond)

He was, by almost all accounts, a tortured and tormented man in the years after "The War." His once-fierce pride had been shattered; his long-held hopes of eternal glory crushed forever. This was George Edward Pickett, major general, Confederate States of America. Once he had been as cocky as a bantam rooster. He believed, like general George Patton in a later war, that he was destined for greatness. He believed this despite the fact that he graduated 59th, dead last, out of the West Point class of 1846. One of his classmates was another George — McClellan — who graduated second.

Pickett was a vain man. Civil War historian Shelby Foote described him as being, "Jaunty, on a sleek black horse, he wore a small blue cap, buff gauntlets and matching blue cuffs on the sleeves of his well-tailored uniform." He carried an "elegant riding crop. His boots were always brightly polished with gold spurs. He was of middle height, slender, graceful of carriage, dapper and alert. "One spoke of his pulchritude," Foote noted. He sported a curly chin beard and a mustache that drooped beyond the corners of his mouth and then turned upward at the ends. It had, said some, "a swashbuckling effect." His dark brown hair hung shoulder length in ringlets which he anointed with perfume. Historian James McPherson said Pickett looked like a "cross between a Cavalier dandy and a riverboat gambler. He affected the romantic style of Sir Walter Scott's heroes and was eager to win everlasting glory."

His chance for such glory came on July 3, 1863, just outside the sleepy village of Gettysburg, Pennsylvania. Although he had distinguished himself somewhat as a young officer during the Mexican War, Pickett ached for heroic action. July 3rd was the third day of the historic battle at Gettysburg. The first two days had been somewhat inconclusive. Commanding General Robert E. Lee ordered a direct frontal attack on the strong, well-fortified position of the Union army.

It would mean crossing open fields for three quarters of a mile to higher ground. General James Longstreet, Lee's right arm after the death of General Stonewall Jackson, pleaded with Lee to reconsider such an open assault. Longstreet believed the Confederates would be wiped out before they could even reach their target. But Lee would not be persuaded. Longstreet later would write: "My heart was heavy. I could see the desperate and hopeless nature of the charge and the hopeless slaughter it would cause. . . . That day was one of the saddest of my life."

Pickett, oddly, did not share Longstreet's pessimism. He saw such a charge as his chance for immortality. It was be the crowning achievement of his, to then, non-illustrious career. McPherson wrote that Pickett's all-Virginia division waited with "nervous impatience" to go in and get it over with.

The result of Pickett's charge is well-known history. Nearly 15,000 men began the attack in the early afternoon. Of that event, historian Bruce Catton wrote: "Men passed the limit of human endurance." Smoke from cannon fire and dust from the fields was so heavy that the battlefield couldn't be seen at times. Catton: "Men fought to the utmost limit of primal savagery."

The Union position was too strong. Canister from lines of cannon tore into the Rebel lines. The few who did reach the Yankee position were soon overrun. Thousands died. Pickett's division was decimated. Foote said: "Pickett came riding back with an expression of dejection and bewilderment on his face. Leading his division into battle for the first time, he had seen two-thirds of it destroyed. Not only had his great hour come to nothing; tactically speaking, it added up to considerably less that nothing."

Lee then ordered Pickett to place his division to the rear of a hill. Pickett then said the famous line, "General Lee, I have no division now." Lee, true to his character, said: "This has been my fight, and upon my shoulders rests the blame. The men and officers of your command have written the name of Virginia as high today as it has ever been written before. . . . Your men have done all that men can do. The fault is entirely mine."

In time, Pickett grew disillusioned about the order to charge, and became bitter toward Lee. When he was asked what he thought of Lee, he uttered: "That old man had my division massacred."

There seems to be some confusion among historians, to this day, about how Pickett personally performed on that fateful day at Gettysburg. A persistent question is how did he alone survive the charge without a scratch when all but one of the commanders under him fell dead or wounded. There was one report that he stayed to the rear of his charging men and then waited for them when they were driven back. Certainly there is nothing to compare Pickett's actions with those of General Lewis Armistead, for example. Armistead led his men up the hill and even crossed over the Union barriers before he was mortally wounded. His courage was exemplary.

Still, Pickett was not charged with cowardice and not relieved of command. He continued fighting, although his heart did not appear to be in it. He lost most of another division at Five Forks, Virginia, near Dinwiddie, on April 1, 1865. Historians have written that he was "out of touch during the battle, behind the lines at a shadbake."

Whether or not this was the final straw, Lee stripped Pickett of his command the day before the surrender at Appomattox. Curiously, Pickett showed up on April 9, 1865, at the surrender site. Lee saw him and said to an aid, "I thought that man was no longer with the army."

Still, in an odd twist of fate, Pickett gained the admiration of Southerners as time passed. Civil War experts say he received the reflective benefit of the heroic spirit his men had exhibited at Gettysburg.

When he died at age 50 in 1875, a decade after the war had ended, he was given a ceremonial funeral. Thousands came to his interment at Hollywood Cemetery in Richmond, where now stands a lasting monument to him. Tens of thousands more still come to Hollywood annually to view his gravesite.

George Pickett could also be considered a ladies' man. Once, when some admiring women asked General Lee for a lock of his hair he suggested that they turn to Pickett. Pickett had married Sallie Minge of Richmond in January 1851, but lost her through death 11 months later.

At the age of 38, after the war had begun, he fell desperately in love with LaSalle Corbell, not half his age. Virginia historian Douglas Southall Freeman wrote of the courtship. "That interesting romance would have been exclusively his affair had not 'the charming Sally,' as he styled her, lived in the very county where Pickett's lines now were drawn. The miles from his headquarters to her home at Chuckatuck (Virginia) were not too long to deter a lover on a good horse; but double that distance between the end of one day's duty and the labors of another was a heavy strain on man and mount. Longstreet would deny Pickett nothing that a chief honorably could grant a lieutenant, and, again and again, he gave assent for Pickett to rush to Chuckatuck to make his avowals and then to come back and get such sleep as he could in the morning."

Finally, Longstreet told Pickett he could no longer go to his sweetheart, but he went all the same. Freeman: "Nothing could hold him back from that pursuit."

Pickett and Miss Corbell eventually married and their deep love for each other is evident in the poignant letters he wrote her during the war. After Gettysburg, he penned: "The battle is lost . . . . Your soldier lives and mourns and but for you, my darling, he would rather, a million times rather, be back there with his dead, to sleep for all time in an unknown grave."

Mrs. Pickett died in 1931. She had requested to be buried beside the body of her husband in Hollywood Cemetery, but this was denied because of a rule against burying women in the "soldiers' section." This so incensed Pickett's grandson, George E. Pickett III, that he threatened to reinter the general in Arlington National Cemetery. There, he hoped to establish "a special shrine" near the site where several hundred Confederate soldiers had been buried. His plan was to erect a large statue of Robert E. Lee and to bury his grandfather on one side of the statue and former Confederate general James Longstreet on the other. Richmond officials appealed to the Pickett family to reconsider, and eventually they did. LaSalle Pickett's ashes were placed in the Abbey Mausoleum outside the Hobson Gate next to Arlington Cemetery.

Over the years, the mausoleum fell into disrepair and Civil War heritage groups, including the Virginia Division of the United Daughters of the Confederacy, arranged to bring her remains to Richmond for a reuniting with her husband. The old rule had been relaxed.

And so, on Saturday, March 22, 1998, Mrs. Pickett got her dying wish. Her remains were laid to rest in a bronze urn inside a silk-lined, 13-side redwood box in front of her husband's monument at Hollywood.

"They've been joined in heaven these many years, now their

mortal remains are joined here," said Nancy Gum, president of the Virginia division of the UDC. Added Dan McGuire, commander of the Virginia Society of the Military Order of the Stars and Bars: "She's home at last in Virginia . . . . She is home at last with her beloved husband."

As with the burial of General Pickett, Mrs. Pickett's reburial was well attended. To the sound of cannon fire and the strains of "Dixie," about 400 people, many dressed in Confederate finery, came to the event. The keynote speaker was Kathy Harrison, a historian with the Gettysburg National Military Park and author of the book, "Nothing but glory, Pickett's Division at Gettysburg."

* * * * *

(Author's note: Call it coincidence. Call it what you will. I was reading a clipping of Mrs. Pickett's reburial one day in March 1998 when I got a call from a man named Dale Davidson, who lives on Hollywood Drive in Richmond. He is a security guard at a funeral home. Here is what he told me.)

"I like to wander around old cemeteries and old Civil War battle sites. I've been all over - Malvern Hill, Spotsylvania, Cold Harbor, Gettysburg, Antietam, Chickamauga, Drury's Bluff, you name it. And I've had a few really weird experiences. I'm Scotch-Irish. Does that mean I have a second sight. I don't know how to explain it.

"About 15 years ago, I was by myself, walking along the Revolutionary War battlefield at Yorktown. I was out by the siege lines at a redoubt, standing on a parapet. The British Union Jack flag was flying. I was looking out to the east, toward the French-Colonial lines, when I saw something out of the corner of my eye. It appeared to be a British soldier in red coat with crossed white belts just off to the left. But when I turned to look directly at it, I saw only the flag. I turned back and again, out of my peripheral vision, I saw the soldier again. I wasn't frightened. But then it just disappeared.

"Another time I was visiting Sherwood Forest, the home of President John Tyler. I was taking a tour of the house and the hostess took us into a room and mentioned the old servant's stairway in the corner of the room. She told the story of the ghost of a former servant who used to go up and down those stairs. Well, I saw something move on those stairs out of the corner of my eye. I saw the hem of an old skirt. It was at eye level. I thought at first maybe it was someone put there to scare us as the hostess was telling her story. But after I thought about it, I don't think so, because there was no sound — no footstep or rustle of a skirt. And the vision was gone in a flash.

"But the real reason I called you was about the burial of Mrs. Pickett in Hollywood Cemetery. I saw it on the evening news — all the reenactors and all that. I said to a friend of mine, Ralph, I saw that same scene 10 years ago. He said 'that's weird. What do you mean?'

"Mr. Taylor, let me tell you. I went to Hollywood Cemetery about 10 years ago, just to wander around. I was alone, and believe me, I was stone cold sober. I remember clearly that I parked by an old gate near Pickett's grave. I walked over to the gravesite and looked around.

"Suddenly, I saw a crowd of people. Some men were in Confederate uniforms and some wore long morning, or frock coats. Women were in fancy hoop skirts. They were all gathered around an old bandstand or gazebo. There were horses and carriages lining the pathway, and there were some drummer boys. It was as if they had all assembled here for some sort of ceremony, maybe a funeral. For some reason I was not frightened. I was intrigued but not frightened.

"I realized what I was seeing was there, but it wasn't there if you know what I mean. In other words, it wasn't real. These were not mortal beings. How did I know this? Everything and everyone I saw was in black and white! And although there seemed to be a lot of commotion going on — people were talking and moving about — there was no sound whatsoever. It was deathly still.

"It was a scene just like the one I had seen on television when Mrs. Pickett was buried there, although it lasted only a few seconds at most. Then everyone disappeared and the site was all in color again. I have asked myself, was it my imagination or was it low blood sugar. No. I saw it. It was there, but I can't explain it, nor do I ever expect to."

Was Dale Davidson somehow, for those fleeting few seconds, enveloped in what parapsychologists have called "a time warp?" Was he transported back in time to the scene of George Pickett's ceremonial burial in 1875? Or was he projected ten years into the future, getting a preview of LaSalle Picket's reunion with her husband in 1998?

Perhaps some questions are better left unanswered!

* * * * *

Pickett's Grave

THE SWEET SCENT OF PHANTOM PERFUME

 ark Muller's mother came to visit him in Richmond in October 1998. On October 31 —

Halloween — they decided to tour historic Hollywood Cemetery. "We were looking for the gravesite of General George Pickett," Mark says, "and we missed the turn and drove around for a while before we finally found it. Once there, we got out of the car and immediately were literally overwhelmed with the strong scent of flowers. And I mean strong. It was overpowering! It centered right around Pickett's grave. We both sensed it. We tried to identify the scent, but it seemed to be a mixed bouquet.

"We walked several yards away and there was no odor. Then we walked back, and when we got near the Pickett site the sensation overtook us again."

George Pickett, it must be remembered, had a penchant for wanting to smell nice. He liberally splashed himself with flowery perfumes and toilet waters!

"We found the incident kind of, well, unusual to say the least," Muller recalls. "But if anyone from the Civil War was identified with flowers, it would definitely be Pickett."

AN APPROVING SPECTRAL ONLOOKER

Second footnote: Billie Burgess Earnest of Virginia Beach, President of the Norfolk County Grays chapter of the United Daughters of the Confederacy, is a huge fan of LaSalle Corbell Pickett and has spent a great deal of time researching her life. In April 1999, she hosted a special memorial service at the Cedar Hill Cemetery in Suffolk, honoring Confederate Colonel James Jasper Phillips. He was LaSalle's uncle. Billie gathered 24 members of the Corbell-Phillips family for the ceremony. She had the event taped by a professional videographer.

Toward the end of the video a ghostly white figure or image appears in one frame, standing back from the crowd, alone. Neither Billie or anyone else knows who this was. "You couldn't distinguish his facial features," she says. "It was more like an apparitional figure. No one saw him that day in person. And the video image appears just in that one frame. When the videographer panned back to that section a few seconds later, it was gone." Could it have been the spirit of Colonel Phillips, lending his approval to the service? Billie smiles and shrugs.

Billie, who has done extensive genealogical research on her Civil War ancestors, tells of another extraordinary incident which she and her sister witnessed sometime earlier. "After a long search, we had traced the gravesite of our great-great uncle, John Arthur Battle, to an unmarked spot in the Oakwood Cemetery in Richmond," she says. "He was a private in the 19th infantry of the second cavalry in North Carolina.

"It was a beautiful, bright, sunny day. As we stood over his unmarked grave and said a little prayer, a light shower of raindrops suddenly fell on my sister and me. There was not a whisper of a cloud in the sky. Where did it come fram? I said 'it's his teardrops. He knows we have found him at last'."

GHOSTLY STRAGGLERS IN THE WOODS

here is another curious sidelight to the Pickett phenomena. A few years ago, during the filming for the movie, "Gettysburg" at that site, a strange thing happened. As the cameras began rolling, capturing the start of Pickett's charge, one cameraman stationed at Spangler's Woods, suddenly stopped filming and yelled, "cut." Reenactors stopped in their tracks. The man said that as he looked through his lens he could still see some Confederate forms "milling around back in the woods." Not all the reenactors, he claimed, had charged forward as they should have.

The scene was reset and the cameras rolled again. Once more, the one cameraman shouted "cut." He said he could still see some figures lurking among the thick trees. A production assistant was dispatched to search the woods and scold the offending reenactors. He looked.

There was no one there.

The Spectral Return of a 'Mosby's Ranger'

(Flint Hill, near Front Royal)

He was known as the "Gray Ghost."

But the nickname, given in admiration, had no supernatural overtones. He was a real living man and more. He was a legend. Although small in physical stature, at about five foot eight inches tall and less than 130 pounds, he was a giant in deed. Like his more famous contemporary in the Civil War, J. E. B. Stuart, he was charismatic, daring, dashing, absolutely fearless, unorthodox, unpredictable . . . and extremely effective.

This was Colonel John Singleton Mosby.

In the middle years of the War Between the States, he commanded two battalions of less than 200 men and yet wreaked unholy havoc on Union forces that often outnumbered him ten to one or better. He did it by what became known as guerrilla warfare. He hit and ran, darted and parried, surprised and conquered.

Historian Shelby Foote said of Mosby: "(He was) A former Virginia attorney, 33-years-old and sandy haired, in his thigh-high boots, red-lined cape and ostrich plume, was utterly fearless, quite uncatchable, and altogether skillful in the conduct of operations." Robert E. Lee himself became a devoted fan of Mosby's even though he had little general regard for the fighting of "partisans." Perhaps Mosby's greatest compliment came from Union commanding general U.S. Grant. After the war, he said, "There were probably but few men in the South who could have commanded successfully a separate detachment, in the rear of an opposing army and so near the border of hostilities, as long as he did without losing his entire command."

Mosby's most noted raids came in and near his native territory, in Loudoun and Fauquier Counties, cradled between the Bull Run and the Blue Ridge Mountains. Most of his carefully recruited men were farmers by day and conducted their attacks against the Yankee forces at night. They often struck when least expected: in pre-dawn hours; during rain and snow storms; and at heavily guarded sites thought impregnable. And their lightning strikes brought astonishing results: the capture of thousands of Union soldiers; thousands of horses; huge quantities of guns, ammunition and equipment; and untold amounts of Federal payrolls, including one of $173,000.

But perhaps their greatest effect cannot be measured in mere statistics. It was the fear they drove into the hearts of their enemies; the demoralization they created when even the name "Mosby's Rangers" was circulated in Union camps.

So devastating was this effect that northern General Philip Sheridan sought unusual and cruel means to curb Mosby's influence.

He asked for, and received, from General Grant, permission to hang without trial any of Mosby's men he captured. This was carried to its barbaric end in September 1864, when General George Custer's men captured six rangers in Front Royal. They summarily shot four of the men, and hanged the other two, leaving them dangling before the shocked town's citizens. A crudely lettered placard was placed around the neck of one of the rangers. It said, "This will be the fate of Mosby and all his men." Soonafter a seventh ranger was captured and hanged in Rappahannock County.

Although appalled at this, Mosby nevertheless thought the only way to prevent more hangings of his men was to retaliate in kind, and he received such permission from General Lee. Over the next several weeks Mosby captured more than 700 men and sent most of them to prison in Richmond. But he kept 27 men from General Custer's command. He then lined them up and had them draw slips of paper from a hat. Twenty slips were blank. Those who drew these would be sent to Richmond. But the ones who drew numbers one through seven would be executed. One of those who drew a deadly number was a young drummer boy barely in his teens. Mosby let him go and had the men redraw for the seventh death sentence.

These ill-fated soldiers were taken out into the countryside at night at a place then known as Grindstone Hill. There, three were hanged from a large red oak tree that for years afterward was called "Mosby's Hanging Tree." Two were shot, and two managed to escape in the darkness. Mosby didn't seem to mind this too much, believing they would get back to Custer and Sheridan to let them know any further killings would be countered equally. And it worked. Sheridan rescinded the order to execute any captured rangers.

But before the "truce" became effective, a particularly sad and curious sequence of events occurred. Near a place called Flint Hill, also in the Front Royal vicinity, a captured Union deserter was shot and killed attempting to escape. Shortly after this, two of Mosby's men were captured at a nearby blacksmith shop. In reprisal for the shot deserter, the Union soldiers declared that one of the two Mosby men must also die. The men were told to draw straws to see who would be executed. The man who drew the fatal straw had a wife and five children. The other man was unmarried. His name was Albert Gallatin Willis, a 20-year-old ministerial student.

Willis, in a rare display of courage, stepped forward and offered the ultimate sacrifice. He said since he had no family of his own, he would take the other man's place. And so, on October 14, 1864, Willis, at the last minute asking forgiveness for his executioners, was hanged. He was buried in a small cemetery behind the Flint Hill Baptist Church. State highway marker J 26, at the site of the hanging, documents Willis' heroism.

One hundred and one years later, in 1965, a family moved into a large old house near the church. The father, mother, and four sons requested to remain anonymous. Upon learning the legend of Willis, they went to the cemetery and cleared his grave from the thick underbrush which covered it. The young children often visited and grave and "talked" to Willis. They developed a special rapport with him.

Willis apparently repaid the visits, in spiritual form. First the mother, and then others, began hearing the distinct sounds of someone in heavy boots walking across the upstairs bedrooms of the boys. It would move from one bedroom to another. The mother said the footsteps were so real she at first feared an intruder in the house. But careful investigation found no one there, and the boys and her husband sound asleep.

Over a period of months the ghostly boot steps were heard a number of times, often after the boys had paid a visit to the cemetery. In time even the father, a skeptic, believed them to be from another world. He had searched for a source on several occasions, but found none.

They both then believed Albert Gallatin Willis was returning from the dead to make sure their sons were all right.

Verification of a Vision
(Northern Virginia)

(Author's note: In most instances, it seems, a ghost or ghosts are sighted by one person. Sometimes several members of a family, living in the same house, may sense such phenomena. But it is rare for there to be multiple witnesses. A notable exception was the legendary black ghost dog of the Blue Ridge Mountain foothills in Bedford County. It is alleged that hundreds, perhaps even thousands saw the phantom canine when it appeared 300 years ago.

The following account is also highly unusual. It tells of a ghostly sighting, itself a bit out of the ordinary, by two men, who learn that another witness has seen what they saw — five years later! I am indebted to that indefatigable Civil War historian, Dr. Kenneth Stuart McAtee, formerly of Berryville and currently of Fairfax, for the following account. Dr. McAtee is the author of three books on "Ghost Stories and Legends from the Old Confederacy." They can be found in such shops as the Loudoun County Museum in Leesburg. Because of the sensitive nature involved, and out of respect for the participants, who requested anonymity, no names are used. But the occurrences themselves are sworn to with convincing sincerity. The exact location of the ethereal sighting also remains confidential, although it obviously was at or near a Civil War battlefield in northern Virginia, possibly Manassas. The time frame was about 30 years ago.)

arly one morning two young men decided to go relic hunting for Civil War artifacts on what was then mostly vacant farmland. They were using metal detectors. It was believed that a Confederate tent hospital had once occupied this patch of land.

Dr. McAtee quoted the narrator on the thrill of relic hunting: "There is an indescribable feeling in getting a signal from your detector and then carefully removing the earth to expose a button, thimble, knapsack, hook, belt buckle, or some item lost in the far distant past. A similar feeling exists while hunting the battlefields when you dig a fired bullet and realize brave boys have stood there in the open, exchanging shots with the enemy until one side claimed victory. You can stand there holding a flattened bullet, examine the surrounding terrain, and know that a lot of personal bravery had occurred there in the past."

He said the two were successful in the hunt and found a number of horse harness buckles, some buttons of both Union and Confederate issue, and several bullets. In mid-morning they moved to the place where they thought the hospital had been located, and this feeling was confirmed when they uncovered several iron spikes which probably had been used as tent pegs. Here, they also dug up a few charred buttons, and they guessed that they might have come from the uniforms of soldiers who had communicable diseases, hence their clothes were burned and buried. They also came across some old medicine type bottles.

At this point, the two men sat down to rest under the shade of some trees. Here, the narrator picks up the story: "A cold feeling engulfed me as though I had walked into an air conditioned room. Then I noticed my friend's face. He was staring intently at something behind me and a look of fear was on his face. I cautiously turned and then I saw them!

"I couldn't believe my eyes, but walking by us about 50 feet away were two Confederate soldiers carrying a stretcher with what appeared to be a body covered by a blanket! The body was completely covered and I assumed it was a dead comrade. The uniforms were gray, the hats were the kepi type of the period. They were walking along looking neither left or right. Something struck me as strange, for although their legs were moving, I could not see their feet. It dawned on me that they were walking along an old path, now partially filled in some places, and that path headed in the direction of a cemetery used by the Confederates early in the war.

"And then they were gone!

"My heart was pounding and the hair on the back of my neck must have risen like that of a frightened cat! My friend sat in a trance. 'Did you see that?' he asked. 'I saw something and I am glad that you did, too, or people would think I was crazy.' 'Do you think anyone will believe this?' he said. 'I don't think we would be wise to mention this,' I replied. 'There are some who would accuse us of indulging in strong drink, and we know that isn't the case.'

"So that was my strange experience, not afterwards mentioned in public by either or us, and we agreed that this was one incident we preferred to remain private. It remained vivid in my memory over the years, and it was simply an experience one could not forget."

As the years passed, a housing development sprang up in the farm area, and the region where the relics were found and the sighting was made became dotted with new houses. There was no more searching for relics in the area, but the narrator says he jogged along a road through the development five years later.

One day during a run, he met a psychologist he knew, and he stopped and they began chatting. The subject got around to the Civil War, relics, and the tent hospital. The more they talked, the more the doctor seemed absorbed by the subject. He asked the narrator if he had ever seen anything unusual. This seemed odd. Then the psychologist explained his purpose. He said he had treated a disturbed young girl of about 12 or 13 who had had some kind of traumatic experience, and he believed it may have related to the Civil War and to this particular area. She had asked him several questions about what had happened here during the war, but she wouldn't tell him exactly what was bothering her. He then asked the narrator, since he knew Civil War history and the area so well, would he mind talking to the girl. Maybe she would open up to him. The narrator agreed.

A few days later, he met with the girl in the psychologist's office. After a few introductory comments she asked him what he knew about the old hospital that had been on the site in the 1860s. He told her what he knew, and then she asked him: "Did you ever see anything unusual where I live?" (She lived at or near the tent hospital site). She also asked him if he believed in ghosts.

He answered: "Frankly, I don't know about ghosts. Some people have different mental powers than others, and it may be some people see things not visible to others. Or it may be a time warp sometimes occurs and someone just happens to be there." Then he told her the secret he had kept for five years: "I did see something very unusual on that hill. I saw two Confederate soldiers carrying a stretcher with a body under a blanket. I remember it well."

He said tears then came into the girl's eyes, and she seemed somehow greatly relieved, as if a heavy burden had just been lifted from her. "Did they seem to bob up and down out of the earth as they walked?" she asked, with a look of intense anticipation on her face. He nodded.

Then she told him: "I went to get my cat one day, and all of a sudden she arched her back and started hissing, and it got real cold. I looked up and here came two big men in uniforms carrying a stretcher. I knew they were soldiers. I stood there petrified and they went right on by and just walked through the end of the house. I knew no one would believe me. I started to think maybe I was going crazy, and I couldn't tell anyone. I am scared to go in the yard or in that end of the house, and that is why I am seeing the psychologist."

He then told her that both he and a friend of his had seen the same thing, and "since those soldiers never threatened us or looked like they might want to, I do not think it is anything to worry about. . . . The day I saw these soldiers I had some Confederate buttons in my pocket that I had just dug, and since no ghosts attacked me and took them away, I have always considered them to be good luck charms. I have brought you one, and I think you will never be bothered again. You keep it around for good luck, and I know that everything will be all right."

They both then agreed that they would tell no one of their experience, not even the psychologist. Several years later, the girl wrote the narrator: "I am married now," she said, "and just wanted to send along a note of thanks. At my wedding I carried the traditional something old, and something new. The something old was a Confederate uniform button that brought me good luck and that I have treasured over the years.

"I never saw 'our secret' again while we lived there, and I never told the psychologist or anyone else what I saw that day."

To which the narrator closed his account of the experience the three of them shared, five years apart, by saying that . . . "Confederate ghosts still walk the paths of the past. That is, three of us believe that they do!"

CHAPTER 53

Verification of the
Vanishing House

(Manassas National Battlefield Park)

(Author's note: Like Yogi Berra once said, "It's Deja Vu all over again." In the past I have written extensively about the old Stone House in the middle of the Manassas National Battlefield Park. During the Civil War it served as a makeshift hospital and countless young men passed away there decades before their time. A legend persists that a Mr. Starbuck, a resident of the house in the early 1800s, put a curse on the Pridmore family, which lived there later, because he didn't like Mr. Pridmore. Author Robert Goldthwaite Carter, who authored "Four Brothers in Blue," wrote: "Certain it is that out of the Pridmore family six or more died in quick succession, and . . . the house rightfully bears the name of the 'Haunted House'."

A number of mysterious manifestations have occurred in Stone House over the years, and park administrative officer Jane Becker has photographed what appears to be a ghost in the house. Then, in January 1986, I got a letter from a young woman named Kathleen Luisa who lives in Falls Church, Virginia. I included excerpts from her letter in "The Ghosts of Virginia, Volume III" (1996). In essence, here is what she said:

I have traveled down Route 29 through Manassas, Gainesville, and on westward many, many times. I love the battlefields and the Stone House has been a favorite landmark for me at the intersection of 29 and Sudley Road. Many times as I waited for the traffic light there, I gazed at the house and wondered about its stories if it could talk.

"One night in 1986, I suggested we all go for a drive out to Manassas battlefield to see if we could see Halley's Comet. My mom, her mother and father, and I got in the car and set out. As we approached the intersection I was looking in the darkness for my landmark, the Stone House, so I could make the turn onto Sudley's Road and into the little parking area. I drove right through the intersection.

"<u>There was no house!</u>

"Puzzled, I turned around and went back since I was coming into Gainesville and I knew that was too far. We got back to the intersection and sat at the light looking aghast at the empty lot where the Stone House should have stood. The rise of land was empty except that the well or cistern that stands in front and the fences were still there. I remember looking intently at the route markers at the intersection to make sure I was in the right spot, even though I know that area well.

"We were very upset, figuring some land development scheme had led to its being torn down, or maybe there was some move by the Park Service to relocate it. . . . As we drove by looking at this, I do not remember seeing any foundation walls, hole in the ground, or signs of rubble, etc. Just an empty lot and the well. Finally, we left, shaking our heads sadly.

"Imagine my utter shock when, two weeks later, we drove down 29 during the day, dreading the spot where my 'old friend' used to stand . . . <u>and the house was there!</u>

"We sat at the light staring with our mouth open. I immediately asked my mom and grandparents to verify that they really had seen a vacant lot that night. They all swore they had. I know we were not at the wrong location. I know the area too well for that.

"My grandfather passed away in 1989, but my mom and Nan and I still talk about the 'vanishing Stone House' to this day."

Strange? Yes. Now hear this. In November 1997, I got the following letter from a woman named Beverly Kish of Merrifield, Virginia:)

"I experienced a 'ghostly encounter' in January 1997, but didn't know what it was at the time until I read one of your stories. You wrote about a lady who said she drove by that location (the Stone House) and the house had disappeared.

"The same thing has happened to me!

"I was living in Manassas at the time and wanted to take a drive one night. It was clear with a moon out. It wasn't pitch dark. I was alone. I got lost on this drive and ended up on Lee Highway. Having lived in the area 20 years, I know exactly where the Stone House is. In fact, I took a tour there years ago, yet on this night it was gone! I even turned the car around and said to myself, 'that's funny, I'm at the right intersection,' and all I saw was a patch of grass with the glow of the moon on it where the house had been. It was about 1:30 a.m. Nobody on the road but me.

"And you can't miss this house. It's close to the road. Then I figured, 'well I guess they moved it to another part of the battlefield, but I didn't read about it in the paper, and I read the paper everyday. Then I thought no more about it until I read the lady's account in your book.

"So I can vouch for what she saw — or better, for what she didn't see!"

CHAPTER 54

The Lady Who Fell in Love with J.E.B. Stuart

(Gettysburg, PA)

(Author's note: In May 1998 I got a call from a woman named Nancy Sopolinski in Milwaukee, Wisconsin. She said she had a compelling story to tell me about an experience she had at Gettysburg in 1997. When I explained that I wrote almost exclusively about Virginia ghosts, she said her adventure involved a Virginian and that I was partially responsible for it because of something she had read in one of my books, "Civil War Ghosts of Virginia," (1995). So I told her to write down the information in concise form as she remembered. A few days later I got the following letter. I have only used slight excerption and editing.)

"**O**ur lives have changed 100 percent since our first trip to Gettysburg. It's the most wonderful (supernatural), yet horrific (being separated from our generals) experience of our lives!

"I am (also) enclosing some of the poems I wrote (in the past year). I am not looking for you to publish them. I needed to show you how 'Lily' is emerging within me. I have <u>never</u> written such a thing in my life. I have no skills or talent for such. When I sit down to write it, I can actually feel her love and pain. It completely drains me when I finish a poem or short story.

"I truly hope you are interested with this remarkable love story. I feel it must be told, if only to give people hope that true love does carry on.

"On May 15, 1997, my sister Karen and I, along with our husbands, Tom and Dave, went on a four day trip to Gettysburg. Karen saw a picture of General John Reynolds at the tower and was instantly attracted to him. Thinking it was just a simple crush, she had to buy a picture of him. The rest of the trip was uneventful until we were on the plane to go back to Wisconsin. I started crying and couldn't stop and told Karen I felt like I was leaving my home.

"Once back in Milwaukee, I couldn't understand what was wrong with me. I and my sister lost 25 pounds in a month! Two weeks after our trip, Karen had a musical santa in which you must press the hand to activate it. It went off by itself during a thunderstorm. The following day she had a sudden urge to take out John's (General Reynolds) picture and look at it. At that instant, an immense burst of love went charging through her whole body! During this time, we would both smell a sweet cigar odor in our houses and feel a presence with us.

"It was not until June that I found my general — Jeb Stuart. I read about him in your book, and when I did, it hit my heart like a ton of bricks! I read only the first paragraph or two when I had to stop and catch my breath! Right then I knew it was he whom I had been searching for.

"Shortly thereafter we started talking to them (Generals Stuart and Reynolds) on the Ouija board. Before our hands were even on the board the nail was frantically shaking back and forth. Previously, the board had never worked for us. But since we have made contact with them (the generals) it went wild. Jeb and John told us about themselves — things which we had no knowledge of until we researched in books.

"John told Karen that indeed Karen was Kate Hewitt (his fiancèe). Jeb told me that I was Lily Dandridge. She was not his wife, but he said they (we) had fallen in love at the Bower Plantation in West Virginia in 1862 while his cavalry headquarters was located there for a month.

"On August 11th, Karen and I went to see Carol Rushman. She is a famous Milwaukee astrologer. She was amazed as to how active their (the generals) charts were considering they had been dead for almost 135 years. She named the date we came in contact with our past life without knowing of it. From what she read on her charts, she truly believes that we were, and still are true loves.

"The following morning when Carol and her assistant opened her office, they found a mirror, which had hung on the wall for

J.E.B. Stuart

seven years, had fallen and shattered. There were small spears of glass sticking up from the carpet and chairs. It was all over the room, not just below where it had hung. When we asked the generals (on the Ouija board) about it, Jeb said it was his idea to prove to Carol she was right.

"On August 9th, 1997 he (Stuart) appeared to me at night. He stood on the side of my bed. He looked very solid and Jeb was all aglow with a bright whiteness. He was in full uniform and his mustache was curled up as he smiled down upon me. I would have thought it was a dream, but at that instant my husband and our dog, Ginger, walked in. Ginger started barking furiously and he (Jeb) vanished. I know Ginger saw him, too!

"On September 22, Karen and I had an appointment to talk with Patricia Michaels, a world famous psychic. She told us Jeb and John are our 'twin flames.' That is better than a soulmate because there are only two of a kind created as one. She said one of our main purposes was to go back to Gettysburg and find them (the generals), because they were earthbound and in search of us.

"On November 7th, I left my dog outside and forgot about her when I decided to take an afternoon nap. As soon as I lay down, I heard someone pacing back and forth outside my bedroom door. I have wood floors so I could tell 'he' had boots on and it sounded like heavy material brushing against his body as he walked. Then came some very light knockings on my door. This lasted at least five minutes. I knew it was Jeb since no one was home at the time. I just enjoyed the fact that he was with me. He was trying to warn me that Ginger was in danger, for at that moment she was running across a very busy street and almost got hit by a car. The next time we talked to them on the Ouija board, Jeb spelled out 'JEB NO'S U FIND GINGER.'

"On November 12th, our dad, who had died in 1975, talked to us on the board. He told us that everything is true and our generals love us. We told him to give a family member a sign to prove it. The following morning my brother and his wife in California saw a smoky white light dart across their front room and actually made contact with a ceramic seagull hanging from the ceiling. The seagull started spinning and the form darted off to the kitchen and disappeared. The next day our dad talked to us again. He said it was him (who had spun the seagull) to show us it was true. He told us that my brother was wearing a black shirt. I called my brother and indeed he had on a black shirt.

"Unfortunately, we had to burn our Ouija board because the generals told us it was drawing in 'too much evil.'

"March 14th — I gave my poems to my husband's friend, Budda. He said he would try to get them published. He didn't believe in ghosts until he took the poems home with him. Ever since then his house seems to be filled with supernatural activity. It started with the rustling of papers coming from where he had placed my poems. When he looked there, he saw Jeb on the wall. He described him in detail, including how his hat turns up on one side. He had not seen any pictures of him at the time. He was quite frightened.

"We went back to Gettysburg in September. I spent two hours looking for information about the Dandridge family in West Virginia, but I didn't find anything about 'Lily.' This was at the historic Belle Boyd House (she was a Confederate spy during the Civil War.) I was completely discouraged and about to leave when, on a whim, I walked across the room and flipped open a genealogical book. I looked down in amazement. I had turned directly to a page on the family history of the Dandridges, and there was Lily's name! The woman who had been helping me couldn't believe it. I simply smiled and quietly thanked my darling Jeb.

"Following my stay at the Boyd House, the Bower Plantation was next on my list along with my very sweet, loving but grouchy husband. By the way, both my husband and brother-in-law call Gettysburg, "A trip from hell!'

"I learned that Lily was visiting a niece at Bower in September 1862. I remember being there and the feelings that attacked my heart were of complete love and sadness. It was then that I knew just how Lily felt in the poems I wrote. I looked up upon the window Lily had looked down from in years far removed by time. I remember looking down on a beautiful warm autumn night to the general serenading me with songs of love.

"Many months later I read in W. W. Blackford's book of Jeb Stuart, that he indeed put a program together for the women of the Bower. One song he had one of his officers sing was a song called 'Dear Lily.' Blackford also referred to the one month long stay at the Bower as being of such romance that everyone fell in love, including the general himself.

"I strongly feel if not for your chapter about Jeb Stuart in 'Civil War Ghosts of Virginia,' which you wrote, I may not have discovered the connection with him for quite some time. For that, I thank you.

"I'm sure the generals will continue to be a large part of our lives even though we are separated by two worlds. When it is decided that our lives here are accomplished, we will gladly once again enter their loving arms.

"Sincerely, Nancy Sopolinski."

(Author's note: Following is one of the poems Nancy sent with her letter. It is about her "relationship" with Jeb Stuart and is entitled "The Separation.")

"Do I have the right to claim your heart in love? Seemingly distance in war and a commitment to another draws us further apart. I find no favor of what has become of me. Will this appetite for you, which consumes my every waking hour, destroy what righteousness I find so impelling for myself?

"With you by my side, I have found just cause for tranquility and harmony within. How may I stop this feverish sensation each time you enter the room? What has fallen before me is the utmost poetic passion that has set my soul free.

"You enriched my life to a whole new world with an incomparable sense of deliverance and unspoken fondness for nature and creation alike. You warm my days with such daring rushes of seductive glances and arouse my spirit with much zealous laughter. As daylight passes, you cool my evenings as your merciful charm eludes us into a lustful and enchanting paradise.

"Will I discover a pathway of strength to carry on in this hardfilled existence once you depart? I shall forever reminisce the burning desire we have shared as our two forms became one. In the pith of my heart, I fathom only in death will we be unrestrained to love once again."

(Author's note: Several months after first hearing from Nancy Ann, I got a "P.S." — another letter describing further events in her "this world-another world" relationship with Jeb Stuart. Here are excerpts:)

"Patricia Michael, the world renowned psychic, said our story is one of the 'top ten' readings she had ever given — the fact that two sisters are going through the same motions of finding these men whom we have been separated from for over 135 years, and finding them together! She told us we should write a book about it.

"Many supernatural things have happened since my last contact with you. We do not lead an average life any longer. We, my sister Karen and I, have found many similarities between ourselves and the fiancee of General John Morgan, and the love of Jeb Stuart. For example, Karen learned that after Morgan was killed in the battle of Gettysburg, Kate Hewitt, his fiancee, became a nun. This may help explain why Karen has collected nun figures all her life!

"As for me, I had always told my husband that if we had a daughter I wanted to name her Sarah. He said that it was too old fashioned. I have since learned that Stuart's lover's full name was Sarah Lily Dandridge. In 1866, Lily married a politician. So did I. I researched her life as best I could, but she seemed to mysteriously disappear around Winchester in the late 1800s. She just seemed to vanish from the records. She is not buried in the Dandridge family plot, nor is she buried with her husband. On the Ouija board Jeb has told me that I physically resemble her. We have talked (Jeb and I, and Morgan and Karen) from two separate worlds on the board.

"More recently I had an 'aura' picture taken of me. That is a picture taken on special film which produces the life forces that surround you, in color. Before I had this done, the photographer told me I have many spirits around me. When she handed me the picture, there was an image of Jeb's face next to me!

"In August (1998), my husband and I went to the state fair. In a building there I had the overwhelming sense of Jeb being close by. One cannot explain the rush of love and excitement that goes through your body when this happens unless you could experience it yourself. A few minutes later, I literally felt a tap upon my shoulder. It was so intense, I turned around expecting to see someone I knew behind me. There was no one there!"

(Author's note: Nancy Ann went on to describe several other psychic experiences both she and her sister, Karen, have had in recent months — encounters for which there is no rational explanation. They both believe, wholeheartedly, that it is Stuart and Morgan's way of "communicating" with them from the beyond.

Nancy Ann also sent me a photograph she had taken at Gettysburg in May 1997, at a site known as Spangler's Spring. She writes that "there was absolutely no ground fog throughout the park on that particular night," and adds that her husband, a skeptic, believes the images which appeared on the film to be spirits. Only two of the ten photos she took that evening have the "white, misty substance" on them. Her camera was working fine. Nancy Ann says that 252 Civil War soldiers perished during an engagement at Spangler's Spring, and she believes she can see a Union soldier on the left side of one of the pictures.

"It is heart-rending to know these poor souls are still not free from the pain of war, well over a century ago," she notes. "How bitterly sad it is! I know everything I have told you is so bizarre, but I assure you everything is as I have told you.")

Second footnote: Excerpts from a later letter sent by Nancy: "For the past several months, Karen and I have been feeling strange goosebumps and a tingling sensation on the tops of our heads — along with 'someone' touching our hair. When I look in the mirror, my hair is standing straight up, like electricity.

". . . I am growing tired of people not believing me. Can't

rightly blame them, though. The important thing is that I know it to be true and if the story was meant to be told, it will be."

In this letter, Nancy enclosed another poem: "Patience of the Heart," a poignant appeal to her love, J.E.B. Stuart:

"As the evening crawls forth, I am not alone.
Though there may be shadows of darkness surrounding my faith,
I fear not, for what I trust is real.
I may fault the tender touch,
Or purely a brush of your course beard
That tended to scratch thy face when near
Those soft-spoken words of complete enjoyment
Whispered gently within my ear. Only to sedate my heart
And grant such unqualified merriment.
Shall I call your name at nightfall, when by bed is warm
and dry, only to exceed once more another day of tears.
Imploring you to soothe my wounds and take away my pain!
For it is not I who grieves only,
Furthermore, the honor of your heart bleeds within mine.
Until we come together again, life is dark!"

Spangler's Spring

CHAPTER 5 5

The Confederate
Soldier Who Died <u>Twice!</u>
(Malvern Hill, Charles City County)

(Author's note: Strange is not a strong enough word to explain how I sometimes gather ghostly material in Virginia. Consider this: In my book, "Civil War Ghosts of Virginia," (1995), I wrote, in the introduction, how I was surprised that some of the most tragic and traumatic battle sites of that war seemed <u>not</u> to be haunted. One of these places is Malvern Hill, located between Richmond and Williamsburg just off historic Route 5 in Charles City County.

s a preface to the following extraordinary account, let me repeat what I said: "Why are there no spirits, or at least more evidence of spirits at Malvern Hill? It was here, on July 1, 1862, that thousands of Confederates charged up a long, gently-sloping hill in the face of murderous cannon and rifle fire. Many were killed. The dreadful carnage was described by Union Colonel William W. Averell, who, as the foggy dawn broke the next morning, wrote: 'Our ears had been filled with agonizing cries from thousands before the fog was lifted, but now our eyes saw an appalling spectacle upon the slopes down to the woodlands half a mile away.

"Over 5,000 dead and wounded men were on the ground in every attitude of distress. A third of them were dead or dying, but enough were alive and moving to give the field a singular crawling effect.' Yet despite the agony of such a disaster, there have been only a couple of vague reports of witnesses who, more than a century later, told of hearing strange noises and moans across the fields, and of catching fleeting glimpses of distant disembodied figures at Malvern Hill where blood once dyed the ground red."

That is what I wrote in 1995. I have since learned, through Nannette Morrison's fine book, "Echoes of Valor," that there have indeed been a few instances of unexplained ethereal encounters at Malvern Hill. With Ms. Morrison's gracious permission, I quote: "There are two women from the Sandston area of Richmond who are quite drawn to the Malvern Hill Battlefield. The pair always bring their dogs to let them run, but the real affinity for the acreage goes beyond that. 'Every time I come out here, I get a real eerie feeling. Still, something keeps drawing us to this wheatfield.' The older woman points to the wood line on the left, 'See that spot out there? One afternoon last year I swear I saw two Confederate boys running along that edge, coming toward us!' She was adamant regarding the sighting.

"A few folks who live around the Malvern Hill site have also remarked on seeing and hearing unusual phenomena. Tim Fredrikson was a house guest of some friends living only two miles from the battlefield. One July evening in 1994, Tim was driving his car about dark and drawing near the residence. Through a patch of woods on Route 156 approaching Malvern Hill, an event startled him. A caisson and limber were drawn across the road directly in front of his vehicle about 150 yards away! They passed from one wooded side to the other as quick as a flash! Yet, for Tim there was no denying what he witnessed."

Ms. Morrison then described the battle scene, recreating the awful sounds that emanated that fateful day — the chorus of Rebel yells as the infantry charged up the hill amidst the booming roar of General George McClellan's imposing line of cannon. Then she told of another haunting account experienced by a park volunteer named Martin. "Was it these same sounds that Martin heard in July 1993? He is certain that it is true. Martin was alone at his post in early July . . . when he was interrupted by voices. 'I looked around to see who was approaching (he said), but there was no one around. . . The fields all around are wide open. There weren't any cars in sight either. I sat quietly in the shade of the park shelter right where the cannon are now. Then I heard them again. I distinctly heard two men carrying on a regular conversation. I couldn't quite determine complete sentences. Nevertheless, there was a clear exchange of words back and forth only a few feet from me.'

Malvern Hill

(Martin then checked two of the houses that are adjacent to the battlefield and found no one home, and thus no rational explanation for what he was hearing. He returned to the shelter.) He then said, 'This was really puzzling! Anyway, I stayed at my post for the afternoon. Every once in a while I could catch bits of that same conversation back in time once again. And actually, there were many days I spent there that I felt some real creepy things, almost like eyes watching me from all sides'."

In 1997, reenactors of the l2th Virginia Infantry gathered at Malvern Hill to take part in a living history recreation of the battle which had taken place 135 years earlier. For her most recent book, "Warrior Poets and Warrior Saints," (Echo Effects Publishing, Charlottesville, $15.95) Nannette Morrison later interviewed several members of the group when it was learned that strong psychic activity had taken place on the battlefield the night <u>before</u> the anniversary of the battle.

Reenactor sergeant Henry Kidd told author Morrison that the 12th Virginia unit had been portraying camp life that night, and during the evening one young man went from campsite to campsite reading a letter which a Georgia soldier had written to his mother on the eve of the battle in 1862. According to Kidd and others, the reenactor's portrayal was so lifelike that some reported getting chills, and one swore that he saw the images of 15 or so <u>real</u> Confederate soldiers standing nearby during the readings!

At this point Tim Fredrikson, the same person Nannette Morrison had quoted in her earlier book, said that he was "being drawn" toward the tree line flanking the battlefield, about 200 yards away. Several of the men started walking toward the woods, and when they got near they felt a sharp drop in the temperature. They had walked into a cold spot. Such spots are often associated with the presence of spirits. Sergeant Kidd then stepped backwards a few feet and the temperature returned to normal. When he advanced again he was once more enveloped in coldness.

Nearer the treeline, which seemed to be drawing the reenactors closer to it, Kidd said he suddenly smelled the strong presence of body odor. He looked around. There was no one near him. The odor seemed to be hanging in one particular spot, and then, in a few seconds, it dissipated.

Then Kidd had a sighting. Morrison quoted him: "In the treeline under the limbs of the trees where it is dark and the tree trunks are, and between that area and where the brushline starts, is a real dark area. That is the space where I saw silhouetted shapes of men's heads, shoulders and elbows bent back to their sides as though they were holding muskets centered in front of them. It wasn't one or two, but an entire regiment of Confederate soldiers from 135 years ago standing there in front of me! Moving toward the regiment was like observing an Impressionistic painting. As I moved closer to them, I could no longer make out individual forms. If I stepped back, I could again see details. Yet, the entire area was illuminated with an unusual shadowy light. . . I stood near the Confederate ranks and had the sensation of the soldiers closing in around me. 'Thanks!' was the clear message I felt from them."

According to Morrison, a most extraordinary psychic phenomenon also occurred during that evening. Those who witnessed it said that the voice of a 17-year-old Confederate soldier spoke through the body of reenactor Tim Fredrikson! Henry Kidd was one of those who heard this. He said the soldier identified himself as Samuel Edmunds of Tazewell, Virginia (Subsequent research of Civil War Records determined that a Samuel Edmunds of the 26th Virginia Infantry was, in fact, at Malvern Hill for the battle. It was not known whether or not he survived.)

The "voice" let it be known that he was frightened. He was afraid of being killed the next day in battle. He also expressed concern that if he was killed, would he be admitted into heaven?

Sergeant Kidd and others tried to console the shaken youth, and prayed with him. They believe it helped.

There was yet another encounter that night. Reenactor Whitt Smith and his son Christian also felt compelled to approach the mysterious woods. Sergeant Kidd followed them and told Morrison: "As we arrived at the slight rise where you could barely see the treeline, the ghostly unit was still visible and waiting. As he (Whitt) slowly stepped into the midst of them, the Confederate regiment parted ranks as if to admit a fellow soldier . . . the color party for the regiment closed ranks around him, accepting him as a member."

That is what Nannette Morrison wrote. Here, let me add a personal note; one that is shared by a number of historians. Both commanding generals at this site — Robert E. Lee and George McClellan — made monumental blunders at Malvern Hill. Lee's mistake was to overestimate the abilities of his men in ordering them to charge up that fearful hill in the face of such overpowering cannon and rifle fire. It was an order, against all odds, that Lee was to repeat by directing Pickett's charge at Gettysburg a year later. There was simply no way a run up Malvern Hill against such awesome force was going to be successful.

McClellan, on the other hand, did not follow up his advantage. With Lee's men in total disarray, he should have ordered them to march on toward Richmond, barely 20 miles away. Yet, incredibly, despite the severe damage he had caused, he chose instead to retreat and regroup. Had he gone forward, many experts believe, he could have taken Richmond with his far superior forces and possibly shortened the war by two or three years. It was his extreme cautiousness that eventually led to his removal as commanding general of the Union forces.

And now, to one of the most surrealistic encounters I have come across in nearly two decades of researching ghost experiences in the commonwealth. I was at a New Age festival held in Williamsburg in September 1998, giving a talk. In the question and answer session afterwards a young lady raised her hand and asked if I had ever interviewed anyone who had their body invaded by a spirit from the past. I told her of the lady in Charlottesville, who, while living in an old house near Monticello, believed that the spirit of a former slave, circa 1820s, had taken over her body for a few minutes. (See "The Ghosts of Virginia, Volume I," 1993.) The woman said she felt she was that slave; she felt the slave's tiredness from having too many children and from having been worked too hard. The feeling passed in about three or four minutes.

Here then is what the lady, Beth Wells of Richmond, told me about her experiences at Malvern Hill: "It was in June 1998, near the anniversary of the battle. I was in my car, alone, and driving on Willis Church Road. It was mid-afternoon and it was a beautiful day. I remember saying to myself how gorgeous the woods looked, when, at that very instance, I felt the presence of a spirit in the car with me. It suddenly was there, in my body! It was the presence of a young Confederate soldier, and he, or it, said 'That's the last thing I thought,' meaning he, too, had noticed how beautiful the woods were.

"And then, I felt — I knew — that he had just been shot. He had been shot in the solar plexus. The shot tore a hole in his chest. He lifted his hands up in the air, and in that instant he was gone. The presence had left the car. It was like he had taken up residence in my body for a few fleeting seconds. I don't know how else to describe it.

"It was like he had been trying to communicate with me, like he wanted me to know he had been killed. The strangest thing was that it wasn't at all a frightening experience. It was, rather, a sharing kind of thing. He wanted me to know about him. I felt privileged.

"I know it all may sound crazy, but it really happened. I was fully awake and lucid. I guess the sensation lasted only a few seconds, but it was very real. It did happen! I have tried to come up with an explanation. Did I somehow drive through his energy field for those few seconds. I don't know.

"I will say this, however. I feel much less afraid of death now."

A FAMILY BURIAL

There is a fascinating footnote to the battle at Malvern Hill. It was recorded by author Nannette Morrison in her 1998 book, "Warrior Poets and Warrior Saints." Her research uncovered a singular incident that most absorbingly reveals the harsh ironies of war. During the fighting a Union sergeant named Driscoll shot a Confederate officer. He later went to see if the man was dead. As the sergeant turned him over the young man said, "Father?" He then closed his eyes. He was dead. Driscoll had killed his own son, who had moved to the south before the Civil War started! Minutes later the sergeant's unit was ordered to charge. He was mortally wounded. Both father and son were buried in a single grave on the battlefield, marked only with a rough cross.

CHAPTER 56

The Dancing Skulls of Chantilly

(Fairfax County)

(Author's note: Fear can be a strange thing. The anticipation of danger sometimes can be more damaging than the actual danger itself. I believe that is true with ghosts. The fear of experiencing a ghost is greater than the fear felt by an actual encounter with the unknown. The imagination, unchecked, can run wild, creating intense levels of fear in a person. The fear of what is behind that cob-webbed attic door is far superior to anything one might realize by opening the door. In Volume IV in this series on Virginia ghosts (1998), I included a chapter about a man who spent a night in what was alleged to be a haunted house. He neither saw or felt anything supernatural. All that he saw and heard that night in the dark was created by natural causes. Yet the man's jet-racing imagination trig-gered a terror so sharp-edged and profound that one wonders how he survived the night without collapsing into insensibility. Even I shivered a little just reading the account.

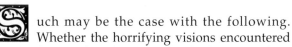uch may be the case with the following. Whether the horrifying visions encountered were actual or imagined is not the true issue. In either case, the sheer fear, the stark terror expressed is all too real.

The account comes from a Civil War veteran named Alexander Hunter. During the four years of the war, as a fuzzy-cheeked young man, Hunter kept a detailed diary. Forty years after the fighting had ceased, he published his diary. It was titled, "Johnny Reb and Billy Yank." It is a thorough and poignant description of what life was like both on the battlefield and off during those hellish years from 1861 to 1865.

In one of the chapters, Hunter tells of experiencing ghosts at a plantation home in Fairfax County. There is a problem with exactly which house it was. He describes it as being known as "Chantilly . . . a famous ancestral place." The site lies within the present-day boundaries of the town of Chantilly, near the Dulles Airport.

Near route 50 is a magnificent 18th century house called "Sully." It was the ancestral home of Richard Bland Lee, a descendent of Richard Henry Lee. Sully has its own intriguing history. In 1839, for instance, it was sold to William Swartout, who was said to once have been a pirate. There is one report that he was apprehended, sent back to England, and hanged there.

At some point around the beginning of the 19th century, Richard Bland Lee acquired some property adjacent to Sully, and he named it Chantilly. This was in honor of the Lee family estate in Westmoreland County.

I could not determine whether or not a manor house was built adjacent to Sully. According to Hunter, the house he describes burned to the ground after the second battle of Manassas, in 1862. Therefore, he could not have been talking about Sully, which is still standing, and open to the public. Likely, the Lee family did erect a house some-where in the vicinity of Sully, and this is what Hunter was talking about.

The time is 1861. The Confederates are in control of the area, and young Alexander Hunter is assigned to guard duty one night at the Chantilly house, to keep looters and pillagers from damaging it. His first thoughts are of all the famous people he believes have passed through the house over the years, and all the gay festivities which have taken place within its walls. He mentions the Lees, Stuarts, Fairfaxes, Mann Page, George Mason, the Carters, Byrds, and others.

His words give a vivid and exquisite picture of what plantation life among Virginia's social upper strata was like.

Here then are excerpts from Hunter's diary:)

". . . What must have been the glory of Chantilly in the Christmas time, when hosts of relations, friends and even strangers gathered around the immense yule log. Even around our camp-fires we had heard of old memories handed down from sires to sons, of those splendid entertainments; the table groaning under the weight of its feast; the rare old china; the massive family plate; the smoking haunch of venison; 'old Virginia cured' hams, sweet as sugar; wild fowl from the Chesapeake; fish from Hog Island, rare old wines from famous cellars; and the silver punch bowl filled with that most delicious of festive brews.

"We had heard, too, of those gay old balls where the proudest, the fairest and best of the Colonists met, where satin rustled, velvets trailed, and brocade swept over the polished floor; where jewels rich flashed in the soft, becoming light of numberless wax candles. And the dress of the cavaliers! Why, the homeliest man would shine 'a thing of beauty' in such arrayal, brought in the big strong chests from across the sea — velvet coats with gold buttons; elaborately embroidered satin vests worked in delicate designs; dainty ruffs of fine old lace; shorts that reached to the knee and tied with a garter; stockings of finest silk, and long, pointed shoes with jeweled buckles. Decked in these, with an embossed belt hung over the right shoulders, to which was attached a slender rapier in bright steel scabbard, and a three-cornered cocked hat, and you have the outfit complete in which shone the cavalier colonist in all his glory.

"A decided contrast to the stiff, ugly, conventional black of our present day (1860s), in which a man hardly can tell himself from his own waiter. Call to mind the stately gallantry, the elegant courtesy that makes the very mention of their names and their son's names, and their son's sons (generations all passed away) synonym of all that is refined and polished, of all that is courteous and chivalrous to women, and we once more people Chantilly with the men who trod its now deserted boards, and woke the slumbering echoes with dance and song and jest.

"Well, I confess the theme has ever had strange fascination for me, and many is the day-reverie in which they have been as present to my mind, in fancy, as if I had seen them with my own eyes . . ."

(Hunter is daydreaming all of this, imagining what life must have been like in past decades at the grand old house. He then arrives at his post.) " . . . I started, collected my wandering senses, and looked up. Before me was Chantilly, a stately old place, with spacious porch and a passage running from end to end, so broad that a four-horse wagon might have driven through it. A wide stairway led up to the apartments above.

"The house was built of brick brought over from England, but the various wings, added at intervals, were of solid oak. Around the house was a splendid park of full-grown chestnut trees that shadowed and adorned the fine old mansion.

"No one inhabited the house when the enemy (the Union) made

the first advance to Bull Run, its owner having collected previously all his Negroes, 'lares and penates,' and started to Richmond. The said enemy had carried off all that was portable, but had had no time to gut and sack the house. To protect if from further plunder by our own soldiers, a guard was placed over it, with orders to allow no one to trespass upon the premises, and so it fell out . . . I was doomed to guard old Chantilly that night."

(Hunter proceeds inside the house. The only major piece of furniture left is) "An ancient spindle-legged piano of German make, whose keys were yellow with age. . . Across the room and directly opposite the piano there hung two portraits, the one of a woman, but so blurred with age as to be nearly indistinguishable; the other a man's, judging from his attire; the features had faded with time, all except his eyes, which shone out with startling distinctness from the shadowy face, with an expression of intense surprise, as if questioning my presence there.

"Leaving this room I went up the broad, handsome stairway leading into a long gallery . . . Evidently all articles of value had been removed and only these few old relics of a century past left as lone sentries at their post. Oh, sad! This dismantled home, with its rich association of years, endeared to its owners by all the refinements of cultured life, left to a ruthless and reckless soldiery! The old King Lear of a house, turned adrift it its old age to bear the raging tempest. Nothing but the body of the old house left — the soul, the life, all gone!

"I explored the building all over, its every nook and corner, its loft rooms; it seemed as if a whole regiment might have found shelter within its spaciousness.

(Hunter is then relieved at his post at eight p.m. He is to get four hours off, and then is to return at midnight. Just before his relief arrives, however, something happens, a portent of what is to come.) "Eight o'clock and dark as pitch! I was getting nervous, I could swear that I heard a door slam. But, thank heaven! there came the sound of the advancing relief. (Hunter goes back to camp and falls asleep immediately — but not for long.)

"The quick, stern cry of 'Guards, turn out!' brought us to our feet at once. Sergeants and men were talking in an excited tone and for a few moments no one could tell what was the matter. But the officer of the day came, and in the silence that then fell, the cause was soon understood. One of the relief was brought in the tent by two guards, and if ever there was a man literally frightened out of his senses, that man was before us then.

"His hat was gone, his hair hanging over his face, half hiding his wide, protruding eyes; his features were deadly pale, huge beads of perspiration were dropping down upon his jacket and he trembled like an aspen leaf. But he could answer no questions, and only begged that we would spare him the details of that which he had seen. Even after we had given him a heavy drink, and his pulse had assumed its wonted beat, and the color had returned slowly to his face — even then he said he could not put in words the terror of the past two hours. He had been detailed to guard Chantilly, and it was there at his post that he had heard and seen what he would never forget. And this was all we could learn — or ever learned.

"Again the trembling seized his limbs, again we noticed the deadly paleness of his face, when even the officer was moved to pity, and instead of having him handcuffed and tried in the near future for one of the most serious infractions of military law a soldier can commit — that of leaving an outpost without permission — was so much struck with the man's abject condition that he only ordered him back to his post.

"But with this command the soldier positively refused to comply. He said without equivocation, he would be shot first, and that nothing earthly could induce him to go into that house again, or even near it after dark. He said he knew it was now his business to try and put some people out of the world, but once out, he considered he had no further use for any of them; and that he was willing to stand a court martial any day, but that he was not willing to stand up against ghosts!

"'Ghosts,' said the officer contemptuously; 'ghosts! Why, are you such a baby? Some old woman's tales have been frightening you!'

"'Maybe they have and maybe they haven't; but I am not going into that house again. You know yourself, Lieutenant, I don't sing second to any soldier on the battlefield.'

"'Yes, that is so,' cordially assented the officer, 'and that is why I had thought better things of you; but go in the guard tent and consider yourself under arrest.'

"Then turning to me, he continued, 'Hunter, get your musket and take his post.'. . . I stood speechless and almost petrified. What! When a full-grown man, and one of the most daring soldiers in the regiment, had been scared almost to death at Chantilly, that I, a mere boy, should be sent into that ghost-haunted place! Me! Ordered to go! Me!"

(Hunter protests, but to no avail. He asks for a second guard to go with him, but the request is denied. The officer admonishes

Hunter, "don't be a coward!") "That word stung me and settled the matter so far as I was concerned. I would have gone inside a tomb and lain down, as Romeo says, 'amid dead men's bones, reeky shanks and yellow, chapless skulls' in a charnel house, much less Chantilly. (Hunter goes back to the house.)

"It was a moonless night, though the sky was brilliant with stars . . . Passing through the gloom strange figures seemed to glide in and out among the tree trunks; spectral arms reached out toward us (Hunter and his sergeant); the breeze, which had sprung up since night-fall, sounded like boding voices from the grave. I began to quiver with long, low, creeping shivers that curdled the blood like a congestive chill. I thought 'Of shapes that walk at dead of night, And clank their chains and wave the torch of Hell around the murderer's bed.'

(Hunter and his sergeant enter the house. Hunter pleads with the sergeant to stay, but the sergeant tells him he has other duties to attend to. However, he will come back as soon as he can. Hunter enters the house and lights a candle.)

"Ugh! How chilly the cold air felt inside the room; and how the old villain's eye glared from the portrait, to see me there again. I glared back, while the dip flared ominously, as if it meant to leave me in utter darkness. . . .

"I looked at my borrowed watch; it was just twelve — the mystic hour when spirits most do walk abroad. . .

"The old cavalier (in the portrait) never ceased to look at me with those fierce, questioning eyes, as if bent on draining every secret of my soul. I struck some chords on the piano and the reverberations came back, it seemed, from every chamber in the house. I began to feel uncomfortable. The candle did not fully light the great room with the little ghostly glare it shed, and in the distant corners, lying in shadow, mystical spirits seemed to congregate, pointing and gibbering at me. . .

"I grew so fancifully nervous that I went out in the open porch once more; and there I heard singular muffled voices upstairs — voices as of women talking, it seemed to me. I turned cold, and back into the house I wandered in my restlessness, only to feel an added thrill as the eyes gleamed threateningly at me from the canvas. Again those sounds from the upper rooms, screams of laughter and — I could stand it no longer.

"Forming a desperate resolution, I grasped the candle in one hand, the musket in the other, and marched up the stairs. Each step woke a separate echo, and it seemed as if feet long since moldering in the grave were walking along the floors and ascending the back stairway, and all the stairways at once, up into the gallery, where the high old clock stood like a specter on the landing — I could swear that it was ticking. Nothing there. Through the front rooms — farther up, and I was appalled by a furious noise somewhere. I started to run, but knowing if I once took to flight I would never stop this side of camp, I retreated slowly. I saw nothing — not even a shadow. I turned to descend, and as I did so, I became conscious that something was following me. I could not hear it nor could I feel it or touch it; but my sixth sense told me the shape was there, dogging me close behind.

"For the life of me I could not look around, so I kept on increasing my speed until I burst into the parlor with a rush, and then I turned and stood at bay. Nothing was there! Absolutely nothing; and though I felt sick, I tried to laugh it off but could not. Once more placing the bayonet candlestick in the piano top, I sought the open air of the porch and then lighted my pipe.

"O sweet and noble comforter, what a friend thou art in need! for as the smoke curled up from my lips it left in its wake sweetest and purest comfort. The bounding heart-beat became quiet and shaken nerves firmer, and I began to smile at the vivid imagination which made my ear take note of sounds that never smote the air. So I seated myself on the steps and watched the campfires which were fast smoldering out. . .

"Hark! What sound was that! The piano - yes! the piano as I live! There goes a running scale, and now a full crash!

"I could scarcely get my breath and my heart thumped like a trip-hammer. I rose to my feet and stood like one turned to stone, and then by a strong effort of will I went across to the window and looked in. Everything was just as I had left it, only the candle was nearly burned up, and there remained but a death wick hanging down to chronicle departed time. The old fellow on the wall was scowling menacingly, and thrilled me with horror. I went back to my place again on the steps, again relit my pipe and sought to restore my shattered equilibrium."

(Here, Hunter's imagination takes over, intensifying an ever-deepening fear.) "But my thoughts were far beyond my control and refused to be soothed by tobacco. They dwelt defiantly on every ghost story I had ever heard. 'Banquo' shook his gory locks at me with eyes that had no speculation in them, and I remember how Macbeth said: 'It was a bold man that dare look on that which might appall the Devil.' Old Mr. Hamlet, Sr., walked abroad with his slugged-up ear, rattling his 'canonized bones hearsed in death.' Clarence sat heavy on my soul; and all his fellow shadows struck as much terror to my heart as ever they did to Richard's. I hardly know whose ghost the Witch of Endor brought up, or whether somebody brought up hers, but I am pretty certain she was at her worst and favored with her company.

(Hunter recalls the lines of an old poem.)

"'We have no title-deeds to house or lands.

Owners and occupants of earlier dates
From graves forgotten stretch their dusty hands
And hold in mortmain still their old estates.'

"Shades of Erebus! How many of those hapless landlords of Chantilly might take it into their heads to stalk abroad tonight.

"Here I was brought to my feet more quickly than if a whole salvo of artillery had been fired in the yard, for the crashing tones of the piano came again slantingly clear to my ear. There was no ground for a mistake now. I felt as if an icy hand encircled my heart; my head spun so I could not see. My brain teemed with horrid, hideous images, and skeleton hands seemed to grasp my throat.

"Rising to my feet with a spasmodic step like a sleep-walker, I turned toward the point from whence the sound proceeded. Yes! Yes! Clear and loud the piano keys were being touched by ghostly fingers! My eyes seemed to fill with blood; and then like a felon walking from the cell door to the steps of the gallows, I moved to the window and looked in.

"I saw, or fancied I saw, a brilliant company in gorgeous array — but, oh horrors! Instead of smiling, beautiful faces, there grinned each skull with awful cavities where eyes and nose should have been, and every toothless mouth was gaping wide.

"A dozen skeleton fingers suddenly pointed to me, and a burst of hideous laughter followed. By the expiring flicker of the candle wick it looked to me like a scene from the Inferno.

"Unless I could break the spell I felt I should go mad; so with a last convulsive movement I raised my gun, leveled it and pulled the trigger. A burst of light — a stunning report — and darkness! A shriek! A long, loud shriek! I turned and fled!

"How I reached camp I never knew. I suppose I ran myself clear out of breath. I reached camp without hat, gun, or cartridge-box, and speechless.

"I told my tale by degrees to a believing audience — none doubted me.

"That night the lieutenant went with a guard and examined the premises. In the garret they found half a dozen swallows that had just tumbled down the chimney, and so those mysterious noises that had frightened my brave predecessor and myself were explained. So far so good. And now must I spoil my ghost story — they generally all end as did mine, so I had better add a few words more before we turn in for the night.

"In the parlor were found the remains of the candle, and on the keys lay a huge rat which my bullet had struck before it had embedded itself in the solid wood. The explanation now is easy.

"Frightened when I started, I became wrought up to such a state of nervous excitement by the noises upstairs and my own vivid imagination that when the old rat sounded the keys of the piano by jumping on them, I believed that beings of another world were present in bodily shape. Nay, I actually saw them, for superstitious terror had made me as mad as any patient in Bedlam, and with my own voice ringing in my ears, I broke away from the scene.

"You will say it was because I was a mere boy, but that had nothing to do with it — a boy can be as brave as a man. And every man is a coward in the dark. . .

"Thereafter the doughtiest warrior would not stand guard at Chantilly, and it was left to be pillaged. The bad name it received remained with it.

"In 1862, just after the Second Battle of Manassas, the fine old house was burned to the ground; and in a short while the forest was laid low by soldiers; and so faded from earth even the slightest trace of its site. . . ."

(Author's footnote: And so ends private Alexander Hunter's narrative. On September 1, 1862, writes Civil War Historian Bruce Catton: " . . . there was a wild, brief, and bloody fight near the country house of Chantilly, with a mad, gusty wind and a driving rain, and an overpowering thunderstorm which made so much noise that the gunfire itself could not be heard at Centreville, three miles away . . . (Union General) Phil Kearny - galloping through the dark wood with the lightning gleaming on the wet leaves, his sword in his hand and the bridle reins held in his teeth (he had lost an arm in the war with Mexico), rode smack into a line of Confederate infantry and was shot to death."

Hunter says he "fell headlong, with a bullet through his heart, but a few steps from the historic mansion . . ." Hunter adds that he wondered at the "strange destiny" that had brought Kearny to die in the shadows of the haunting Chantilly.)

CHAPTER 57

A Quaint Custom From the Civil War

(New Market)

letter from Rob Taylor of Arlington, Virginia: "Three years ago (1995), I relocated from upstate New York to New Market. In a way, moving to the Shenandoah Valley felt like a homecoming since my grandmother was a native Virginian. I started my own computer business. One of the services I offered was onsite instruction. As a result I frequently found myself in the homes of computer owners. Some of those customers lived in historic old homes. I've held a lifelong interest in ghosts and the paranormal, so as I would get to know my customers, quite often I'd ask them about the history of their houses, and, if it seemed appropriate, whether there might be any ghosts in residence. I was a bit surprised, for a town as rich in Civil War heritage as New Market is, it seems incredibly devoid of ghostly phenomena? I did, however, hear one interesting tale.

"Joyce and Frank Winfree of New Market own a lovely stone farmhouse on the edge of town that predates the Civil War (1846). I had suspected that the home may have served some purpose during the Battle of New Market, and when I asked Joyce about it one day, she replied in the affirmative, having been told by the former owner that it had served as a hospital during the battle. Naturally, that gave way to me asking about any Civil War ghosts that might be lingering about, but Joyce said no. They'd never seen, heard, nor felt anything out of the ordinary there.

"Then, almost as an afterthought, she did produce from memory a peculiar incident from some years ago — one for which she and Frank never came up with a satisfactory explanation. On a spring day they returned from a trip to Harrisonburg and were startled to find the pictures that normally hang on the downstairs walls resting on the floor, all of them propped at similar angles against the wall, directly below their normal positions. Joyce indicated that the front door had been locked, but that there was no evidence of forced entry. A cursory review of their valuables found nothing missing, and nothing else out of place. All the same, Frank searched the premises for a possible intruder. Again, he found nothing amiss.

"The next thought was that a minor earthquake or a sonic boom may have knocked the pictures from the wall, but no knick-knacks had teetered off their shelves, and no china had toppled over in the cabinet. And besides, what were the odds that all of the pictures would fall in such a manner, all carefully lined up as they were? None were lying face down, none had broken glass from a fall.

"Later that night, I was corresponding via an Internet chat program with a friend in Pennsylvania. She, too, holds a fascination with the paranormal. When I passed the story on to her, she immediately recognized this phenomenon, and proceeded to tell me that there are several homes in Gettysburg where this occurs periodically, most often on the anniversary of the great battle there.

"It seems that at the onset of a Civil War conflict, it was relatively common practice for housewives to remove all of their pictures from the walls and lower them to the floor, so that the percussion caused by artillery fire wouldn't drop them in slightly more violent fashion.

"On my next trip back to visit Joyce and Frank, I asked if they recalled the exact date of the incident. Unfortunately neither did, but I would not have been the least bit surprised to learn that the date was May 15th, the anniversary of the Battle of New Market. It isn't hard to convince oneself that the ghost of a prior resident was taking care to protect the Winfrees' pictures in their absence!"

CHAPTER 58

The Disaster of Dahlgren's Raid – Part II

(Richmond)

(Author's note: In "The Ghosts of Richmond" (1985), and repeated in "Civil War Ghosts of Virginia" (1995), I included a chapter on an extraordinary but little known slice of commonwealth history which occurred during the Civil War. It involved a daring but ill-conceived raid on Richmond in early 1864, that, had it succeeded, might well have shortened the conflict by a year. It did not succeed, however, and the entire episode was frought with horror, including an unjustified murder, desecration of a Union officer's body, and accounts of a trio of evolving ghosts.

In the past year, 15 years after doing the initial research, I have come across some additional material which adds even more to the overall weirdness of the event.

To briefly recap, here is what I initially wrote, mixed in with the later additions:)

It is unclear who first hatched the plot. Some historians give the credit (or the blame) to Union General Judson Kilpatrick. Whatever, a plan was devised in the early months of 1864 to stage an assault on Richmond, then lightly defended. With a force of 4,000 men, Kilpatrick would openly test what defenses the city still maintained. As he was doing this, a detachment of 500 men under the command of a 21-year-old colonel by the name of Ulric Dahlgren, would sneak around behind

SA 27

DAHLGREN'S RAID

HERE COLONEL ULRIC DAHLGREN, UNION CAVALRYMAN, RAIDING TO RICHMOND, HANGED A NEGRO ON A TREE BESIDE THE ROAD, MARCH 1, 1864. DAHLGREN PLANNED TO CROSS THE JAMES RIVER IN THIS VICINITY AND ENTER RICHMOND FROM THE SOUTH. A NEGRO GUIDED THE RAIDERS TO A FORD BUT THE WATER WAS TOO HIGH FOR CROSSING. DAHLGREN THOUGHT THE GUIDE HAD DECEIVED HIM.

CONSERVATION & DEVELOP- MENT COMMISSION 1931

Richmond. He would then release some 15,000 Yankee prisoners being held at Belle Island and at Libby Prison. They would then sack and burn the city, and the defenses, mostly home guards and a hodgepodge of others, would crumble, and with the capitol captured, the South might capitulate.

It was a most innovative plan, but one destined to fail. Kilpatrick did not attack forcefully enough. He was hampered by foul weather and by the underestimated fighting intensity of the thin Confederate defenses. Meanwhile, Dahlgren, cut off from communications, became lost in the woods of Goochland County, and was thoroughly confused.

At one point he had planned to cross the James River to carry out his mission of freeing the prisoners. He came across a free black man named Martin Roberson, who told him he knew a place where the fording could be made. According to another black man, named

Jones, who then was a cook under Dahlgren, Martin led them to the spot, but heavy rains had raised the water level to a dangerous height. Jones quotes Dahlgren as saying, "Roberson, this does not look like a ford. Boys, I'll lead the way." Dahlgren then waded in and both he and his horse disappeared beneath the surging waters.

The drenched colonel swam back to shore and said: "Roberson, you have already delayed me by poor direction and I think you are guilty of treachery. You can prepare to die." Jones said when the rear of the column passed near St. Mary's Church, Roberson's body was swinging from a limb of a tree. The strap, said to be from Dahlgren's own bridle, remained on the limb for "a good many years after the war was over," and a skull, said to be Roberson's, could be seen on the side of the road.

Unable to cross the river, Dahlgren and his men continued down River Road, in the vicinity of Tuckahoe Plantation. They ran into an ambush. Here, the story is taken up by Edward Halbach, who then was a school teacher in the area. He wrote that he had formed "a company of my pupils between the ages of 13 and 17, as a local defense."

Halbach and his boys were in the woods on both sides of a road at Walkerton, on the Pamunkey River on the evening of March 2, 1864. At about 11:30 p.m., as Dahlgren's column of troops approached, the schoolboys fired a volley of shots in the dark. One Union soldier fell from his horse while the others scattered. A 13-year-old boy named William Littlepage then went out to examine the fallen man. It was Ulric Dahlgren. Littlepage had killed him. The boy, went through the dead colonel's pockets and retrieved a cigar case and a memorandum box.

At daylight the next morning, Halbach read papers found in Dahlgren's memorandum box. They were the colonel's orders. He had written: "We hope to release the prisoners from Belle Island first, and having seen them fairly started, we will cross the James River into Richmond, destroying the bridges after us, and exhorting the released prisoners to destroy and burn the hateful city, and do not allow the rebel leader Davis, and his traitorous crew to escape."

Subsequent publication of these orders created near panic in Richmond. The Richmond Examiner, for example, wrote: ". . . turning loose some thousands of ruffian prisoners, brutalized to the deepest degree by acquaintance with every horror of war, who have been confined on an island for a year, far from all means of indulging their strong sensual appetites — inviting this pandemonium to work their will on the unarmed citizens, on the women, gentle and simple, of Richmond, and on all their property."

The furor rose to such heights that Confederate General Robert E. Lee sent Union General George Meade a message asking for an answer to the charges of intended barbarity. Meade swiftly replied that no one had ordered any cities burned or civilians harmed. This led to the immediate question of just where did the orders come from.

Meanwhile, some of the pent-up fear and hatred spilled over into extreme ugliness. One man allegedly cut off one of Dahlgren's fingers to get a ring. Another took his artificial leg — he had lost a leg in an earlier battle — as a souvenir. In 1929, Mary James Tabb of Gloucester County, wrote an article entitled "Memories of War Days." In it she said, "One of Mother's most thrilling experiences of these days was in connection with Dahlgren's raid. About dusk one evening Dr. Taylor came rushing into our room in his exciting way, bearing a package, which he seemed to value very highly. 'Mrs. James,' he exclaimed, 'I want you to take care of Dahlgren's leg!'

"Dr. Taylor explained that he wanted to take the leg to the hospital to show the other doctors, as it was the most remarkable artificial limb in existence at this time. He wanted the Confederate surgeons to see the wonderful mechanism before it was buried with the owner. Mother agreed to take care of the leg for him, and it was placed under my crib in our crowded room. So it was that I slept over Dahlgren's leg for one whole night."

According to one account, the colonel's body, stripped of clothes and all other belongings, was carted to Richmond in a lidless pine box, where it was displayed in a railroad station.

Later, as Dahlgren's rude coffin was being lowered into a grave, orders came to send the body for interment at Oakwood Cemetery. Sometime later the remains were again dug up and moved to the neighborhood of Laurel, at the request of Union sympathizers. After the war, his body was exhumed once more by his family for final disposition.

Another account of the interments of Dahlgren's body was recorded in an edition of the Southern Historical Society Papers. Here, there is this: "Dahlgren's body was brought to Richmond for identification. It was buried in Oakwood Cemetery, and was afterwards taken up and carried to Miss E. H. Van Lew's house on Church Hill. From her house the body was carried to <u>Chelsea Hill</u>, where it remained several days; then carried on a wagon covered with fruit trees and buried near Hungary Station. After the War it was taken up and carried North and buried among kindred."

Perhaps the most definitive treatment of what happened to Dahlgren's body is told in Ernest B. Furgurson's 1997 book, "Ashes of Glory - Richmond at War." According to the author, when Dahlgren fell, dead, his left little finger was cut off to steal a ring and his artificial leg was taken. "Then they dumped his body over a fence to protect it from hogs roaming the road. When a rough coffin was completed, they buried him in a shallow grave near the junction since called 'Dahlgren's Corner'."

The body was soonafter dug up and taken to Richmond where "curious citizens looked on the young colonel's face as the open coffin lay in a boxcar at the York River railroad depot." He was then reburied in an unmarked grave somewhere below Oakwood Cemetery on the northeastern edge of the city. Of this event the Richmond Examiner reported: "Where that spot is no one but those concerned in its burial know or care to tell . . . It was a dog's burial . . . Friends and relatives at the North need inquire no further; this is all they will know - he is buried, a burial that befitted the mission upon which he came."

At this point Union General Benjamin Butler requested that the body be returned to Federal hands. Confederate colonel Robert Ould ordered this to be done, but when the grave was opened - the body was gone! Here, northern sympathizers intervened. They finally found a black cemetery worker who had seen where Dahlgreen's remains had been taken. A month after Dahlgren had been killed his body was disinterred once more, placed in a metal coffin, and was put on a wagon and covered by a load of young peach trees. It was then surreptitiously carried through Richmond to a farm 10 miles north of the city and laid to rest yet another time. The site was marked by a single peach tree.

After the war Dahlgren's father finally retrieved his son's body and took it home. Curiously, author Furgurson noted, the colonel's missing leg was recovered in November 1865 in Albermarle County, where it was being worn by a Confederate veteran. Dahlgren's missing ring was also found.

The poor man was thus buried three, four, or five times, depending upon which account one follows.

As to the overall raid, the Richmond Sentinel, on March 3, 1864, had this to say: "Thus has passed away Kilpatrick's . . . attempt at raiding into Richmond . . . As far as the grand objects of his undertaking were concerned, he has reason to feel very foolish. . . They have failed in everything except some temporary damage of our railroads, the burning of some barns and mills, the seizure of some horses, the hanging of one Negro, and the stealing of some spoons. For these he has paid, probably, 250 picked men, and he has thoroughly broken down the rest, both men and horses, for a time."

If ever there were cause for a spirit to rise, in the face of such abject failure, and/or because of what happened to his body in the immediate days following his sudden death, one might expect Dahlgren's to appear.

And perhaps it does.

For there are indeed some intriguing footnotes to this account, and the possible return of not one, but three separate ghosts!

* During Dahlgren's march around the outskirts of Richmond, his men learned that a Confederate general named Wise was visiting a house known as Eastwood in the area. They set out to capture him, but Wise, who knew the region intimately, bolted on horseback into the woods and escaped to the city.

It is an ironic twist of coincidence that General Wise was the man in charge of the hanging of John Brown.

* An article in a Richmond newspaper more than half a century ago concerned "an old house on Three Chopt Road owned by Ben Green." Some of Dahlgren's men had stopped here during their foray, seeking the location of the household silver, which was "known to be extensive," and thought to be buried nearby. When a "faithful" old slave named Burwell refused to disclose the hiding site he was strung up by his thumbs. This house, according to the article, "is known to be haunted." Some believe it is the spirit of Burwell who remained, seeking some form of retribution for the brutal pain he suffered so long ago.

* Another legend centers around one of Dahlgren's young officers. When the column of Union soldiers was attacked, he rode his horse into a dense patch of honeysuckle thicket surrounded by trees somewhere on Cary Street Road in an area where an old ice house once stood. He immediately fell, mortally wounded by a sniper's bullet. It has been reported that on calm nights "are frequently heard moans from the luckless victim."

* And finally, the author's more recent research has turned up this: On Sunday, December 29, 1929, the Richmond Times-Dispatch ran an article by Edward L. Ryan titled, "Tenth Governor of Virginia Beloved by All for His Character and Services to His State."

In part, the article noted: "One hundred and sixteen years ago, General James Wood, the tenth of the Governors of Virginia, died at 'Chelsea,' now Wood Street, on Chelsea Hill, and was buried in St. John's Churchyard, beloved by all the people of Virginia, etc. . .

(Chelsea, remember, was the place where Dahlgren's body "had remained for several days.")

"He (Wood) died June 16, 1813.

"Grandfather, Phillip Meisel, bought Chelsea just before or just after the War Between the States and his widow owned it until approximately 1905. The purchaser let it fall into ruin, unfortunately, as it was a very fine old house, the materials said to have been brought from England, not a nail in the house, all dovetailed."

And then came the kicker in Ryan's article: "There was a story current among the Negroes nearby that . . . Dahlgren's ghost haunted it. Mother heard it as a child."

CHAPTER 59

The 'People of the House' at Colesville

(Charles City County)

(Author's note: I guess at this point, after 17 years of research, ten books, and hundreds of interviews, I shouldn't be surprised or amazed at anything anymore. But I am. At the Newport News Fall Festival in October 1997, where I was autographing books, a lady came up and asked if I had ever written about Colesville Plantation. Where was it, I inquired. In Charles City County just off Route 5, she said. Are there spirits there, I asked. She nodded. I couldn't believe it.

Route 5, now the John Tyler Highway, and once known as the Old Indian Trail, is a scenic, tree-lined, two-lane road that runs from Williamsburg west to Richmond - about 50 miles. It is dotted with historic mansions and plantations along the James River. When I was working on my first book in this series, "The Ghosts of Williamsburg and Nearby Environs," in 1982, I rode up and down Route 5, and included ghostly encounters at: Sherwood Forest, the former home of President John Tyler; Westover Plantation, the former domain of William Byrd, II; Edgewood, which dates to 1849; and Shirley, home of the Carter family for 10 or 11 generations. Each house had an intriguing and individual haunting associated with it. I had inquired at other famous homes, but found nothing more at the time.

After the book came out, in 1983, I got a call from the late Malcolm Jameson, owner of Berkeley Plantation, adjacent to Westover. Why hadn't I included their ghost, he wanted to know. I told him the historical interpreters there had informed me they had no ghost. "Oh, yes," he replied. And he told me the story of the psychic phenomena that occurred there. I wrote a chapter on it and included it in a second book, "The Ghosts of Richmond," which was published in 1985.

After that came out, I received word that Miss Evelyn Byrd, the daughter of William Byrd, II, who died in 1737, and apparently reappears occasionally at Westover, also has been seen at Evelynton Plantation on Route 5! So I did a chapter on her in the third book, "The Ghosts of Tidewater." Now I was sure I had covered every haunt possible. That's why I was surprised when the lady told me about Colesville. So, 17 years later, here it is.)

*C*olesville Plantation today is a 350-acre working farm located approximately two miles west of the Charles City County courthouse and near Indian Fields Tavern, which is a charming place to dine on fine Virginia country fare. This was all part of an original 10,000-acre tract known as Swinyards and named after Thomas Swinhowe. It is also documented that the first land grant here was made in 1617, and that five years later, seven early settlers were killed on the site during the infamous Indian raid of 1622. In the mid-1700s William Cole, after whom the plantation was named, bought some of the property, and later traded this portion to three brothers named Clarke. They owned Colesville for more than 100 years before moving away in 1880.

According to family records, the noted explorers William Clark and Meriwether Lewis stayed at Colesville just prior to their departure from Charlottesville for exploration of the western territory.

Union General U.S. Grant used the house as temporary headquarters in June 1864 as he was preparing to chase Robert E. Lee and his army south, leading to the siege of Petersburg. In mid-June 1864, Grant and about 100,000 of his men crossed the James River at Wilcox Landing over a pontoon bridge near Colesville. A state historical marker notes where they crossed.

Little is known of the house history from 1880 well into the 20th century. In 1983, Roger and Bonnie Sizemore bought the land and house and later began renovations. Colonial Williamsburg experts helped authenticate the history of the house. It is a two-story structure with original floors and trim. The earliest part of the house dates to 1730, and another part was added in 1820. Thus, it is

Colesville

actually two houses joined together. There are six rooms downstairs, including a kitchen, and four bedrooms upstairs plus an attic. From one bedroom one can walk up to the attic and come down in an adjacent bedroom. This secret passageway was probably built as an escape route should Indians attack. A smokehouse and an outhouse flank the main house.

Roger and Bonnie Sizemore moved into Colesville in 1996. Their daughter, Arden, then was about four years old. Mysterious manifestations began the second night they were in the house. "I had heard there had been a lot of tragedy here," Bonnie says. "Several people, including some children, had died in the house. On the second night we were there, I was in the bedroom when I heard someone walking about in the bathroom. The floors here creak real bad when somebody walks on them, so there was no mistaking what I heard. Roger wasn't there. The footsteps came toward me. They entered my bedroom, walked around the bed and then went out the door and down the hall.

"I got up to look and prayed that I wouldn't see anything. I didn't. There was no one there. When Roger wasn't at home I would sometimes have Arden get in bed with me at night. We both heard the same sounds a number of times. Once it stopped right at the edge of our bed. Arden was asleep and about to fall out of the bed. I think whatever or whoever it was, was trying to alert me that she was about to fall. When I pulled Arden beside me, the footsteps left the room and went down the hall.

"I told a friend about the experiences, and she said I should talk to the ghost or ghosts. So I did. I said they were scaring me and I'd appreciate it if they wouldn't walk into my room. After that I would hear doors shut upstairs and someone walking around in the attic. But at least they weren't in my room."

Bonnie continues: "Arden had never talked to herself before, but she began doing this right after we moved in. Normally, when a child does this, they carry on a full conversation, but Arden didn't. It would be like she was listening to someone. She would say, 'uh huh, uh huh.' I asked her who she was talking to and she said, 'the people of the house.' She said it was a boy and a girl. Arden almost seems like she is in a trance during these conversations.

"One time Roger and Arden were in the car ready to go somewhere and Roger forgot something and left Arden in the car alone. She didn't like to be left alone and started crying. When Roger came back to the car, she told him the boy and the girl had stayed with her while he was in the house and she was okay. She described the girl as having on a long blue coat and hat, and shoes with buttons on them. The boy wore a brown hat and pants. Of course, Roger and I never saw anything, but they say sometimes a child can see spirits no one else can."

In restoring the house and attempting to get it listed on an historic register, the Sizemores called in a specialist from Chesterfield to hang some curtains. The man had never been to Colesville before and, Bonnie believes, knew nothing of its history. The moment he walked in the front door, before he even said hello, he said, "Do you know you have two ghosts in this house?" Bonnie was astonished. He then told her that Arden talks to the ghosts all the time, "and when she gets a little older, she will have lots of stories to tell you."

The man said that his family was sensitive to supernatural phenomena. Bonnie: "He told me that the boy ghost used to play in the attic all the time and that he used to hide stuff in a secret place in the attic, behind a loose brick. Roger went up to investigate, and he found the loose brick and an open space behind it! The man then said that I shouldn't be afraid of the spirits, that they wouldn't harm me. They were just looking after the house. He said that there was a strong box somewhere on the property. I felt a chill up my spine when he said this, because I had been having recurrent dreams about such a strong box. He said I should find it. We haven't found it yet, but Roger is into metal detection and we have found all sorts of Civil War relics.

"We also had some contractors during the renovation who said strange things happened to them. They said someone or something would turn lights on and off, and that their tools and materials would get 'moved around' when they weren't there."

Roger and Bonnie have opened a bed and breakfast at Colesville. Their scrumptious breakfasts include pear jams and dried apples from the trees on the farm. Wheat, barley and corn are grown on the plantation. Whether or not visitors will sense the spirits of a boy and girl, as the Sizemores have, is not known.

Who are these children of the past? Bonnie has a clue. The amateur psychic who came in to hang the curtains, said the girl's name was Emily and the boy's name was Trent. Bonnie did some research. She wrote to a Clarke family descendent in Alabama. He told her the last Clarke to live in the house was named Alexander <u>Trent</u> Clarke!

"The curtain hanger told me that the boy and girl have remained here because they felt this was still their house, says Bonnie. "They would be friendly to us because we had faithfully restored Colesville. "But to be on the safe side, we have hung a picture of Mr. Clarke in one of the rooms. We hope he likes that."

CHAPTER 60

The 'Legend' of Rippons Hollow

(Charles City County)

(Author's note: As Halloween 1998 approached, I was struck by the impressive and steadily growing number of historic houses, beds and breakfasts, and plantations which featured haunting tours. One involved three sites in Charles City County between Williamsburg and Richmond. Now, I had worked with the owners of such famous mansions as Shirley, Evelynton, and Sherwood Forest in the past, doing signings on or near October 31.

But here was a new tour, or at least new to me. Actually, it had been going on for the past four or five years, but probably was under-publicized. One of the three houses, Edgewood, was thoroughly familiar to me. I had written extensively about the alleged ghost of s "Miss Lizzie," who has been seen peering out a third-story bedroom window searching for her lost lover who rode away to fight in the Civil War in the 1860s. The indefatigable owner of Edgewood, Dot Boulware, had persuaded me, on more than one occasion, to come out and sign books for her.

I knew about a second house on the tour as well. It is a B & B called North Bend. I had received one report of a scary encounter there by a guest who was so spooked she got up in the middle of the night and left the premises, vowing never to return. The third place, another B & B, was Piney Grove, and I knew virtually nothing about it. A newspaper teaser, plugging the tour, mentioned "The Legend of Rippons Hollow," would be told at Piney Grove. This looked promising, so I called Brian Gordineer one evening and asked him about it. His family owns Piney Grove.

I was at first disappointed when Brian said the legend was "kind of made up" and related by a story teller. But then he told me about a "real" ghost in the main house on the grounds, and added information about the interesting history of the plantation. Here is what he said:)

he original part of the house was built as a corn crib. It dates to 1790, and the plantation then included 300 acres. It was owned by Furneau Southall who then served as sheriff of Charles City County. Brian says in the latter part of the 19th century, and well into the 20th, a doctor and his family lived here. One of the rooms was used to operate on people. If it was a complex or complicated operation, doctors from Richmond were sent to the house to participate.

Curiously, relatively close to the original house, to which several additions have been made over the years, there is a small graveyard belonging to the doctor's family. Here, there are five grave sites for children. Halloween tour attendees are taken to this area.

Today, Piney Grove offers guests a quiet overnight stay, a history of the area, and a candlelit plantation-style breakfast. The B & B rooms are not in the main house, where Brian's parents live, but

Piney Grove

in other buildings. One is a house that was dismantled in Caroline County and reassembled on the grounds. It dates to 1857. Another was moved from a site where the Colonial Golf Course is now located. It is circa 1835. And, if one asks, Brian or one of his family will talk about their resident spirit.

The original house stood vacant and abandoned for 20 years, between 1964 and 1984. Then the Gordineers bought the property and began extensive renovations. One day, after working, Brian's father and brother were leaving when his father realized he had left his watch in the house. They went back to get it. The house was sealed tight and there was no way anyone could be inside. They had just left it.

They went inside, and both of them heard distinctive footsteps upstairs. Something was in the house. The two men searched every inch of the structure, but found nothing.

"We've not had any other experiences," Brian says. "We wonder if it was someone who might have lived here in years gone by and is there to protect the house."

There are other possible causes. Could it be the doctor who once operated at Piney Grove? One of his patients, unpleased at the outcome of his treatment? Or one of the children buried nearby? How did they die?

Perhaps it might be old Furneau Southall himself, the 18th century sheriff. For it is documented that when he died his heirs fought over ownership of the plantation for 50 years before his grandson was finally able to buy the property at auction. Would not that be enough to bring back a long-tormented spirit — to see that his house was finally in good hands?

THE RETURN OF GENERAL SHERIDAN?

(Author's note: The day after I interviewed Brian Gordineer I got a call from Ridgely Copland. She and her husband own North Bend. This impressive house — 6,000 square feet — was built in 1819, and was the home of Sarah Harrison, sister of William Henry Harrison, the ninth President of the United States, who himself was born at Berkeley, a few miles to the west. General Philip H. Sheridan used North Bend as a temporary headquarters during the Civil War, and it is said that during a temper fit in the house, he stuck his sword in one of the panel doors, splitting it.

Today, the plantation is a bed and breakfast, complete with some historic furnishings. A solid mahogany queen tester bed,

North Bend

circa 1810, belonged to Edmund Ruffin, the controversial Virginia soil expert, and the man who fired the first shot at Fort Sumter to begin the Civil War. Also here is General Sheridan's desk, among illustrious other period antiques.

George Copland, incidentally, is the great-great-grandson of Ruffin, and also the great-great-nephew of William Henry Harrison. The Greek revival style home features original mantels, staircase carvings, and woodgraining on the pocket doors. There is a fireplace in each room, three porches, a billiards room, and a swimming pool. Overnight guests are treated to a lavish breakfast of bacon, sausage, homemade waffles, juice, melons and strawberries.

They may also experience a paranormal event, because both Ridgely Copland and an out-of-state guest have reported ethereal happenings, but of entirely different manifestations. Ridgely says in the past during the Halloween tours, they had an actor portray General Sheridan, but there really wasn't anything ghostly in the presentation. "We would take people through the house by candle light and then we would go up and see 'the general'," she says. "There was nothing out of this world, so to speak, but when we would enter the bedroom and the actor, dressed in a Civil War uniform, would get up to speak, the guests, not expecting it, would be scared to death."

Ridgely had her own encounter about ten years ago. Her husband was on a trip in Canada, and she was at North Bend alone. She was in her bedroom when she heard the sound of someone in boots tromping across the floor in the Rose Room above her. "It scared the bejammers out of me," she says. "I had never heard of anything like that before. I called my son and told him someone was in the house. He just lives a short way, and drove his truck up the lane in a matter of minutes.

"Just as I heard his truck, the stomping stopped. He searched the house from top to bottom, but found no one. He then left, and as soon as he had cleared the driveway, the heavy steps began again. I called my son back, and when he arrived, the steps ceased once more. This time he spent the night, and nothing further happened." Ridgely says this phenomenon only occurred to her that once, although a visitor also heard the footsteps one night. Ridgely wonders if the restless spirit of Philip Sheridan may still linger.

"I should add one other incident," she says. "We were doing renovations on the house in the early 1980s. An old man once came inside and asked if we had any ghosts here. I thought it was rather curious. At the time we didn't know of anything and told him so, and he reacted very strangely. He said 'don't tell me you don't have any ghosts here! I'm getting the hell out of this house,' and he left abruptly."

And there is this final note. A lady in Fairfax called the author one night and related the following:

"I don't know whether I am psychically sensitive or not. Perhaps so. I do know that my first husband died 14 years ago, and I saw him one night five years later! He was standing in the corner of a room.

"Anyway, my second husband, Richard, and I spent the night at North Bend some time ago. Mr. Copland gave us a tour of the house and then we went out to have dinner at the Indian Fields Tavern. Later, we came back and went to bed. Sometime about midnight, I noticed that Richard was still awake. I asked him what was wrong, and he told me his shoulder was bothering him.

"Shortly after that, I got the strangest feeling. I felt there was someone else in the room. I sensed there were evil spirits present. I said 'in the name of Jesus Christ, get thee behind me.' Then I clearly heard the sound of a child crying. I guessed it was someone seven or eight years old. It was a 'hurt' cry. I also saw a white wreath of live doves. And I know it was real. I wasn't dreaming.

"I bolted upright in the bed and told Richard that we had to leave here. Richard was already awake. After I told him my experience he said that he had not been able to sleep, not because of his shoulder as he had said, but because of what he was encountering in the room. He said that he had the weirdest feeling that he was 'susceptible.' Then he felt something pushing on his chest! He said it was like somebody trying to grab him. He pushed something away from him.

"Neither one of us could sleep the rest of the night. We got up at six in the morning and left. We both knew we couldn't stay there."

Oddly, one of the prized antiques at North Bend is an oriental porcelain Foo Dog dating to 1801. It is said to ward off evil spirits.

Footnote: Whether one is met by an actor or a "real" spirit at Piney Grove and North Bend, the Halloween tour has become a popular annual event. In 1998, Ridgely Copland says more than 100 people attended.

CHAPTER 61

Aunt Pratt Surfaces Once More

(Charles City County)

(Author's note: Apparently the ghost of Aunt Pratt, or at least accounts of the ghost of Aunt Pratt, will not be stilled. I have written extensively about this venerable lady, or rather the portrait of her, in the past, first in "The Ghosts of Williamsburg and Nearby Environs," (1983), then in "The Ghosts of Virginia, Volume I," (1993), and I added a postscript in "The Ghosts of Virginia, Volume IV," (1998). Now comes more.

To refresh memories, Aunt Pratt was a member of the Hill-Carter families who have lived in historic Shirley Plantation on the James River halfway between Richmond and Williamsburg for the past ten or so generations. At some point in the 1700s a portrait was painted of auntie. For eons, it hung in a prominent spot in a downstairs room. But when it was removed from that room and relegated to the attic by a later generation relative, all hell broke loose. Furniture would be banged around in the attic and the sounds of a woman sobbing could be heard. Finally, the portrait was restored to its proper place and the psychic phenomena died.

Then, in the 1970s, Aunt Pratt's portrait was loaned to a Virginia tourist bureau exhibition on the supernatural being held in New York City. Here, the "uncomfortable" portrait was:

— Seen swinging wildly on the wall.

Aunt Pratt

— Found one morning off the wall and, in the words of workmen, "heading toward the exit."

— Locked in a closet at night for security reasons. Sounds of a woman crying were heard in the closet, and one morning the portrait was found outside the secured room and again heading toward the door.

When the exhibition was over and Aunt Pratt was shipped home and rehung, everything was quiet again. That is, until recently when her story was being told to a group of tourists, and one man said it was all a bunch of bull. As he said this, while standing beneath her portrait in front of an armoire, the doors of the cabinet swung open forcefully, banging him in the backside. He abruptly left the house.

Here is more that has surfaced in recent times. Aunt Pratt, it is now believed, was actually Martha Hill, a family member who died in England in 1752. According to one account, before her portrait was banished to the attic, it was first taken down from the front room and placed in an upstairs bedroom. A distant relative came to visit and was given that room. After several restless nights, she complained that Aunt Pratt's "gaze" followed her around the room, causing her great stress. So she finally confronted the portrait, and as she did, she heard "someone moaning," and an arm chair began to rock with no one in it. Once the picture was placed in the attic, one of the sounds heard there was of the same chair rocking.

There are a couple of curious footnotes, too. At some undetermined point, it is not specified exactly when, art experts came to the mansion to inspect the portrait. They found that Aunt Pratt had actually been painted over the earlier image of another woman. A psychic told the Carters that this woman's name was "Cynthia." Subsequent research revealed that indeed there was a Cynthia in the family tree!

In 1986, two alleged "ghost hunters" came to Shirley Plantation to see what they could find. When they entered the room where the portrait hung, chandelier lights flickered off. When they left the room the lights came back on. One of the psychic experts said she felt "the strong presence of a woman in the room, but for some reason she didn't want to communicate with us."

Aunt Pratt, it seems, is perfectly happy at Shirley as long as no one messes with her!

CHAPTER 60

Is Jamestown Island
Forever Cursed?

reasonable case could be made that Jamestown Island, the site of the first permanent English settlement in America, could be cursed. Certainly, there has been more than enough tragedy and misfortune over the past nearly 400 years to warrant such a foreboding claim. Two-thirds of the first 105 Englishmen who landed here on May 14, 1607, were dead within eight months, and of the first 500 settlers who survived the long and arduous crossing of the Atlantic Ocean to reach Jamestown, only 60 survived.

Despite Captain John Smith's initial observation that the island was "a verie fit place for the erecting of a great cittie," it was, instead, a horrible location. Consider some 17th century accounts:

— Mrs. Ann Cotton: ". . . It is low ground, full of marshes and swamps, which make the aire especially in the summer insalubritious and unhealthy. It is not at all replenished with springs of fresh water, and that which they have in their wells, brackish, ill scented, penurious and not grateful to the stomack."

— George Percy: "Our men were destroyed with cruell diseases, as Swellings, Flixes, Burning fevers, and by Warres (with Indians), and some departed suddenly, but for the most part they died of meere famine. There were never Englishmen left in a forreine Countrey in such miserie as wee were in this new discovered Virginia."

— David Pietersen de Vries: "They say that during the months of June, July, and August, it is very unhealthy; that their people who have lately arrived from England, die during these months, like cats and dogs . . . "

The disastrous toll in human life was further advanced by the fact that most of the first settlers were ill equipped for such a harsh environment. Many were "refined gentlemen," who had few skills or the inclination to cope with the forging of a colony in the wilderness. This alone caused much strife and hardship. As John Rolfe, the husband of Pocahontas, wrote in 1620: "I speake on my owne experience for these 11 yeres, I never amongst so few, have seene so many falsehearted, envious and malicious people . . ." And Governor Dale said, in 1611: "Everie man allmost laments himself of being here, and murmers at his present state."

In January 1608, a terrible fire ravaged Jamestown, and, two years later most of the survivors died during a period known as "the starving time." Starvation drove some to cannibalism and others to madness. So many died so fast that they were hastily buried, without benefit of coffins, in mass shallow graves, in an effort to hide the vulnerability of the precarious colony from Indians.

In 1622, an Indian massacre killed more colonists, but even this was less threatening than rampant disease which claimed a greater number of victims. Historian Lyon Gardiner Tyler wrote: "Jamestown was literally the grave of the first settlers. The fatality among them, produced by famine and diseases of the climate, was almost unprecedented." To this, Carl Bridenbaugh, author of "Jamestown, 1544-1699," added: "The story of Jamestown is one of continous tragedy — wars, disease, death, fires . . . " Indeed, it is a wonder that _any_ early Jamestowners made it.

The town burned to the ground again in 1676, when rebellious Nathaniel Bacon and his men torched it. It was rebuilt, only to once more succumb to flames on Halloween, 1698. As Lyon Tyler put it: "The evil genius of misfortune still pursued the unfortunate methopolis."

It was only then, as the 18th century approached, that the colony leaders, perhaps believing that there was indeed a curse on their site, decided to move the capitol inland to what was then known as Middle Plantation — Williamsburg. Most of Jamestown Island then lapsed into a tomb-like silence that has lasted for 300 years. In 1716, John Fontaine wrote: "The town (Jamestown) consists in a church, a court house and three or four brick houses . . . but all is gone to ruin."

Sometime early in the 18th century, probably in the 1720s, a family named Ambler acquired a sizeable tract of land here and built a formidable home. Despite the isolation, the Amblers were

335

The Ambler Ruins

prominent citizens. Richard Ambler, for example, ran the ferry from Jamestown Island across the James River to Surry in the 1740s, and another Richard Ambler, in 1766, was an esteemed member of the Virginia House of Burgesses.

In an article in the Southern Literary Messenger, published in 1837, the writer notes: "The greater part of the island was in possession of the Ambler family for several generations . . . The soil is well adapted to the growth of corn, wheat, oats and palma christi. The island and surrounding country abound in game of almost every description — partridges, pheasants, wild turkeys, waterfowl and deer."

The mansion itself was Georgian, with a dominant central structure flanked by dependencies "to give the whole edifice line, proportion and balance." One author reported that "a surviving photograph of the plantation house . . . showed it to be a bleak and grim pile devoid of any environmental embellishment save for a dirt path flanked by rows of paper mulberries, trees renowned for their gnarled and forbidding appearance."

There is, too, a sad legend associated with the Ambler home, that is reminiscent of an earlier "love tragedy" nearby at the James River plantation — Westover. Here, in 1737, Evelyn Byrd, the daughter of William Byrd, II, pined away and is said to have died of a broken heart because her father would not let her marry the man she loved. (See "The Ghosts of Virginia, Volume I, 1993). Evelyn is said to occasionally reappear, in ghostly form, at Westover.

On Jamestown Island, a young lady named Lydia Ambler allegedly fell in love with a soldier named Alexander Maupin during the time of the American Revolutionary War. They were hastily married in August 1776, and he left, soonafter, to fight for American independence. He never returned. It is not known if he was killed in battle, or just abandoned his unhappy bride. Tradition says she waited anxiously for him, often spending the day on the banks of the James River, peering ever hopefully for him to return. Finally, in despair, she took her own life.

The curse continued when, in 1781, American hero-turned-traitor, Benedict Arnold sailed up the James and destroyed a number of plantation houses, including the Ambler mansion. It was rebuilt, only to be burned again during the Civil War. Once more, it was reconstructed. Then, in the 1890s, flames razed it again, leaving only ruins which still stand as silent sentinels to the cruel fates.

And, in recent years, there have been "incidents" recorded that the pale and desolate wraith of Lydia Ambler returns to the site, still searching for her lost lover. National park employees have told of seeing the apparition of a woman, wearing a gown of the 18th century, roaming the grounds. They know this is not a reenactor dressed in period costume, because the woman vanishes before their eyes!

One person who has had frightful experiences here is Traci Poole of Hampton, Virginia. Traci is a psychic. She sees and senses things others do not. She is, in paranormal terms, gifted . . . or cursed with such abilities.

For example, in 1991, when Traci's step-mother died of cancer, her vision appeared to Traci, who was miles away at the time. At the moment of death, the step-mother was visible to Traci, her arms outstretched, smiling, and surrounded by a purplish-colored aura. She had previously made a pact with Traci, telling her if she could come back from the beyond to communicate, she would.

Three years later, when Traci was pregnant with her daughter, Amber, Traci began hemmoraghing. Doctors told her that either she or her daughter would not make it alive through the birth. Traci told them to save the baby. As they were preparing Traci for a C-section, her step-mother's apparitional figure appeared to her, again smiling and with her arms outstretched. Traci thought her step-mother had come "to get her." The next conscious thing she remembered was someone touching her and saying, "Traci, you have a beautiful baby girl." "It was a miracle both of us were alive," Traci says today.

Traci, for some inexplicable reason, is drawn to Jamestown Island and the Ambler mansion. "I can't tell you why, but I am obsessed with the place," she says. "I've had some very strong sensations there. There have been times when I've been on the island and I had to get out of there. I could hardly breathe. At the foot of the large cross memorial there, I have heard children and women talking, and I don't mean tourists. These voices were from another time. I have seen Indian images there of barebreasted women, with bits of shell and bone necklaces. It freaked me out."

Traci also is deeply moved each time she visits the Ambler ruins. "I get the profound impression that the house never should have been built, that it was doomed from the start. Sometimes I can see people dancing there, but there also is a very dark side.
There is a feeling of a presence against the liveability of the house. I know there was much sadness and tragedy here. I get goosebumps just thinking about it."

Amid the mass graves of America's first settlers, and the ghosts of past residents, the curse — or as Lyon Tyler put it, "The evil genius of misfortune" — apparently lives on at Jamestown Island.

CHAPTER 63

The Charismatic Cavalier and the Vengeful Governor

(Jamestown and other sites)

he contrasts between the two men couldn't have been greater. One was 70-years-old and was the long-time governor of the Colony of Virginia. He was growing deaf, had a mercurial temper, harbored grudges, and ruled with a tyrannical hand. Some suspected he was approaching the early stages of senility. Once loved and respected, he was now feared and hated.

The other was young, 28, high-spirited, charismatic, intellectual, a masterful orator and a natural leader. Though he had been in Virginia for only a short time, he had already established himself as a fearless, dynamic personality.

The two men were on a collision course which would make an indelible mark on colonial history. In fact, some experts believe their clash was the chief precursor to the American Revolution which would take place a century later.

The year was 1676. The older man was William Berkeley, governor of Virginia. The younger man was Nathaniel Bacon, Jr., a landowner and farmer.

Berkeley had first come to the colony as governor in 1642, and then had been well received. He was a talented young man with a magnetic personality. He encouraged crop diversification, exhibited "statesmanship of a high order," and was considered a fair and able ruler. But he had stayed in power too long. As he grew older, his popularity waned. He had not held any elections for 14 years,

339

William Berkeley

causing widespread dissent.

But perhaps the biggest complaint against the governor, in 1676, was that he seemed to have lost his incentive for protecting the colonists against marauding Indian attacks. Earlier, especially after the great Indian massacre of white settlers in 1644, Berkeley personally led the charge against the attackers. But now, even though nearly 500 colonists had been killed in the early months of 1676, he refused to commission his followers to seek vengeance.

It was this refusal, principally, that forced the young Bacon into a leadership role. Incensed, after his own overseer had been murdered, Bacon, backed by alarmed citizens in what is now Charles

Nathaniel Bacon

City and Henrico counties, took charge. Without approval from the governor, he led an expedition against the Occaneechees, slaughtered 100 of them, and burned their village to the ground. When Berkeley heard of this, he charged Bacon with "treason and rebellion," captured him and brought him to Jamestown. Here, the governor exclaimed: "Now I behold the greatest rebel that ever was in Virginia." But realizing that Bacon had become a popular hero to the people, Berkeley relented and pardoned him.

Bacon did not trust Berkeley, however, and with a force of more than 100 armed men returned to Jamestown in June, where he confronted the governor with his request for a commission to go after the attacking Indians. Berkeley was infuriated, but when Bacon ordered his men to aim their cocked guns at the windows of the statehouse, the governor had little choice but to grant the commission.

But no sooner had Bacon and his men began chasing the Indians, when Berkeley renounced the commission, called Bacon a traitor, and said he would raise an army to go after him. But two things happened which caused the governor to retreat instead. First, Bacon, using fiery oratory, raised a force of 1,300 men, and second, Berkeley's own militia were "completely unwilling" to go after Bacon. Consequently, the governor abandoned both Jamestown and his own palatial home at Green Spring, and fled across the Chesapeake Bay to the Eastern Shore.

Bacon then went in pursuit of the Pamunkey Indians in the Dragon Swamp, and while he was occupied here, Berkeley and his adjutants managed to retake Jamestown. Bacon reassembled his troops and stormed the colonial capitol. The governor's soldiers virtually threw down their arms and ran. They had little heart to fight a man many of them believed was right in his cause. Berkeley again sailed to the Eastern Shore. Bacon then had Jamestown burned.

It was then, in the fall of 1676, that fate intervened and ended what has become known as "Bacon's Rebellion." The months of hard fighting and marching through swamps and thick woods finally took its toll on the young leader. As historian Virginius Dabney phrased it: "He (Bacon) had been under constant strain since the arduous expedition in the spring which took him hundreds of miles through the wilderness against the Occaneechees. Then came the marches and countermarches against Berkeley's forces, as well as the Pamunkeys, across trackless terrain and in abominable weather combining stifling heat with almost uninterrupted rain and enervating humidity. All this lowered his resistance. In the soggy trenches before Jamestown he is believed to have contracted the dysentery which carried him off a few weeks later."

He died on October 26, 1676, at the home of Major Thomas Pate on Portopotnk Creek in Gloucester County, not far from the town of West Point. What happened next has remained an unsolved mystery for more than 300 years. As Dabney wrote: "Bacon was buried secretly, lest perchance Governor Berkeley seek to inflict indignities upon his corpse." But where?

Author Mary Newton Stanard, in her book, "The Story of Bacon's Rebellion," published in 1907, says: "Those who had loved the Rebel in life were faithful to him in death, and tenderly laid his body away beyond the reach of the insults of his enemies. So closely guarded was the secret of the place and manner of his burial that it is unto this day a mystery; but tradition has it that stones were place in his coffin and he was put to bed beneath the deep waters of the majestic York River."

But Philip Alexander Bruce, author of "The Virginia Plutarch," published in 1929, wrote: "His corpse was committed at night to the waters of one of the inlets, and to this day the exact spot where his bones repose is unknown." Over the years there have been several attempts to find Bacon's body, believed by many to be submerged in shallow creek or inlet waters in Gloucester County, but all the searches have been in vain.

With their leader dead, Bacon's followers could not keep up the cause, and the rebellion collapsed. A number of Bacon's key lieutenants were hunted down and captured. It was then that Governor Berkeley openly demonstrated his cruel vengeance. Despite a plea from King Charles II of England for leniency, Berkeley had 23 of Bacon's men executed, after "trials devoid of dignity and fairness." Most were hanged. He also confiscated their estates and harshly treated their wives and children. Such vindictiveness contributed to the end of Berkeley's reign in Virginia. He was called back to England and died a short time later.

As one York County resident summed up the tragic ending for Bacon's men, "the Hangman (was) more dreadful to the Baconians, then their General was to the Indians; as it is counted more honourable, and less terable, to dye like a Souldier, then to be hang'd like a dogg."

Considering all the traumatic deaths involved, the unresolved mission of Nathaniel Bacon, and the undying vengefulness of Governor Berkeley, it might be assumed that such would be just cause for the return, in spirit form, of one or more of the participants. Perhaps.

There are, for example, a number of psychic manifestations which have taken place at Bacon's Castle in Surry County — a 17th century mansion in which Bacon's followers hid out during the rebellion. These have included unaccountable footsteps, "horrible moaning" in the attic when no one is there, objects being flung across rooms by unseen hands, and, most frightening, the occasional appearance of a "pulsating, red ball of fire" which soars 30 to 40 feet in the air over castle grounds and then disappears (See "The Ghosts of Virginia, Volume I," 1993). Some attribute these incidents to the ghosts of Bacon's men who were unmercifully hanged.

There are additional clues at the site of Green Spring, Governor Berkeley's mansion near Williamsburg. Although the house is no longer standing a spirit or two there may still be sensed.

Writing in the Colonial Williamsburg Magazine in 1996, historian, archeologist and author Ivor Noel Hume had this to say: "Those who believe in the supernatural will tell you that places once the scene of great emotional or physical stress retain their energy and can release it years, even centuries, later to those of us tuned to the right wave length.

"I visited the Green Spring site at dusk on January 22, 1996 — 319 years to the day since a victorious Governor Berkeley returned to oust its defenders and begin the reign of terror that so horrified the colony.

"The trees were still; the ground was hard, cold, and crackled under foot. The headlights of my parked car barely carried to the only still standing ruin — the one known as the jail and believed to have housed Berkeley's doomed prisoners. I listened there for the rattle of fetters, of the pleading voices of the weak, the cold, and the hungry. . . . I heard a snapping twig as the fall of a gavel ending the court martial that sent Captain Crewes stumbling past me down the dirt road to his death at Glasshouse Point.

"Suddenly a chill wind blew across the open field rustling the dead grass; I pulled my coat tighter around me and was anxious to be gone. At Green Spring there should be, must be, ghosts."

And finally, there is this, written by a newspaper reporter more than 40 years ago in a Halloween article about the spirits of Colonial Williamsburg . . . "There's Royal Governor Berkeley . . . last seen some 270-odd years ago when his palace (Green Spring) burned . . . not a trace of him until the restoration started here 27 years ago. Now, he's supposed to sit slouched in an armchair at the restored palace smoking his pipe and (disdainfully) dropping an ash or two on the royal rug."

CHAPTER 64

Still More Ghosts in Colonial Williamsburg

(Colonial Williamsburg)

(Author's note: As I have said, one of the things that has continually amazed me in doing the research for this series of books is how and where ghostly encounters turn up. For example, in 1983, I published "The Ghosts of Williamsburg," which included several houses in the historic area of the city. I thought I had covered the subject. Seven years later, when "The Ghosts of Tidewater" came out, I added some previously unpublished material on places in the old colonial capitol which had surfaced in the interim. Then, in 1996, in "The Ghosts of Virginia, Volume III, I had to add an entire section on "The (Re)Haunting of Williamsburg." This included 10 separate entities which had not been aired before, plus considerable additional "fresh" material on the Peyton-Randolph house. And, in Volume IV of "The Ghosts of Virginia," out in 1998, I included a chapter on the King's Arms Tavern. Nothing had been written about it before.

By this time, I should have become used to the idea, yet I continue to be surprised. In 1997, for instance, as I researched for a script for a revised ghost tour down Duke of Gloucester Street, still more material surfaced. The following psychic accounts revolve around the old public gaol (pronounced jail); the Capitol Building; and the Raleigh Tavern.)

PHANTOM SOUNDS AT THE PUBLIC GAOL

 f all the ancient buildings in Colonial Williamsburg, one might well suspect the

Gaol

most haunted would be the public gaol, located on Nicholson Street just across from the capitol. It dates to the early 1700s, and was the scene of the most horrible cruelties and suffering. Conditions, even by 18th century standards, were atrocious and inhumane.

Here, runaway slaves, murderers, cut throats, pirates, marauding Indians, political prisoners and even the criminally insane alike were shackled in heavy leg irons and handcuffs to await their fate. It was thought by many that hanging was almost an "escape" from the harsh life one led in the overcrowded, rodent infested building. In the frigid winters, at best, prisoners shivered beneath thin, worm-eaten blankets. When food was served, it generally consisted of "damaged salt beef and Indian meal." Consequently, more inmates died from starvation and disease than ever reached the awaiting gallows.

One might well suspect that ghostly moans from those about to be executed, or maniacal shrieks from the crazed and tortured would reverberate in the night air surrounding the gaol. But there have been no such reports at that particular site. Yet there have been some inexplicable sounds. A few years ago an historical interpreter, who has asked to remain nameless, was in the gaol early one morning, preparing to open the building for the day. No one else was around.

Suddenly, she heard sounds from the floor above her. She described it as being two women in high heels walking back and forth across the floor. And they seemed to be talking. She could clearly hear them, although she couldn't quite make out what they were saying. The upstairs rooms often had been used as living quarters for jailers in past years. Curious, the interpreter went upstairs to look.

There was no one there!

And while there are no reports of piercing cries in the night echoing from the gaol itself, there have been numerous accounts of ghostly sounds coming from what used to be known as "Hangman's Road." In the 18th century, when a convicted felon was sentenced to be hanged, the procedure was for him to ride in a horse-driven cart from the gaol down Nicholson Street and out to

Blackbeard and His Crew

what was then the far outskirts of town. Hangman's Road is today Capitol Landing Road. To add insult to injury, the condemned criminal rode seated on his own coffin.

And as a final humiliation, hundreds of people from the surrounding area would assemble to witness the ghastly spectacle. In those days, a public hanging had the same drawing power as does a town festival today.

Perhaps the most infamous of the hangings were those of members of the notorious pirate Blackbeard's crew. Fifteen or 16 of the crew (the number varies in historical accounts) were brought to Williamsburg and shackled in the public gaol in 1718. Thirteen or 14 of them were sentenced to be hanged. Two were released. One of them, interestingly enough, was Israel Hands, who was later immortalized in Robert Louis Stevenson's masterpiece, "Treasure Island."

Present day residents along Capitol Landing Road, as well as others on Nicholson Street, have, for years, periodically told of hearing strange and inexplicable sounds in the stillness of the night. The manifestations include horses' hooves clopping at a slow gait. . . the ancient wooden wheels of an old cart groaning over cobblestones . . . and muffled cries of agony. . .

* * * * *

A CURIOUS 'CROWD' AT THE CAPITAL

The original Capitol building in Colonial Williamsburg was completed in 1705, and was gutted by fire in 1747. A second structure, using the original "naked brick walls," was erected in 1753. After the removal of Virginia's government to Richmond in 1780, this capitol fell into disrepair, and it, too, was destroyed by fire in 1832. Colonial Williamsburg has restored it to its initial elegance.

In 1790, Thomas Jefferson, the third President of the United States, and a renowned architectural scholar (among many other things), wrote about the capitol. He obviously had some reservations about it: "The only public buildings in the Colony worthy of mention are the capitol, the palace, the college, and the hospital for lunatics, all of them in Williamsburg, heretofore the seat of our government. The capitol is a light and airy structure, with a portico in front of two orders, the lower of which, being Doric, is tolerably

Capitol

just in its proportions and ornaments, save only that the intercolon-
nations are too large. The upper is Ionic, much too small for that on
which it is mounted, its ornaments not proper to the order, nor proportioned within themselves. It is crowned with a pediment, which
is too high for its span. Yet on the whole, it is the most pleasing
piece of architecture we have."

Much of America's early history is tied to this site.

** It was here that Patrick Henry fanned the flames of revolution in 1765 with his fiery speech against the stamp act. One may
recall that famous line he thundered: "If this be treason, make the

most of it."

** It was here, on May 15, 1776, that the convention of Virginia called on Congress to declare the colonies free and independent states — an action that led directly to the Declaration of Independence.

Today, the British flag flies over the capitol. That's because it was a colonial capitol.

Could this somehow stir the spirits of patriots past?

In his 1938 book, "Old Williamsburg," William Oliver Stevens wrote: "They say that the portrait of Patrick Henry now in the capitol was quite pleasant-looking when it was first acquired . . . but that its present sour aspect of disgust and rage is due to that banner which flies over his head all day."

Stevens added: "Some Williamsburg inhabitants go so far as to say that on the stroke of midnight on every Fourth of July there is an assemblage of Revolutionary ghosts — with Patrick Henry at their head — who stand in front of the capitol and use most reprehensible language!"

* * * * *

PSYCHIC REVELATIONS AT THE RALEIGH TAVERN

he Raleigh Tavern is one of the most famous landmarks in Colonial Williamsburg. It was built about 1717, and it is known from old documentation that the Raleigh served as a center for social, commercial and political gatherings.

The first incident which gave the tavern its historic character occurred in February 1769, when English parliament advised the king to transport persons accused of treason in America for trial in Great Britain. Incensed at this order, the burgesses of Virginia passed "warm resolutions" denouncing it. Then Governor Lord Botetourt immediately dissolved the assembly, so the burgesses met in the Apollo Room of the Raleigh and proceeded to adopt a "non-importation" agreement.

On June 1, 1774, the burgesses met here again and passed resolutions against the use of tea and other East India goods in protest of the British shutting down Boston Harbor following the famous "Tea Party."

On December 5, 1776, the Phi Beta Kappa Society was orga-

Raleigh Tavern

nized at the tavern.

Lyon Gardiner Tyler, the son of President John Tyler, wrote in his book, "Williamsburg, the Old Colonial Capitol," published in 1907: "The Apollo was the main room in the tavern. It was well lit, having a deep fireplace, on each side of which a door opened, with carved wainscoting beneath the windows and above the mantel-piece."

Tyler added, "This room witnessed probably more scenes of brilliant festivity and political excitement than any other single apartment in North America." At least four governors — Spotswood, Gooch, Dinwiddie and Botetourt — supped here. "And with the advent of the Revolution, it grew suddenly popular as a meeting place for the patriots.

"It had long been used for balls and assemblies, and in 1764, we find Jefferson, then a gay young man, studying in the law office of George Wythe, writing from 'Devilsburg,' as he called Williamsburg, that he was as happy on the night before as 'dancing with Belinda in the Apollo could make him.'

"This ancient room saw indeed, at one time or another, all that was brilliant and graceful in the Virginia Society of the 18th century. The Raleigh Tavern continued the place for all extraordinary meetings, balls, banquets, etc., in Williamsburg for three-quarters of a century."

Among the other more famous names associated with the tavern are these:

** George Washington often noted in his diary that he dined here, and he was once given a surprise birthday party in the Apollo room.

** Patrick Henry was honored at a farewell dinner hosted by his Virginia troops

** And the Marquis de Lafayette was feted at an extravagant banquet in the Apollo room during his triumphant return to Virginia in 1824.

Against this background one might readily assume the spirits of some legendary figures linger here.

The apparitions of Washington and Jefferson are linked to the ripped carnation petals at nearby Carter's Grove Plantation.

Patrick Henry's possible spectral return has been tied to his youthful home at Hanover Tavern and his mansion at Scotchtown, both near Richmond.

Lafayette has been said to make an occasional haunting presence at Seawell's Ordinary in Gloucester County.

And the shadow of Washington allegedly has been sighted at his old grist mill in northern Virginia.

But none of these esteemed gentlemen have been seen or heard at the Raleigh Tavern! There have been a few scattered notations by passersby of hearing the sounds of a party taking place within the structure's walls. The pungent scent of pipe tobacco also has been sniffed. Queer, because no smoking has been allowed inside for years. There has been no plausible explanation for the sounds or the smells. Each time those who witnessed the phenomena looked in on darkened, empty rooms. There was no one there.

Perhaps the absence of any famous phantoms lies in the fact that the original tavern burned to the ground in 1859. It was restored more than 70 years later.

And so one wonders what the original walls at the old Raleigh might have yielded had they not been consumed by fire. What magnificent conversations and testimonies, and ringing declarations of freedom they must have held!

Revelations of
Motherly Love

(Appomattox County and Williamsburg)

hat is it about maternal ghosts and babies?
There seem to be several instances where either mothers, nursemaids, or young children have died, and then returned in spirit form to check on the care and welfare of someone departed or left behind.

Covered in past volumes in this series, for example, there is the intriguing study of the Gray Lady at Sherwood Forest, John Tyler's ancestral home in Charles City County halfway between Williamsburg and Richmond. Here, an infant died sometime in the mid-19th century while in the care, it is believed, of a servant woman. Apparently, the woman felt somewhat responsible for the child's death. Whether this was the case or not, the servant is still seen or heard occasionally rocking in a chair in the house. Although she was not the actual mother in this instance, she must have had a strong bond with the baby and couldn't let go.

One of the classic cases, recorded 70 years ago by Margaret DuPont Lee in her book, "Virginia Ghosts," involved a famous family in Appomattox County. Dr. and Mrs. Joel W. Flood lived here in the middle of the 1800s, and adopted their infant grandson when his young mother tragically died. The grandson was Major Joel W. Flood of the Confederacy. He, in turn, was the grandfather of Governor Harry F. Byrd of Virginia, who later became a United States Senator.

Joel Flood's grandmother raised him. She placed his little crib in the center of the large, old-fashioned bedroom in her house, and hired a nurse to help her care for him.

Joel's grandfather was a doctor who had a large practice, and in those times he was often out late at night making house calls (remember those "good old days?). Consequently, his wife often went to bed before he came home. One evening she awoke with a strange feeling that someone was in the room. She thought it was her husband. She peeped out from between the curtains of her big four-poster bedstead and gasped. It was not the doctor! It was the transparent form of a young woman bending over the crib. She was weeping.

Mrs. Flood, too frightened to speak, fell back on the bed and covered up her head. She trembled and shivered until her husband came home. When she told him about her ethereal experience, he just said she must have been dreaming and asked her what she had had to eat for supper. The next morning Dr. Flood chided his wife again, but he could not shake her from the belief that she had seen something supernatural.

A week or so later, the apparition reoccurred. Again, Mrs. Flood was badly shaken. The form of the woman peered over the edge of the crib, looking intently down at the baby. In a while the woman vanished. Mrs. Flood became convinced that "God had permitted the young mother (who had died) to visit her baby." Mrs. Flood was determined to address the woman if she appeared again.

Sometime later, she did. Mrs. Flood raised up from her bed and said, "Daughter!" The ghostly woman looked at her. "Don't be grieved my dear," Mrs. Flood stammered. "I promise you I will be a good, kind mother to your child." The woman looked at her again, "and, smiling sweetly, bent over the baby for a moment, then disappeared.
She was never seen again.

Mrs. Lee wrote: "The grandmother lived to be an old woman, and to her dying day was firm in the belief that she had seen and spoken to the baby's mother; and the baby, who grew to middle age and past, would mention the occurrence with the greatest reverence and faith in its veracity."

* * * * *

(Author's note: At a ghost talk I gave to the faculty at Clara Byrd Baker Elementary School a year or so ago (note the Byrd coincidence), a teacher named Linda Woodard came up to me afterwards and related the following experience:)

A few years earlier, Linda and her husband had lived in a dependency building adjacent to the famous Bassett Hall in Colonial Williamsburg. Bassett Hall is the magnificent mansion in which John D. Rockefeller, Jr., lived when he came to Williamsburg to supervise the restoration of the colonial area, which he had endowed.

The Woodards had a 14-month-old child. The infant toppled out of its crib one day, but was not harmed.

Shortly after this, Linda came into the child's room one afternoon to check on it, and suddenly was paralyzed with fear. She clearly saw an apparitional woman leaning over the crib. The woman appeared to be quite elderly. Before she could react, Linda said, the woman dematerialized before her eyes.

Later, Linda again approached the room and saw another "old lady" bending over the crib. This woman was different, and, according to Linda, appeared to be "covered in ivy!" Again, this woman evaporated before her eyes.

"Somehow, I felt as if these two ladies were checking on my baby to make sure it didn't fall out of the crib again," Linda says. "I just had that feeling. They didn't appear threatening or to be harmful in any way. I wasn't really afraid of them, although I must admit it was pretty unsettling."

Sometime afterward, Linda learned, to her astonishment, that two ladies, matching the description of the figures she had seen, had, in fact, lived in the same dependency building decades before, but both had died long ago!

Were they indeed, like the Gray Lady of Sherwood Forest and the spirit of Joel Flood's dead mother, there to check on the child? You can't convince Linda Woodard otherwise.

CHAPTER 66

Active Spirits at the Cole Digges House

(Yorktown)

(Author's note: In October 1998, I received a letter in a thick envelope from Carter R. Allen of Waynesboro, an attorney. I am always leery when I receive mail from lawyers. You never know, some descendent of a ghost I had written about might have taken offense and wanted to sue me. However, in this instance, I was pleasantly surprised. Here is what Mr. Allen had to say: "My wife's aunt and her husband lived in the Cole Digges House in Yorktown the last years of their lives and experienced a ghost, which my daughter, Mary Dudley Allen Eggleston (also a member of the Virginia Bar) wrote about in her high school days. I thought you might find it interesting so I am taking the liberty of enclosing it."

I did find it interesting. Here not only was an historic house, allegedly haunted, of which I had not heard of or written about previously — but there were also some unusual phenomena, and I had done a short article in "The Ghosts of Tidewater" (1990) on another member of the Digges family.

In reviewing what I had covered (admittedly more legend than documented fact), the piece was about Elizabeth Digges, a daughter of Edward Digges, who served as governor of the Virginia colony in the 1650s. It was believed that she was on her way home from a party, to Bellfield Plantation which was located on what is now part of the Naval Weapons Station not far from the Colonial Parkway between Yorktown and Williamsburg. Here is what I wrote:

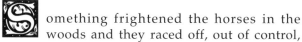 omething frightened the horses in the woods and they raced off, out of control, plowing headlong into a quagmire called the Black Swamp. The riders' terrified screams were muffled, as the dark, muddy quicksand swallowed them all, including the coach, without leaving a trace.

"Although the Weapons Station officially denies it, there have been persistent stories of military men hearing screams coming from that murky area, and catching fleeting glimpses of the ill-fated coach sinking. In fact, the reports date to the 1920s, when mention of the sightings was made in the Navy Mine Depot's official log. In more recent years, a government spokesperson did tell a newspaper reporter that although he had not personally experienced the phenomenon, and there was no physical evidence to support it, that 'there have been so many reports, some of them must be true'!")

Cole Digges was a direct descendant of governor Edward Digges — and he was the son of Dudley Digges and Susannah Cole Digges, she being the daughter of Colonel William Cole of Warwick County. The house Cole inherited was built in 1705 at the corner of Main and Read Streets in Yorktown. The Digges family remained here until 1784, three years after the American Revolutionary War ended.

Mary Dudley Allen Eggleston wrote her paper on the house in August 1977. She said it was an "Early American styled home, accompanied with high, pine paneled ceilings, large beautiful old oaken doors, and magnificent interior woodwork." She added that after the Digges family left, the house, at various times, served as a general store, a bank, a restaurant, and a hotel.

"My great aunt, Mary Louise Williamson, lives (1977) in Yorktown. Her husband, Charlie A. Williamson, died this past March. Before Charlie died, he and Mary Louise told me in great detail the events leading up to an acute description of the ghost they have been housing. Being such an old home and having so many different kinds of people building the character of the Cole Digges House, (here Mary Eggleston quotes her late uncle, Charlie Williamson) . . . 'it is expected, I suppose, that some things might occur in it which would be out of the ordinary'."

Mary Eggleston continues: "Mary Louise presently lives alone in the house. Two previous tenants who have lived in the home moved away because of ghosts. Mary Louise and Charlie courageously stayed in the home, being interested and curious of the mysterious ghost. They have experienced a series of strange incidents during the 16 years they have lived there." Following are excerpted highlights of these happenings.

** In the fall of 1963, "The full moon made it possible to see objects very clearly. Mary Louise was sleeping on her good ear, but something woke her. She saw a figure of a man enter their room from the door on the right, walk across the room, and exit through the door on the left. He proceeded down a short hallway and disappeared from sight. Having much time to examine him, she described him as 'a servant in colonial times . . . a full shirt and baggy trousers all seemed to be a light color. The sleeves of his shirt were gathered in at the wrists, and his hair was white and cut, seemingly, in sort of a bob-type haircut.'

"Thinking Charlie had gone to the bathroom, she thought it was he, however, when she looked in his bed, which was next to hers, she found him in it — sound asleep!"

** On another occasion, Charlie saw the figure of a woman slip into the kitchen. He assumed it was his wife, Mary Louise. He called to her but she did not answer. He then looked in the kitchen. There was no one there. He then searched the living room and in the front yard. Nothing. He finally found Mary Louise in the bedroom — upstairs! She had been asleep for an hour. Who then had he seen?

** The couple had three German Shepherd dogs. According to Charlie: "Each one has apparently been able to see something that we have not been able to see, and to hear something that we haven't been able to hear." Mary Eggleston: "Lying in front of them, the (dog) would be sound asleep while Mary Louise and Charlie read or watched television. Suddenly, the dog's head would rise, growls would emerge from deep within his throat, and the fur surrounding his neck would bristle. His attention would be directed toward the ceiling above the piano, located on the left side of the living room. For a few moments, the dog would mysteriously watch something on the ceiling, then follow it down and over into the dining room. Cautiously, he would tip-toe toward the dining room and peek around the love seat. He would go no farther though, unless Mary Louise and Charlie would advance with him."

** On a cold night, Mary Louise, unable to sleep, decided to go downstairs, build a fire, and write some letters. She got a shovel and cleaned the fireplace of ashes, put them in a bag and placed it

The Coles Digges House

on the hearth. She then laid a fire with paper, kindling, small pieces of wood and a large log. She did not light the fire, however. By this time she felt sleepy, went upstairs and slept soundly.

The next morning she came back down to light the fire and write her letters. She was astounded to find that instead of the kindling and logs, there were only ashes in the fireplace. Yet the bag of ashes she had filled the night before was still there on the hearth!

** Mary Eggleston: "Returning from an outing, Mary Louise and Charlie ascended the stairs to go to bed. Undressing, Mary Louise placed her black undergarment across her pocketbook. The next morning, Mary Louise picked the slip up to put it away." Here, Mary Louise is quoted: "The strap of the slip was inside the handle strap of the pocketbook. The threads, the original threads that were on the slip at both ends, I mean the straps of the slip at both ends, were intact. They were just as they were when they were bought from the store. To have gotten into the strap of the pocketbook, the slip would have had to have gone through a metal ring and then a leather opening before it could get into the inside of the strap of the pocketbook." Mary Eggleston adds that people from NASA, William and Mary College, and Colonial Williamsburg came "to see this amazing proof of a strange inhabitant. I personally have seen this phenomenon. I saw no evidence of broken seams in either the pocketbook or the slip!"

** Of all the eerie encounters Mary Louise and Charlie experienced over the years while living in the Cole Digges house, perhaps the most frightening occurred to Mary Louise on a hot summer night in 1963. Charlie was out of town. As she walked toward the dining room door she became enveloped in some sort of ethereal encasing. Here is how she described it: "My face, shoulder and arm became enwrapped in a flimsy, filmy sort of material, like fine veiling, or, I thought at the time, a curtain of cobwebs like you would see in an old barn. My face was covered so that it gave me a sort of smothered feeling!" She turned the light on, but saw nothing.

Such an experience would terrify most people, but Mary Louise apparently accepted it calmly, and both she and Charlie seemed unafraid of their resident spirit or spirits. Here is how Mary Eggleston quoted her great aunt on this: "You're afraid to believe what you wish about these happenings. . . Something does happen, for it happens to others. People often ask us if we're afraid to live here, or if we mind living here with these ghosts. We always tell them no, that we think it's rather interesting, and I hope that another time I have contact with one that I will be able to say something to it and maybe have a conversation. But anyway, we're looking forward to our next experience with them."

Who Haunts Cornwallis' Cave?

(Yorktown)

ere it not for the intervention of fate, relatively few people would ever have heard of the sleepy little town of Yorktown Virginia. But what transpired there for a few days in the middle of October 1781, etched Yorktown indelibly in the annals of American history. It was here, on the banks of the York River that General George Washington and his allies hemmed in the British army of Lord George Cornwallis, surrounded them, laid relentless cannon siege to the town, and forced a surrender that led to independence for the beleaguered American colonies.

The Revolutionary War had droned on for six years, and before this fretful lapse of military strategy on Cornwallis' part, there appeared to be no end of hostilities in immediate sight. Washington's rag tag army, half starved and ill clothed, was in danger of falling apart. Meanwhile, Cornwallis had stormed through the Carolinas with his elite corps. But as he marched northward he made the fateful decision to camp at Yorktown, believing the British Navy would fully support him by commanding the York River.

When Washington and his allies realized this, he saw an unprecedented opportunity to hem the British in, and with the support of French admiral Comte de Grasse, who with his ships beat the British to the river, Washington moved quickly. Nearly 9,000 Americans were joined by 8,000 Frenchmen, and they formed an impenetrable ring around Cornwallis and his 6,000 soldiers. The great allied bombardment began at 3 p.m. on October 9. In a curious twist of irony, American general Thomas Nelson was asked to "point out a good target toward which the artillerists could direct their fire." Stoically and without hesitation, he pointed to a large brick mansion which he suggested might be serving as Cornwallis' headquarters. The house Nelson indicated was his own! It was a magnificent act of patriotic self sacrifice which greatly impressed the Marquis de Lafayette and others. For several days the little town was shelled unmercifully. American and French cannons and mortars roared at full blast. American doctor James Thacher, a front line observer, wrote of the effect: "The haze of a soft Virginia fall day was thickened by welling cannon smoke, by the geysers of loose red dirt thrown skyward. . . " He figured at least 100 guns were at work. "The whole peninsula trembles under the incessant thunderings of our infernal machines. . . We are so near as to have a distinct view of the dreadful havoc and destruction of their works, and even see the men in their lines torn to pieces by the bursting of our shells."

Cornwallis was professional soldier enough to write to the British authority, on October 14: "My situation now becomes very critical. We dare not show a gun to their old batteries, and I expect that their new ones will open tomorrow morning . . . The safety of the place is, therefore, so precarious that I cannot recommend that the fleet and army should run great risque in endeavoring to save us."

In a move of great desperation, on the night of October 16, Cornwallis made a bold attempt to escape the trap. His plan was to try and cross the York River with as many able men as possible, leaving the wounded behind, fight his way through French troops at Gloucester Point, and proceed north to reunite with other British forces. Wrote Dr. Thacher: "A more preposterous and desperate attempt can scarcely be imagined. Boats were secretly prepared, arrangements made, and a large proportion of his troops actually embarked . . ."

Then fate struck again. Dr. Thacher: "From a moderate and calm evening, a most violent storm of wind and rain ensued. The boats with the remaining troops were all driven down the river, and it was not till the next day that his troops could be returned to the garrison at York." Many soldiers drowned.

Cornwallis now knew that he was doomed. There was no escape.

Then, at 10 a.m. on October 17, a strange sight was seen when the fog and smoke of the guns rose from the fields. A red-jacketed little British drummer boy appeared above the haze standing atop a parapet. As the firing ceased, the clear sound of the beat of his drum was heard. It was a signal to halt the battle. As one American officer wrote: "I never heard a drum equal to it — the most delightful music to us all."

The surrender was sealed on October 19, 1781, thus, in effect,

Cornwallis' Cave

ending the war and ensuring American independence.

There are many ghostly overtones at Yorktown, attributable to the historic fight that took place there. Tourists have reported seeing apparitional soldiers appear on the battlefields. The sounds of booming cannons have been heard by visitors more than 200 years after they roared incessantly at Yorktown. There is, allegedly, the ghost of a trapped British soldier in the Nelson House at Yorktown, and there is another spirit who is said to haunt the Moore House, across the battlefields, where the terms of surrender were signed.

And there are also suspected supernatural "happenings" at a natural tunnel-like opening on the banks of the York River historically known as Cornwallis' Cave. This cavity of 12 by 18 feet, known to have existed at least as far back as the 18th century, may well have been a smugglers' hideout in pirating days. There is another theory that the excavation was enlarged during the siege of Yorktown by townspeople who took refuge there, and hid their valuables as the shells blasted all around them. It also has long been rumored that General Cornwallis himself, and members of his staff, scurried to the cave to escape the intensity of the shellings, although there is no definitive proof of this. He may, in fact, have sought another dug out haven a quarter of a mile away.

Regardless of the difficulty of separating fact from legend, however, the cave stands today on the embankment and is closed off at the entrance by a barred gate. One can only peek in now and see a few feet inside. For at least the last half century or so, some Yorktown residents insist that there is something in there, possibly something evil. Here again, there are differing hypotheses as to what it might be.

Foreboding sounds seem to emanate from inside the cave, especially at night. They have been variously described as men talking or whispering, groans, moaning, and "incantations."
A number of people, both visitors and residents alike, have reported hearing them. Since the cave has been closed for years, no one has been able (perhaps no one wanted to) to venture inside and investigate.

Some believe they are the voices of the spirits of long-dead British soldiers who sought shelter here. But there also is a persistent feeling that the "voices" may be of a more recent origin. Years ago, before the cave was gated, it was said that a group of "devil worshipers" used the place to hold Satanic rituals. Many feel that is a plausible answer to the incantations heard there.

Two Hampton residents who have not only heard these eerie

sounds, but have tape recorded them, are Belinda and Richard Thomas. Both are amateur ghost hunters who track haunting legends with their recorders and cameras. "It definitely is what I would call 'a power place'," says Belinda. "We have photographs showing a vortex in there." She describes a vortex as being a place where spirits can move in and out. "When we went there, we stuck the tape recorder inside the bars of the gate, and we definitely got some strange sounds," Belinda says. (The author has heard the sounds and seen the photographs, and they are, while not conclusive that ghosts exist in the cave, still, intriguing and impressive.)

"We believe they are chantings, but, of course, the sounds are open to interpretation," she concludes.

"I stuck my hands inside the bars and took some photos with my camera one night," Richard adds. "I was scared. I definitely sensed something in there."

The National Park Service, which operates the Yorktown Battlefield, has no official comment on Cornwallis' Cave. They refuse to speculate on the ethereal sounds so many people have reportedly heard there.

The entrance to the cave is a forbidding sight, and . . . who knows?

CHAPTER 68

The Ghost Who Saved
His Grandson

(Newport News)

(Author's note: Can a ghost be physical? That is can it communicate from the beyond by being felt physically by a mortal being?
And I don't just mean breath on the neck, or the creation of a cold
spot. I mean physical physical. The answer may be yes, but such
experiences are exceedingly rare. At Aquia Church north of
Fredericksburg, a lady reported she was once slapped by someone
or something she could not see. Whatever it was, it was invisible.
Others have told of: being pushed or shoved at the top of staircases; being held in place by unseen hands; and being blocked
from entering or leaving through a door by some sort of invisible
force. A classic example of this occurred many years ago to a friend
of mine, the late Martin Caidin (author of "Marooned," and more
than 100 other books.) He once told me that as he was boarding an
airplane, such a force prevented him from entering the cabin. He
took it as an omen, turned back, and caught a later flight. The
plane he couldn't board crashed, killing all passengers.

Perhaps the best known case of a ghost's "physical" presence
was the famous Bell Witch of Tennessee, where, before scores of
witnesses over a prolonged period of time, an angry spirit was said
to have slapped and pinched a young girl named Betsy Bell, and to
have literally choked her father. Visible red marks and welts were
raised on their faces and necks each time this happened.

All of this serves as a prelude to the following incredible
account told to me by Sam Watkins, a retired fireman from

Newport News, Virginia. Sam is psychic, and many, many strange things have happened to him, so much so, in fact, that he wants to someday write a book about his paranormal experiences. For one thing, he steadily gets premonitions of things that are going to happen in the future. "Most of the time when the phone rings, I know who is calling, and I don't have any phone service that tells you that," he says. "I just know." Another time, as he and his brother were about to enter a tavern one night, Sam got the strong feeling that they shouldn't go in. Danger was inside. He couldn't talk his brother out of it, however, and in a barroom brawl they both narrowly escaped death.

"I know when someone is sick, when they are going in a hospital and when they are going to die," he says, matter-of-factly. On one occasion, in the early 1970s, Sam took a photograph of his dog. When the print was developed, there was a image of his brother in it, although his brother had been in another town when he took the picture. His brother was holding his elbow and his side. At first, Sam didn't understand. Then he got word that his brother had just been in an auto accident and had injured. . . his elbow and his side!

In the following interview, Sam tells of a life-saving supernatural experience he had in 1996.)

"**I** was always very close with my grandfather. Very close. He died in 1991, and I miss him. But I still feel, on occasion, that he is still with me. He used to love egg sandwiches. Now, every once in a while I find myself making egg sandwiches, and sometimes when I am eating them while sitting on my bed, I can see my grandfather's image there.

"What I am about to tell you, you won't believe, but it really happened to me. I think my grandfather is my guardian angel. I have no other way of explaining what happened. It was in the winter and it had been snowing. I was in Mechanicsville and I had been in a bar having a couple of beers one night. When I left to go home I was in good shape. I wasn't drunk or anything like that. Well, I was driving down Meadowbridge Road, and I was going a little too fast. There was a turn up ahead and I had to brake pretty hard, and when I did the car hit a patch of ice or snow and began skidding.

"The car turned sideways. I was out of control, and I was heading straight toward a telephone pole. And I didn't have my seatbelt on. I was scared. Just as I was about to collide with the pole, something <u>physically lifted</u> me out of the driver's side of the front seat and pulled me into the back seat!

"The impact of the collision was tremendous. The telephone pole snapped in two places. The car was totaled. The steering wheel broke off and the steering column was jammed into the back of the front seat. It would have killed me instantly had I not been lifted into the back seat.

"I walked away from that crash with barely a scratch on me. People who saw the car and the pole and the damage couldn't believe how anyone could have survived. It was that bad.

"But I know how I did. My grandfather saved me. He was the one who pulled me out of the front seat just before the car hit the pole. I felt his presence. I know he was there. He was watching out for me. You can say what you want — lucky, a miracle, or anything else. But I know it was my grandfather. If I live to be 100 you'll never convince me otherwise!"

CHAPTER 69

Cape Henry's Haunted House

(Virginia Beach)

t may well be Virginia's most unknown historic site. Its rich traditions, dating to the earliest arrival of Englishmen in America, are all but forgotten in today's high-tech, electronic, computerized society. In fact, thousands of motorists, both tourists and residents, pass by this spit of land daily with little or no knowledge of its storied past.

This is Cape Henry, the present-day location of Fort Story at the tip of Virginia Beach. It was here nearly 400 years ago, on April 26, 1607, that three storm-driven little ships — the Susan Constant, the Godspeed, and the Discovery — first touched land following their arduous voyage from England. It was here where this hardy band of settlers opened the box containing the sealed instructions of the London Company, directing them to establish a colony in America.

Virginius Dabney, author of "Virginia, the New Dominion," eloquently described the event: "Having been plagued almost interminably by winter storms off the English coast, they now found themselves violently assailed by the thunder, lightning and wind of a strong tempest. But they rode out the gale and at 'about foure a clocke in the morning' on April 26, they sighted the low-lying Virginia shoreline.

"Newport, Gosnold, Percy, and other leaders went ashore with about 20 men. They would soon erect a cross there and name the spot Cape Henry in honor of the Prince of Wales. The men were enchanted with the sights, smells and sounds of springtime in Virginia — 'Faire meddowes and goodly tall trees, with such fresh waters running through the woods'."

It was from this point, which separates the Atlantic Ocean from the Chesapeake Bay, that the settlers, a few days later, pushed off, sailed up the great river soon to be named the James, and disembarked at Jamestown, where they commenced the first English colony in the "new world."

But Cape Henry was not forgotten. It was recognized early on by the colonists as a most strategic point. Here, in the 1700s bonfires were lighted to warn passing vessels they were nearing land. In 1791 the first lighthouse was erected, and this was supplanted, in 1879, by a more permanent structure, a towering edifice which dominates the skyline today.

Cape Henry also served, in the early part of the 20th century, as a weather station.

It was here, too, that a military base was built that has served the nation steadily for more than 200 years. It is ideally situated to guard against enemy ships, and, along with Cape Charles to the north, protects the Chesapeake Bay. Thus, it has stood as a silent sentinel, a unit of a defense system that stands watch over the important naval bases, shipyards and ports of greater Hampton Roads.

Such service extended through the years of the second World War when enemy submarines and other ships threatened the area. Today, Fort Story is a training center for a number of inter-service functions including: Army amphibious operations; a Naval ordnance disposal school; a Marines training site equivalent to the Navy's Seals; and even a Department of Defense music school.

Long an independent U.S. Army installation, Fort Story now is classified as a "sub-installation" to Fort Eustis, which is located near Newport News. The Cape Henry-Fort Story site is surrounded by other interesting visiting points. Just off route 60, for instance, is the First Landing Seaside State Park and Natural Area. Just down the road is the Association for Research and Enlightenment (A.R.E.), the institution founded by Edgar Cayce, perhaps the greatest psychic of the 20th century (see "The Ghosts of Virginia, Volume I," 1993). And nearby is the Life Saving Museum of Virginia.

It is the three-story, brick post commander's quarters at Fort Story, known as Cape Henry House, that is said to be haunted, not only by an aged male apparition, but also by the ghost of a little

GLOSTER Co.

YORK Co.

York River

CHESAPEAK BAY

WARWICK Co.

CHARLES CITY

SURREY

James

POINT COMFORT

RIVER

Cape Henry

LOWER NORFOLK Co.

Cape Henry Lighthouse

dog. Colonel Ed English was post commander at the fort from 1991 to 1993. His wife, Andra, says although she never experienced any supernatural activity in the house, she was visited one day by a woman named Zilla Newsom Johnson, who had lived in the home years earlier. Mrs. Johnson said the spirit of her dog, "T.C.," still romped around in the house. Long after T.C. had died, the Johnsons would find "things amiss."

Carefully folded fresh laundry, for example, would be strewn all over a room — when no one had been in the house. Bed covers would be found ripped off the bed. And T.C. was blamed for "tearing up the garden" when the Johnsons were away. "He (T.C.) still doesn't want to be forgotten," Mrs. Johnson explained.

While Andra English didn't experience anything out of the ordinary, one of her close friends did. Debbie Bowman was, at the time, the wife of the post's executive officer. She lived near Cape Henry House. One day when Colonel and Mrs. English were out, Debbie noticed they had left the upstairs windows open. A storm was brewing. Debbie had a key. She went upstairs in the house to close the windows. As she walked across the bedroom floor, she tripped over a pair of shoes. She shut the windows, turned around, and the shoes were gone! Debbie and others who lived in the house said weird things were not uncommon there. There were reports of items being misplaced, and sometimes being thrown down the stairs.

Some attribute such mischievous acts not to T.C., but rather to the ghost of a mysterious figure known as "Chief Thornhill." His apparition has been sighted by more than one witness, usually in the upstairs master bedroom. According to legend, the chief, then 70 years old, was called back to active service during World War I in 1918. He was a Coast Guardsman, and his job was to work in the old weather station. His watch station was on the top floor's front room, now the master bedroom.

One day Chief Thornhill got new orders. He was assigned to go overseas. He became despondent, and hanged himself. It is his sad spirit, past residents of Cape Henry House say, that lingers on at this most historic site.

The Mad Poltergeist of Portsmouth

I t was known simply as the house on Florida Street in the Mount Hermon section of Portsmouth.

It was torn down several years ago. It probably is just as well.

There was a time, nearly 40 years ago when the old house at 949 Florida Avenue was the talk not only of the town, but of the entire country. For a brief period, in September 1962, the residence became a whirlwind of psychic activity which lasted several days, frightened the wits out of the chief of police and newspaper reporters, among others, and drew unruly crowds of hundreds who demanded to see what was going on.

It had begun, simply enough, on a Thursday afternoon about 4 p.m. Charles and Annie Daughtery were living in the house at the time with their great-great-grandson. The Daughterys were described as being very old; Annie was said to be close to l00. A little horse vase, sitting on a sewing machine in the hallway, fell on the floor three or four times. Annie, who said she didn't know what ghosts or haunted houses were, and was not afraid of them, told her great-great-grandson to take the vase and set it outside. Just then a bottle of hair lotion inexplicably sailed through the air and struck her in the back of the head.

By the next day accounts of the mysterious happenings had circulated through the neighborhood and beyond, and came to the attention of local newspaper reporters. It had been alleged that: a carpet eerily rose off the floor by itself; vases jumped from mantlepieces and hurtled over people's heads; and a mattress slid off a bed and onto the floor, all in front of the incredulous Annie Daughtery. But the phenomena had not been witnessed by her alone. Friends and neighbors had seen these occurrences, too, although many didn't stay long. They had fled in stark fear. One who reportedly had run out of the house was the local chief of police!

By Saturday the events had become so celebrated that when Joseph Phillips, a Virginian-Pilot staff writer, entered the house along with a photographer, a mob of more than 200 people had gathered outside. "I didn't believe in ghosts — until Saturday," Phillips began his front page article. But, he added, he "got goose pimples while dodging flying household objects that crashed to bits on the floor. I saw weird things happen, but I don't know what caused them." When Phillips entered the house, he stood by a buffet with Mrs. Marion Bivens, a neighbor. She asked him if he had felt the buffet move. She looked scared. He hadn't felt anything. Suddenly a vase that had been on the mantlepiece in the living room crashed into the hallway wall at the front of the house, apparently rounding a corner in the process. Phillips and the photographer ran to the living room. There was no one there. As they did, a cup from the buffet in the dining room shattered at their feet. At this point, Mrs. Bivens ran from the house in terror.

"Then I saw an empty tobacco can fly toward me from the buffet," Phillips said. "It was in the air when I saw it. It crashed and rolled to the floor at my feet."

Phillips' subsequent story of his experience drew even more people to the area, and when a wire services article ran a day or two later, crowds grew to enormous proportions. Police estimated 20,000 people congregated there one day, and they ordered out the fire department, hoses ready, in case a riot broke out. Some in the horde of people stormed inside the house and demanded to "see the thing." A number were arrested, and finally the Daughterys had to move out of the house themselves and stay with relatives until the excitement died down.

William G. Roll, a scientist with the Parapsychology Lab at Duke University, showed up to investigate. He said there were enough witnesses to support the likelihood that the disturbances in the house were caused by Recurrent Spontaneous Psycho-kinesis, or RSPK. But Roll claimed the flying objects and loud noises were not necessarily the work of a ghost. Rather, he believed they were the work of the living not the dead.

"Our focus on RSPK eruptions has been on the individual who

is at the center of the disturbances," he told a reporter, adding that usually such occurrences are sparked by tension or certain neurological features.

Maybe so, but that would have been a difficult theory to swallow by any of the dozens of people who were in the little house on Florida Avenue during the few days all hell broke loose. They didn't have a rational explanation, but they knew what they saw. As reporter Joseph Phillips summed it up, "I didn't believe this nonsense before. Now I'm not so sure."

The Girl Who Was "Born To See"

(Portsmouth)

"**S**he was," says Gabrielle Bielenstein, "'born to see.' Isn't that a marvelous expression? It means, of course, that a person is psychic. Some are born with perfect pitch, and some can play the piano by ear. She was 'born to see'."

Gabrielle is talking — in the darkened, high-ceilinged parlor of her magnificent Art Nouveau home at 328 Court Street in Olde Towne Portsmouth — about the teenage black girl who worked for Gabrielle's mother nearly half a century ago.

It is called the Maupin House, the family name, and it was built in 1885 because Gabrielle's grandmother, Edmonia, wanted to live on Court Street since it was the most fashionable section of the city. And it was erected on the last available lot in that section of Portsmouth, over a creek bed. The house has "20-odd rooms, including six bathrooms," a beautiful spiral staircase, exquisite wood paneling throughout, and was built at a cost of the then-princely sum of $7,000. Behind it was a splendid walled garden which was a showpiece of the area.

Gabrielle and her identical twin sister, Florence Mary Maupin, grew up in these fashionable surroundings, and the young girl came to work there in the early 1940s, during World War II, when most of the other servants had gone to work in the Norfolk Naval Shipyard nearby.

Almost immediately, she began to "see" things others didn't.

"There had been some strange occurrences in the house before," says Gabrielle, "but we had never paid much attention to them. One would hear tales. Some of the other servants would talk occasionally about a rocking chair rocking on the front porch. We would hear noises that sounded like someone descending the staircase. Things like that."

But the new young girl, whose name escapes Gabrielle, saw, felt, and sensed presences in and around the house almost from the day she began work there. And, with uncanny accuracy, they perfectly fit descriptions of past residents, both animal and human.

Consider, for example, the instances of the buried pit bulls. "My mother, Florence, had about given up on having any children, before my sister and I came along, so she had a number of pit bull dogs," Gabrielle says. "Now you have to understand, this was at a time when these dogs were very rare. Few people knew what they looked like. They hadn't got all the notice they have in recent years.

"But my mother didn't have much luck with them. Most of them died very young, and they were all buried in little pine coffins in a corner of the yard. When the young girl came to work for us, there hadn't been any pit bulls around for years, and I don't believe she had any way of knowing what they looked like. Yet, she told us she saw the dogs playing in the yard. When she was asked to describe what they looked like, she said they were just like Miss Julia's dog. Miss Julia was a neighbor who had a Boston Terrier, which closely resembles the pit bull. How did she know what those dogs looked like unless she saw them?"

The girl also saw the apparition of Miles Portlock. Born a slave before the Civil War, he had been a servant to Gabrielle's great grandmother. "We considered him a part of the family, and as a child, I can remember him sitting at the kitchen table and drinking ice tea. Someone had given him a gold or silver headed cane and he used to use it to dig out the grass that grew between bricks. When I was a little girl, he was so old then that this was about all he could do."

Gabrielle says he died about 1939 or 1940 somewhere around the age of 90, well before the girl came to Maupin House to work. Yet she said she saw him in the garden with his cane, and she described him perfectly, too.

And then there were the sightings of Miss Edmonia, Gabrielle's grandmother. The girl said she saw an "old woman" on the staircase at times. "We had a lot of photos in the house in those days," Gabrielle notes, "but there were no recent photos of Edmonia

The Maupin House

before her death, because she refused to have any taken after she reached middle age. She had been a beautiful woman.

"We took the girl around to view all the photos, and she immediately picked out an earlier portrait of Edmonia, and said that was who she saw. She said it was the same person, only she was much older now. How did she know? How did she pick that one picture out of all the ones in the house. She had no way of knowing what Edmonia looked like. I can't explain it, other than she was born to see!"

The girl only worked at the house for a short period. Her psychic ability unnerved the other servants and they demanded that she leave. In the intervening years there have been a few other haunting occurrences. Gabrielle's husband, Hans, a native of Estonia who now teaches Chinese at Columbia University once woke up in an upstairs bedroom and saw an apparition of a woman appear at an open door.

"They're still here," says current house sitter Emily Mossberger of the ghosts. 'They are friendly, but strange things go on." Her daughter was taking a nap one day in a room on the third floor when she was awakened by "something" that was moving her bed. It kept moving as she sat up.

The Maupin House is one of the most popular ones on the annual Olde Towne Ghost Walk at Halloween. Either an actor or a local resident usually plays the part of old Miles Portlock and tells the story of the ghostly legends, and the young girl who was "born to see".

CHAPTER 72

Some Ghosts That Should Have Been

(Various Sites)

(Author's note: In doing the research for this series of Virginia ghost books, I have often found it curious that there are no reports of lingering spirits at a number of sites where one might well expect them. This would include certain Civil War battlefields, the scenes of terrible disasters, and occasions where great wrongs - including premature and/or questionable deaths, such as suicides and unsolved murders, have occurred. I have written about some of these in the past. For example, why are there no haunting moans or screams heard at the site of the great railroad tunnel collapse in Richmond on October 2, 1925? Why does one not hear the anguished cries of the victims of the tragic 1811 theater fire in Richmond which killed 71. Many of the bodies were buried enmasse beneath historic Monumental Church on Broad Street, yet all is silent there. And on and on.

Here following are some additional unusual cases for ghost candidates:)

THE PIRATES WHO TRIED TO COME BACK

One may wonder, for example, why there are no reports of the ghosts of three Spaniards — Pepe, Couro, and Felix — who were tried for piracy and murder in Richmond, and then hanged together on August 17, 1827. It surely ranks as one of the most gruesome chapters in the city's history, especially the way the bodies were treated. Here, excerpted, is an account of that most strange incident, as told by W. Asbury Christian in his book, "Richmond - Her Past and Present," published in 1912. He called the event "The Carnival of Death."

"This was the day on which they were to die. They were taken from Henrico jail at 11 o'clock a.m., in the presence of thousands of people. Clothed in purple gowns with hoods over their heads and ropes around their necks, they started to the gallows seated on their coffins in a wagon and guarded by the military companies. All seemed to be enjoying the occasion except the three culprits; it was rather distasteful to them . . . The procession extended nearly the whole length of the city.

"Here was a great multitude of people, estimated at 7,000, on the hills surrounding the gallows . . . After the ropes around their necks were fastened to the cross beam of the gallows, the officer pulled the cord which dropped the platform. Felix was left hanging in the air, but the ropes holding Pepe and Couro broke, and they fell strangling and struggling to the ground. A chill of horror went through the great multitude. There were loud screams, and many thinking that their friends had come to rescue them, ran home in great dismay.

"The officer took them up and again conducted them to the platform by the side of their dead comrade. He then adjusted the rope and again dropped the platform. Their bodies shot down, but the ropes held and they were strangled to death. Their bodies were allowed to hang there in full gaze of the morbid multitude for one hour.

"Then they were taken down and buried in one grave on the hill near the penitentiary. After some hours they were disinterred and taken to the armory, where they were experimented upon with galvanism, as the electric current was then called.

"They were not brought back to life as some thought the wonderful power would do, so they were reinterred and remain even to this day in the one grave, probably under the house of some citizen who lives on the hill."

* * * * *

In Chesterfield County, sometime in the mid-19th century, a man named Dick Jones lived at an imposing house called Bellvue. It is thought he died sometime around 1870 as an old man who was deeply in debt. Apparently, there was a law on the books at the time that said if someone died owing money, his debtors could put his body in jail until the debt was settled. Dick Jones' body was thus incarcerated, for how long it is not clear. Eventually, his debt was paid, presumably by a relative, and Mr. Jones was finally buried near the front yard of his house. He was later disturbed once more and his gravesite moved further away across a field.

WHAT A WAY TO GO!

If a bizarre way of dying might be cause for a ghost to return in protest, certainly an aged gentleman who lived in Bristol would qualify, but there are no reports of his spectral return. In 1883, an elderly man was living in a house with his son and daughter. He was asleep in an upstairs bedroom one night when a flaming meteorite crashed through the roof of the house, nearly severed the man's body, then rocketed downward through the building and tore a hole five feet deep in the ground. The incredibly unlucky victim was buried in the Sharrett Cemetery and the meteorite was placed at the foot of his grave. It was later stolen by a morbid souvenir hunter.

OVERKILL!

Oddly, one of the most brutal, bizarre and bloody episodes in the history of Wise County, in fact, in the history of the entire commonwealth, has no haunting associated with it, although one wonders why. It occurred on November 29, 1927, and ranks — along with the infamous Hillsville courtroom shootout in 1912 — as a tragic and sad black mark in state annals.

It began two days earlier, November 27, 1927, a Sunday, when Hershel Deaton, a well-liked and prominent citizen of Dale Ridge, just outside the town of Coeburn and two of his co-workers were enroute from their homes back through the Cumberland Mountains, to their weekly jobs at the Elkhorn Coal Company in Fleming, Kentucky. At about 11 p.m., halfway up a steep mountain grade, their car was hailed by a black man named Leonard Woods and two black women who were standing by the side of the road.

It is not certain exactly what happened next — either Woods

and the women jumped on the running boards of the car as it labored up the ridge, or Deaton stopped and they loaded themselves on the car. (Cars in those days had running boards which could be ridden on.) It also should be pointed out that in 1927, more than 70 years ago there still was a strong prejudicial feeling between whites and blacks, and the Ku Klux Klan was still quite active in the area.

Whatever happened, Deaton stopped his car, got out and either asked or ordered the three off his car. At this point one of the women handed Woods a gun and he shot and killed Deaton, and asked his two passengers "if they too wanted to die." Woods and the two women then fled into the dark woods. Deaton's body was returned to Coeburn and laid to rest in Laurel Grove Cemetery in Norton.

A subsequent manhunt was organized and Woods and the two women were "promptly captured" and jailed in Fleming, Kentucky, just across the state line. When a maddened crowd began to form there, the three were transferred, first to Jenkins and later to Whitesburg, Kentucky for safekeeping. Here, Mrs. Fess Whitaker was the acting jailor in place of her husband.

It didn't take long for the word to get out about where the captives were, and on the night of Tuesday, November 29, as historian Roy Sturgill phrased it, "it seemed like the earth opened up and there were over 500 people in a motorcade of approximately 150 cars that converged on Whitesburg jail." When Mrs. Whitaker refused to turn over the cell keys, the men "attacked the jail with axes, hacksaws, cross ties, battering rams, and every conceivable tool needed to wreck the jail and take the prisoner. The mob finally succeeded in gaining entrance through the roof and brought the prisoners out."

The women were whipped and then thrown back in jail. A chain was placed around Woods neck and he was put in a car. The men fired pistol and rifle shots into the air and then sped away, heading for the state line at Pound Gap. Here, Woods was placed on a platform, surrounded by the mob, and was asked about the killing of Deaton. When he replied, showing no remorse whatsoever, something to the effect that "he would do the same thing again," he instantaneously signed his own death warrant. All hell broke loose.

In the next minute or two, "no less than 500 bullets struck his body." The body was then hanged, burned beyond recognition, and left on the roadside. Road workers buried what was left the next day. Author Sturgill said that he visited the site shortly after the lynching and found small sticks stuck all over the grave. On each stick there was an empty cartridge.

Although Virginia Governor Harry Flood Byrd condemned the action, there was confusion as to exactly where the fatal hail of bullets was fired — on the Kentucky or Virginia side of the line. Consequently, no one was ever prosecuted for the heinous crime. Sturgill wrote: "It is felt that if one is to record any of the violent days of Southwest Virginia and Eastern Kentucky, then surely this event in historic Pound Gap could not be omitted." There have been no reports of the resurrection of Leonard Woods' ghost in the area. Curious.

WHERE IS THE GHOST OF MERIWETHER LEWIS?

Of all those Virginians with ample justification to come back to "set things straight," perhaps none would be more qualified than the famous explorer, Meriwether Lewis. If his ghost were to make itself known, perhaps it could clear up an enduring mystery that has lasted for nearly 200 years — and is still debated to this day.

Lewis was born at Locust Hill in Albemarle County, at Ivy, near Charlottesville in 1774. He displayed strong intellectual and leadership qualities from his youth, and in 1801 was selected to be the private secretary of the new President of the United States — Thomas Jefferson. The Sage of Monticello chose him, three years later, to lead the dramatic expedition across the wild wilderness of the west. In recommending him, Jefferson cited his "high character, courage, inflexible perseverance, intimate knowledge of the Indian character, fidelity, intelligence, and all those peculiar combinations of qualities that eminently fitted him for so arduous an undertaking."

The four-year journey he led, with William Clark, opened up the frontier from St. Louis to the Oregon coast, and made him a national hero of the first rank. Jefferson, in fact, was so impressed that, in recognition of his services, he appointed Lewis governor of the Louisiana Territory. One writer at the time said, "finding it (the territory) the seat of internal dissensions, he by his moderation, firmness, and impartiality, brought matters into a systematic train."

But here, at the pinnacle of his fame, historical fact comes to a halt and "mysterious circumstances" enter. It began when Congress questioned expense vouchers Lewis had filed for pay-

MERIWETHER LEWIS
1774-1809
KENTUCY

NASHVILLE

LEWIS
BURIAL

NATCHEZ TRACE PARKWAY

65

TENNESSEE
ALABAMA

MISSISSIPPI

GEORGIA

ment. These were challenged, and Lewis, then 35 years old, feared, if they went unpaid, he would be broke and become destitute. He started on a trip to Washington to "straighten things out," and, enroute, died a horrible death at an obscure tavern in Tennessee. The circumstances of his death have never been resolved. Some historians believe he shot himself. Others contend he was murdered by ruthless bandits who frequented the area.

In November 1997, I got a letter from Sam Black of Millboro, Virginia. He asked if I "knew anything about Meriwether Lewis in Tennessee?" Then he added, "I wonder if he roams about."

In subsequent research, I found that the great explorer's last days are shrouded in as much confusion and mystery as were the last days of Edgar Allan Poe who died in Baltimore in 1849. Here is what is known:

Lewis was traveling to Washington with a Captain Gilbert Russell, and they camped at a site about 120 miles from Nashville on October 9, 1809 (coincidentally, the year Poe was born). The next day Lewis struck out on his own and told Russell, who stayed behind to gather some lost horses, he would stop "at the first house he came to."

It turned out to be a tavern known as Grinder's Stand. Robert Grinder's wife met him there. She was to say later that Lewis had acted very strangely. After dinner he had retired to a crude cabin for the night and she said she heard him pacing back and forth and talking to himself, "talking aloud like a lawyer."

Several hours later, Mrs. Grinder heard a shot ring out from the cabin, a thud that sounded like a body falling, and then a second shot. Minutes later, Lewis, severely wounded, had crawled to the kitchen door of the tavern and pleaded, "Oh, madam! Give me some water and heal my wounds." Inexplicably, Mrs. Grinder ignored his call for help. She saw him stumble away, lean against a tree trunk, and then go back to his room. Again, he managed to come back to the tavern, begging for water. Again ignored, he dragged himself back to the cabin.

The next morning Lewis was found barely alive. He was bleeding from one bullet wound in his side, and another which had blown off a piece of his forehead. He begged Mrs. Grinder, her children, and a servant to "take his rifle and blow out his brains." Lewis died a short time later.

Even in death, he found no peace. He was buried nearby in an unpretentious grave. In 1848 his remains were disturbed when the grave site had to be opened for the installation of a monument. The coffin itself was opened and the upper part of Lewis' skeleton was examined to "make sure it was him."

From the time of his death, speculation ran wild. The Grinders said he committed suicide. Some said the Grinders themselves had killed him, believing him to have a map pinpointing a treasure he had allegedly found during his expedition in the west. Still others believed he had fallen victim to murderous robbers who infested the area.

In the "suicide camp" were those who pointed out Lewis suffered from a "congenital melancholia" compounded by hard drinking and the prospect of financial ruin because of the refused expense vouchers.

Historians who believe Lewis was murdered say he had every reason to believe the vouchers would eventually have been paid, which they were. They noted that Lewis, an expert in firearms, would certainly have been able to kill himself had he so chosen. Why, for instance, would he shoot himself in the side? Also, if his aim was to die, why did he struggle so valiantly to seek Mrs. Grinder's help? They added that his entire life had been marked by courage in the face of adversity. And, as many have reported, that particular area was "notorious for the savagery of marauders" who frequented it. In fact, the region was known as "the Devil's Backbone."

How did Meriwether Lewis die? Will we ever know? There are two possible ways to clear up the long-standing mystery. One has been suggested by James Starrs, professor of law and of forensic sciences at George Washington University. He told a magazine reporter in 1996 that, "records can't tell us what happened because there are no records. It's all speculation." Starrs traveled to the Lewis burial site where the gray stone base of the monument has disappeared into the ground. "That's where the answer is. All the rest in insubstantial. Nothing remains but the remains."

Starrs, and other modern-day experts believe an exhumation of the remains and an examination of the body, through DNA analysis, might well tell whether or not Lewis killed himself or was murdered. So far, he has been unsuccessful in getting permission to reopen the grave. "Historians have had their day," he contends. "Science has not. Lewis's bones hold the answers, and even after nearly 200 years they can tell us the truth."

What is the other means by which the enigma may someday solved? There is precedence for it. It has happened before. There are on record instances where the spirits of the fallen have reappeared to point to clues which led to the identity of their murderers.

Where is the ghost of Meriwether Lewis?

Skull & Crossbones

(Various Sites)

(Author's note: The following chapter includes a variety of psychic-related items of general interest.)

SOME CURIOUS NOTES ON COFFINS

In many rural sections of Virginia, coffins were handmade up to and into the early years of the 20th century. Less expensive coffins were generally made of pine or poplar and were cloth lined. Pricier items were fashioned from walnut and oak, and often were covered with white brocade velvet. Top line coffins 150 years ago went for anywhere from $13 to $50.

In those days, nearly everyone "died at home in their own bed," according to a report by the Carroll County Genealogy Club in Hillsville, Virginia. Relatives, friends and neighbors shared in the responsibility of preparing the body for burial (before embalming was done). They also "sat up with the corpse," filled the grave, and conducted the burial service. Sometimes services took place months after the actual burial, "a custom which grew from the felt need to have something more than a brief burial service."

ROBERT E. LEE'S WATERLOGGED COFFIN

ccording to Charles H. and Paul C. Chittum, one of their ancestors, Charles Chittum, then

22-years-old, played a key role in the burial of General Robert E. Lee in Lexington. It happened like this. On October 9, 1870, a shipment of coffins had come from Richmond and had arrived at Alexander's Wharf in Lexington for undertaker C. M. Koones. High flood waters, "of enormous proportions," in the North River swept away the wharf and three coffins on it.

Lee died three days later, on October 12. Koones was then faced with a most distressing dilemma. He had no proper coffin for the general's burial! That was when young Charles Chittum and his friend, Harry Wallace, came to the rescue. They began a search for the missing caskets, and finally found one, several hours later, two miles down the river. It had washed up on a small island. The coffin was cleaned up and Lee was buried on time.

WHERE IS THE BODY?

One of the strangest funeral processions in Virginia's storied history occurred sometime in the 1820s in or near the village of Collierstown, a few miles west of Lexington. A man named Dove, a broom maker, passed away, and, as was the custom at the time, mourners gathered at his house for a wake. Everyone got drunk. Meanwhile, a heavy snow fell, so a two-horse sleigh was rigged up as a makeshift hearse. Billy Moody was given the responsibility of driving the hearse to the little Oxford Cemetery, several miles away. Instead of waiting for him, the mourners, on horseback, scampered on ahead and waited at the grave site, probably continuing to fortify themselves with liquid spirits.

Sometime later, Moody arrived, and several men, acting as pallbearers, went over to the sleigh. To their amazement, there was no coffin! It had somehow fallen off the sleigh during the bumpy ride and Moody had not noticed its absence. Then a man named Bob Houston pronounced that, "Dove should have a Christian burial, and he would see Moody at the 'divil' before he would give up Dove as lost." So the mourners mounted up once again, retraced their route, and found the casket laying upside down beside the road in a bank of snow. They then proceeded back to the cemetery and buried the broom maker without further incident.

DOOM'S DAY COMETH!

The following passages are taken from W. Asbury Christian's book, "Lynchburg and It's People," published in 1900.

"In 1833 there were two phenomena that caused much anxiety. The first was an earthquake, August 27, which shook the town considerably. But this was as nothing compared to the sight witnessed on the morning of November 13. The first part of the night the air was very transparent and the stars were exceedingly brilliant. The thermometer stood at 54 and the barometer at 23.

"At two o'clock the horizon suddenly became luminous with a burning meteoric shower. They came down like snow-flakes, and when within three or four feet of the ground disappeared. The shower continued until daybreak. It was a beautiful and awful sight. It looked like a snow-storm, with flakes of fire instead of snow.

"The whole town was excited. Some said the stars were falling and that Judgment Day was at hand. The Negroes began to moan and pray, the abandoned women rushed to the Methodist Church and wept and prayed until day, and many covered their heads to keep out the fearful sight.

"At the Franklin (Hotel) a few citizens were sitting at a card-table gambling, when one looked out and said, 'Doom's Day has come!' Immediately the table was overturned and one that stammered called out to the others to pray. No one knew how, so he, trembling with fear and stammering, attempted to sing:

"'Show pity, Lord, O Lord, forgive;
Let a repenting rebel live'"

RAISED FROM THE DEAD!

"Sawney Early, a well-known Negro character, was attracting a good deal of attention (in 1875). He claimed to be the 'second Christ,' and went about the streets with feathers in his hat, red and gilt letters and peculiar figures on his coat, and a Bible under his arms. The Negroes and small boys looked upon the queer character with a feeling of half fear and half veneration.

"Times got hard with Sawney and he decided to appropriate a citizen's cow. He killed the animal and was in his house dressing it when the owner called. The 'prophet' refused to be interrupted, saying that the Lord had told him to rise, Sawney, slay and eat.

"He offered a stout resistence to the men, even threatening their lives, whereupon they shot him. The Negro was badly wounded, but turned it to some account, for when he recovered, he presented a new claim to the belief of the credulous, declaring that he had been killed and raised from the dead.

"After causing more trouble, Sawney was landed in the insane asylum."

DOUBLE, DOUBLE, TOIL AND TROUBLE

"Dr. L. W. Bates, the newly assigned pastor of the Methodist Protestant Church, and nearly his whole family, were taken desperately ill immediately after breakfast one April morning (in 1881). The doctors were called in and pronounced it a case of poisoning, most probably from the meat eaten at the morning meal. Later it was found that only those who had drunk coffee were sick, and at once the coffee was analyzed and found to contain poison.

"Then the question arose, who had tried to kill the preacher and his family? Suspicion pointed to the cook Margaret Fogus, and when questioned she confessed to putting a certain mixture in the coffee, but denied attempting to poison the family. Margaret was superstitious and believed in the effects of herbs, potions and the like, so she applied to 'Dr.' Huckstep, who professed to be familiar with the art of conjuration. He promised to furnish the needed 'conjur' and went to work to prepare it.

"'Double, double, toil and trouble
Fire burn and caldron bubble,
Fillet of a fenny snake
In the caldron boil and bake,
Eye of a newt, and toe of a frog,
Wool of a bat and tongue of a dog,
Adders' fork and blind worms' sting,
Lizard's leg and owlet wing,
For a charm of powerful trouble,
Like a hell-broth and bubble.'

"Thus the 'doctor' fixed the 'conjur' and gave it to Margaret, who thought that all trouble between her and her employer would vanish and she would hold a high place in their esteem, and be able to fix whatever terms suited her.

"Her venture into the region of the recondite proved a dismal failure, for she soon found herself, with the 'doctor,' in the clutches of the law, to answer the charge of attempting to kill a whole family. Her faith in 'conjurs' was now gone, and she went to jail weeping over the effects of her folly."

DARE NOT CHALLENGE A WITCH!

That superstition still ran strong in southwest Virginia well into the 19th century is evidenced by the following account, published by Henry Howe in his book "Historical Collections of Virginia," published in 1845.

". . . There resided, in 1838, in the hills, a few miles from Abingdon, a man by the name of Marsh, who was deemed by his neighbors not only honest and industrious, but possessed of as much intelligence as most people . . . This man was severely afflicted with scrofula (a swelling of the lymph glands of the neck), and imagined his disease to be the effects of a spell or pow-wow, practiced upon him by a conjurer or wizard, in the neighborhood, by the name of Yates.

"This impression taking firm hold of Marsh' mind, he was thoroughly convinced that Yates could, if he chose, remove the malady. The latter, being termed an Indian doctor, was sent for, and administered his nostrums. The patient, growing worse, determined to try another remedy, which was to take the life of Yates. To accomplish this, he sketched a rude likeness of Yates upon a tree, and shot at it repeatedly with bullets containing a portion of silver.

"Yates, contrary to his expectations, still survived. Marsh then determined to draw a bead upon the original, and accordingly, charged an old musket with two balls, an admixture of silver and lead, watched an opportunity, and shot his victim as he was quietly passing along the road, both balls entering the back of the neck. Yates, however, survived, and Marsh was sent to the penitentiary."

AN INTERVENTION OF DIVINE PROVIDENCE?

he following episode occurred at an undisclosed location in the Shenandoah Valley in the year 1764, and was duly recorded in Samuel Kercheval's book, "History of the Valley," published in the 1830s. Following an Indian attack which killed a number of settlers, several others, including a woman named Mrs. Thomas, were taken prisoner and led to an encampment by a flood-swollen river.

"The next morning a party of white men fired off their guns, which alarmed the Indians, and they hurried across the river, assisting all their female prisoners except Mrs. Thomas, who being quite stout and strong, was left to shift for herself. The current, however, proved too strong for her, and she floated down the river — but lodged against a rock, upon which she crawled, and saved herself from drowning.

"Before her capture she had concealed a half a loaf of bread in her bosom, which, during her struggles in the water, washed out, and, on her reaching the rock, floated to her again. In this instance the text of Scripture, (Ecclesiasties, II: I.) 'Cast thy bread upon the waters, for thou shalt find it after many days,' might have some application. It was not 'many days,' but there appears to have been something providential in it, for it saved her from extreme suffering." (She was rescued the next morning.)

A MEMORIAL SERVICE MOST STRANGE

uthor Henry Howe once visited the fabled coal mines of Chesterfield County. He told of a terrible mine disaster and a most curious memorial service which was held afterwards, as follows:

"Some years since (presumably the first or second quarter of the 19th century), when ventilation was less understood than at present, an explosion took place in a neighboring mine of the most fearful character. Of the 54 men in the mine, only two, who happened to be in some crevices near the mouth of the shaft, escaped with life. Nearly all the internal works of the mine were blown to atoms. Such was the force of the explosion, that a basket then descending, containing three men, was blown nearly 100 feet into the air. Two fell out, and were crushed to death, and the third remained in, and with the basket, was thrown some 70 or 80 feet from the shaft, breaking both his legs and arms. He recovered and is now living. It is believed, from the number of bodies found grouped together in the higher parts of the mine, that many survived the explosion of the inflammable gas, and were destroyed by inhaling the carbonic acid gas which succeeds it.

"This death is said to be very pleasant; fairy visions float around the sufferer, and he drops into the sleep of eternity like one passing late into delightful dreams.

". . . Shortly after we were at the Midlothian mine, the Rev. Mr. Jeter, of Richmond, made it a visit, and having held divine worship there, published an interesting and graphic narration of the scene. A part of his description here follows:

"'The intelligence of the meeting had spread throughout the cavern, and all had gathered for the service. The news had gone beyond the pit, and brought down several from above. By means of logs, puncheons and boxes, the congregation were mostly seated in a wide and well-ventilated drift. The small brilliant lamps, of which every collier has one, were suspended along the walls of our chapel, creating a dazzling light. The congregation consisted of about 80 colored, and 10 white persons. The blacks at my request sung a song. Their singing was greatly inferior to that of their colored brethren in the tobacco factories at Richmond. I lined a hymn, which was sung, offered a prayer, and preached from John III. 10. The circumstances were impressive and awful. I desired to do good — I spoke without premeditation and I was listened to with devout attention.

"'Many of us felt that God was present.

"' . . . A few words of advice and encouragement closed the service. The like had never been known in these parts. Mr. Marshall, who had spent many years in the English mines, said that he had frequently heard social prayer in the pits, but had never before known a sermon delivered in one.

"To address the living, on the solemn subjects of death, judgment and eternity, 800 feet beneath the sleeping-place of the dead, in a pit which bears so striking a resemblance to that region of outer darkness into which the impenitent shall be cast, cannot but interest and affect the heart'."

A SAMPLING OF VIRGINIA GHOST TOWNS
(Various Sites)

uthor Charles Mills, in his book "Treasure Legends of Virginia," includes some intriguing notes on towns of yesterday which have, in most cases, vanished. Among them:

** Albemarle, Mills says, was founded around 1700 on a sharp bend of the James River, near Scottsville. It vanished "without a trace" sometime after the Revolutionary War.

** Several settlements once surrounded the Chiswell lead mines near Austinville on the banks of the New River. The author says during the Revolutionary War many forges and furnaces were built in this area. They became the main sources of lead shot for the American army. Although ruins of the mines can be found today, none of the settlements survived.

** One of the "great ghosts," Mills declares, is Corotoman Plantation which once stood on the Rappahannock River near Kilmarnock. It was settled in 1650 and was once one of the largest and richest plantations in the colony. Curiously, however, its exact location has never been found.

** In northern Virginia, at a site due west of McLean and north, northwest of Fairfax, there was a "big scare" reported about 30 years ago. Several teenagers said they could hear "mysterious footsteps" following them when they walked the streets of a certain section at night. They never found the source. Each time they would turn back, they would see nothing, even though the steps seemed to resound within a few feet of them. It was such a frightening experience that some youngsters even armed themselves with baseball bats.

The location was in the middle of what, more than a century ago, had been planned as a master suburban center, but became instead, yet another Virginia ghost town. Here is the story:

In the 1880s, a German-born successful physician named Carl Adolph Max Wiehle, moved his family from Philadelphia to Washington. Dr. Wiehle bought thousands of acres in Fairfax County and retired there. He was then only 35 years old. In 1888, he built a large, Victorian-style frame "summer" house, complete with an elaborate white gazebo.

Described as a man of "prodigious energy and imagination," Dr. Wiehle, bored in retirement, decided to develop a town to surround his property. He envisioned it having a luxury hotel, parks, local industry, a community center, and a post office. He believed the site, being only 20 miles or so from Washington, would thrive as an appealing "bedroom community." The only trouble was, Dr. Wiehle was about 80 years of so ahead of his time.

He did commission the building of a two-story brick town hall, including an 80-pound bell in its steeple. His initial plan called for 800 private residences. But transportation being what it was in those days, Washington commuters felt the planned community was too far from their work, and only a handful of houses was built. A prolonged recession also helped dash the hopes for the fledgling town.

Undeterred, the doctor went ahead with plans to erect his own "castle," a 25-room brick mansion, which was completed in 1902. Unfortunately, however, Dr. Wiehle died, at age 50, of pneumonia in 1901, before the house could be finished. Dying with him was the dream of his town.

Weeds grew on once-cleared lots, construction of half-built homes was halted, and area industry never developed. What was left of the old buildings was purchased in 1923 by a distillery company which produced Virginia Gentlemen bourbon. This lasted until prohibition, and once again the area was, to a large extent, abandoned.

Thus, some who live in the area today think perhaps, if there were ghostly footsteps traipsing about in the 1960s, as was reported, they might well have been made by Dr. Wiehle himself. And if so, he would undoubtedly be a happy ghost. For the site where he had envisioned a thriving community more than a century ago is today — the bustling city of Reston!

WHAT TO DO IF YOU MEET A GHOST

hat do you do if there is a ghost in your house? Several people have told me over the years that the most effective way to deal with the phenomenon is simply to talk to the spirit, as if it were a mortal being. Mrs. Payne Tyler at Sherwood Forest in Charles City County east of Richmond, the home of President John Tyler, said their ghost, known as the "Gray Lady," got so bothersome at one point that she had a talk with "her." "I said you may have lived here at one time, but I live here now, let's try to peacefully co-exist." Mrs. Tyler said the manifestations quieted down considerably after that.

Of course if you want to get rid of the "hant" altogether, you could try calling in a professional psychic who could try to persuade the entity to move on to whatever its next plateau is. Meanwhile, here are some other suggestions as gleaned from the anthology, "Great American Folklore."

** Ghosts hate new things. If you have a persistent ghost, hang something new over your door."

** Say, 'What in God's name do you want?' when you first see a ghost, and you will know no fear."

** "Never strike at a ghost; never get mad at it. You will have very bad luck and the ghost will resent you and plague you for it."

** "Ghosts enjoy people singing and will listen."

** "When horses and other animals start acting strange, it's because they see a ghost. Horses that snort at night are seeing a ghost."

** "If someone sees a ghost, look over their left shoulder and you'll see the ghost."

** "Graveyards at night are lucky places if you stay quiet. Talk and you will be haunted for a week."

** "Christmas Eve is the favored time for ghosts to walk on earth."

** "Always settle an argument before you sleep, or ghosts will come and bother you."

(Come to think of it, that's not such a bad idea anyway!)

Here are some more tips by experts. Parapsychologist Hans Holzer, says: "Relax, if you can. Be a good observer, even if you are scared stiff. And remember, please — ghosts are (or were) real people. There but for the grace of God, goes someone like you."

The late ghost hunter, Harry Price, author of "Blue Book for Psychic Investigations," offers this: "Do not move, and on no account approach the figure. If the figure speaks . . . ascertain name, age, sex, origin, cause of visit, if in trouble, and possible alleviation. Do not move until the figure disappears."

HOW TO FRIGHTEN EVIL SPIRITS

ant to get rid of a ghost, or an evil spirit? One way might be to attend the annual Wassail held each October at the Claude Moore Farm at Turkey Run in northern Virginia near McLean. This is an ancient winter farm tradition where attendees sing and drink cider. It is said to drive the evil spirits from the farm's apple orchards. There must be many who want to learn the tradition. In 1998 more than 400 people came to participate.

A STAKE THROUGH THE HEART

In ancient lore, the way to kill a vampire was to drive a stake through its heart. Curiously, 300 or so years ago in certain parts of Virginia, this quaint and cruel custom also applied to those early settlers who committed suicide. According to superstitious custom prevalent in the 1600s, stakes were driven through the hearts of some suicide victims and their bodies were buried at a nearby crossroads as a demonstration of public disgust.

In the Westmoreland County Courthouse files there is a document telling of such a case which occurred to a slave who had been found dead in a creekbed. It was suspected that he had taken his own life. The incident was reviewed by a 12 man jury on August 25, 1661, which resulted in the following decision:

"Wee whose names are hereunder written being summons & sworn upon a jury Concerning ye death of a man servant of Mr. William Frekes who was drowned in ye Creek near his masters plantation doe finde that hee hath willfully Cast himself away, having viewed diligently Accordingly to our Oathes & Conscience, & that Caused him to bee buried at yet next Cross Path as ye Law Requires with a stake driven through ye middle of him in his grave hee having willingly Cast himself away."

THE PARSON'S GHOST THAT WASN'T

(Author's note: The following was found in the April 1852 issue of "The Virginia Historical Register." Seems a young man was living in Suffolk, England, during the first half of the 19th century. He was in love with a young lady and asked permission of his father to marry her. The father said he would grant such a request only under one condition: that his son would go to Edinborough to complete his education, and thus be separated from his new bride for a period of three years. (For some reason unexplained in the account, the bride would be in Virginia.) The son agreed. Here is what followed:)

"Three years rolled away, as they will, whether of joy or sorrow; and he was preparing to return home, when he had a dream (a premonition?) that revealed to him the death of his wife. He arrived in Virginia — the dream was a reality! The shock made him a maniac. The madness gradually wore away — melancholy succeeded. He would escape from his home, and spend night after night on her grave, praying to have one — but one look at her. He trusted that the earnestness of his prayer would meet with acceptance.

"Mr. Agnew, a Scotch clergyman, was pastor of his church; he asked him if he thought that departed spirits were ever permitted to visit this earth. (The preacher answered.) 'I'll tell you a Ghost Story, and you may judge how near I was in believing that they (ghosts) might — that they did. I was invited to preach in Gloster (presumably Gloucester), and was a guest in a large house. There was a great simmering among the young members of the family when they saw me. I, a minister! — my youth made it ludicrous in them — even the servants joined. I had experienced something like it before — had disturbed their associations — a young and gay clergyman; I should have been the reverse — old and grave.

"'I retired. All was comfortable, and I was soon asleep. Towards morning I awoke. The curtains were parted; in the opening I saw a tall figure shrouded in white. I fainted. On recovering, the eyes of the figure seemed to gaze on me. I felt that prayer was my only defence. I struggled to put myself in the attitude of prayer. Never did I supplicate with greater earnestness. Prayer gave me courage. I stretched forth my hand, and touched something — 'twas cold. I recoiled — again I fainted. How long I remained insensible, I know not. I touched the object — spirits are not material, therefore there was no spirit!

"'The morning had dawned — objects were distinct. I opened my eyes, the curtains were still parted, and there stood — a Barber's block, on which mine host's wig was displayed.

"'The truth, the whole truth flashed upon me — the children and the servants wanted to play the young Parson a trick. With the wig, the dredging-box, and a morning-gown, a Ghost was gotten up.

"'So ends my Ghost Story — as veritable a Ghost as can be met with'."

C H A P T E R   7 4

A Soupcon of
Spectral Snippets

(Author's note: One of the few frustrations of this ever-interesting job of tracking down ghostly legends and lore is that I sometimes hear hints of intriguing encounters, but I am unable to learn any further information about them. Someone will call and say, "Did you hear about the ghost at . . . . . ?" Or a letter writer will mention a certain house he or she has heard is haunted, but can offer no more details. Some leads prove invaluable, but others may lead to a (pardon the pun) dead end.

I include a sampling of these here, for although they are tantalizingly short, maybe they will stir a reader's memory and lead me to the full story.)

* There is, or was, an old Victorian house somewhere in Suffolk that, earlier this century or perhaps even in the 18th century, was reputed to be a bordello. It is said to be haunted by a man who was once caught in the house by his wife. He allegedly jumped out of an upper story window to escape and was killed by the fall. He is still seen roaming the halls of the house.

* Sometime about 1970 a man sailed out of the Langley, Virginia, marina, had an accident at sea, fell overboard and drowned. Afterwards the marina seemed to experience all sorts of unexplained problems. Curious, an area "ghost-buster" went out one day with a tape recorder to the spot where the man had gone down. He recorded sounds of a man gurgling, as if drowning.

* At the Stonewall Jackson Shrine near Guinea just off Interstate 95 south of Fredericksburg, a Canadian couple took a photo through the window of the house where Jackson died. When they had the picture developed there was an apparitional image of a female figure on it. They sent a copy to the park rangers at the shrine. They said it bore a striking resemblance to Jackson's wife!

* At an Eastern Shore Coast Guard Station, a man "blew his brains out" about 20 years ago. Since then, guardsmen have reported seeing phantom legs with blood all over them, and the sounds of someone following them around. When they look back no one is there.

* The four-year-old daughter of a woman in Mechanicsville said a "man in a gray uniform with blond hair and a goatee" washed her hair one day. Her mother scolded her for making up such a story. But afterwards she wondered. Because one day she was spanking her daughter when she herself saw the apparition of such a man approaching her and shaking his finger at her. She said as he neared her he just "faded away." She hasn't spanked her daughter since!

* Cathy Clark, a Colonial Williamsburg employee at the famous Williamsburg Inn, says a guest once took a photo which clearly showed an apparitional figure on it. Clark kept the photo in a file, but when I checked with her about it, the photo had mysteriously disappeared.

* At Bach Tavern in Midlothian, Bob Draucker operates a tea room and antique clock shop. He says that whenever he was out, a ghost — or something — kept raising the deadbolt lock from inside the front door, locking him out of the house. He finally had to take the top of the bolt off.

* There apparently was a lot of past tragedy at an old house somewhere in Buckingham County. An old woman allegedly lost her mind, and a man once hanged himself in the barn. The house is now used as a hunting lodge, and a hunter who slept there one night said "a ghost slept on top of him!"

* At Redlands, a stately, 200-year-old house in Albemarle County, descendants of the original builder, Robert Carter, have seen what they believe to be the spirit of a Civil War soldier in their attic. The house was used as a hospital during that war. Members of the family say they occasionally get, near dusk, "a brief glimpse of a gray-bearded face peering down from one of the attic windows. He has a long beard and is always dressed in Confederate gray."

* Nearby, outside of Crozet, mysterious lights are sometimes

seen 3,000 feet up on Buck's Elbow Mountain. A Piedmont airliner crashed in this vicinity 40 years ago killing all aboard. While the appearance of the lights remains unsolved, a unusually large black cat has been sighted on occasion, seated on a stump in the area. Some have speculated it represents an evil spirit.

* In May 1983, Margaret Synor of Fredericksburg was touring a part of the Fredericksburg Battlefield near Mary Washington College when she suddenly heard some strange sounds. There was a "tinkling of bells, then flutes, and the strains of a fife and drum corps." She thought of them as "preludes to a battle." She then heard "men shouting, horses snorting, and guns going off." There was no reenactment that day, and no one in sight.

* Lillian Gobble, a Wise County Historical Society staff member, tells of two of her relatives who once worked in a coal mine in Esserville. She says, "While coming home from work one night, the two men met a lady ghost who said: 'If you know what I know, you won't go to work in the morning.' The ghost appeared later that night at one of the men's houses and said the same thing. That man didn't go to work the next day. The other man did — and was killed by a falling rock!"

* Sometime in the 1930s, a bus reportedly careened out of control and plunged head-long into the James River near the town of Hopewell. Several people drowned. Local residents say that on certain dead still nights they can hear moans and screams coming from the site where the bus entered its watery grave.

* At the immense Luke Mansion, near Covington, (40 bathrooms!), the appearance of a young woman in white each Christmas so spooked caretakers of the house that they moved out and refused ever to come back.

* At Sherwood, a large house in Gloucester County, it is said that if one rides up to the front porch on horseback, even to this day, a ghostly figure will appear, shake its finger, and tell the rider, "you shall not burn this house down!" The origin of this legend dates back to the Civil War when a badly wounded Union officer was taken into this house and nursed by the Robert Selden family. When Yankee soldiers came to plunder and burn the house, the young officer, still shaky on his feet, struggled to the porch and reproached the men, saying, "You shall not burn this house down." Sherwood was spared. The Union officer died shortly afterward, but county residents say they have seen his apparition a number of times over the past 135 years.

* At historic Warner Hall, also in Gloucester County, there is a

long-standing tradition that late in the 19th century, a mistress of the house, unhappily married, decided to commit suicide — but not alone! She talked her maid-servant into joining her. They ingested laudanum, a poison. When the two women were found, a doctor was summoned. The maid was revived but the mistress died. Residents and guests at Warner Hall, over the years, have sworn they have seen the disembodied image of the lady, strolling around the house at night, a sad frown implanted on her face.

(Author's note: For years I had been teased or tantalized with the sketchy accounts of a ghostly cat in or near Danville — a cat that talked! Or at least that is what some people claimed. I never could run down the details, or the origins of the legend.

However, late in 1998 I corresponded with a young man named Michael Renegar of East Bend, North Carolina. Michael was collecting haunting tales from his region for a possible book. He said he had gathered encounters including: "A World War I soldier who came home one last time;" haunted college dormitories; a headless horse; and "the Devil's Cave."

I asked him if he had ever heard of any accounts in Virginia. He replied that he had a friend who once lived in Ridgeway (south of Martinsville near the Carolina line, and just west of Danville). She told him that "they had a cat that could actually talk! Whenever it would get shut into the bathroom, they'd hear a voice distinctly calling, 'Let me out! Let me out!' It would also say things like 'hello' and 'goodbye'." Michael said he believed her because she wasn't the kind to "pull his leg."

And so it goes.

CHAPTER 75

A Hodgepodge of Haunting Humor

Satisfying a Hunger from the Beyond

(Newport News)

(Author's note: The following was told to me in April 1998 by Stephen Goens of Newport News:)

"A few years ago I went to a black church funeral service for a man named Brown who I had known. The preacher was in the middle of his eulogy when, suddenly, a large woman appeared at the door and began walking down the aisle toward the casket, which was draped with flowers. The woman was carrying what appeared to be a large casserole dish, and even from where I sat, in the middle of a pew, you could smell a pungent odor wafting in the air.

"When she got close to the front the preacher asked her what she was doing. She said, 'I'm taking some chicken and dumplings to Mr. Brown.' 'You don't understand, sister,' the minister answered, 'Mr. Brown has gone on to his great reward.'

"The woman stopped in front of the coffin and huffed, 'it is Wednesday, isn't it?' The minister said, 'yes it is.' 'Well, I have fixed chicken and dumplings for Mr. Brown every Wednesday for the past 30 years!' The somewhat frustrated minister said, 'that may be, but he can't eat it now.'

"To this, the woman huffed, with righteous indignation, 'if

that's the case then, I guess Mr. Brown can smell the damn flowers, too!' She then placed the dish next to the bank of flowers and seated herself for the service.

THE 'CORPSE' THAT SAID 'DON'T SHOOT!'

October 1998, the Virginia Museum of Transportation in Roanoke held their first ever "Haunted Railyard" tour during Halloween week. Education director Judy Hensley said they had no idea what to expect. As it turned out, they were overwhelmed. More than 360 people came. Among the "stories" they related was the Wreck of Old 97 which occurred in Danville in 1903 (see separate chapter in this book).

Another incident recounted is not ghostly, but is nevertheless rather humorous. Seems a crook who thought he was clever, concealed himself on an express train in 1886 by hiding in a coffin. The plan was to extricate himself from the box along the train's route and rob it.

But an agent, either alertly, or perhaps scared to death, foiled the attempt. He heard noises coming from the coffin. It is probable that he might have believed someone was coming back from the dead. Whatever, he piled some heavy freight on top of the casket, and when it arrived at the next station, the agent had it placed on the platform. He then yelled, "if anyone is in there, you'd better come out. I'm going to shoot through it!"

A sheepish voice inside cried out, "I'm in here, don't shoot!" The chagrined would-be bandit was promptly arrested and later received a three year prison sentence.

THE WALKING SKULL

he following is excerpted and paraphrased from a letter to the editor published in the July 27, 1739, issue of the Virginia Gazette (Williamsburg).

The letter writer told of an incident which occurred when two men were digging a grave in a country church cemetery. One of their shovels hit something solid. It was a human skull. They brushed the dirt off it and laid it beside the grave on some grass.

To their utter amazement, both men saw the skull moving on

its own! They raced to the little church and stammered what they had seen to the parson. He suspected the men may have been imbibing some alcohol while digging, but came out to see for himself. Sure enough, the skull moved. The wide-eyed parson shouted, "it's a miracle!"

He immediately sent for a cross and some holy water, and ordered the church bell to be rung. Curious parishioners flocked to the church. The skull was taken inside the building and laid on the altar. . . . and there, the mystery was quickly solved.

A tiny mole crawled out of one of the skull's eye sockets!

The gathered congregation abruptly dispersed.

A SCARY MOMENT AT ROSEWELL

There are hauntings enough at the ruins of Rosewell, the once-magnificent 18th century plantation home of the Mann Page family, which was gutted by fire in 1916. One does not have to manufacture manifestations here, but such apparently was the case a few years ago, as recorded in Claude Lanciano, Jr's. fine book, "Rosewell, Garland of Virginia."

Seems a group of tourists were on their way to visit the ruins one day. A Colonial Williamsburg employee named Joe Nicolson was on his way home in Gloucester County, and decided to stop by Rosewell to take some photos. He was garbed in his colonial costume, complete from buckled shoes to ruffled collar. It should be added that Joe was a gaunt, spare man, 110 pounds and five feet nine inches tall. Lanciano wrote that Joe had "a facial aspect that might be described as half-way between somber and cadaverous."

Anyway, Joe was milling about in the ruins when he heard the tourist group arrive, chattering away. He decided to have some fun. As the tourists lined up facing the ruins, he suddenly sprang up from out of the shadows behind a still-standing chimney, and announced: "Good evening ladies and gentlemen. I'm Governor Page!"

His reception was a stunned silence. The tourists froze in their tracks, and two ladies nearly fainted.

A QUICK CURE FOR LAMENESS?

(Author's note: The following anecdote was told to me by a gentleman at the 1998 Hanover Tomato Festival in Mechanicsville. He said it was a story his father had often told him when he was a child, and although he could not absolutely vouch for its truthfulness, it was such an amusing vignette, that I include it here strictly for entertainment purposes.)

It occurred, it is believed, somewhere in Hanover County early in the 20th century, and involved two old friends known only as John and Amos. John had been wheelchair-bound for about 15 years and Amos often would take him places. John liked to visit a local cemetery, presumably to "visit" a departed relative or friend.

Some acquaintances of John and Amos knew of these frequent excursions and decided to play a Halloweenish-type trick. So one evening when Amos was pushing John towards the graveyard, they hid in the bushes, and as the two passed, they leaped out at them, covered in white sheets.

Terrified at the sight, Amos immediately abandoned John in his chair and took off running as fast as his feet would carry him. He ran a good long distance to a rural church, dashed up the stairs, entered the building and attempted to shut the door tight behind him. However, the door wouldn't shut. Something was holding it. Amos looked around and was astonished to see John right behind him.

"Don't close the door on me," John shouted.

The wheelchair was nowhere in sight!

A MOST DRAMATIC CURE

Sam M. Hurst, author of "The Mountains Redeemed," a book about life in Southwest Virginia during the "early days," and published in 1929, tells a humorous story about two "Hardshell" Baptist "apostles" who had a fondness for moonshine liquor back in the 1920s. Nothing, it seems, could discourage them from their regular binges. Nothing, that is, until some sober-minded members of their congregation decided to scare the hell out of them - figuratively and literally.

So one night after both imbibers had passed into a drunken stupor, the members swung into action. They tied them up inside the skeleton of a long-deceased mule! When the two men awoke, they were staring directly into the bleached-white, grinning skull of the dead beast - a most frightening experience to say the least, especially, when in their hungover condition they became convinced they were face to face with "his Satanic majesty."

The ploy worked. Not only did they give up all forms of alcohol, but they also became the ministry's most outspoken advocates of abstinence!

CHAPTER 76

The Tour Guide Who Wasn't There

(Randolph Macon College, Ashland)

ll is reasonably quiet these days, at least on a paranormal basis, at the Sigma Alpha Epsilon fraternity house at 109 College Avenue, Randolph Macon College in Ashland. But such was not always the case. The building burned to the ground in the late 1980s, and was later rebuilt. But before the fire frat brothers reported some strange happenings.

It was originally built in the early 1800s, and during the Civil War, it was made into a makeshift hospital. One of the rooms in the back was used for surgery and it even had a slanted floor with a drain in the middle for the blood to wash away. There is no telling how many young arms and legs were amputated, and how many men died here well before their time.

And there is more. A number of tragedies occurred in the house in the years after the war. For a time it was known as the Ray house. There were two, three or more Doctor Rays who lived here and a prevalent rumor contends one or more of them committed suicide. Eventually, the Ray family gave the house to the school. Such a background should be enough to nominate the structure for a haunting or two . . . and there is evidence that such was the case before the fire.

"I know a lot of eerie things happened there, some to me personally, and I've heard a lot of others had weird experiences, too," says Mark Hamby, a Richmond stock broker who attended Randolph Macon in the 1980s. "I know I was scared out of my wits one day. I was at the house doing odd jobs during the summer break. I was painting. I started up one of the old outside staircases, when I heard a loud noise behind me. I thought it might be another student painter. I looked around and there was no one there. I kind of hurried up the steps and something, or someone followed me into one of the rooms upstairs. I heard it follow me, but I didn't see anything. It's hard to describe, but I felt like there was a presence there with me. I don't mind telling you it was a little frightening. It got so I wouldn't go in the house at night during that summer. And I wasn't the only one who had such an encounter."

Mark says there was a basketball player who was on the third floor studying one night. He was by himself. During the summer there was rarely anyone about. He heard someone knock at the door. He got up and opened the door. There was no one there. He went back to his books, and in a few minutes there was another knock. He got up again and when he found nothing, he assumed someone was playing a joke on him, so this time he stood by the door. Several minutes later, when the rapping reoccurred, he jerked the door open expecting to unmask his tormentor. But the hallway was empty! He hastily gathered up his stuff and ran out of the house.

"I know when I was a student there," Mark says, "sometimes when we would go out to a party, we'd leave all the lights on in the house. It would be empty. And then when we would come back a few hours later, all the lights would be off, and the pictures on the walls would be found scattered all over the floor. Now, obviously, this could have been done by some rival fraternity men, but we didn't think so. Why would they just do that? If it was a joke, they would have sprayed shaving cream, or tossed toilet paper rolls about. This was something else."

Mark says that students living in the house reported hearing mystery footsteps at night, and some said, in a certain upstairs room, they saw wispy apparitions peering over their beds. The manifestations were witnessed by a number of residents over a period of 15 years or more, right up until the house burned.

But perhaps the most chilling episode was experienced by a student named Scott Tilghman. He walked up to the house one summer when it was unoccupied. He said an elderly man wearing glasses and of medium build just seemed to appear in front of the place from out of nowhere. The man smiled and asked Scott if he would like a tour of the house. Scott nodded. The man then took him through it, showed him the old surgical room and told him about the past history there. After the tour, the man walked out the front door and seemed to vanish.

Scott later told Mark about the tour and described the man in explicit detail. Mark told his father, and he said that the description perfectly matched the last Doctor Ray who had lived in the house.

Then Mr. Hamby said that this was odd, because that Doctor Ray . . . . had died more than 30 years earlier!

CHAPTER 77

The Return of Ellen Glasgow

(Richmond)

The sound is usually heard late at night. It is a distinct sound, the soft clacking of keys on an old manual typewriter. And it is heard only in one place in the house — in the northwest room on the second floor. That was her den, where she did all her work.

A number of people have heard the midnight typing over the years. Others have claimed that people's imaginations have run wild; that these tapping sounds can be rationally explained. It is, they say, the bursting of seed pods from magnolia trees hitting against the windows. But this does not explain the fact that each time anyone has investigated the source of the sound by opening the door to this particular upstairs room, the tapping mysteriously ceased, only to begin anew once the door was shut again.

Among those who have heard it, some are convinced it can be only one thing — the ghost of famed Richmond novelist Ellen Glasgow — back to complete the novel she left unfinished when she died November 21, 1945, at her longtime home at One West Main Street.

Ellen Glasgow has been described as among the most significant of this nation's 20th century novelists. She wrote 19 novels, all but one set in Virginia. Together, they comprise a social history of the state from 1850 through the author's lifetime. Miss Glasgow won the Pulitzer prize for the best novel of 1941 — "In This Our Life." Critics have said her works have a scope, wit and realism

The Glasgow House

which give them enduring interest, and which made them an influence on the development of American letters. The theme which unified her work was the survival of essential values in the face of adversity, pretension and change.

The critic J. Donald Adams once wrote of her: "I rank her among the best we Americans have produced. In one respect she stands preeminent. She is the wittiest novelist in our history, bar none, and one of the best stylists."

Ellen Glasgow was born in Richmond in 1873. In 1888 her family moved to the residence at One West Main Street, which came to be known as "The Glasgow House." It is a Greek Revival house which was built in 1841 by David M. Branch, a tobacconist. It was purchased in 1846 by Isaac Davenport, one of Richmond's industrial pioneers. He helped build the Franklin Manufacturing Company, the first of the great paper mills of Richmond. His daughter inherited the house when he died, and it was she who sold it to the Glasgows.

Constructed of lightly scored stucco over brick, the house incorporates two stories over a full basement. The interior of the Glasgow House displays the elegance of Greek Revival detail. The most positive trace of Miss Glasgow's former presence is the unusual wallpaper in her second floor study. Imported from England, the paper was so highly prized by the author that she went so far as to insure its preservation in her will. The paper depicts, in an almost Impressionistic manner, the red tile roofed houses of the Mediterranean.

After Miss Glasgow died in 1945, her brother, Archer Glasgow, presented the house to the Virginia Historical Society. Two years later the Association for the Preservation of Virginia Antiquities purchased the house with money collected from friends and relatives who gave generously to preserve it as a landmark to the noted writer. The University Center of Virginia occupied the house from 1947 to 1971, and it was during this period that a number of people saw, heard and felt the presence of what they believed to be Ellen Glasgow's ghost.

One who felt this was Roy Carter, an assistant professor of dramatic art at Virginia Commonwealth University. While a student at Richmond Professional Institute, he lived in the house for awhile, and later, in 1954, returned for a visit.

"I was downstairs with a friend when a compulsion suddenly came over me to get the key and go up to Miss Glasgow's old office," he recalls. "I went upstairs, opened the door, and from that point until my friend called to me about 30 minutes later, I don't remember anything about the room itself. It was almost as though I had gone to sleep. In that time a story was revealed to me concerning Miss Glasgow and another Richmond literary figure. I later checked it, and though I had known nothing about it before, found the story to be true," Carter says.

"When my friend called, I was acutely aware of a clock ticking loudly - but there was no clock in the room. I felt very close to 'Miss Ellen' without knowing why. I felt her presence. I didn't hear any voices, nor did I hear or see anything else. But I perceived something."

Another who has experienced the ghostly manifestations at Glasgow House is Dr. W. Donald Rhinesmith, formerly head of the University Center, and later associated with the state library. He lived in the house for a period, slept in Miss Glasgow's old bedroom, and used her study for a living room.

"I believe in ghosts, but not as anything unfriendly or malignant that can do you harm," he said in a newspaper interview some years ago. "I am convinced that there is a spirit in this house on occasion. I don't know that it stays here all the time. There's something walking around at night, methodically walking, a rather heavy tread as if a troubled spirit is walking in her study, and one night . . . in my bedroom I definitely felt a presence.

"It was about 12 o'clock at night," Dr. Rhinesmith says, "and I had just gone to bed when I heard footsteps coming around the four poster bed, walking toward the window, where I heard a foot stamp. I immediately got up and turned on the lights. "Why," he asks, "would she stamp her foot?" Then he answers, "Well, there used to be handsome Greek Revival houses across Foushee Street. Now there's an ugly parking lot.

"There's a push button buzzer on the wall near the bathroom that Miss Glasgow used to ring for the servants. it's been disconnected for years, but sometimes it rings," he adds. Oddly, none of these happenings aroused the interest of Dr. Rhinesmith's two dogs, who lived in the house with him. Dogs generally can sense anything supernatural and often react to it violently, with snarls, barking and raised hair on their backs. These dogs just slept peacefully. He explained this by noting that Miss Glasgow was a great lover of dogs throughout her life and gave a tremendous amount of support to the SPCA. Two of her pet dogs, in fact, were dug up from their backyard graves and reburied near her gravesite in Hollywood Cemetery, which is adjacent to that of Confederate General J. E. B. Stuart.

Michael Christopher, former owner of the Barn Dinner Theatre, was a student in 1965 when he lived in the basement of Glasgow house. On Thanksgiving evening of that year he returned to the empty house and saw a woman facing him on the stairway landing. He looked to the wall on his right at a picture of Miss Glasgow, and when he looked again at the woman facing him, she was gone. The woman's resemblance to the picture was so real that it totally unnerved him. He left the house immediately and would not return, not even for his possessions!

Earlier in the year, Christopher and others heard a typing sound coming from Miss Glasgow's study. The noise stopped, he said, when the door was opened, and it began again when it was closed. Ruth Norris, who worked in the house once, remembers sensing the "feeling of a benevolent spirit" there. She once heard a woman's voice singing three notes on the musical scale. But when she searched for the source she found no one else there.

A recent call to Dr. Rhinesmith brought his reaffirmation that something ghostly exists in the house, which currently is occupied by the law firm of McCaul, Grigsby, Pearsall, Marning and Davis. "I definitely heard the stamping feet on the floor," Dr. Rhinesmith says, "when no one was there. Others claimed to see a woman on the landing. Most of us just assumed it was Miss Glasgow, but some believed it may have been another woman who lived in the house earlier.

"In fact, in her autobiography, 'The Woman Within,' Miss Glasgow mentions having had a horrible vision on the stairs, so she could have seen the figure, too." Indeed, in this volume she states in one passage that "ghosts were my only companions." She went on: "This is not rhetoric. This is what I thought or felt or imagined, while I stood there, in that empty house, with the few strident noises floating in from the street, and my eyes on the darkness of the garden beyond the thick leaves on the porch. I felt, literally, that I was attacked by fear, as by some unseen malevolent power."

So, the question remains: is the ghost of Glasgow House that of Ellen Glasgow, who endured a number of deep personal tragedies while living there, and who died in her sleep before finishing her last novel? Or is it that of another woman who suffered some unknown sorrow and unpleasantness more than a century ago? Is it possible that there are *two* ethereal beings that co-exist; one who types late at night and rings a disconnected buzzer for ancient servants to answer; the other who appears periodically on the stairway landing, and occasionally is heard singing?

CHAPTER 78

The Reappearance of the 'Governor's Ghost'

(Richmond)

(Author's note: In 1985, in "The Ghosts of Richmond," I included a chapter on a rather mysterious spectral visitor at the Governor's Mansion. She allegedly was first witnessed during the administration of Philip W. McKinney in the 1890s. He is said to have encountered a young lady in an upstairs bedroom sitting by a window. He left the room for a moment to ask his wife who the guest was. She told him they had no guest, and when he reentered the bedroom, the lady had vanished.

S ince then, off and on, there have been a number of curious manifestations at the mansion. These have included footsteps, slamming doors, windows that frosted over in the middle of summer heat waves, and several sightings of a phantom female. One capitol police officer quit his job on the spot after he felt a chilling touch on his cheek by an unseen hand in the mansion basement one evening.

The ghost lady seems to make her presence known during certain administrations and is quiet during others. Governor Linwood Holton told of a haunting experience in the 1970s, but when Chuck Robb was the head of state, he and his family and staff encountered no "unusual sights or sounds." In the more recent tenure of Governor George Allen, however, Mrs. Allen hosted a Halloween television show at the mansion, telling the story of the ghost lady.

And, in volume IV of this series (1997), I told of a letter I received from a Richmond radio personality who claimed she found, on a tour of the mansion, an antique locket hidden in a chest of drawers in the same bedroom the spirit was seen 100 years earlier. There is no record of such a locket.

Then is the summer of 1997 I gave a talk to a delightful group of ladies belonging to the Suffolk Women's Club. One of the attendees was Governor James Gilmore's mother-in-law. She took me aside after the talk and told me that her two grandsons, then living in the mansion, were occasionally frightened in their beds at night by unexplained sounds and the feelings of a "presence" in their room.

Roxane Gilmore, the Governor's wife, confirmed this. She said, in a newspaper article, that she believed there may be ghosts in the house, and that it well might be the lady who first appeared there in the 1890s. She noted that there was a long-standing legend that this particular lady stayed at the mansion one night during a terrible storm. The next day, while on her way home, she was killed in an accident.

"She comes back to the mansion because that was the last place she had joy," Roxane Gilmore surmises. As to her two sons, Mrs.

Governor's Mansion

Gilmore added that one boy's bed had been moved halfway across the room one night and on another occasion her other son's bedspread was found outside the bedroom and in the hallway. A rational explanation could not be found for either incident.

It appears that the lady ghost seems to be more comfortable, and more expressive, during Republican administrations.

CHAPTER 79

Providence &
a Presentiment

(Richmond)

(Author's note: In the "Ghosts of Richmond," (1985), and repeated in "The Ghosts of Virginia, Volume III, (1996), I included chapters on the devastating Richmond theater fire of 1811, one of the worst tragedies in the history of the commonwealth. Governor George Smith and 71 others perished in the flames which quickly gutted an entire building after stage curtains caught fire during a performance of a play called "The Bleeding Nun."

On the afternoon of December 26, 1811 — the date of the play — a 15-year-old girl was walking down Broad Street. As she passed a ravine she heard a ghostly voice call out to her: "Nancy, Nancy, Nancy Green, you'll die before you are 16!" She looked around but saw no one. Terribly frightened, she ran home. She was to attend the play that evening with her "adopted" mother, a Mrs. Gibson. Nancy begged her to cancel the engagement. She deeply believed she had received a warning from "the other side" that afternoon, and that something catastrophic was going to happen.

Mrs. Gibson chided Nancy for having such ridiculous thoughts, and insisted on attending the play. Both she and Nancy Green were among those consumed in the flames that evening.

Nancy Green would have been 16 on December 27, 1811!

I had discovered the above "incident" in 1984, in an unpub-

lished manuscript in the files of the Richmond Historical Society. Fifteen years later, I was scanning through "A History of Richmond," by John P. Little, which was published in book form in 1933. It was reprinted from a series that initially appeared in the magazine, "The Southern Literary Messenger," in serial form from October 1851 through June 1852.

The following is extracted from Little's account of the 1811 fire:)

"Lieut. Gibbon, in his death, illustrated one of those singular instances we have of the presentiment of danger; he had promised to accompany some young ladies this evening to the theater, yet in a dream the night previous, had been so fully impressed with danger, of some unknown character, in going, that he endeavored to relieve himself from the engagement.

"The ladies, however, made light of his fears, and so rallied him, that he consented to go; yet, during the whole play, so firmly was the impression made on him, that he was observed to be restless and uneasy, like a man expecting danger from an unknown source, or by ambuscade.

"When the cry of fire rose, and the flames rushed out, he became perfectly cool and composed, and prepared to meet, and escape from, the danger, which, in uncertain expectation, had disturbed him. Leading one young lady, and followed by another, he had gained the door before the crowd rendered the passage impossible, and then returning to save Miss Conyers, perished with her in the crowd of sufferers."

* * * * *

(Author's note: The second intriguing occurrence involves an historical episode that is virtually unknown to Richmonders today, yet but for a "direct interposition of Providence," could have had devastating results for the capitol city. In "The Ghosts of Virginia, Volume I" (1993), I wrote a chapter about the infamous slave insurrection of 1831 in Southampton County led by Nat Turner. More than 50 residents were slaughtered in that uprising, and a number of the slaves were later hanged. That rebellion, a century and a half later, was forever etched in our consciousness through the best-selling book "The Confessions of Nat Turner," by Virginia author William Styron. Turner believed he had been guided to carry out his bloody mission by "divine Providence," and when a solar eclipse occurred in August that year, Turner saw it as a signal to launch his attack.

Far lesser known, however, was an attempted insurrection, on a much larger scale, that <u>almost</u> took place in Richmond in the year 1800. Both John Little, in his Southern Literary Messenger serial, and author W. Asbury Christian, in his 1912 book, "Richmond - Her Past and Present," covered the event. Oddly, it, too, occurred in August. Here is what happened:)

Christian wrote: "The year 1800 would have been known as the great year of horror in Richmond had it not been for an act of Providence which averted the calamity. Led by mean and desperate Negroes, a thousand or more slaves in and around the city armed themselves with axes, scythe blades, knives, guns, and whatever instruments of death they could lay their hands upon, and prepared to attack Richmond at night that they might murder and rob."

Little wrote: "On a night late in the month of August 1800, intelligence was suddenly brought to the city of Richmond, that an insurrection of slaves in the neighborhood had broken out, and that the insurgents were marching on the town. One thousand slaves had organized a rebellion under the command of two intelligent leaders (one was known as "Gabriel"), and in secrecy had perfected their plans. They were to attack the city by night, kill all who resisted, and all the males, divide the women and the spoil, seize on arms and munitions of war, and free all the Negro race throughout the state."

It was here that fate stepped in. . . or coincidence . . . or Providence . . . or whatever one wants to call it. Christian called it "an act of Providence." Little said it was "a direct interposition of Providence."

Christian: "A violent storm came up, and for hours the rain poured in torrents. The streams overflowed their banks and the roads became impassable with mud and water."

It was at this point that a young slave, in awe, convinced the storm was a warning signal (much like the solar eclipse that appeared to Nat Turner 31 years later), leaped into a surging stream, at the risk of his life, swam to the opposite shore, and ran to his farm where he awakened his master and told him of the murderous plot.

The alarm soon spread throughout the city. Governor James Monroe called out the Richmond Light Infantry Blues, and citizens armed themselves in time. Seeing that their planned raid would obviously fail against such overwhelming odds, the slaves scattered and fled. Gabriel and several other "ring leaders" were caught and hanged.

And thus Richmond was saved.

Had not "Providence" intervened, as Little penned: "The police were feeble, the town small and scattered, the militia and citizens totally unprepared, and the attack would have been terribly disastrous."

CHAPTER 79

Evil of Another Kind

(Richmond)

ennifer (she prefers that her last name not be used) is no stranger to evil. As a detective and nine-year veteran in the Richmond Police Department, now assigned to the third precinct in the west end of town, she has seen her share of vice, drugs, robbery, murder and other crimes. She can deal with that. "I have been trained to handle bad situations," she says.

Nothing, however, in her training, job experience, or anything else for that matter, has prepared her for some chilling encounters she has been confronted with over the past few years. These incidents, one in an historic house, she believes, involve another kind of evil — one that is not easily explained. In fact, to her, it's not explainable at all!

Jennifer says one such occurrence was right in her third precinct headquarters building. She explains there was a lot of ruckus raised when plans for the four-year-old structure were announced. "There was an old lady in the area who said if we built here, something terrible would happen," Jennifer says. "She was adamant about it. She wrote an article in the paper warning everyone. Why, I don't know. Maybe our headquarters was built on an old Indian burial ground, or a long-forgotten cemetery. I think there were row houses here before."

Apparently, the lady knew something about what she was saying, because during construction there was a terrible accident. A contractor was crushed to death when walls collapsed on him.

Jennifer was on midnight shift one night during the summer of 1996. She walked down the hall toward the ladies' room.

"Suddenly, I had this real eerie feeling that someone was watching me, that something was behind me. I looked back but I didn't see anything. At first, I ignored it. But then I got this awful feeling of the most evil presence. I don't know how to describe it. There was nothing visible. I didn't hear anything, and nothing touched me, but still, it was an overpowering feeling. Tears were streaming down my face.

"I had to get out of there. I said out loud to whatever it was, 'don't worry. I'm leaving, and I'm not coming back.' And I did! I wouldn't come back into the building until daylight the next day.

"Later, I was talking to one of the officers downstairs and I told her about my experience. She said, 'that's strange, because the most unusual thing happened to me in here last night.' She had been working at a computer terminal when an electric typewriter next to her started typing — all by itself! She didn't think too much about it right away. She thought it might be some sort of electrical surge or something. But then she reached over and unplugged the typewriter. And it continued typing!"

Jennifer says it was all so unsettling that she sat down one day and had a "talk" with whatever it was. "I just said I had a job to do and this was where I worked, and please leave me alone." It seemed to work.

As frightening as that was, however, it pales to what happened to Jennifer a couple of years earlier in one of Richmond's most historic shrines — the Maggie Walker House at 110 1/2 East Leigh Street. Maggie Walker was a dynamic, charismatic black woman who was born in 1867. Her mother, a washerwoman, had been a slave. Maggie arose from the depths of stark poverty and rampant racism, in a male-dominated world, to become one of the most respected and revered women of her time.

She is perhaps best known as having founded the St. Luke's Penny Savings Bank. She was the first woman in the United States to be the president of a bank. It later evolved into the Consolidated Bank & Trust Company, and is the oldest bank in the nation operated by blacks.

But Mrs. Walker was much, much more. She was nearly a century ahead of her time in fighting forcefully and effectively against segregation and for women's rights. She was active in many civic and charitable causes. She helped found the Independent Order of St. Luke, a fraternal mutual help society which provided a wide range of health and education benefits for the city's blacks. She also was founder and president of the Richmond Council of Colored Women.

The Maggie Walker House

Maggie Walker did all this despite all the obvious obstacles inherent in her era, but she also overcame a series of tragic, and somewhat mysterious incidents that would have discouraged or depressed a lesser person. In 1876, for example, when she was nine-years-old, her step-father was found drowned in the James River. Although murder was suspected, the case was never resolved.

In 1904, she and her husband, Armstead, moved into a house on Leigh Street in the Jackson Ward district. It was an Italianate town house that had been built in 1883. The house today is preserved and furnished exactly as she left it and has been acquired by the U.S. Department of the Interior for exhibition as a National Historic Site.

But tragedy followed Maggie Walker here. In 1907, she severely injured a kneecap — some say as a result of a fall down a flight of stairs — which crippled her and caused her to wear leg braces. Then, on a hot summer day in June 1915, neighbors reported seeing a prowler on the roof of the house. Maggie's son, Russell, ran upstairs, grabbed a gun, and when he saw a figure through the bamboo sunshade at the end of the porch, he fired. He killed his father, Armstead! The shooting was at first ruled accidental, but then a murder charge was brought against Russell. Legal

Maggie Walker

wrangling went on for five agonizing months before the trial got underway. Russell finally was found not guilty.

But an indelible stigma had been marked on the house — one that has lasted long after Maggie Walker died in 1934. Some believed it to be haunted.

Against this background, a few years ago, detective Jennifer was on midnight patrol when, sometime after midnight, she got an alarm call from the Walker House. She and a fellow officer "rolled up," and were met by a ranger from the Interior Department. Here, Jennifer tells what occurred next: "Nothing really happened until we got to the base of the front hall staircase by the front door. Then I started to get this crushing feeling. It was real scary. I sensed some presence lurking. It was a horrible, crushing feeling. It was like a super emotionally-charged atmosphere. I felt like it was riding my back.

"I didn't see anything, but I didn't want to look back behind me. I didn't want to see anything! I didn't feel anything, yet it was so real, it was almost tangible. I was really afraid. It was like there was another person there, hanging with me, on the stairs. I couldn't stand it. I shoved the officer in front of me and said, 'get up those stairs, fast!' He looked at me like I was looney tunes, but I couldn't help it. It was the strongest feeling of an evil, terrifying presence. It was oppressive. I felt the worst hate and rage coming up right after me. My heart was racing. It felt like something was breathing down my neck, and it was definitely not my imagination. It was a real feeling.

"I've been in difficult and dangerous situations on the street, and I've been nervous, but never scared like this, never scared where I couldn't do my job. This was a different feeling. I had a gun, but how do you shoot a ghost?" Jennifer says the feeling passed when she reached the top of the stairs. She got out of the house as fast as she could.

A year of so later, Jennifer and her partner got another alarm call from the house. Her fellow officer, knowing what had happened before, told her to check the outside of the building. She looked up to an upstairs window. "I saw something staring out of that window at me," she exclaims. "It was a shadow-like figure. I can't explain it, but no one was found inside the house.

"I'm not psychic, but I am sensitive," Jennifer notes. "I pick up on things. I believe there are such things as guardian angels — and also such things as unhappy souls. Such things may co-exist on different levels from us, and sometimes these levels collide. Sometimes I get benevolent feelings, but in that house all I got were malevolent feelings! I believe there is such a thing as evil, and if there is, it exists in the Walker House, or at least it existed that one night on the stairs.

"I know I never want to go back there."

Postscript: (Author's note: In February 1999, my son Tony and I visited the Maggie Walker House. It was a cold day and there was no one else around at the time. So long-time national park ranger Jim Bell gave us the full, unabridged tour. Bell was ready to retire a couple of years earlier, but when the Walker House assignment came up, he extended a career in which he takes great pride. He showed us every nook and cranny of the house and even played a short piece on the grand piano that belonged to the family.

I asked him if there had been any reports of ghostly activity. He smiled. "As a matter of fact," he said, "I was taking a couple of ladies through the house one day and a strange thing happened. When we got to the place upstairs, where Russell had fired his pistol and accidentally killed his step-father, one of the women shrank away and walked over to a corner where she seemed to be cowering in fear. I asked her what was wrong, and she said, 'are there any spirits associated with this house.' She added that she had felt a strong supernatural presence in the hallway overlooking the porch. I then told her about the accident. She had not known about it.")

The Baffling Case of the Brooding Nun

(Richmond)

I n Salem, Massachusetts, centuries ago, fear so overcame town residents that they publicly burned witches. And in Richmond, more than100 years ago, there is a recorded instance where citizens were so terrorized at the specter of "a woman in a window" that they eventually demolished a house on Fifth Street in an effort to rid themselves of the haunting apparition.

This was, in the annals of psychic phenomena, a highly unusual case, because the ghost was "seen" not by a single person, or a handful of people. It was witnessed by thousands! In fact, when word spread about town of the mysterious woman, the abandoned house became somewhat of a tourist attraction, much to the consternation of a local real estate agent who was trying to sell it.

Although the legend was passed rapidly through the community by word of mouth, probably with a new layer of embellishment in each recounting, the facts of the occurrence were set in print in June 1890 by a newspaper columnist identified only as "Felix." Here, in part, is what he wrote:

"Late upon a shadowy evening . . . a young man was walking out Fifth Street, when some uncertain distance beyond Leigh (Street), where the houses are all grey and tottering with unkept old age, he absently turned his gaze upon a vacant and silent looking house. At an upper window his astonished eyes discerned the solemn face of a sad-eyed, hooded nun peering out. He stopped and looked long and carefully, but no closer scrutiny proved an error in his sight or impression. Unmoved, and with melancholy steadiness, the solemn eyes of the nun looked down at him from out their frame of black veiling, looked beseechingly and longingly until he was conscious of no impulse but to release a prisoner, who seemed to be one by some strange chance or accident, so he bounded up the dust-ladened, trackless steps to try the front door in vain.

"A yellow, rain-smeared card, tacked upon the wall, told that it (the house) was 'For Sale.' The ragged, overgrown weeds choked the side entrance to the yard, but forcing that, he bravely tried to get in the back way, but the locks, at least, were still on duty and resisted his efforts. It was growing late then, so he again walked around and looked up at the window, to see in the gathering darkness the same face of the beseeching, saint-like nun at the window.

"Still believing it to be a human being imprisoned, he sought the agent of the deserted house and told his story, but he only found an incredulous listener, who assured him that it was nonsense, that that was 'one of the most desirable houses in town, nice and quiet, away from the bustle and noise, yet convenient to business.' Having thundered out this formula of his business, which is kept in readiness like a ready-loaded cartridge to fire off at whatever rises in the field, he thought the matter ended. But the young man was importunate, and finally persuaded him to get the keys of the house and to go with him, and if he confessed to seeing the face there they both would go in and make a search.

"Even by the stingy, pale light of the moon and a fitful lantern they carried, the agent, too, could not help seeing that in verity there was the face of a nun pressed close to the glass and looking out. They entered bravely, with the heavy, forward tread which marched over the carpetless floor and rickety stairs and resounded in all the empty space with some sound akin to echo, but the heart of each fluttered with an unmanly nervousness that neither of them would have liked to confess.

"They, however, came to the room from whose window the face peered, confidently expecting to there find a miserable, frightened woman for them to release and remove to some more cheerful quarters. They entered, and the ray of the lantern fell directly upon the window they came to search, but it only fell upon a vacant, cobwebbed sill, and lit with a sickly, pallid shine the empty, glaring window panes. No so much as a shadow did the lantern there reveal, but only the weird shine of the dim, smoky light on the glass.

"There seemed an insufferable silence in the room, and something more dread than fright seemed to make it impossible for either of them to speak a word. They moved about the room, but even their foot treads had a smothered, distant, far-away sound, and while neither of them could discern the faintest trace of any object in the room, however, after they turned the lantern in the corners and around its walls, there was a strong feeling with each that there was something undefined, which moved around with them just sufficiently to disturb the waves of air that came in contact with their bodies.

"They left the house without further search that night, both of them more unstrung and over wrought than they knew. The next day in the full glare of the noon-tide sun, in the unimaginative clearness of afternoon light, or at whatever hour of the day that one looked, there was to be seen that same unmovable steady, pleading stare of the solemn black veiled nun.

"It did not take many hours for the news of the advent of the strange and sudden apparition to spread. The neighborhood was in a riotous state of nervous tumult, and fled the vicinity with more rapidity than if the small-pox flag had hung from the window instead of the shadow image of a pale-faced, sad-eyed woman.

"From morning until night crowds of curious and awestricken people gathered around the house, thousands sometimes going a day to look at the haunted window. Some few were brave enough to explore the room, the incredulous ones, but such would come out trembling and convinced. There were a few attempts made to burn the disturbing phantom home, after which policemen were placed on continuous guard. The reporters had a 'Widow's Crew's' supply of material, and interesting matter seemed to increase for them regarding it day by day.

"At last it was thought expedient to tear down and ruthlessly destroy such a useless element of annoyance and mental discord. From the heavy felling blows of the pick-axe and the spade, the haunted house was mutilated and the sad-eyed, solemnly-veiled nun shattered in her image existence upon the window pane and (was) driven back into her proper sphere, in the shades of some deserted cloister, or the clammy realms of a ceiled vault, where she could look out through rusted iron bars and win the sympathy of bats and owls, while peace once again reigned on Fifth Street, and despair ceased its hold upon the mind of the real estate agent."

CHAPTER 82

Bodiless 'Things' Can't Hurt You

(Richmond)

(Author's note: Throughout this series of Virginia ghost books I have made a conscious and concerted effort not to repeat any of the material. True, I have taken excerpts from the five regional books I did and incorporated them into the state-wide volumes. And I have updated certain chapters when additional material was discovered. But there is no substantial repetition in the Virginia series, volumes I through V.

I am now going to make an exception to that rule — and here is why. In Volume I, I included a chapter on "The Skeleton with the Tortoise Shell Comb." It concerned a ghost at the Hawes House in Richmond; an episode which occurred in the 1850s. It had special significance because it was first told by one of the Hawes' daughters, Mary Virginia, who later became Mrs. Edward Terhune. Under her pen name of Marion Harland, she was one of Virginia's most noted writers of the 19th century.

In Volume IV, I had a chapter titled "The True Story of the Trueheart Ghost." This was, in effect, another version of the Hawes family ghost which Ms. Harland wrote about in a book called "Judith - A Chronicle of Old Virginia," which was published in 1883. I added this because it was more detailed, involved, and different from the original storyline.

In October 1998, at an antiquarian book show in Williamsburg, I came across "Marion Harland's Autobiography." In it, she had a chapter headlined, "Our True Family Ghost-Story." Here, Mary

Virginia Hawes, aka Marion Harland, again covered the haunting encounters she and her family experienced a century and a half ago — only this was yet the most definitive accounting of all. She told of still more manifestations, of different ones, and how all this affected her well-to-do, well-educated family; how they coped with phenomena they could not understand. The Hawes did not believe in supernatural occurrences, but they were subjected to so many inexplicable demonstrations, over a period of years, that they reluctantly had to come to the conclusion that some things just cannot be explained.

Although some of this material, as I said, has been in previous volumes of Virginia ghosts, I am going to include Marion Harland's own vivid and detailed account of the ghostly activity in her house. I do this because: this version not only is more inclusive and descriptive, but also creates a picture of how such hauntings can affect those who encounter them; and it is so well written. I found it compelling — a true ghost story told by a master craftsperson. I have excerpted it slightly. The setting is the Hawes House, a large colonial brick house built early in the 19th century. It was located at 506 East Leigh Street, but is no longer standing.

It begins on a cold winter evening in 1851. Mary Virginia has just seen a long-time friend of hers to the door, and she is ready to retire for the evening. Enjoy.)

"I carried a careless spirit and a light heart with me as I went off in the direction of my bedroom, having extinguished the hanging lamp in the hall, and taking one of the lamps from the parlor to light myself bedward.

"It was a big, square Colonial house, with much waste of space in the matter of halls and passages. The entrance-hall on the first floor was virtually a reception-room, and nearly as large as any apartment on that level. It was cut across the left side by an archway, filled with Venetian blinds and door. Beyond this was a broad, easy stairway, dropping, by a succession of landings, to the lower from the upper story. Directly opposite the front door was a second and narrower arch, the door in which was, likewise, of Venetian slats. This led to the rooms at the back of the house. The plan of the second floor was the same.

"On this eventful night I passed through the smaller archway, closing the door behind me. It had a spring latch that clicked into place as I swung it to. The bedroom I shared with my sister, who was not at home that night, was directly across the passage from that occupied by our parents." (Mary Virginia then describes how she looked in on her mother, said goodnight, and then went on.)

"The lamp in my hand had two strong burners. Gas had not then been introduced into private dwellings in Richmond. We used what was sold as 'burning fluid,' in illuminating our houses — something less gross than camphene or oil, and giving more light than either. I carried the lamp in front of me, so that it threw a bright light upon the door across the passage, here a little over six feet wide.

"As I shut the door of my mother's room, I saw, as distinctly as if by daylight, a small woman in gray start out of the opposite door, glide noiselessly along the wall, and disappear at the Venetian blinds giving upon the big front hall.

"I have reviewed that moment and its incident a thousand times, in an effort to persuade myself that the apparition was an optical illusion or a trick of fancy.

"The thousandth-and-first attempt results as did the first. I shut my eyes to see — always the one figure, the same motion, the same disappearance.

"She was dressed in gray; she was small and lithe; her head was bowed upon her hands, and she slipped away, hugging the wall, as in flight, vanishing at the closed door. The door I had heard latch itself five minutes ago! Which did not open to let her through!

"I recall, as clearly as I see the apparition, what I thought in the few seconds that flew by as I stood to watch her. I was not in the least frightened at first. My young maid, Paulina, had more than once that winter fallen asleep upon the rug before my fire, when she went into the room to see that all was in readiness for my retiring. The servants slept in buildings detached from the main residence.

"The house was locked up by my father's own hands at ten o'clock, unless there was some function to keep one or more of the servants up and on duty. Therefore, when I had twice awakened Paulina from her unlawful slumber, I had sent her off . . . with a sharp reproof and warning against a repetition of the offense. My instant thought now was:

"'The little minx has been at it again!' The next, 'She went like a cat!' The third, in a lightning flash, 'She did not open the door to go through!' Finally — 'Nor did she open the door when she came out of my room!'

"I had never, up to that instant, known one thrill of supernatural dread since I was old enough to give full credence to my father's assurances that there were no such things as ghosts . . . I had never been afraid of the darkness or of solitude. I would take my doll and book to the graveyard and spend whole happy afternoons there, because it was quiet and shady, and nobody would interrupt study or dream.

"It was, then, the stress of extraordinary emotion which swept me back into the room I had just quitted, and bore me up to the table by which my mother sat, there to set down the lamp I could scarcely hold, enunciating hoarsely:

"'I have seen a ghost!'

"My father wheeled sharply about.

"'What!'

At that supreme moment, the influence of his scornful dislike to every species of superstition made me 'hedge,' and falter, in articulating, 'If there is such a thing as a ghost, I have seen one!'

"Before I could utter another sound he had caught up the lamp and was gone. Excited, and almost blind and dumb as I was, I experienced a new sinking of heart as I heard him draw back the bolt of the door which the Thing had passed, without unclosing it. He explored the whole house. . . In a few minutes the search was over.

"He was perfectly calm in returning to us.

"'There is nobody in the house who has not a right to be here. And nobody awake except ourselves.

"'Now, daughter, try and tell us what you think you saw?'

"Grateful for the unlooked-for gentleness, I rallied to tell the story simply and without excitement.

"I really saw it, father, just as I have said! At least, I believe I did!'

"'I know it, my child. But we will talk no more of it tonight. I will go to your room with you.'

"He preceded me with the lamp. When we were in my chamber, he looked under the bed (how did he guess that I should do it as soon as his back was turned, if he had not?) Then he carried the light into the small dressing-room behind the chamber. I heard him open the doors of a wardrobe that stood here, and try the fastenings of a window.

"'There is nothing to harm you here,' he said. 'Now try not to think of what you believe you saw. Say your prayers and go to bed, like a good, brave girl!'

"I was ashamed of my fright — heartily ashamed! Yet, I was afraid to look in the mirror while I undid and combed my hair and put on my night-cap. When, at last, I dared put out the light, I scurried across the floor, plunged into bed, and drew the blankets tightly around my head.

(The next morning) "After breakfast he took me aside and told me to keep what I had seen to myself.

"'Neither your mother nor I will speak of it in the hearing of the children and servants. You may, of course, take your sister into your confidence. She may be trusted. But my opinion is that the fewer who know of such a thing that seems unaccountable, the better. And your sister is more nervous than you.'

"Thus it came about that nothing was said to Mea (the sister), and that we three who knew of the visitation did not discuss it, and tried honestly not to think of it.

"Until, perhaps a month after my fright, about nine o'clock, one wet night, my mother entered the chamber where my father and I were talking, and said, hurriedly, glancing nervously behind her:

"'I have seen Virginia's ghost!'

"She saw it, just as I had described, issuing from the closed door and gliding away close to the wall, then vanishing at the Venetian door.

"'It was all in gray,' she reported, 'but with something white wrapped about the head. It is very strange!'

"Still we held our peace. My father's will was law, and he counseled discretion.

"'We will await further developments,' he said, oracularly.

"Looking back, I think it strange that the example of his cool fearlessness so far wrought upon me that I would not allow the mystery to prey upon my spirits, or to make me afraid to go about the house as I had been wont to do. Once my father broke the reserve we maintained, even to each other, by asking if I would like to exchange my sleeping-room for another.

"'Why should I?' I interrogated, trying to laugh. 'We are not sure where she goes after she leaves it. It is something to know that she is no longer there.'

"Mea had to be taken into confidence after she burst into the drawing-room at twilight, one evening, and shut the door, setting her back against it and trembling from head to foot. She was as white as a sheet, and when she spoke, it was in a whisper. Something had chased her down-stairs, she declared. The hall-lamp was burning, and she could see, by looking over her shoulder, that the halls and stairs were empty but for her terrified self.

"But Something — Somebody — in high-heeled shoes, that went 'Tap! tap! tap!' on the oaken floor and staircase, was behind her from the time she left the upper chamber where she had been dressing, until she reached the parlor door. Her nerves were not as stout as mine, perhaps, but she was no coward, and she was not given to foolish imaginations. When we told her what had been seen (by others in the family), she took a more philosophical view of the situation than I was able to do.

"'Bodiless things can't hurt bodies!' she opined, and readily joined our secret circle.

"The crisis came in February (1852) of that same winter.

"My sister Alice and a young cousin who was near her age — 14 — were sent off to bed a little after nine one evening, that they might get plenty of 'beauty sleep.' Passing the drawing-room door, which was ajar, they were tempted to enter by the red gleam of the blazing fire of soft coal. Nobody was there to enjoy it, and they sat them down for a school-girlish talk. (At ten o'clock, they left the room to go to bed.)

"Going into the hall, they were surprised to find it dark. We found afterward that the servant whose duty it was to fill the lamp had neglected it, and it had burned out. It was a brilliant moonlight night, and the great window on the lower landing of the staircase was unshuttered. The arched door dividing the two halls was open, and from the doorway of the parlor they had a full view of the stairs.

"The moonbeams flooded it half-way up to the upper landing; and from the dark hall they saw a white figure moving slowly down the steps. The mischievous pair instantly jumped to the conclusion that one of 'the boys' — my brothers — was on his way to get a drink of water from the pitcher that always stood on a table in the reception-room, or main hall. To get it, he must pass within a few feet of them, and they shrank back into the embrasure of the door behind them, pinching each other in wicked glee to think how they would tease the boy about the prank next morning.

"Down the stairs it moved, without sound, and slowly the concealed watchers imagined, listening for any movement that might make retreat expedient. They said, afterward, that his nightgown trailed on the stairs, also that he might have had something white cast over his head.

"It crossed the moonlit landing — an unbroken sheet of light

— and stepped, yet more slowly, from stair to stair of the four that composed the lowermost flight. It was on the floor and almost within the archway when the front door opened suddenly and in walked the boys, who had been out for a stroll.

"In a quarter-second the apparition was gone. As Alice phrased it:

"'It did not go backward or forward. It did not sink into the floor. It just was not!'

"With wild screams the girls threw themselves upon the astonished boys, and sobbed out their story. In the full persuasion that a trick had been played upon the frightened children, the brothers rushed upstairs and made a search of the premises. The hubbub called every grown member of the household to the spot except our deaf grandmother, who was fast asleep in her bed upstairs.

"Assuming the command which was his right, my father ordered all hands to bed so authoritatively that none ventured to gainsay the edict. In the morning he made light to the girls and boys of the whole affair, fairly laughing it out of court, and, breakfast over, sent them off to school and academy. Then he summoned our mother, my sister, and myself to a private conference in 'the chamber.'

"He began business without preliminaries. Standing on the rug, his back to the fire, his hands behind him, in genuine English-squirely style, he said, as nearly as I can recall his words:

"'It is useless to try to hide from ourselves any longer that there is something wrong with this house. I have known it for a year and more. In fact, we had not lived here three months before I was made aware that some mystery hung about it.

"One windy November night I had gone to bed as usual, before your mother finished her book.

"'It was a stormy night, and I lay with closed eyes, listening to the wind and rain, and thinking over next day's business, when somebody touched my feet. Somebody — not something! Hands were laid lightly upon them, were lifted and laid in the same way upon my knees, and so on until they rested more heavily on my chest, and I felt that someone was looking into my face. Up to that moment I had not a doubt that it was your mother. Like the careful wife she is, she was arranging the covers over me to keep out stray draughts. So, when she bent to look into my face, I opened my eyes to thank her.

"'She was not there! I was gazing into the empty air. The pressure was removed as soon as I lifted my eyelids. I raised myself on my elbow and looked toward the fireplace. Your mother was deep in her book, her back toward me. I turned over without sound, and looked under the bed from the side next to the wall. The firelight and lamplight shone through, unobstructed.

"'I speak of this now for the first time. I have never opened my lips about it, even to your mother, until this moment. But it has happened to me, not once, nor twice, nor 20 — but 50 times — maybe more. It is always the same thing. The hands — I have settled in my mind that they are those of a small woman or of a child, they are so little and light — are laid on my feet, then on my knees, and travel upward to my chest. There they rest for a few seconds, sometimes for a whole minute — I have timed them — and something looks into my face and is gone!

"'How do I account for it? I don't account for it at all! I know that it is! That is all. Shakespeare said, long before I was born, that 'there are more things in heaven and earth that are dreamt of in our philosophy.' This is one of them. You can see, now, daughter,' — turning to me — 'why I was not incredulous when you brought your ghost upon the scene. I have been on the lookout for what our spiritualistic friends call 'further manifestations.'"

"'You believe, then,' Mea broke in, 'that the girls really saw something supernatural on the stairs last night? That it was not a trick of moonlight and imagination?'

"'If we can make them think so, it will be better for them than to fill their little brains with ghostly fears. That was the reason I took a jesting tone at breakfast-time. I charged them, on the penalty of being the laughing-stock of all of us, not to speak of it to anyone except ourselves. I wish you all to take the cue. Moreover, and above everything else, don't let the servants get hold of it. There would be no living in the house with them, if they were to catch the idea it is 'haunted.'"

"'You girls are old enough to understand that the value of this property would be destroyed were this story to creep abroad. I would better burn the house down at once then to attempt to sell it at any time within the next 50 years with a ghost-tale tagged to it.

"'Now, here lies the case! We can talk to outsiders of what we have seen and felt and heard in this, our home . . . or we can keep our own counsel like sensible, brave Christians. 'Bodiless spirits cannot hurt bodies,' and the little gray lady seems to be amiable enough. I can testify that her hands are light, and that they pet, not strike. She is timid, too. What do you say — all of you? Can we hold our tongues?'

"We promised in one voice. We kept the pledge so well that both the girls and the boys were convinced of our incredulity. Our father forbade them positively to drop a hint of their foolish fancies in the hearing of the servants. Young as they were, they knew what stigma would attach to a haunted house in the community. As time passed, the incident faded from their minds. It was never mentioned in their hearing.

"A year went by without further demonstration on the part of the little gray lady, except for two nocturnal visitations of the small, caressing hands.

"The one comic element connected with the bodiless visitant was introduced, oddly enough, by our sanctimonious clerical uncle-in-law, who now and then paid us visits of varying lengths. As he came unannounced, it was not invariably convenient to receive him. . . . He was good for a week at the shortest.

(This time, however, he stayed only one night.) "It was a delightful surprise when he announced, next morning, his intention of going out to Olney that day, and to remain there for — perhaps a week.

"The wife of my mother's brother (Aunt Sue) drove into town to spend the day with us, a week after the close of his stay at Olney.

"'Did any of you ever suspect that your house is haunted? (she asked.)

"'How ridiculous!' laughed mother. "Why do you ask?'

(Aunt Sue) "laughed yet more merrily. 'The funniest thing you ever heard! The old gentleman had an awful scare the last night he was here (the Hawes House). . . He was standing at the window, looking out into the moonlight in the garden, when somebody came up behind him, and took him by the elbows and turned him clear around! He felt the two hands that grabbed hold of him so plainly that he made sure Horace (one of the family) had hidden under the bed and jumped out to scare him.

"So he looked under the bed and in the wardrobe and the closet, and, for all I know, in the bureau drawers and under the washstand. There was nobody in the room but himself, and the door was locked. He says he wouldn't sleep in that room another night for a thousand dollars.'

"Passing over what might or might not have been a link in the true, weird history of our bodiless tenant, I leap a chasm of a dozen years to wind up the tale of the 'little gray lady,' so far as it bears directly upon our family. After the death of her husband and the marriages of sons and daughters left my mother alone in the old colonial homestead, she decided to sell it and to live with my youngest sister.

"The property was bought as a 'Church Home' — a sort of orphanage, conducted under the patronage of a prominent Episcopal parish renowned for good works. In altering the premises to adapt buildings to their new uses, the workmen came upon the skeleton of a small woman about four feet below the surface of the front yard. She lay less than six feet away from the wall of the house, and directly under the drawing-room window. There was no sign of coffin or coffin-plate.

"Under her head was a high, richly carved tortoise-shell comb, mute evidence that she had not been buried in cap and shroud, as was the custom 100 years agone. The oldest inhabitant of a city that is tenacious of domestic legends, had never heard of an interment in that quarter of a residential and aristocratic district.

". . . The grave was dug in the front garden, and so close to the house as to render untenable the theory that the plot was ever part of a family burying-ground.

"The papers took inquisitive note of all these circumstances, and let the matter drop as an unexplained mystery. Within the present occupancy of the house, I have heard that the gray lady still walks on moonlight nights, and, in gusty midnights, visits the bedside of terrified inmates to press small, light hands upon the feet, and so passing onward, to rest upon the chest of the awakened sleeper. I was asked by one who had felt them, if I had 'ever heard the legend that a bride, dressed for her wedding, fell dead in that upper chamber ages ago.'

"My informant could not tell me from whom she had the gruesome tale, or the date thereof. 'Somebody had told her that it happened once upon a time.' She knew that the unquiet creature still 'walked the halls and stairs.'

"She should have been 'laid' by the decent ceremony of burial in consecrated ground, awarded to the exhumed bones.

"I have talked with a grandson of our former next door neighbor, and had from him a circumstantial account of the disinterment of the nameless remains. They must have lain nearer the turf above them, a century back, than when they were found. The young man was a boy when he ran to the hole made by the workmen's spades, and watched the men bring to light the entire skeleton. He verified the story of the high, carved comb. He told me, of a midnight alarm of screaming children at the vision of a little gray lady, walking between the double row of beds in the dormitory, adding:

"'I told those who asked if any story was attached to the house, that I had lived next door ever since I was born, and played every day with your sisters and brothers, and never heard a whisper that the house was haunted.'

"So said all our neighbors. We kept our own counsel. It was our father's wise decree.

"I have told my ghost-story with no attempt at explanation of psychical phenomena. After all these years I fall back, when questioned as to hypotheses, upon my father's terse dicta:

"'How do I account for it? I don't account for it at all!'"

THE DOG THAT WAS(N'T) THERE!

here is a doggy footnote to the Marion Harland story. After Mary Virginia Hawes married Edward Terhune they lived for a time at a home called Sunnybank, in New Jersey. This was later the home of Albert Payson Terhune who lived there in the early 1900s. He was the son of Mary Virginia and had a ghost encounter with an animal, a beloved pet crossbreed dog named Rex. And what is so curious is how he viewed the experience — in a vein strikingly similar to how the Hawes family looked upon their ghostly experiences.

Rex was a creature of habit, and was "slavishly devoted" to his master. When the Terhunes dined, the dog would stare at Albert through the French windows on the veranda, and when Albert was at work in his study, Rex always used to lie in one particular spot in the hallway just outside the study door.

Rex died in March 1916; a sad event which Mr. Terhune wrote about in his book, "Lad: A Dog." Over a year later, a friend of Albert's came for a visit. They sat at the dining room table. The man asked about the large short-haired, fawn-colored dog with a scar on its forehead. He said it was out on the veranda looking in. Mr. Terhune told him he had no such dog. (Rex was a large short-haired, fawn-colored dog — with a scar on his forehead!)

A year later a close friend visited the Terhunes. After dinner they sat in the firelight. As the man was leaving he commented that he wished he had a dog as devoted to him as Rex was to Albert Terhune. He told Albert that the whole time they had been in the room Rex had sat next to Albert, looking up into his face. Albert said Rex had been dead for more than two years.

His friend replied that he knew that, but just the same he had seen

Rex lying in the firelight at Albert's feet all evening!

Albert had a collie after Rex. He said the dog would never lie in the spot that had been Rex's favorite. The collie would always walk around the spot, eyeing it as if something was there.

How did the one friend see a dog peering in through the window from the veranda? Albert answers succinctly: "I don't know." What did the other friend see lying at Albert's feet in the firelight? He answers again: "I don't know."

Such observations seem to run the in Hawes-Terhune families. In each case entities were seen, but no explanations were offered.

* * * * *

ROXIE'S LAST GOODBYE

(Author's note: Speaking of canines, Matt Paust, a staff writer with the Newport News Daily Press, called one evening early in 1999, as I was finishing this manuscript, and suggested I get in touch with Myrna Splan, a respected local criminal defense lawyer. She had a "ghost dog" experience, Paust said. I called. Here is what she told me:)

"I had a rottweiler named Roxie. I got her in 1987. She was a wonderful dog. We had a special bond. But I gave her up in 1992. The reason was, I had a close friend who was having problems, and had decided to move to Florida. He loved Roxie and Roxie loved him. I thought Roxie might help him solve some of his problems, so I let him take her with him to Florida. Once or twice each year, he would return to the area for a visit and bring Roxie with him. She was always thrilled to see me, and I her.

"Then, shortly after New Years 1999, a strange thing happened. I have another rottweiler now, named Corrie. One morning I let Corrie out into the fenced yard. As I watched, I was astonished to see an amorphous gray shape following Corrie. I believed it to be another dog, but the features were not distinguishable. Somehow I got the feeling it was Roxie, or maybe the spirit of Roxie. It didn't frighten or upset me. I went back into the house to make some coffee.

"A few days later, I heard from my friend in Florida. Sadly, he told me that Roxie couldn't stand on her hind legs anymore and he had to put her to sleep. He had done this the same morning I had seen the gray shape follow Corrie into my yard. I know that I am an attorney who has been practicing law for 12 years and I am supposed to be practical, sensible and logical. Still, I am convinced what I saw that morning was Roxie coming back to say goodbye."

C H A P T E R   8 3

The Vision in the Vineyard

(Beaverdam)

(Author's note: I was all set to go to the printers with this book when I got a call from Tim Trivett in Beaverdam, Virginia, a few miles northwest of Ashland, adjacent to the North Anna River. He manages a winery there and told me that a beautiful ghost lady sometimes roams through the vineyards at night. It sounded intriguing, doubly so since the area was a key site during the Civil War. Beaverdam Station then was an important railroad junction and a major storehouse for Robert E. Lee's supplies. It was here, in May 1864, that General Phillip Sheridan's Union army came charging through, battling Confederate soldiers, and threatening to capture Richmond. While Richmond was saved, the cost at Beaverdam was heavy. The South lost a million rations of meat, half a million rations of bread, and a huge reserve of medical supplies. When the warehouses were torched on May 9, 1864, it was said the pungent aroma of bacon could be smelled for miles around.

At the Windy Hill Winery, just off state road 738, Tim gave Roger Zoccolillo, a friend of mine, and me a tour of the estate and told us of its brief history.)

he winery is owned by Randy and Judith Rocchiccioli, and was started in 1994. Randy's grandfather was a winemaker in the Tuscany section of Italy. Despite its youth, Windy River features an interesting (and award winning) array of wines. In addition to the Cabernet Sauvignons, Chardonnays and Roues, there are some unusual varieties, such as the Wolf — a hearty, robust red featuring a blend of

Virginia grapes, predominantly Chambourcin.

To promote their wines, the Rocchicciolis offer a number of special events during the year, such as a red wine and chili cookoff, a chowder weekend, jazz in the vineyard, and an annual Mardi Gras ball.

Prominently displayed on bottle labels is a rendering of a beautiful lady with long-flowing hair cradling a wine glass. The "label lady" is strikingly similar to the ghost lady seen walking through the vineyards at night.

One might have cause to wonder whether she may be a malevolent spirit, because Windy River has experienced a series of mini-tragedies that might well have discouraged less enthusiastic owners. Consider: There was a terrible drought in 1994, the first year of plantings. A blizzard hit in 1995, and a late frost hurt the crop a year later. In 1997, a plague of birds descended and devoured grapes, and in 1998 lightning damaged 400 vines during a severe electrical storm.

Several people say they have seen the ghost lady and there are various theories as to who she might be and why she occasionally appears. Tim has not seen her, but he admits to some queasy feelings at times. "Sometimes when I am in the old house where we have wine tastings (1920s vintage), I get this strong sensation that someone is outside watching me through the windows. I never see anyone, but it's like someone is there."

Tim says that the "lady" has been seen walking from the vineyards into the woods in back of the owners' house and then emerging from the trees up to the front of the house. "We have some horses here, and they will not go into those woods," Tim asserts. "They will bolt and shy away every time they are taken near the woods."

Field worker Rick Slater has seen the ghost a number of times, always at night and always in or near the vineyards. "Sometimes I see her just staring at the old house, but when she sees me watching her she fades away," he notes. "Once I went after her, but she ran away and then when I got close, she disappeared."

Rick has his own conjectures about her. "I think she may be a lady who lived during Civil War times. Often she is wearing a long flowing dress that seems to be from that era." Rick believes some tragedy befell her, like maybe she was in love with a young man who was killed, or maybe she herself was killed. "It's just a thought," he says.

Randy Rocchiccioli has not seen the vision, but he is convinced in the sincerity of others who say they have, including Judith, his

Windy Hill Winery Poster

wife. "They all seem to agree in the sightings," he says. "It is a young, beautiful woman with long auburn hair, and wearing a long dress. She must have had some connection with the land here at one time. Why else would she keep appearing?

Judith has had the most interesting experiences. "The first time I saw her was in November, 1996," Judith recalls. "My mother had been ill and I had been to see her and was late coming home one night. It must have been about two in the morning. As I was driving up the road past the vineyards I clearly saw a woman walking down one of the rows. At first I thought it was Kathryn, my sister-in-law, but then I realized it wasn't her. I wondered why anyone would be out in the fields at this hour. Oh, before harvest time we sometimes are out at all hours because of frosts or storm damage and the like. But the harvest was already over.

"I stopped the car and got out. I walked toward the woman. She was tall, slender, and appeared to have auburn hair done up in a bun and she was wearing a long flowing garment. It could have been an evening dress or perhaps some sort of fancy night dress. It looked like it was of the Civil War era. Anyway, as I approached, when I got within 15 yards or so, she just disappeared. I rubbed my eyes. I thought maybe I was seeing things. I was tired.

"I really didn't think much about it until the next summer. One day we were hosting one of our events at the winery, and the subject of the ghost lady came up. A neighbor couple who live just down the river from us said they had experienced her, too. The husband said he had seen her and his wife said she hadn't, but she had felt an icy hand brush her forehead one night. Then, Rick, our fieldhand, announced he had seen the mystery lady also. We call her the 'Windy Lady'. I What amazed me was that when we compared notes, we obviously all had seen the same apparition! We all described her in exactly the same way.

"The next time I saw her," Judith continues, "was in the fall of 1998. One night I couldn't sleep, so I got up and went to the kitchen. I was going to read. It must have been about four a.m.

Suddenly, I looked up, and there, staring at me from outside the window, was this lady! We looked at each other, and then she started walking off, toward the barn. She waved at me. I waved back, and then she was gone. The only difference in this sighting, was that her hair was down.

"Who is she? I have no idea. I haven't done any exhaustive research. We do know that some Civil War skirmishes were fought on the grounds, and we had been told that the woods in back of the house were haunted. There is a small graveyard out there someplace. I haven't seen anything there, but our horses absolutely refuse to go into that patch of the woods. They will bolt and really freak out when they get near that section. I also know that I am not frightened by the lady by any stretch. She seems friendly, and I feel almost a sort of kinship with her."

Judith hesitated, laughed, and then said, "I probably shouldn't tell you this. I haven't even told my husband about it, but there is something else. It happened in February 1999, and I cannot explain it. It was the night we had our annual Mardi Gras ball in Richmond. When we came home, Randy, my husband, went on up to bed. I was sitting in the living room with Eric, our CPA, who sometimes stays over here. We were having a drink and talking. I was still in my evening gown.

"Suddenly, the room got very cold to me. I said something about that to Eric, but he said he didn't feel any chill. I started to get up, but I couldn't. It was like I was paralyzed or something. I know this sounds crazy, but I was trapped in my own body. And then I looked over into the adjacent great room, and there, seated in the two Queen Anne chairs, were two men, dressed in Civil War Confederate uniforms!

"I managed to stammer this out to Eric, but he said he didn't see them. One of them had a beard and the other one didn't. They appeared to be very tired and worn out. I could hear them talking. They were talking about the war. They said things looked 'dismal and grim.' Then I heard them say they wanted some coffee. I tried to get up to go into the kitchen and get some coffee, but I couldn't move. This time I was scared, really scared.

"Then they got up and walked out of the house through the French doors. They headed toward that patch of woods in the back. Eric said he never saw anything. But I did. They were there as plain as day. I didn't sleep much that night at all. The next morning when I came down, there was mud and dirt in the foyer! It was where the soldiers must have entered the house. That's the only explanation I can think of. Was it from their boots? Had there been a Confederate camp here?"

And, finally, there is this. Last fall, Rick, came into Randy and Judith's house. It was the first time he had been in the house. Judith: "He walked into the dining room and seemed transfixed at the portrait hanging on the wall. 'That's her,' he exclaimed. 'That's the lady who I have seen walking through the vineyards. Who is she?'

"It was a portrait me, taken about 15 years ago! I, too, have auburn hair."

Dining Out With A Ghost
(Chesterfield County)

(Author's note: Should one want to dine on gourmet cuisine in an historic old house, and possibly experience a ghostly encounter, he or she might well make reservations at one, or both of two elegant restaurants, within only a few miles of each other in Chesterfield County, south of Richmond. one is primarily an upscale steak house where servers are dressed in tuxedos, and the other is a more informal but nevertheless an exquisite seafood emporium.

Ruth's Chris Steak House, 11500 Huguenot Road, off route 60 in Midlothian, features "the finest custom-aged prime Midwestern beef" hand cut, broiled at 1800 degrees, and served "sizzling on a heated plate." Other specialties include lamb, veal and pork chops, chicken, salmon, lobster and barbecued "Shrimp Orleans." Desserts range from Creme Brulèe to a chocolate praline torte.

Down the road a short distance south, right on route 60 opposite Coalfield Road, is the Crab Louie Seafood Tavern. Entrees include fresh fish, oysters, shrimp and crab. (The author enjoyed mahi-mahi grilled in a Jamaican jerk sauce with pineapple-mango chutney.) On the dessert menu is a Bananas Foster Sundae.

Here is the history of the two houses, and the haunting legends:)

THE RETURN OF ROBIOU AND HIS YOUTHFUL BRIDE

uth's Chris Steak House is located in Bellgrade Plantation, a magnificent manor home built in 1732, the same year George Washington was born. In 1824 the house was sold to a family by the name of Friend. A Dr. Friend who once lived here assisted Dr. Hunter McGuire in the amputation of General Stonewall Jackson's arm during the Civil War.

In fact, during that war the legendary Confederate General A. P. Hill used Bellgrade as his headquarters during the fighting between Petersburg and Richmond. When Union soldiers broke through southern trench lines outside of Petersburg, Hill was shot and killed by a northern soldier. It was said tears came to Robert E. Lee's eyes when he was told. In a curious request, Hill, in his last will and testament, asked that he be buried <u>standing up</u> at Bellgrade. And so he was. After the war ended, his body was reinterred at Hollywood Cemetery and again buried in a vertical position.

But it was sometime before the Civil War that Bellgrade gained notoriety. In the 1840s a French bachelor named Anthony Robiou bought the house. He met a 14-year-old girl who lived nearby on Old Gun Road. She was the daughter of John S. Wormley, a prominent lawyer and wealthy land owner. Despite the difference in their ages, Robiou asked for, and was given, her hand in marriage. According to author Francis Earle Lutz, who wrote "Chesterfield,

Ruth's Chris Steak House

an old Virginia County," the wedding took place in 1851. The couple lived at Bellgrade.

After only a few weeks of marriage, Robiou arrived at his home unexpectedly one afternoon and found his new bride in a "compromising position" with her former boyfriend, 19-year-old James Reid. Incensed, Robiou threw the girl out of the house and demanded a divorce.

Angered and humiliated, her father, Wormley, talked Reid into retaliation. Late one evening they hid in front of Bellgrade, and when Robiou reached his porch, Wormley shot and killed him. Both Wormley and Reid were arrested for murder and jailed in the Chesterfield Courthouse.

Clay Thomasson, owner of Ruth's Chris Steak House, says Reid was later released because it was deemed he had been duped into the plot. Wormley subsequently was tried for murder, but as he had made many friends during his long years in the area's judicial system, he cunningly concocted a plan to get a mistrial. He arranged for a deputy sheriff to "liquor up" two of the jurors. It worked.

However, a second trial was ordered. This time, since the case had become so well known locally, jurors had to be summoned from Petersburg, Richmond, Amelia and Dinwiddie. Wormley was found guilty and sentenced to hang. On the day of the execution a crowd estimated to be from 4,000 to 6,000 came to witness what became a bizarre spectacle. Three ministers came and preached for nearly two and a half hours! Wormley, dressed in a new black frock coat, a black silk shirt, new boots, and a silk hat, was then placed in a wagon and driven to the gallows, a quarter mile west of the courthouse in an open area near the woods. This was done to accommodate the huge crowd. He then spoke for another 15 minutes before he was "swung into eternity."

But the saga was not over. The new young widow soon after married Reid. Within two weeks, however, she fell down the front stairs of the plantation home and died. Thomasson says there are two varying accounts. One is she fell on a sewing basket, and scissors punctured her heart. The other is she broke her neck.

In either case, both she and her murdered first husband, Robiou, apparently occasionally return to the site of their tragedies. "A number of people have said they have seen their apparitions in the boxwood gardens in back of the house," Thomasson says. One who saw them often was a former employee at the steak house, a woman named Willamena, who died a couple of years ago. But there have been several others who have witnessed the spectral figures.

Which raises some pertinent questions. If one is Robiou, is he back to scold his bride, or to seek vengeance for his murder? Does the girl appear in remorse for what she did, or is she looking for her lover, James Reid? And why does the ghost of John Wormley not join them?

Whether or not a present-day patron will see such images is, of course, chancy. But the dining experience alone is well worth a visit. Try the New York strip!

THE GLASS THROWING LITTLE GIRL — AND OTHERS

*C*rab Louie's Seafood Tavern is located in a house formerly known as "Midlothian," circa 1745. The name was also given to the coal mines nearby, owned by a wealthy family named Wooldridge. Later, Midlothian became the name of the town. Abraham Wooldridge, an officer during the War of 1812, had a reputation for hospitality that was so widely regarded, drivers traveling the old Lynchburg-Richmond stagecoach route used the home as a refreshment stop for their passengers. A later resident was Colonel William Wooldridge, a Civil War hero who fought with Jeb Stuart's cavalry.

In 1875, John Jewett purchased the property, and he and his wife had six children here. They ran a popular boarding house and renamed the property "The Sycamores" because of the abundance of sycamore trees in the vicinity. In the mid-1900s a descendent operated a nursery school in the building. In 1975, a restaurant, the Sycamore Inn, was opened, and the surrounding acreage was developed into the Sycamore Square Village Shopping Center. A year later, a fire partially destroyed the east wing of the house. This was rebuilt, and in 1981 Crab Louie took over.

"Actually, I think we may have several different ghosts here," says owner Floyd Sinkler. One is the figure of a man Sinkler and others have seen. "I believe it was the summer of 1985," he says. I was sitting at the bar one night after we had closed and I suddenly got this feeling that someone was behind me. I turned and saw him. Well, maybe not all of him. I saw the upper half of a man wearing clothes that seemed to be from the 19th century. He had on a black suit with a white collar and his face was all powdery. He turned and disappeared heading toward the attic. It scared the

bejabbers out of me."

Several other inexplicable incidents have occurred over the years.

* A few years ago a truck jumped a nearby curb and knocked the power out. While it was out Floyd started doing some book-work by hand, when he heard a loud crash. A load of ice had dropped in the ice machine. How? The power was still out. Then, as he watched in astonishment, a roll of paper began pouring out of an electric adding machine — by itself. Floyd assumed the power had been turned back on, but when he asked a lineman, he was told it was still out!

* On two or three occasions people have run into the restaurant saying that it was on fire — they had seen flames shooting out of the chimney. There was no fire.

* There may be a haunted table at Crab Louie — table 10. One night a group of 10 or 12 people lingered late. Everyone except Floyd and a waiter had gone home. After the party left, they went to table 10 to reset it. Floyd told the waiter, Scott, to go to the kitchen and bring out the bread plates. Scott looked dumbfounded. "Floyd," he said, "we already brought those plates out." Floyd then remembered that they had. But the plates had somehow vanished before their eyes.

* On another occasion, again late at night just before closing,

Floyd and another server were stacking paper napkins on table 10. Incredibly, the napkins, in sequence, fluttered off the table and landed neatly in a single pile on the floor! The window was closed and there was not even a hint of a breeze. "If I hadn't been there and seen it for myself I never would have believed it," Floyd says.

* One night Floyd clearly heard some small children singing "Happy Birthday" at table 10. A waitress passed by, and he asked her where the children were. She turned pale and said, "that's not even funny, Floyd." He asked her what she meant, and she told him she had heard the singing, too, but there was no one there.

Two new employees, on their first day on the job, asked about the "ghost stories." They soon became believers. Right in front of them, three drawers on a bread warmer cabinet opened and slammed shut.

But of all the manifestations at Crab Louie, perhaps none can match the "shenanigans" of what employees have come to know as "Rachel." They occurred in the 1995-96 era. Glasses began sailing off the bar racks. "They just didn't drop out of the racks onto the floor," Floyd says. "They moved. They would land several feet away." One night a glass flew right over a man's shoulder and hit another man in the foot. They were both sitting about 10 feet away from the bar. Both diners and employees experienced this phenomenon.

One evening, a busboy and two servers decided to do some "research" on the mischievous poltergeist. They went into the attic and, on a Ouija board, asked for the ghost to tell who it was. The name Rachel was spelled out. She "told" them, through the board, that she was a little girl of about six or seven, and that they couldn't see her because she was afraid and wouldn't come out in the open.

When Floyd told his own six-year-old daughter, Kelsey, about the incidents, she said Rachel "was lonely." So she gave Floyd one of her dolls, and told him to put it in the restaurant. He did. Rachel's glass-throwing manifestations ceased, and have not recurred since!

In 1993, an airline pilot came into the tavern and told Floyd he was a direct descendent of the Wooldridge family which had initially owned the house. Floyd told him about Rachel. "When I mentioned the name, he turned, pardon the pun, as white as a ghost," Floyd says.

"He then told me that one of the first Wooldridge daughters

who lived in the house, died when she was about six or seven years old."

Her name was Rachel!

CHAPTER 85

The Extraordinary, Incredible, Unbelievable Doll House Ghost

(Bermuda Hundred, Chesterfield County)

(Author's note: Just when you think you've heard it all, that nothing can surprise or shock you anymore — along comes a bizarre encounter that knocks the pins right out from under you. Such was the case early in 1998 when I received a call from a congenial lady in the Richmond area named Phyllis Thurston. I had met her the year before at a Christmas craft show. She said I wouldn't believe what she was about to tell me (a lot of people tell me that), and then she proceeded to relate that a friend of a friend had a miniature ghost in her <u>doll house</u>. And that she had "captured" the ghost on video tape. Now, that got my interest!

Phyllis referred me to Jean and Leonard Bell, who run a miniature store in Highland Springs, east of Richmond. They sell the kits from which rather elaborate doll houses are put together. Phyllis said they sold the doll house to the lady and they had seen the video she had taken with the ghost in it. I called the Bells. They confirmed what Phyllis had told me and said they would call the lady and give them my number.

I heard nothing for three or four months and had about given up hope, when Cherie Edwards called me toward the end of May. Not only did she give me the complete details about the doll house episode, but she also told me all about a real life-size ghost who has appeared in her house in Bermuda Hundred, off and on, over the past 26 years!

So in effect this is two chapters in one. The first part is about Cherie's more "conventional" spirit, and the second half covers what I consider to be one of the most extraordinary cases I have ever investigated.)

THE CONFEDERATE CAVALRYMAN

o better understand the historical significance of Bermuda Hundred, one needs to brush up on the important part it played during the War Between the States. First of all, Bermuda Hundred is a spit of land, a peninsula, that lies between the James River and the Appomattox River, at a point less than 20 miles from Richmond, and even closer to Petersburg. It is nearest to City Point and the town of Hopewell.

In early May 1864, Union commanding general U.S. Grant met in Norfolk with one of his most controversial field commanders, General Benjamin Butler. He looked like anything but a military leader. He was once described as having a head set "immediately on a stout, shapeless body, very squinting eyes, and a set of legs and arms that look as if made for somebody else and hastily glued to him by mistake." For his crude insults to southern women and for his hangings of southern patriots, Butler had gained the non-affectionate nickname of "Beast."

Grant ordered Butler to head up the Virginia peninsula with an army of between 30,000 and 40,000 men and to go as far as he could. If he could take Richmond or Petersburg, fine. If not, okay. But push as hard as possible. Butler chose Bermuda Hundred as his destination. He figured, rightly, he could well defend such a position with rivers on both flanks, and from here he could plan and mount an all-out assault on either Richmond or Petersburg.

How he arrived, in spectacular fashion, is best described by one of Butler's generals, William Farrar Smith. He wrote: "The James River will never again present such a scene as that of the fifth of May 1864. An army of 40,000 men was afloat on its waters, convoyed by various vessels of the navy. It was a motley array of vessels. Coasters and river steamers, ferry boats and tugs, screw and side-wheel steamers, sloops, schooners, barges and canal boats raced or crawled up the stream toward the designated landing. General Butler . . . took the lead, followed by the fastest transports in what seemed to be some giant national pageant."

There were more than 200 vessels in all. It was, simply put, a dramatic spectacle to behold, and it threw the fear of God into Richmonders. Here was Butler, practically at their doorstep, and Robert E. Lee and his army were some 80 miles to the north trying to fend off a hard charging General Grant.

But what Butler had not realized when he chose Bermuda Hundred as his camp site — yes, it could be easily defended — but he was more or less stuck there. He and his army could also be easily caged there by a much smaller Confederate force.

A day or two later there was another incredible scene on the James. A hidden Rebel torpedo (mine) exploded directly under the Union ship, Commodore Jones. One eye witness said: "It seemed as if the bottom of the river was born up and blown through the vessel itself. The Jones was lifted entirely clear of the water, and she burst in the air like an exploding firecracker. She was in small pieces when she struck the water again." For days, bodies and parts of bodies floated and were fished out of the James; 69 men perished.

With the fear of more such blasts, and practically surrounded by southern forces, Butler found himself, as historian Bruce Catton put it, "locked up as securely as if he and all his soldiers had been in prison." A frustrated General Grant fumed that Butler "was as completely shut off from further operations directly against Richmond as if he had been in a bottle strongly corked."

That is the historical background of Bermuda Hundred. And that is why Cherie Edwards, who lives there today, thinks there is a Civil War ghost in her house. "There were thousands of soldiers all over here during the Civil War," she says, "and many were killed before their time. You find relics from the war all the time."

Cherie and her husband, Steve, moved into their tri-level home in 1972. She felt the presence of something supernatural while the house was still under construction. There were noises inside she couldn't explain. During their first night in the house, Cherie saw the apparitional figure of a Confederate soldier, wearing the uniform of a cavalry officer.

"At first it was like a mist," she recalls. "And then this man seemed to form out of it. He appeared to be in his early thirties, maybe, and he was good looking. He was there just for a second or two and then he was gone."

Cherie has seen him many times. "But by the time my brain registers, and I realize what it is I am seeing, he has disappeared," she says. Others have seen him, too. Once, the Edwards had six or eight people over for a cocktail party and the Confederate spirit appeared amidst all of them. "The party broke up pretty fast," Cherie chuckles.

There are other manifestations as well.

— Cherie had a rocking chair that seemed to rock all the time with no one visible in it. It finally got on her nerves so much she gave the chair away.

— Frequently, there are distinct odors filling the house. "There are, at different times, strong scents of bay rum, of smoked ham, cinnamon, and freshly cut boxwood," she says. "And many people have smelled them. There is no rational source for such odors."

— Someone whispers in the house. "I used to have two West Highland terriers," says Cherie. "Sometimes when I heard the whispering, they would be staring at something, like someone was talking to them. Their eyes would be fixed on something I couldn't see and their ears would be perked up.

— There are occasional unexplained cold spots in the house.

— A few years ago the wife of a local minister visited the Edwards. When she heard the story about the ghost, she insisted on going upstairs to a front room where the soldier most often materialized. In a few seconds she came racing back down the stairs clutching her neck. She told Cherie that something up there had choked her and she had to get out of the house right away. She wouldn't come back.

"That's the only instance I know of where 'he' was harmful or threatening," Cherie says. "I have never really been frightened of him, but he does get on my nerves sometimes. You know, it appears when you least expect him and if you're having a bad day, you don't want to put up with that. And sometimes his humming bothers me. He hums. Once in a while I will come downstairs at night to play gospel music on the piano or organ. My husband will either be out or upstairs asleep. I'll be playing and suddenly I will hear this humming. Sometimes I just shout, 'shut up, I can't take it anymore,' and usually the humming will stop.

"I really don't know why he's here. Maybe he was killed at this site during the war. I can't think of any other reason. You know, I never believed in this sort of thing before we moved here. But there's definitely something weird here, and whatever it really is, it must like this place, because he's been here as long as we have."

- And there is this postscript. Sometime after the initial interview with Cherie, she reported yet another strange occurrence. In

January 1999, she went one day to the Sunset Memorial Cemetery near Hopewell to place fresh flowers on her father's grave. As she was there, tidying up the site, she heard a "rustling" sound behind her in the dried, dormant grass. She turned around and saw two little stuffed animals, a dog and a mouse. They hadn't been there when she had approached the grave. Where had they come from? There was no one else in sight. Odd, she thought.

Cherie reasoned that someone must have left the toys, either for placement on a burial site or by a young child who had brought them to the cemetery and forgotten them. Fearful that if she left them on the ground they would be thrown away, she picked them up and walked over to a brick ledge several feet away. She placed them on the ledge. She noticed that if she pushed a button on the little dog, it would play a tune - "White Christmas."

She walked back to her father's grave and pulled some weeds. Then she heard the same rustling sound again, looked back, and the two stuffed animals had "followed" her. They were laying behind her on the grass! Once more, Cherie replaced them on the ledge, and, understandably unnerved, she says, "I got out of there quick." As she left, she looked back. The animals were again off the ledge and on the ground!

THE DOLL HOUSE GHOST

(Author's note: As they say, art sometimes imitates life, or sometimes it's the other way around. Consider the following:

FICTION: One could say that Algernon Blackwood was the Stephen King of his day — that is 75 or so years ago. Blackwood wrote scary stories about the unexplained. Some of them are classics, and rank in the same company as Ambrose Bierce and, with a little stretch, even Edgar Allan Poe.

One of Blackwood's most spellbinding tales was titled, simply, "The Doll." This involved a man named Colonel Masters. He was a retired military officer who had, years before, served with the British army in India. He had committed some atrocious crime there, but the nature of it was never revealed. However, he had long feared someone would find him some day seeking revenge.

One evening while the colonel was out, during a stormy, rainy

Doll House

night, there was a loud rap at the front door of the colonel's manor house. The housekeeper answered, and was frightened at the sight she beheld. There was a fierce looking, dark-skinned man at the door. He thrust a package toward the housekeeper and told her it was for Colonel Masters. Then he quickly vanished into the wet blackness.

"The package contained an unusual looking doll. It was a wax doll with flaxen hair, yet there seemed to be something mysterious about it. Nevertheless, the housekeeper and a governess decided the doll must be for the colonel's daughter, and they gave it to her. The doll and the girl, Monica, became inseparable. She slept with it tightly clutched in her arms. One night the governess, checking on Monica before she went to bed, was shocked to see the doll <u>walking</u>!

Later, red splotches were observed on the doll. The housekeeper insisted it was blood. The governess tried to convince her it must be red paint, but the doll was not painted. And then, several nights later, both the housekeeper and the governess heard strange sounds coming from Monica's room. There were voices. One was Monica's, but the other wasn't. It was <u>different</u>! The two ladies learned, to their utter horror, that the doll itself was speaking!

They had not, to this point, told Colonel Masters about the

doll, or how and when it had arrived. But now, terrified, they told him. He somehow sensed, when he heard about the dark-skinned man and his package, that this related to the revenge he had so long feared.

Finally, one night after midnight, he and the governess slipped up to Monica's bedroom and opened the door. The doll then moved swiftly straight toward the colonel, who stood frozen in absolute horror, and attacked him! As Blackwood described it, (the doll) "savagely, its little jaws were bitten deep into Colonel Master's throat, fastened tightly.

The doll then dropped to the floor, limply. And at that instant, a dark-skinned arm stretched through a half-open window, snatched it up, and then disappeared.

The next morning, Colonel Masters was found dead on his bed, with a "swollen, blackened tongue!"

* * * * *

FACT: In "The Ghosts of Tidewater," and repeated in "The Ghosts of Virginia, Volume I," the author wrote about a Virginia Beach woman who had a lifelong love affair with a charismatic man. When he learned he was dying of cancer, he told the woman he would try to communicate with her from the beyond, to convince her of his eternal love. A few months after he died, the woman decided she wanted to write a book about this unusual man and their relationship. One day she was reminiscing about events by talking into a tape recorder. She got to one incident where she couldn't remember the facts and the tape ran blank for about 30 seconds. Sometime later, as she played the tape back, <u>his voice filled in the missing facts!</u>

FACT: A few years ago there was a movie called "Three Men and a Baby." Tom Selleck was one of the stars. In one of the scenes, the apparitional image of a young boy appeared in a doorway in the background. No one had seen such a boy during the filming. He appeared, unaccountably, after the film had been processed. No one knew who the boy was or what he was doing there. It became a national news item; a ghost boy on the clip of film. It was never satisfactorily explained.

All of this is a prelude to the following incident.)

Cherie and Steve Edwards, of Bermuda Hundred, have a hobby. They like to build, from unassembled kits, complex doll houses. These houses are on a one-twelfth scale, one inch to one

Ghost?

foot. They take these kits and improvise or redesign them to their own individual tastes. In 1996, they bought such a kit from Jean and Leonard Bell, who run a miniature store near Richmond.

They assembled it. The house was fully furnished, but there were no dolls in it. This particular house was like a granite block house similar to the old New Orleans style architecture. It had a large sweeping veranda. About a year later, Cherie was making a video tape of some of their houses. Steve, who works for the Virginia Department of Transportation, wanted to take it into the office to show it to his co-workers. Nothing out of the ordinary transpired during the taping.

Sometime later, Cherie and Steve sat down to view the tape. As the camera panned across the veranda, the Edwards suddenly sat up, stunned. "Did you just see what I saw," Cherie exclaimed. "I think I did," Steve replied. "Run the tape back and let's see it again." Cherie did. It was there again!

What they saw, clearly, was a figure seated at a table on the porch! It was the miniature figure of a woman!

Here is how Cherie describes it: "As the camera panned down the veranda, there was a woman sitting at a table. She is wearing a flowered dress and is miniature sized, fitting perfectly with the scale of the house. She is looking down and her hands are on the table. She has gray, curly hair and a rather large nose for her face. She is just sitting there. Then, in a few seconds, she gets up from the table and walks out of camera range! We couldn't believe what we had just seen."

The Edwards ran the tape over and over, and each time the vision appeared. They invited the Bells over. They confirm the sighting. Leonard said you could see through the woman.

"I didn't see her at all when I was doing the filming," Cherie adds. "It's all so weird."

(Author's note: Cherie Edwards graciously invited me to view the video. I did. I saw the ghost lady. I cannot explain it.)

THE MYSTERY OF THE MISSING DOLL HOUSE
(The Appalachian Plateau near the Virginia - West Virginia line)

(Author's note: While the following is not a ghost story, per se, it nevertheless is an enduring enigma that remains unsolved to this day, although there have been many attempts over the years to solve it. It involves a cryptic search for a lost treasure, and has been told in a variety of newspaper and magazine accounts and in the book, "Buried Treasures of the Appalachians," by W. C. Jameson. It is in the genre of such legendary, believed to be true, folktales as the lost Swift silver mine, and has enticed and tantalized mountain adventurers for more than a century.)

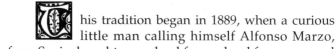his tradition began in 1889, when a curious little man calling himself Alfonso Marzo, allegedly from Spain, bought some land from a local farmer named Shahan, and built a house on the property. It was not an ordinary house. It was rather more like a miniature house like one children would play in. Everyone in the region referred to it as the "doll house."

Marzo proved to be equally as strange as the abode he built. He was a recluse. He shunned any visitors, and was said to even run and hide in the woods when anyone approached. Few people even caught a glimpse of him. Then suddenly, four years later, the quizzical little man disappeared without a trace.

Then, oddly, in August 1911, Shahan got a weird letter from Marzo, postmarked from Madrid, Spain. The letter was difficult to decipher, but the gist of it seemed to be that Marzo was saying he had secretly hidden a fortune of some $330,000 in or around his "doll house;" that he could not return to retrieve it; but if Shahan would recover the money he would share it with him. Marzo indicated that if Shahan would agree, he would send him directions to retrieve a document that would describe where the treasure was hidden.

The farmer never responded, and never heard from Marzo again. He did learn, however, that during the time Marzo was in the region an area bank had been robbed of precisely the amount of money the Spaniard said he had hidden. This would have been, local residents believed, an astounding coincidence.

In time, Shahan and his neighbors began to believe that Marzo may have buried the money beneath the doll house. So several residents began to search for the place.

They could never find it!

There was, said author Jameson, no evidence that it had burned or been destroyed. Like Marzo himself, there simply was no trace of the tiny house.

And so, the questions remain: Why did Marzo build such an unusual structure in the first place; what happened to it; what happened to Marzo, who apparently never returned to the site; and where was the money?

The legend has endured for more than 100 years.

Author L.B. Taylor, Jr., and illustrator Brenda Goens.

About the Author

L. B. Taylor, Jr. – a Scorpio – is a native Virginian. He was born in Lynchburg and has a BS degree in journalism from Florida State University. He wrote about America's space programs for 16 years, for NASA and aerospace contractors, before moving to Williamsburg, Virginia, in 1974, as public affairs director for BASF Corporation. He retired in 1993. Taylor is the author of more than 300 national magazine articles and over 30 non-fiction books. His research for the book "Haunted Houses," published by Simon and Schuster in 1983, stimulated his interest in area psychic phenomena and led to the publication of five regional ghost books, five covering the entire commonwealth, and one on Civil War Ghosts of Virginia.

Personally autographed copies of the following books are available from L. B. Taylor, Jr., 108 Elizabeth Meriwether, Williamsburg, VA 23185 (757-253-2636). Please add $3 for postage

and handling, $5 for multiple book orders. Also, please specify to whom you wish the book(s) signed.)

"The Ghosts of Williamsburg" - 84 pages, illustrated, $7

"The Ghosts of Richmond" - 172 pages, illustrated, $12

"The Ghosts of Tidewater" - 232 pages, illustrated, $12

"The Ghosts of Fredericksburg" - 177 pages, illustrated, $12

"The Ghosts of Charlottesville and Lynchburg" - 188 pages, illustrated, $12

(All five books above are available for $45)

"The Ghosts of Virginia" (Volume I) - 400 pages, illustrated, $15

"The Ghosts of Virginia" (Volume II) - 400 pages, illustrated, $15

"Civil War Ghosts of Virginia" - 225 pages, illustrated, $13

"The Ghosts of Virginia" (Volume III) - 450 pages, illustrated, $15

"The Ghosts of Virginia" (Volume IV) - 465 pages, illustrated, $15

L. B. Taylor, Jr., is available (depending upon his schedule) to speak on the subject of Virginia ghosts to civic, social, fraternal, business, school, library and other groups. Call or write with dates and details.

If you have a ghostly or unusual psychic encounter you would like to share with L. B. Taylor, Jr., (for possible future publication), please call or write the author.

OTHER BOOKS BY L. B. TAYLOR, JR.